ECOCIVILIZATION

ECO CIVILIZATION

MAKING A WORLD THAT WORKS FOR ALL

JEREMY LENT

MELVILLE HOUSE
BROOKLYN • LONDON

Ecocivilization : Making a World That Works for All
First published in 2026 by Melville House

First Melville House Printing: February 2026

Distributed by Penguin Random House LLC,
1745 Broadway, New York, NY 10019
www.penguinrandomhouse.com

Melville House Publishing
46 John Street
Brooklyn, NY 11201
and
Melville House UK
Suite 2000
16/18 Woodford Road
London E7 0HA

mhpbooks.com
@melvillehouse

ISBN: 978-1-68589-233-3
ISBN: 978-1-68589-234-0 (eBook)

Library of Congress Control Number: 2025950073

Designed by Beste M. Doğan

Printed in the United States of America
1 3 5 7 9 10 8 6 4 2

A catalog record for this book is available from the Library of Congress

To future generations, and those
working to leave them a better world

CONTENTS

Introduction *ix*

SECTION 1

HOW DID WE GET HERE?

CHAPTER 1 Careening Toward a Precipice *3*

CHAPTER 2 The History They Didn't Teach You at School *11*

CHAPTER 3 The Windigo Diagnosis *42*

CHAPTER 4 The Need for System Change *59*

SECTION 2

PRINCIPLES OF AN ECOCIVILIZATION

CHAPTER 5 Core Principles of Life, Ecosystems, and Humanity *79*

CHAPTER 6 Principles of an Ecocivilization *88*

SECTION 3

ENVISIONING AN ECOCIVILIZATION

CHAPTER 7 Economy: How to Live within the Doughnut *105*

CHAPTER 8 Industry: Structuring Enterprise to Serve the Common Good *124*

CHAPTER 9 Agriculture: Diversifying Food Production for Sustenance and Sovereignty *141*

CHAPTER 10 Wealth: Regaining the Commons for a True "Commonwealth" *158*

CHAPTER 11 Finance: Transforming Money to Work for Us All *174*

CHAPTER 12 Technology: Distributed Information for Collective Empowerment *191*

CHAPTER 13 Infrastructure: Designing Built Systems for Communal Wellbeing *210*

CHAPTER 14 Governance: Redefining Democracy through Direct Participation *227*

CHAPTER 15 Law: A New Relational Paradigm Interweaving Rights and Responsibilities *249*

CHAPTER 16 Global Governance: Guiding Principles for Steering a Planetary Community *267*

CHAPTER 17 Living Earth: Mutually Beneficial Symbiosis with All Our Relations *286*

CHAPTER 18 Culture & Community: Cultivating Care, Dignity, and Planetary Consciousness *304*

SECTION 4

HOW DO WE GET THERE?

CHAPTER 19 How Change Happens: Models of Societal Transformation *327*

CHAPTER 20 Making Change Happen: Moving Toward an Ecocivilization *343*

EPILOGUE

TOWARD THE SYMBIOCENE *361*

Notes *365*

INTRODUCTION

Few people have had as much effect on the recent direction of the world as Tina. In virtually every major policy decision considered in just about every country on the planet, Tina has been the one to shape the debate. It's Tina who tells people what they can, and can't, talk about.

How come you've never heard of Tina or seen her picture in the press? Because Tina isn't a person, but an idea. Or perhaps more accurately, a killer of ideas. TINA is the acronym of the famous statement made by Margaret Thatcher in 1980, "There Is No Alternative," as she pushed through an unyielding assault on the delicate balance between government and private enterprise that had evolved in Great Britain since the end of the Second World War.

But the underlying creed of TINA was not limited to Thatcher's Britain. Following the ascendancy of Ronald Reagan to the presidency of the United States, the duo unleashed onto the world an ideology that had been incubating for decades, and has since become the de facto governing doctrine of virtually every aspect of human endeavor, infiltrating its core beliefs into areas as wide-ranging as politics, finance, culture, education, technology, and agriculture. This ideology, generally referred to nowadays as neoliberalism, holds that humans are individualistic, selfish, calculating materialists, and because of this, unrestrained free-market capitalism provides the best framework for every kind of human activity.

A decade after neoliberalism took hold of the world, the Berlin Wall fell, signifying the end of the Cold War that had defined global politics for nearly half a century. It was a jubilant moment, liberating millions from the ruthless grip of a morally bankrupt regime. In the battle between capitalism and communism, capitalism had won. As one triumphant commentator infamously proclaimed, it was "the end of history." There was no longer any alternative. Game over. TINA now reigned supreme.[1]

Since that time, neoliberal adherents have succeeded in transforming the world into a gladiatorial arena where markets have become the ruling force of human activity. Regulations have been shredded across the globe. Billions of people are malnourished while mega-billionaires vie for planetary domination. Profit-seeking corporations have surpassed nation-states in economic power. Animal populations have been decimated worldwide. And each year brings our civilization ever closer to the cataclysm of climate breakdown.

People increasingly intuit that the system is not working for them. Angry and desperate, they turn to the only voices that seem to recognize their plight—extremist authoritarians promising to dismantle the structures that have immiserated them.

Yet, most people—even those concerned about the dire state of the world—accept TINA unquestioningly. The only way to structure society, it is assumed, is in the form of growth-based consumer capitalism—a system in which corporate profits ultimately drive the decisions that affect the lives of everyone on the planet, the health of the living Earth, and the destiny of future generations. Virtually all policy proposals under serious consideration to fix our grave problems work within the framework of the current system rather than examining the system itself.

This book constitutes the dethronement of TINA. There is, in fact, an alternative.

A FAULTY OPERATING SYSTEM

The alternative we'll be exploring, though, is not the kind that Thatcher, Reagan, and countless adherents of market-based capitalism had been railing against. Back in those days, and in fact throughout the entire twentieth century, the battle lines were clearly drawn between capitalism on one side and socialism (or, in its extreme form, communism) on the other. A society could either be organized primarily by the market or by the state. There were, of course, many countries that attempted a blend between the two, most notably European nations after the Second World War that explored possibilities of a welfare state with a meaningful safety net for those who fell through the holes ripped open by the market. In the United States, after FDR's New Deal, the state played a significant role in people's lives. But the choice was always between the poles of market and state, closing off any other possibility for organizing human activity.

Surprisingly perhaps, these opposing sides shared considerable common ground. Both prized their particular ideology over the dignity of normal human lives: Submit, people were told, either to the invisible hand of the market or the authoritarian fist of the state. Both worshiped at the altar of economic growth as the supreme aspiration of policymaking. And perhaps most consequentially, both viewed the entire Earth as nothing more than a resource to exploit in the interest of pursuing that growth.

This pursuit of endless growth on a planet with limited resources has propelled human civilization onto a terrifying trajectory. The uncontrolled climate crisis is the most obvious danger: Even as we reel from the impact of little more than one degree Celsius of global heating, the world's current policies have us on track for a staggering three degrees increase by the end of this century—and climate scientists publish dire warnings that amplifying feedbacks could make things far worse than even these projections.

But even if the climate crisis were somehow brought under control, continued untrammeled economic growth in future decades will bring us face-to-face with a slew of further existential threats. Our civilization is already running at forty percent above its sustainable capacity. We're rapidly depleting the Earth's forests, animals, insects, fish, freshwater, and even the topsoil we require to grow our crops. Animal populations worldwide have declined by a staggering 73 percent since 1970. In the oceans, coral reefs are on track to be virtually annihilated by the middle of this century. At this rate, we're well on the way to causing the sixth great extinction of species since life began on Earth—except this is the first driven by the actions of a single species. Surveying this devastation across the board, in 2017 over fifteen thousand scientists from 184 countries issued an ominous warning to humanity that time is running out: "Soon it will be too late," they wrote, "to shift course away from our failing trajectory."[2]

Rather than shifting course, however, we've been going pedal to the metal full speed ahead. The growth imperative underlying this juggernaut of destruction is built into the very fabric of our global economic system. Because of this, even in the face of this despoliation of the living Earth, global production and consumption levels are projected to more than double by 2060. Yet there is virtually no discussion in the mainstream media about this conundrum. Even those policymakers who profess to care about our civilizational crisis propose solutions that merely tinker with specific elements of the system rather than considering the system itself as a whole.

We can think of our entire economic and political setup like a faulty operating system with multiple bugs. Each time the software engineers fix a bug, it complicates the code, leading inevitably to a new set of bugs requiring even more heroic workarounds. Ultimately, it may become clear to someone that the problem isn't just the software: An entirely new operating system is required. But nobody wants to hear that, because they're all so busy working on their particular piece of the puzzle.

It doesn't, however, take a software engineer or even a PhD in economics to see what's wrong. Like the folk tale of the emperor who had no clothes, it just takes someone with the courage to call it out. Someone like fifteen-year-old Greta Thunberg who told world leaders at a UN Climate Conference in 2018, "If solutions within this system are so impossible to find, maybe we should change the system itself."[3]

A CIVILIZATION BASED ON LIFE'S DESIGN PRINCIPLES

In this book, we'll begin answering Greta Thunberg's call. We'll embark on a journey of discovery to map out the contours of a fundamentally different way of organizing human activity—one that is so far-reaching that it encompasses not just economics but every major domain of modern civilization.

At first sight, this might seem like a daunting task, akin to exploring an uncharted wilderness, but in fact we'll have plenty of guides to help us. Around the world, activists, changemakers, scholars, and community organizers are assiduously laying down pathways toward a life-affirming future. In many cases, they may not see themselves as part of a larger movement, but they're driven by a shared set of core human imperatives to care for others around them, nurture the living Earth, and leave a healthy world for future generations to inherit.

Increasingly, people are putting a name on this burgeoning global movement that might just have the potential to become the greatest collaborative human project in history: a transition toward an ecological civilization. In the chapters that follow, we'll home in on these diverse strands of visionary ideas, grassroots movements, and community initiatives, and see how, in every domain of society, life-enhancing alternatives exist that, woven together into a cohesive fabric, could intertwine to form a fundamentally different society.

What does it mean to change the operating system of the entire world? We'll discover how our civilization is based on a foundation of extraction, exploitation, and elite wealth accumulation. These are not unfortunate side-effects of our way of doing things—they are founding principles. An ecological civilization, by contrast, would be one that's designed from the bottom up on life-affirming principles, setting the conditions for all people to flourish on a thriving, living Earth.

As its name implies, an ecological civilization (or "ecocivilization" for short) takes its inspiration from the principles of life itself. Without human disruption, ecosystems can thrive in rich abundance for millions of years, remaining resilient in the face of adversity. Clearly, there is much to learn from nature's wisdom about how to organize ourselves. This is a central idea underlying an ecocivilization: using nature's own design principles to help us reimagine the basis of our own world system.

One central principle of life is known in biology as *mutually beneficial symbiosis*. Living systems are characterized by both competition and cooperation. However, the major evolutionary transitions that brought life to its current abundance were all the results of dramatic increases in cooperation through symbiosis: the process by which both parties in a relationship give and take reciprocally, reflecting each other's abilities and needs. There is no zero-sum game with this type of symbiosis: The contributions of each party create a whole that is greater than the sum of its parts. We'll see in the pages ahead how the pursuit of mutually beneficial symbiosis naturally leads away from extractive and exploitative behaviors, and toward life-enhancing policies and practices throughout society.

Look around the natural world, and you will see fractal patterns everywhere. From microscopic living structures to the entire Earth system, nature uses a fractal design with similar patterns manifesting at different scales. You can see them in the shapes of tree branches, coastlines, cloud formations, lung brachia, and neural networks, to name just a few. Ecologies are themselves fractal, with tiny cells that are part of an organism, which is nested in a population, which is embedded in an ecosystem, which is integrated into the living Earth. In all cases, the long-term health of the larger system requires the flourishing of each of its parts. This universal principle of *fractal flourishing* inspires the ultimate objective of an ecocivilization: to create the conditions in which the flourishing of each of us naturally contributes to the greater wellbeing of the systems in which we're embedded.

Within an ecosystem, every species has its evolutionary niche: a particular constellation of conditions and behaviors that give rise to its unique form of wellbeing. As humans, we have our own evolutionary niche. We didn't evolve to find happiness in taking orders from the boss, eating Big Macs while stuck in traffic, or gazing for hours at a screen. We spent 95 percent of our species' history in nomadic hunter-gatherer bands, where our welfare depended primarily on how well we got along with those around us. Over many thousands of generations, we evolved to become a highly cooperative species, thriving in egalitarian communities that valued fairness and generosity. As a result of our evolutionary heritage, most of us continue to prize qualities that are core principles of an ecocivilization, such as justice, respect for others, mutuality, and dignity, along with a sense of belonging both within our community and as part of the living Earth.

LET'S GET REALISTIC

Go ahead, say it. By now, if a part of you feels inspired by the idea of a civilization actually designed for human welfare, there's probably another part saying something like: "Nice idea, but seriously . . . This is so far from our present reality that there seems little point in even considering it. Let's get realistic."

There are two ways to think about the meaning of "realistic." One way is to begin with what's happening right now, and try to improve things a bit. If fossil fuels are burning up the Earth, maybe it's realistic to attempt to use less and invest in renewables. If vast inequality is ruining most people's lives, perhaps it's realistic to advocate for higher taxes. But if we find that, in spite of our best efforts, the very situation we're trying to fix is continually getting worse, then it's not "realistic" to believe things will magically get better if we keep doing the same thing. We cannot continue to expect infinite growth on a finite planet, and yet that's what passes for realistic in today's mainstream discourse.

The other way to think about "realistic" is to sketch out the conditions that might realistically allow human civilization to prosper into the indefinite future, and then do all that we can to achieve those conditions. The word used for this process in planning circles is *backcasting*. This approach is very different from imagining some utopian paradise and hoping that it might just happen. The framework for an ecocivilization we'll be charting in these pages is based on grounded research, empirical studies, and efforts that have already delivered successful outcomes. But by focusing attention on a genuinely desirable future and then working backward to see what's needed to achieve it, we avoid constraining the imagination into the narrow parameters of what appears possible from where we now stand.

This is what Greta Thunberg was referring to when she spoke truth to power at that UN Climate Conference in 2018. "Until you start focusing on what needs to be done rather than what is politically possible," she declared, "there is no hope." That's what this book focuses on: what needs to be done for humanity to experience a sustainably flourishing future.

As we focus attention on what's required for that desirable outcome, we'll come across some remarkable possibilities that exist beyond the reach of our daily feed of TINA-constrained options. We'll find out how societal institutions we all take for granted as if they were naturally ordained, such as law, money, and education, were designed from the outset to reinforce the power of wealthy elites, and can instead be redesigned for the benefit of us all. And we'll discover alternative modes that communities may use to function, with venerable pedigrees going back millennia, that naturally evoke our better qualities rather than selfishness and greed.

We'll see how advanced technology can be reconfigured to empower each of us rather than a few mega-corporations, how cities can be redesigned to promote wellbeing rather than consumerism and traffic, and how democracy might be reconceived so that regular citizens, rather than wealthy oligarchs, can thoughtfully determine the best policies for society. We'll envisage a world where corporations have been legally restructured to work for people and the planet rather than merely profits, and where enforceable Rights of Nature legislation looks out for the welfare of the other sentient beings with whom we share our world.

This is the kind of hope that Greta, along with the millions of other young people around the world inheriting the mess left by earlier generations, is calling for. It's a directional beacon in the darkness of our times that's based on a grounded realization of what's possible rather than a wistful yearning for an ideal utopia.

But let's be clear—it's not a "hopium" dream filled with encouraging aromas of optimism telling you not to worry, that somehow everything's going to turn out okay. The gap between the beckoning future of an ecocivilization and today's grim repertoire of suffering is only too clear. As the juggernaut we're on accelerates ever closer to the precipice, we might ask whether structural societal transformation is even possible before civilization comes apart. When we discuss this crucial question in the final section, we'll see how, to the extent meaningful hope does arise, it emerges out of the very ruptures of our present breakdown. As the weave of our dominant system unravels, possibilities emerge to reweave our societal fabric into a new design.

A leading systems scientist, Ilya Prigogine, once famously described how complex systems transition from one stable state to another. At first, things look very messy, like the mush inside a cocoon comprising the dissolved flesh of a caterpillar. But within the mess, inklings begin to appear of a new stable state into which the system might transform. Prigogine called these inklings "small islands of coherence in a sea of chaos" which, he explained, had "the capacity to lift the entire system to a higher order."[4]

We'll chart some of these islands in the pages ahead. Whether they can rise high enough from the sea of chaos to combine with each other and form a new landmass will only be known on the other side of the turmoil that lies ahead in this century. But if we can map them out, and join with others in the grand project of weaving them together, we just might succeed in laying the groundwork for a new chapter in humanity's story—an ecocivilization that could allow humans and our nonhuman relatives to flourish together into the indefinite future.

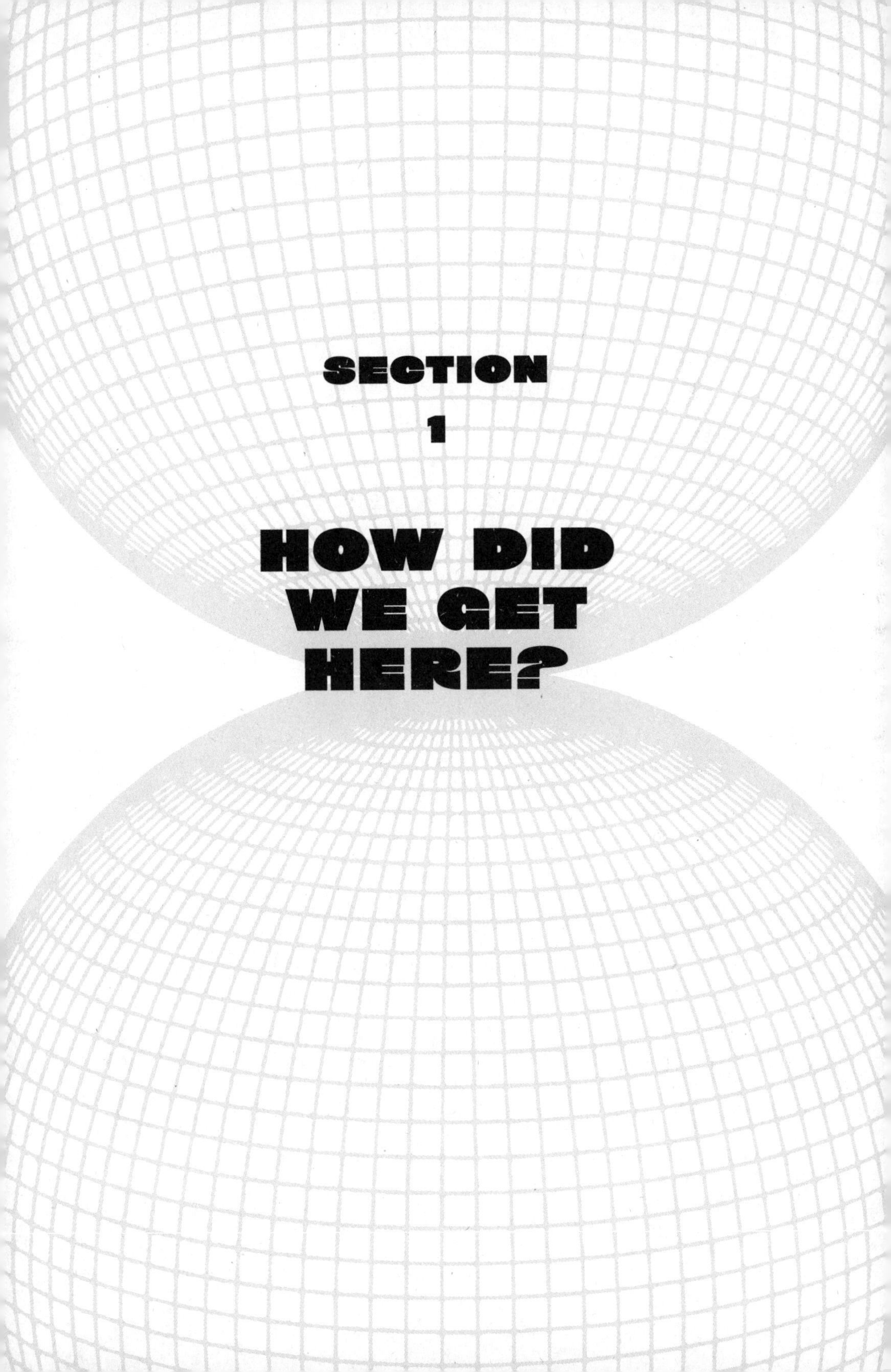

SECTION 1

HOW DID WE GET HERE?

CHAPTER 1

CAREENING TOWARD A PRECIPICE

It was Christmas Eve, back in 1968, when something extraordinary happened, first to a small group of people, and then to all humanity. Three astronauts on board Apollo 8, the first piloted mission to orbit the Moon, had completed their day's task of photographing the Moon's surface. When they turned around the spaceship, suddenly Earth appeared in the window. "Oh my God," Frank Borman exclaimed, as he became the first human being to see his entire home planet floating, alone and tenderly fragile, in infinite space.

The picture they sent back, known as "Earthrise," has since become iconic. It offers a tantalizing hint of the awe many astronauts experience when they come face to face with our only home—a profound experience so widespread that the Overview Effect, as it's now called, has become the subject of academic study. "The Earth," in the words of the Chinese astronaut Liu Yang, "is like a vibrant living thing . . . I said to myself: this is the place we live, it's really magical."

Along with awe and wonder, many of those granted the precious gift of this spectacle are struck by what the Russian cosmonaut Yuri Artyukhin describes as "a strong sense of compassion and concern for the state of our planet and the effect humans are having on it . . . You are standing guard," he felt, "over the whole of our Earth." German cosmonaut Sigmund Jähn concurs: "Before I flew I was already aware how small and vulnerable our planet is; but only when I saw it from space, in all its ineffable beauty and fragility, did I realize that humankind's most urgent task is to cherish and preserve it for future generations."[1]

If this is, indeed, humankind's most urgent task, so far, we have been failing miserably. The "pale blue dot" that is our home planet is the only place we know of in the universe where life exists. Life emerged early in our planet's history, about four billion years ago, and over untold millennia of evolutionary trial-and-error, it gradually unfurled into the dazzling plethora of its present abundance, filling virtually every nook and cranny of the planet with its splendor in innumerable forms of flowers, trees, fungi, bacteria, birds, fish, dragonflies, lions, elephants, and gazelles.

Into this panoply of abundance, in the most recent episode of Earth's epic chronicle, modern humans emerged. If we imagine Earth's entire history compressed into a day, our species has been around for just a second or so. And yet, in that infinitesimally small flicker of time, the amount of damage we have wrought on our home is staggering.

There are many hopeful, even inspirational, ideas and initiatives that we'll encounter in this book. But before we get there—and to understand why an ecocivilization is not only desirable but necessary for humanity's future welfare—it's essential that we first delve into the darkness and come face-to-face with the havoc our civilization has wreaked. As we take these initial harrowing steps, you may feel a sense of despair at this dismal state of affairs. If so, you're not alone. It's an appropriate response to our current situation. Hold it; feel it—but don't let it overwhelm every part of you. You're beginning a journey that will take you through some dark patches, but there are powerful beacons beckoning on the other side.

LURCHING INTO THE ANTHROPOCENE

Most likely, you already know about the devastating effects of climate breakdown. Nowadays we regularly see extreme climate events that used to be called "once in a century." It's impossible to avoid the drumroll of record-breaking heatwaves, droughts, fires, and floods that now make up a sizable portion of our daily news feed. What is rarely discussed in mainstream media, though, is how much worse things will get as the world heats up further.

What is perhaps most terrifying is that these disasters are all happening at a global temperature that is destined to keep rising. Although the world's nations had agreed in Paris in 2015 to target a maximum of 1.5° global temperature rise this century, we're already breaking through this ceiling, and it's widely believed by climate scientists that a minimum two-degree rise is already locked in by the inaction of the world's leaders. The pledges made to reduce emissions have us on track for a temperature rise between two and three degrees this century, but our governments are nowhere close to achieving even those inadequate commitments.

In a two-degree world, the sporadic disasters that now emblazon news headlines will become the grim, continuous backdrop of an ever more precarious daily struggle for survival. Billions of people will suffer severe water shortages with protracted droughts becoming ever more common, and frequent widespread floods and famines will stress global food supplies to breaking point, while marine life dwindles in hot, acidifying oceans. The most alarming aspect of a two-degree world, though, is the increased likelihood of triggering climate tipping points that take us even further into a hellish future.

A climate tipping point is the term scientists use for a condition that kicks off a new set of reinforcing feedback effects making the climate emergency even worse. The melting of permafrost in the Arctic, for example, releases methane, which is a greenhouse gas thirty times more potent than carbon dioxide. When ice melts in the oceans, it reduces the reflection of sunlight, which further heats the water. As the Amazon rainforest dies back, it goes from being a carbon sink to a new source of carbon emissions. Out of fifteen known tipping points, scientists believe that nine have already begun to be activated. What's the worst thing about a tipping point? You guessed it—it increases the risk of further tipping points, leading to what scientists call a "tipping cascade," potentially driving the climate into freefall, and turning our planet into an unrecognizable world that scientists have grimly termed "hothouse Earth."[2]

The climate emergency is bad enough. But if we pause for a moment and look around at the bigger picture, we see that, even with its terrifying implications, it's merely a symptom of a far larger predicament: the pervasive and accelerating devastation of the living Earth caused by the unrestrained activities of modern civilization. Nature is unraveling all around us, and rather than try to halt the damage, our entire system is organized to increase the destruction.

Wherever we look—the atmosphere, oceans, forests, wetlands, or rivers—the basic components of Earth's life support systems are all under severe pressure, and in many cases are approaching breaking points. Several of the world's largest rivers now fail to reach the ocean, and when they do, their waters are frequently so polluted with fertilizer runoff that they cause massive dead zones in the ocean through algae overgrowth suffocating all other life. Around the world, we're experiencing "insectageddon" with insect populations crashing, sometimes by as much as 90 percent, primarily from overuse of insecticides. Rainforests are vanishing everywhere, with the Amazon rainforest alone disappearing at the rate of an acre every second. But of all statistics, perhaps the most mind-boggling is that, at current rates, by the middle of this century there will be more plastic by weight in the ocean than fish. At this point, we're well on the way to causing the sixth great extinction of species since life began on Earth—except this is the first driven by the actions of a single species.[3]

The vast majority of this destruction has taken place since the end of the Second World War, as the modern world system emerged and began what Earth scientists have called The Great Acceleration—an explosive increase in just about every measure of human enterprise. The scale of human impact has become so massive that our actions rival or exceed the great forces of nature. The weight of all the material we produce—such as concrete, steel, and plastics—now surpasses the weight of all living biomass on Earth. Many geologists agree that we have launched a new epoch in Earth's history: No longer are we in the Holocene—the twelve-thousand-year period of relatively stable climate that gave rise to agriculture and civilization—but we have now entered the Anthropocene, an inherently unstable period characterized by massive disruptions in the planet's ecology. Millions of years from now, if another intelligent species were to examine the archaeological record, they would quickly realize that something unprecedented in Earth's history occurred during our time here.

GREEN, SMELLY WATER . . . AND BILLIONAIRES

If you live in one of the world's more affluent countries, there's a good chance that, apart from the emotional impact of reading about distant disasters, you have so far experienced only relatively manageable effects of this onslaught on Earth's life-support systems. Perhaps you've experienced smoky days from forest fires burning in the distance, endured unpleasantly hot nights during a heatwave, or had your basement flooded from an unusually heavy storm. Maybe you've been taken aback by the high price of fresh fish as the oceans empty out. Or you drove for hours through the countryside in the summertime and realized you didn't need to clean dead bugs from the windshield—because there weren't any.

The barely mentioned truth underlying our global crisis is that, while it's been caused primarily by the consumption of the wealthiest nations—frequently referred to as the Global North—the harmful effects are suffered overwhelmingly by those who live in the Global South, which people are beginning to call the Majority World, since that's what it is. Because many of those who live in the Majority World have very little to buffer them against adversity, abnormal weather and degraded ecosystems can wreak havoc on their lives. Floods may wipe out the crops they rely on for subsistence and obliterate their homes. Droughts may cause starvation and death. The resulting chaos may lead to the terror of armed violence.

There is an equally striking contrast in the relative responsibility of the Global North and Majority World for causing this growing cataclysm. When economists analyzed carbon emissions by country to determine which nations have contributed the most to increasing greenhouse gases above safe levels, they discovered a shocking disparity: The Global North has been responsible for 94 percent of the excess emissions since 1970. On this basis, large countries such as India, Nigeria, and Indonesia bear no historic responsibility whatsoever for climate breakdown, since the amounts of carbon they have emitted is still below their "fair share" of what would be a sustainable level.[4]

To the billions of impoverished people barely eking out a living in the Majority World, however, the dire effects of the climate crisis are often difficult to distinguish from the many other sources of ecological devastation and economic hardship that comprise their daily existence. Even though the world produces enough food to sustain the entire human population, roughly two billion people go hungry every day, while about 4.6 billion people—roughly 60 percent of humanity—earn less than the minimum considered necessary for a child to have a reasonable chance of surviving to their fifth birthday and reaching normal life expectancy.[5]

As we'll see in the next chapter, this is not a natural condition of humanity, but rather the result of a systematic centuries-long program of exploitation that has led to the greatest inequality in history. The gap between the wealthy elites and the rest of humanity has grown to such astronomical proportions that is difficult to fully grasp. While most people in the world face a daily struggle to keep a roof over their heads and food in their stomachs, a mere couple of dozen billionaires own as much wealth as half the entire world's population. The richest one percent of humanity possesses more wealth than the other 99 percent—and the gap is only increasing. Since 2020, the richest one percent have captured almost two thirds of all new wealth. Another way of looking at it: For every dollar of new global wealth gained in this period by someone in the bottom 90 percent, one of the world's billionaires gained $1.7 million.[6]

Around the world, inequality has increased dramatically in recent decades. Within individual countries, the gap between the average incomes of the top 10 percent and the bottom half of the population has almost doubled. In the United States, along with many other countries, the gains in wealth and income have gone overwhelmingly to the richest one percent (earning on average about $1.3 million/year), and within that group, the ultrarich—those in the top 0.001 percent—have been getting wealthier at triple the rate of the other one-percenters.[7]

It's important to understand that—just like the impoverished conditions of most of humanity—this chasm between rich and poor is not an inevitable part of the human condition. It is a political choice. From the early decades of the twentieth century until roughly 1980, income and wealth inequality were consistently shrinking in most countries. By 1980, the share of national income claimed by the top one percent had declined dramatically from about 20 percent in 1920 to about seven percent. But with the rise of neoliberal ideology, led by Reagan and Thatcher telling us "there is no alternative," the trend line moved powerfully back in the other direction.[8]

This massive recent accumulation of wealth by the elites has come, not just at the expense of other individuals, but also by sucking public wealth into private hands. National institutions such as health services, education, and public transport have been starved of the very same funds that have fed the extravagant lifestyles of wealthy elites. In 1980, among Global North countries, the wealth held by public institutions was about one fifth of the amount in private ownership. Since that time, while private wealth has roughly doubled, public wealth (the sum of all assets held by governments net of debt) has dwindled toward zero and, in many cases, negative territory. States have become penniless, forced to borrow to fund public services, while new billionaires get minted at the rate of one every thirty hours.[9]

Statistics are a necessary tool to grasp the outlandish state of inequality in our world, but ultimately, it's the quality of life experienced by most human beings that is being eroded. A comprehensive study by the social scientists Kate Pickett and Richard Wilkinson reveals that societies with a more equal wealth distribution are predictably healthier and happier. It may not surprise you that greater inequality in a country leads to lower life expectancy, poor health, and higher rates of depression, violence, and infant mortality. But what's remarkable is that it benefits almost everyone to live in a more equal society, not just the poor. Even wealthier people in more equal countries, such as the Scandinavian nations, report higher levels of wellbeing than equivalently wealthy people in unequal countries. Above a certain threshold of economic attainment, the level of equality in a society is a much stronger predictor of social wellbeing than national income.[10]

But let's not forget that those who suffer the most from inequality are the billions of people worldwide who don't have access to the bare necessities of life. Every day, unnoticed among the headlines of celebrity antics and political bluster, twenty-five thousand people around the world die from starvation and malnutrition. Many live in the slums that have grown up around the world's major cities, such as São Paulo, Jakarta, and Lagos. Often forced by hunger and desperation to leave their dying villages, they set up flimsy shanties in the unstable hillsides, garbage heaps, toxic dumps, and railroad sidings that no one else will go near, to endure what a Baghdad slum dweller describes as a "semi-death." This is what these statistics ultimately mean. In the words of Lovly Josaphat, a resident of Port-au-Prince's largest slum, Cité Soleil:

> I've suffered a lot. When it rains, the part of the Cité I live in floods and the water comes in the house. There's always water on the ground, green smelly water, and there are no paths. The mosquitoes bite us. My four-year-old has bronchitis, malaria, and even typhoid now . . . The doctor said to give him boiled water, not to give him food with grease, and not to let him walk in the water. But the water's everywhere; he can't set foot outside the house without walking in it. The doctor said that if I don't take care of him, I'll lose him.[11]

The fear in Lovly Josaphat's heart about losing her four-year-old, and the love she feels for her child, is just as deeply felt and matters just as much as that felt by an affluent mother in the Global North who has the luxury to give her children all they need for a life of health and prosperity. Why should Lovly, and the billions of others like her, have to endure this suffering in a world of plenty? How did we arrive at this grotesque situation? Where did humanity's path go so wrong?

We can't begin to formulate a vision of an ecocivilization without answering these questions, and to do so, we need to turn our attention to history. Not the history of presidents, diplomats, and glorious battles you'll find in the standard textbooks, but a different kind of history—the chronicle of how small groups of powerful elites systematically stole Earth's abundance from the common people. We must confront head-on the history they didn't teach you at school.

CHAPTER 2

THE HISTORY THEY DIDN'T TEACH YOU AT SCHOOL

Cecil Rhodes was worried. He was one of the wealthiest and most powerful men in the world at the pinnacle of imperialist fame and fortune in the year 1895. As the owner of the De Beers diamond monopoly, Prime Minister of the Cape Colony in southern Africa, and basking in such popularity that Rhodesia (now Zimbabwe) had just been named in his honor, he could do virtually anything he wanted. Yet, Rhodes was beside himself with worry.

He had just returned from a meeting of unemployed workers in the East End of London where, he confided to his diary, he had listened to "wild speeches, which were just a cry for 'bread! bread!'" The mass impoverishment of most Britons as a result of the Industrial Revolution was coming to a head, and Rhodes feared the onset of a "bloody civil war." What could he do to save himself and the elite class to which he belonged? The master plan he envisioned would help define the next century, while continuing to haunt us to this day. "I became more than ever convinced of the importance of imperialism," he wrote, as he laid out what he called his "cherished idea." "We colonial statesmen must acquire new lands to settle the surplus population, to provide new markets for the goods produced in the factories and mines . . . If you want to avoid civil war, you must become imperialists."[1]

Powerful as he was at that time, Rhodes was merely one link in a chain of oppression that had materialized centuries earlier and continues to structure the world we inhabit. His "cherished idea" is notable, not because it led to a directional shift in the strategy of the British Empire, but because in a lucid moment of fear, he crystallized the dynamic that had driven European imperialism for generations into a simple logic: Exploit those around you as much as you can; when the pressure gets too great, find others more vulnerable to exploit further, then dole out just enough of the bounty to relieve the threat from those closer to home.

This logic, in one form or another, is the essential driving force underlying five centuries of conquest and devastation that European imperialists wreaked mercilessly on the rest of the world. There's a reason why they don't teach it at school: It's a disturbing story that subverts core beliefs about the virtue of Western civilization that the dominant culture holds sacrosanct. Even worse, it's a history that bleeds uncomfortably into the present. Once we become aware of it, the harrowing implications stare us in the face through virtually every aspect of our lives, peeking through every cup of Starbucks coffee, every cheap vacation in the tropics. It calls for a moral reckoning—one that would be most inconvenient for business as usual.

This is, however, the very reason why any authentic consideration of an ecocivilization must begin with an accounting of the inequities that brought us here. Only by recognizing the historical forces that underlie our current global system can we begin to conceive of changing them.

THE GREATER FELON

Where does the story begin? Every story has a prequel, but a natural place to start is a surprising one: the Black Death that erupted in Venice and Genoa in 1348 and quickly spread like wildfire throughout Europe, wiping out about a third of its population.

Europe at that time was a cultural backwater compared to the wealth and sophistication of China, India, and the rising Ottoman Empire. Following the fall of the Roman Empire, it had settled into a mostly feudal system, in which a landed gentry maintained a regime of patronage over peasants compelled to work on their overlord's land while subsisting on whatever they could cultivate for themselves. For most common folk, life was tough. Diet was limited, disease was ever present, and life expectancy short. But it was manageable, and offered a rich experience of belonging in community. Peasants had access to the land they needed for subsistence, either through ownership, usage rights, or management of shared land—the "commons."

However, the relationship between landlords and peasants, generally a stable if uneasy one, was transformed by the demographic disaster of the Black Death. With far fewer peasants now available to work on the aristocracy's land, the balance of power shifted to the common people. Peasants, often united with craftspeople, joined waves of popular uprisings demanding compensation for their labor, freedom from taxes and tithes imposed by the nobility and the Church, and greater self-determination. Across Europe, armed rebellions threatened the entire feudal system, inspired by the calls of radical preachers such as John Ball, who famously declared, "Now the time is come in which ye may (if ye will) cast off the yoke of bondage, and recover liberty."[2]

For a while, it looked like they might succeed. In cities across Europe, such as Bruges, Ghent, and Florence, commoners took control of their own governance, temporarily establishing egalitarian communities until they were eventually crushed by well-armed militias. But the peasants continued to struggle, and by the middle of the fifteenth century, their power had grown further. In places such as England, serfs became free farmers, wages doubled or tripled, workers bargained for shorter hours, rents declined, and nutrition improved. As a result, this period has been called by one historian "the golden age of the European proletariat."[3]

Not surprisingly, the nobility was less than enamored of developments. "The peasants are too rich," wrote one in the early 1500s, "and do not know what obedience means; they don't take law into any account, they wish there were no nobles . . . and they would like to decide what rent we should get for our lands." This sentiment catalyzed a backlash by the elite that would reverberate to this day. Using brute military force, they evicted peasants from their land and fenced off the commons that had previously been collectively managed for the benefit of the whole community. This process, known as "enclosure," has been aptly described by the historian Karl Polanyi as "a revolution of the rich against the poor." Jettisoning ancient customs, through organized violence and intimidation, the elites stole land from the peasants, left them destitute, and then harshly punished those who had dared to take back their heritage. In the words of a popular rhyme from that period:

The law doth punish man or woman
That steals the goose from off the common,
But lets the greater felon loose
That steals the common from the goose.[4]

The peasants were far from willing to accept this incursion on their ancestral rights. Across Europe they put up fierce resistance lasting for generations, but eventually they succumbed to the ruthless violence of the aristocrats' armed forces. In Germany, a large-scale peasants' revolt in 1525 ended in the massacre of over a hundred thousand commoners. In England, several major rebellions took place over the course of a century in London, Norwich, and the Midlands. Each one ended in the mass slaughter of the peasants who had dared to defend their rights to land and subsistence.

It is hard to overstate the magnitude of the enclosure movement. While there have been numerous cases in history of powerful elites taking land from those more vulnerable, the scale of this expropriation was unprecedented. In England, where it was most pronounced, it led to the privatization of tens of millions of acres over a couple of centuries, displacing large swathes of the population and destroying over a thousand villages.

By the seventeenth century, the English monarchy, concerned by the transformation of the nation, tried constraining the nobility's power in an attempt to protect what was left of the commons. By this point, however, the balance of power had shifted to the landowners. A civil war ensued, culminating in what became known as the "Glorious Revolution" of 1688, which severely weakened the monarchy and entrenched the authority of the landowning class through their control of Parliament. Now, the organized violence of the enclosure movement was given the imprimatur of the law of the land. In thousands of separate acts of Parliament over the next two centuries, about seven million more acres—the final one-fifth of England's land still available for commoners—were enclosed. The expropriation was complete. As a result, in Britain today, half the land is owned by a mere twenty-five thousand landowners representing just 0.06 percent of the population.[5]

A MODEL FOR THE WORLD

The millions of peasants who were forced off their land, losing their communities and means of subsistence, faced a grim reality. Starving, homeless, and bereft of any support system, they were refugees in their own country. Quantifying the magnitude of this catastrophe, economic historians estimate that wages declined by as much as 70 percent between the sixteenth and eighteenth centuries, causing average life expectancy at birth to deteriorate from 43 years to the low 30s.[6]

New words such as "poverty," "paupers," and "vagabonds" became commonplace in the English language to describe the results of this cataclysm. But rather than responding compassionately, the authorities classified these new categories of destitution as crimes requiring draconian punishments. Vagabonds (defined as anyone who could work but chose not to) were to be whipped for a first offence, with capital punishment for a third offence. In Germany, a simple theft would lead to cruel forms of execution such as quartering or being burned alive.

Along with the physical devastation came a loss of community. Old-style peasant villages had made up for their meagerness in material wealth with a richly complex fabric of relationships based on established customs of mutual aid and cooperation. Now these were gone, leaving people unmoored both materially and spiritually. Prisons and mental hospitals—unneeded in traditional rural communities—were invented in the late eighteenth century as holding pens for those whose lives had been pulverized by their newly desperate circumstances.[7]

For the peasants who remained on the land, the old patronage relationship with the landlord was replaced by a new system of market leases, allocated only to those who were the most productive. In a process known as "improvement," peasants had to compete with each other to extract more produce from the land to satisfy the landlord and avoid being evicted. As the anthropologist Jason Hickel points out, here was the beginning of capitalism: a system in which maximizing the return on capital investment became the governing imperative, eclipsing any consideration of human welfare.[8]

For the desperate millions evicted from their land, there was frequently only one alternative to starvation and death: moving into an urban slum and surrendering oneself to the misery of factory employment. In the "dark Satanic Mills" of William Blake's depiction, families including small children were forced to labor, often for sixteen hours a day, in dangerous, noxious conditions, to earn just enough for their bare survival. This was the birthplace of the Industrial Revolution, described by Polanyi as "a veritable abyss of human degradation." On the other hand, for the industrialists enriching themselves from this misery, there was a double benefit from their workers' plight. Because of their desperation, they could pay them starvation wages, keeping maximal profit for themselves; and since the newly landless workers could no longer provide for their own food, clothing, and housing, they now depended on the market economy for virtually every aspect of their survival, thus becoming what Hickel calls "the world's first mass consumer population."

Through this bleak process of violent dispossession, landowners and industrialists had stumbled upon a model, known as "artificial scarcity," that would be replicated and perfected as Europeans expanded their control through the world. Until the advent of enclosure, peasants were mostly self-sufficient. They might choose to work extra hours for their lord to bring in some extra funds, but they might also prefer to spend any spare time they had with their families or gathering with friends in the village square. They would certainly never dream of uprooting their lives to work for long hours in a grimy factory.

How then, could they be forced to relinquish their lives for the enrichment of landlords and industrialists? Brute force was one way, but was inefficient if it had to be continually applied. A far more effective approach turned out to be creating scarcity by removing the peasants' original source of livelihood, driving them to such desperation that they had no choice but to sell their labor for sheer survival.

By the eighteenth century, this had become a conscious, widely discussed strategy. The agriculturalist Arthur Young declared in 1771 that "everyone but an idiot knows that the lower classes must be kept poor, or they will never be industrious," while Reverend Joseph Townsend concurred in 1786 that "it is only hunger which can spur and goad them on to labour." Hunger, he concluded, "will tame the fiercest animals, it will teach decency and civility, obedience and subjugation to the most brutish, the most obstinate, and the most perverse." The Scottish merchant and magistrate Patrick Colquhoun saw artificial scarcity as the foundation of civilization:

> Poverty is therefore a most necessary and indispensable ingredient in society, without which nations and communities could not exist in a state of civilization . . . It is the source of wealth, since without poverty, there could be no labour; there could be no riches, no refinement, no comfort, and no benefit to those who may be possessed of wealth.[9]

This odious doctrine was not confined to academic theorizing but became the driving force of social policy. In rural Berkshire in 1795, a group of kindhearted justices held an emergency meeting to respond to widespread hunger among the people. Oblivious to the theorizing of Townsend and Colquhoun, they instituted a policy of financial subsidies for the poor based on the price of bread, known as the Speenhamland Law, designed so that no one should go hungry. The policy proved so popular that it quickly spread through the countryside and factory towns. However, the industrialists, with increased political power in Parliament, would have none of it. In 1834 they abolished this policy, substituting it with a Poor Law which the historian Rutger Bregman has called "perhaps the most heinous form of 'public assistance' that the world has ever witnessed." Now, rather than receive a subsidy for bread, impoverished folk were committed to virtual slave labor, forced to perform meaningless work such as breaking stones, spouses separated from each other and their children, and kept in such hunger that inmates would gnaw on bones that were meant to be ground for fertilizer.[10]

Buoyed by their success in using artificial scarcity to force dispossessed commoners into soul-destroying work, Europe's landowners and industrialists learned to apply this model to other parts of the world. As they colonized India and Africa, European imperialists faced a similar obstacle to that presented by villagers back home. How could they force Indian peasants, who were satisfied with their lives, to break their backs producing cash crops such as cotton, indigo, or opium? Colonists in Africa similarly pondered what they called "the Labor Question": How could they drive contented villagers underground to mine copper, gold, and diamonds for them? In each case, artificial scarcity provided the answer. Just as they had done back home, but with even greater brutality, they forced peasants off their land, dismantled their systems of mutual aid, and imposed taxes that could only be paid in European currency, thus mercilessly turning people into commodities for colonial expansion.

HOW THE COLONIES DEVELOPED EUROPE

Throughout most of recorded history, the pinnacles of civilization in Eurasia could usually be found in China, India, or the Middle East. This began changing dramatically a few hundred years ago. The story taught in most schools today is that the Age of Enlightenment, originating in Europe in the seventeenth and eighteenth centuries, generated spectacular and unprecedented progress for humanity. Europeans, we are told, brought material, economic—and even moral—development to the rest of the world.

It is certainly true that Europe's Scientific Revolution, followed by the Industrial Revolution, transformed the world, engendering many beneficial developments. What is frequently left out of the conventional history, though, is the vast devastation unleashed by Europe's increased power on the rest of humankind. Europe's scientific and industrial advances gave them a military edge over other societies, but the ascendancy of the Global North to dominance in wealth and power resulted primarily from how they took advantage of that military edge to conquer, enslave, and plunder other nations.

Until they were assaulted by European powers, most people in the world lived longer, healthier lives than European norms. Asia in particular enjoyed better sanitation, higher levels of nutrition, health, and literacy, more sophisticated cities, and superior transportation systems. China and India alone accounted for about two-thirds of the world economy. Europe's relentless onslaught would change all that. European conquerors engaged in a centuries-long, worldwide campaign of looting the wealth they discovered, subjugating and enslaving populations, expropriating their resources, and forcing them to organize their societies around European priorities at the expense of their own sustenance.

The magnitude of this global theft is monumental. To focus on just one commodity: The amount of silver stolen from South America from the sixteenth to nineteenth centuries, if invested at historical interest rates from 1800 to the present, would now be worth $165 trillion—about one third of the world's total private wealth. The havoc caused by European colonists was equally prodigious. In the Americas, in the sixteenth century alone, close to 100 million Indigenous people died through slaughter, starvation, or disease. Fifteen million Africans were transported over three centuries from their homelands to suffer the torment of slavery. Living standards in India and China collapsed—their combined share of the global economy shrinking to 10 percent while the European share tripled to 60 percent. As Jason Hickel pithily remarks, "Europe didn't develop the colonies. The colonies developed Europe."

When Rhodes came up with his "cherished idea" in 1895, he was merely describing a system of global appropriation that had been developed over centuries. When the British first colonized India, for example, their fledgling textile industry was a minnow compared with India's, which was world renowned for its fine cloth. The British used a plethora of dirty tactics to turn things around, sometimes brazenly destroying looms and even crushing weavers' fingers. Most significantly, they established protective tariffs on imported Indian textiles, while flooding the Indian market with their own. As a result, India's share of the global textile market collapsed from over 25 percent to a mere three percent by the end of British rule. When Dacca, the capital of Bengal and center of the textile industry, was conquered by the British in 1757, it was a wealthy, bustling city as large as London. A hundred years later, having lost 80 percent of its population, it had become a hotbed of malaria and jungle fever. Today, it is one of the most impoverished cities in the world.[11]

Frequently the wealth transfer to the colonists took the form of unbridled plunder. In one particularly egregious episode, when Clive of India defeated the rulers of Bengal, he loaded the entire contents of their treasury onto a hundred boats, sending them down the Ganges to the Calcutta headquarters of the East India Company—a for-profit company that was given license by the British to rule the territory as absolute despot, killing, stealing, and even waging war for the benefit of its shareholders back home.[12]

One of the most devastating aspects of colonization was how systems of collective care, developed over untold generations, were demolished to make way for a market economy. In India, property rights were usually held informally by villagers who managed their land as a collective commons, allocating critical resources such as water through long-established traditions, and storing grain reserves communally as a buffer against lean years. Applying the principle of artificial scarcity, the British replaced this system with one of private ownership, extracting rent from the peasants and forcing them to convert to cash crops. The results were calamitous. During a series of droughts over two decades in the late nineteenth century, nearly 30 million Indians are estimated to have died unnecessarily from starvation. India was producing enough grain to feed its population even during the drought years, but the wheat was kept in heavily guarded silos before being exported to Europe, enriching traders speculating on rising prices while indebted, starving peasants were unable to find the two cents a day they needed for survival.

There were no apparent moral limits to the mayhem Europeans were willing to inflict for profit. The British desired Chinese products such as tea, porcelain, and silk, but couldn't afford enough silver to buy them at the prices the Chinese set. So, they entered the narcotics trade, growing opium in India to sell illegally on China's black market, using the funds to buy the goods they wanted. When the Chinese understandably curbed this illicit trade, the British initiated a series of attacks that became known as the Opium Wars, sending the first steel, steam-powered ships with cannons to terrorize the Chinese, and culminating in the destruction of the Imperial Summer Palace in Beijing. Thus began a century of China's humiliation at the hands of Western powers. Forced to pay "reparations" that bankrupted the nation, and wracked by warring drug lords, China devolved into a vortex of a failed state, enduring a bloody civil war that took the lives of up to 30 million people, while tens of millions became addicted to the opium now supplied plentifully by the British.

The brutality of the European imperialists was rivaled only by their boundless hubris. As European nations began competing with each other to extract the prolific natural resources of Africa's interior, they agreed in the

Berlin Conference of 1884 to coordinate their assault by parceling out the entire continent for each colonizing nation to exploit. The arbitrary lines they drew on the map to delineate territories frequently conflicted with traditional ethnic boundaries, leading to a jumbled outcome whereby some populations were split, while other dissimilar groups were forced into a political fusion—a disarray that haunts Africa to this day.[13]

Freed to focus on their own territories, the European powers now had a new continent to ravage. The copper Europe needed for the electrification of its infrastructure came extensively from land in Rhodesia that belonged to the Ndebele tribe. When the Ndebele rose up to protect their ancestral land, they were helpless against the newly invented machine guns of the British, which Cecil Rhodes's private army utilized to massacre sixty thousand tribespeople. In the Congo, which King Leopold II of Belgium claimed as his private possession, the prized material was rubber to make tires for the booming automobile industry. Leopold stopped at nothing to maximize production. Enslaving much of the population, his military would chop off the hands of those who didn't meet their production quotas. Another diabolical tactic was to take women as hostages, shooting them if their men didn't fulfill their allotment. Ten million Congolese—about half the country's population—died under Leopold's vicious regime.

By the time colonialism reached its denouement, at the end of the Second World War, it had set in place the defining structures of the world we inhabit today. Western nations had amassed vast wealth and power at the expense of most of the world's population, who were left impoverished and bereft of their ancestral cultural and economic traditions. With the horrors of colonialism now foregone, there was hope that a new order might be built to more equitably organize and distribute the world's wealth. Could that be possible?

MAINTAINING "THIS POSITION OF DISPARITY"

Even before the Second World War was over, the United States and its allies were hard at work organizing the new world order. At the Bretton Woods conference in 1944, plans were finalized for the World Bank and the International Monetary Fund (IMF) to enable the global economic system to grow smoothly from the ruins, avoiding the mistakes that had led to the Great Depression before the war.

In his 1949 inaugural speech, two years after India's independence, President Harry Truman struck a hopeful note, ushering in a new global era defined by a fresh watchword: *development*. "We must embark on a bold new program," he declared, "for making the benefits of our scientific advances and industrial progress available for the improvement and growth of underdeveloped areas" filled with people "living in conditions approaching misery. Their food is inadequate. They are victims of disease. Their economic life is primitive and stagnant." No mention was made of the centuries of colonial oppression that had brought them to this misery. Rather, the prevailing sentiment was that the enlightened, advanced Western powers could apply their social, political, and technological superiority for the betterment of what became known as the Third World, and help them develop their societies in the model of their superiors.

There was another dark side to this aspirational vision. Truman went on to emphasize the importance of supporting "freedom-loving nations against the dangers of aggression," announcing plans for the formation of NATO and offering "military advice and equipment to free nations which will cooperate with us in the maintenance of peace and security." The Cold War was coming out of the shadows.

In fact, the prime directive of the postwar era had been more clearly elaborated the previous year by the US diplomat and Cold War strategist George Kennan in a memorandum to colleagues, using the kind of straight talk that was unfit for presidential speeches:

> We have about 50 percent of the world's wealth, but only 6.3 percent of its population. In this situation, we cannot fail to be the object of envy and resentment. Our real task in the coming period is to devise a pattern of relations which will permit us to maintain this position of disparity. To do so, we will have to dispense with all sentimentality and day-dreaming; and our attention will have to be concentrated everywhere on our immediate national objectives.[14]

The IMF and World Bank were set up with these "immediate national objectives" in mind. Voting power in both institutions was structured on the basis of financial ownership, giving majority control to the wealthiest nations and allowing the US to veto any decision. The institutions enjoy legal "immunity" status which means they cannot be sued for any reason, and their leaders are not elected but appointed by the US and Europe.

Even the most high-minded strategies of the victorious Americans were arranged "to maintain this position of disparity." The Marshall Plan, a $13 billion aid program to fund the reconstruction of post-war Europe, dubbed by Churchill the "most unsordid act in history," was designed to facilitate a partial takeover by American corporations of the European economy. By the 1960s, American firms controlled large portions of Europe's markets in industries ranging from petroleum to farm machinery and telecommunications. American-controlled investments in Germany accounted for more than half the value of the entire German stock exchange.[15]

Elsewhere, American forces were less "unsordid" in their efforts to maintain the disparity. Whenever leaders of "developing" nations attempted to throw off the shackles of domination by Western nations and pursue their own path of development, they were met with violent opposition. Using a combination of bribery, economic coercion, and clandestine military assistance, the US ensured that only its model of development remained supreme.

Iran was one of the first countries to experience the new world order when its democratically elected leader, Mohammad Mossadegh was overthrown in a military coup in 1953 masterminded by the US. Mossadegh had drawn the Americans' ire with a series of reforms intended to improve the welfare of his nation: introducing unemployment compensation, abolishing forced agricultural labor, raising taxes on the rich and, most egregiously, attempting to regain ownership of the country's oil reserves. His replacement, Mohammad Reza Pahlavi, was installed as the Shah of Iran, a friend of Western oil interests, who ruled for decades in absolute power supported by a military government.

The next year, it was the turn of Jacobo Árbenz, democratically elected president of Guatemala, who attempted to nationalize tracts of unused private land for distribution to starving, landless peasants. Half a million acres of this land was owned by the United Fruit Company, to which Árbenz offered full compensation for its purchase. This was, however, unacceptable to their executives, who worked with the CIA in what was code-named Operation PBSuccess to bomb the capital and install a military dictator in his place. Thus began four decades of military rule in Guatemala, coupled with brutal suppression of the indigenous Mayan population systematically forced off their land, some two hundred thousand of whom were killed over decades of resistance.

Country by country, continent by continent, the Americans and their European allies ensured that the massive economic and political disparities established by colonialism would not be dislodged. The first elected president of Ghana, Kwame Nkrumah, succeeded initially in nationalizing mines, investing in manufacturing infrastructure, and providing free healthcare and education to the people. As a visionary pan-African leader, he called for continent-wide unity and cooperation. A year after his iconic book, *Neo-Colonialism*, was published in 1965, which denounced continued meddling by the Americans and Europeans in the developing world, Nkrumah was ousted by a CIA-backed coup. The military junta they installed reversed his reforms, crushing the welfare of ordinary Ghanaians by an estimated 80 percent, and invited foreign corporations to return to Ghana to mine resources for export.[16]

President Sukarno of Indonesia, newly independent from Dutch rule, suffered a similar fate. In response to his policies to nationalize Western-owned oil and rubber operations and redistribute wealth to the poor, the CIA backed General Suharto in a bloody coup, resulting in the deaths of nearly a million of Sukarno's supporters. The new regime, guided by economists trained in the US, gave up the country's natural resources for Western corporations to exploit as they pleased.

Overall, it's estimated that the US has attempted to overthrow approximately seventy governments since the end of the Second World War. But it's important to realize how powerfully the effects of these violent interventions were felt even in those countries that avoided direct attack. In *Confessions of an Economic Hitman*, whistleblower extraordinaire John Perkins describes the arsenal of nefarious practices—including fraudulent financial reports, payoffs, and extortion—routinely used by a cadre of highly-paid professionals to coerce Majority World political elites into doing what the US wanted. He describes how he and others would darkly point to the violent ends of leaders in neighboring countries, while motivating them with kickbacks to open up their nations for extraction by Western corporations.[17]

In spite of this rigged game, many Majority World leaders continued to be driven by the urge to relieve their countryfolk from grinding poverty. Even though the IMF and World Bank were controlled by Western powers, their activities were guided by Keynesian economics, which saw governments and markets as balancing each other, and regarded decent wages and workers' rights as important aspects of economic development. To a moderate degree, this worked. Through the 1950s and 1960s, economic growth was unprecedented, while inequality decreased markedly throughout the world. Inspired by a vision of independent development, a group of nonaligned nations proposed what they called a New International Economic Order, claiming the rights for developing countries to nationalize foreign-owned assets if necessary, protect their economies with tariffs, and regulate transnational corporations. When the General Assembly of the United Nations passed their proposal in 1973, it seemed that perhaps a new dawn had indeed arisen.

Alarmed, the Western powers created their own economic alliance, which came to be called the G7, to counteract this threat to their dominance. Additionally, they had a new secret weapon to wield, one that had been quietly developed in academic institutions and think tanks over decades and was now ready for release onto an unsuspecting world. The opportunity for its deployment would present itself later the same year in Santiago, Chile.

"GREED IS GOOD!"

Chileans at that time were enjoying the first fruits of what the New International Economic Order was striving for. Their president Salvador Allende, elected in 1970 on a Socialist platform, delivered on his promises with a minimum wage, free school meals, expanded low-income housing, and nationalizing the copper mines. He capped private land ownership at eighty hectares, fully compensating owners, and redistributed the land to peasant farmers. While wages and school enrollment rose and poverty declined, this was unacceptable to the US. After three years of economic and financial intimidation to no avail, they backed General Augusto Pinochet in a violent military coup culminating in bombers shelling the presidential palace. Following Allende's death, Pinochet murdered or imprisoned up to a hundred thousand of Allende's supporters, and brought in a group of economists educated at the University of Chicago, dubbed "the Chicago boys," to unveil their new secret weapon—neoliberalism.

Five decades after these events, we are so immersed in the precepts of neoliberalism that it's hard to realize how bizarre they appeared when they were first unleashed in Chile. Neoliberalism was the name given to a set of ideas that had their origins in a meeting, held in Switzerland in 1947, of a group of economists, historians, and philosophers who called themselves the Mont Pelerin Society. Concerned that developments such as the welfare state in Britain and the dominance of Keynesian economics would lead inexorably to communism, they set out to promote a diametrically opposed doctrine based on the principle of individual liberty. In the ensuing decades, through a transatlantic network of academics, businessmen, and journalists, and supported by wealthy backers who funded university departments and a collection of think tanks, they refined and advanced their ideology.[18]

The defining characteristics of neoliberal ideology began with the twin concepts of the individual and liberty, which together are viewed as towering above all other values. An individual's drive to outcompete others is considered supremely virtuous, while liberty is the elimination of any constraints on achieving his or her success. "Greed is good!" in the phrase immortalized by the fictional Gordon Gekko in the 1987 movie *Wall Street*, encapsulating the subversive view of morality first popularized by the novelist Ayn Rand decades earlier.[19]

These precepts lead to a fundamental belief in the value of unrestrained competition, with free markets, free trade, and minimal rules or restrictions. Private property is paramount, and the role of government, whether through regulation, market intervention, or state ownership of assets, should be eliminated to the greatest extent possible. Wealth is the ultimate measure of achievement, as manifested in personal riches, business profitability, or a nation's gross domestic product (GDP). Inequality, therefore, far from being pernicious, is a sign of a society's health, because it permits those who are most accomplished to be maximally rewarded.

Neoliberal economics is built on classical economic theory from the nineteenth century, which models a "perfect market" composed of greedy, selfish, lazy individuals who act rationally to maximize their material consumption above any other consideration. Based on a selective reading of Adam Smith's eighteenth-century classic *The Wealth of Nations*, neoliberals argue that encouraging people to act in this way leads to the best possible outcome for society. However, as many experts have demonstrated—and as will be discussed later in the book—this view of humans and society is fundamentally wrong. The only people who act to maximize their desires without regard for morality, empathy, mutual care, or social norms, are clinical psychopaths, who represent no more than one percent of a normal population.[20]

When these ideas were first advanced in the 1950s and 1960s they were dismissed as ludicrous in any serious economic conversation. But over decades of assiduous effort, the Mont Pelerin Society and allies succeeded in shifting what became known as the Overton window—the set of ideas that are considered acceptable discussion topics in mainstream political discourse.

By the time of Allende's demise, they were ready for action. One of their founding members, Milton Friedman, had built a neoliberal command post at the University of Chicago, and along with his Chicago Boys he became a key advisor to the Pinochet regime. Chile was an experimental subject for them, presenting an opportunity to apply their radical, untested theories to an entire nation. They privatized nearly five hundred state companies, sold the public schools and social security system to private investors, removed tariffs, eliminated subsidies, and removed price controls. The results were catastrophic for ordinary Chileans. Unemployment shot up from three percent under Allende to as high as 35 percent. With average wages down and the minimum wage 42 percent lower, the poverty rate reached 41 percent and hunger was rife. But for the wealthy elites, the experiment was a splendid success. Even as poverty became rampant, their share of national income soared dramatically, causing Chile to become one of the world's most unequal nations.

With their first quarry bagged, the next challenge the neoliberals faced was how to roll this model out to the rest of the world. The same fateful year of 1973 dealt them another hand that they skillfully turned to their advantage.

THE RACE TO THE BOTTOM

"Only a crisis," Milton Friedman famously wrote, "produces real change."

> When that crisis occurs, the actions that are taken depend on the ideas that are lying around. That, I believe, is our basic function: to develop alternatives to existing policies . . . until the politically impossible becomes the politically inevitable.

The crisis he was waiting for materialized just a month after the coup in Chile, when Arab nations attacked Israel in the Yom Kippur War. Once the Israelis successfully counterattacked, threatening Damascus and Cairo, the Arabs discovered how to wield an entirely new weapon—oil. The embargo initiated by the oil cartel OPEC caused seismic upheavals through the global economy, kicking off years of stagflation which in turn led to a new series of international disruptions.[21]

As they kept raising the price of oil through the 1970s, OPEC nations found themselves awash in cash (known as petrodollars) which, in return for security guarantees from Washington, they invested in the United States. Other developing countries, unable to afford the high price of oil, now turned desperately to the US banks for those petrodollars as loans to keep their economies going. The Iranian Revolution in 1979, which led to a second oil price shock, further exacerbated these imbalances. Developing countries' debt quadrupled in a decade to $1.6 trillion. The fact that the interest on this debt was denominated in dollars delivered a final blow when the US Federal Reserve raised interest rates up to 20 percent to fight inflation back home. Countries around the world could no longer afford interest payments and hurtled toward bankruptcy.

Friedman and his comrades had, not just one, but multiple intersecting crises to work with. In the US and UK, Keynesian economics had fallen from grace, and the radical neoliberal alternative boosted the popularity of leaders such as Ronald Reagan and Margaret Thatcher. Meanwhile, the desperate straits of nations teetering on the verge of bankruptcy opened them up to the same kind of structural disembowelment that had been foisted on Chile, without having to fire a single gun or bomb a presidential palace.

In place of soldiers in combat fatigues wielding machine guns, Western powers could now rely on bankers in pinstriped suits wielding loan agreements. But the results were every bit as devastating, if not more so, to the lives of billions of people across the world. The IMF and World Bank were repurposed from their relatively benign earlier role of stabilizing the global economy to become enforcers of neoliberal policies throughout the developing world. Their ammunition was a set of requirements called Structural Adjustment Programs (SAPs) that they foisted on countries facing bankruptcy in return for further loans.

Countries were forced to redirect most of their assets and cash flows toward servicing the debt. This meant selling public assets such as railways or mines to private investors, eliminating subsidies on food and farming, and cutting expenditures on healthcare and education. They were also required to open their markets to foreign corporations, cut tariffs, eliminate capital and price controls, and weaken workforce and environmental regulations. Any cash flow remaining after debt service had to be invested in export-oriented industries—cash crops such as wheat, rice, or coffee, and commodities such as copper or aluminum—to earn the foreign exchange required for continued debt service. As these requirements were applied worldwide, markets were flooded with oversupply of raw materials leading to lower prices. This, in turn, created a reinforcing feedback loop: The financial crisis of the Majority World worsened while wealthy countries enjoyed lower raw material costs which curbed inflation and further enriched them.

The test case of Chile proved a reliable indicator for the rest of the world. As the Global North reaped the benefits of enhanced access to the markets and commodities of the developing world, the lives of regular people in those countries were decimated. In the 1960s and 1970s, economies in the Global South had been growing at an annual rate of over three percent. Over the next two decades, those rates plunged to just 0.7 percent, and in sub-Saharan Africa (where a total of 31 SAPs were imposed) per capita income actually declined by 0.7 percent per year, doubling the number of Africans living in extreme poverty. Structural adjustment, in the words of Jason Hickel, "turned out to be the greatest single cause of impoverishment in the 20th century," leading to an increase of over a billion people subsisting on less than $5 per day. Global inequality widened even further: In 1965, the per capita income of the G7 countries was twenty times that of the poorest nations; by 1995 it was thirty-nine times larger—and is over fifty times larger today.[22]

Effective as the SAPs were in spreading neoliberal policies worldwide, they had a limit: They could only be imposed piecemeal on nations facing bankruptcy. However, by the 1990s, a new delivery system was devised that would complete the job, leaving virtually no country immune from the neoliberal takeover. The wealthy nations imposed on the world a new entity under their control called the World Trade Organization (WTO), which developing nations had to join to avoid being shut out of the world economy. The price of membership, though, was to agree to essentially the same package of economic disembowelment that the SAPs had enforced. The scope was now expanded to include intellectual property rights which, among other things, banned poor countries from producing their own low-priced generic pharmaceutical products. While other countries were required to eliminate agricultural subsidies, the US and EU applied a blatant double standard, continuing to pay massive subsidies to their own farmers (mostly large corporations) which allowed them to undercut farmers in the rest of the world with cheap food exports.

The launch of the WTO signaled the beginning of globalization: the opening up of the world into one seamless playing field for large corporations and financial institutions. With impediments to the free flow of capital eliminated, corporations could choose where to invest for the highest returns. Workers, however, did not have the same mobility. As a result, nations now found themselves competing against each other, offering lower wages, tax breaks, and stripped-down regulations to entice corporations to invest in their region. This kicked off what became known as the "race to the bottom" as states and municipalities vied with each other in a downward spiral of concessions. It also transformed the relationship between corporations and their employees in the developed world: Workers became more compliant, knowing that, if they demanded too much, their employers could simply move their operations elsewhere.[23]

We can get a feeling for the effects of globalization from the example of the North American Free Trade Agreement (NAFTA) which eliminated most tariffs between Canada, Mexico, and the United States in 1994. Subsidized corn from the US flooded the Mexican market, undercutting domestic farmers and driving two million out of business over the next ten years, vacating millions of hectares of farmland that transnational corporations bought up cheaply for industrial agriculture and mining. Instead of cheaper corn reducing food prices for ordinary people, deregulation of retail markets caused the cost of tortillas to nearly quadruple, resulting in widespread hunger and malnutrition. Like the European peasants driven off their land by enclosure centuries earlier, displaced farmers had no choice but to accept low-paying factory jobs in the tariff-free maquiladora factories set up near the US-Mexico border. Before long, though, the jobs dried up as corporations relocated to even cheaper Asian sites in the race to the bottom. As desperate workers struggled to survive, criminal drug cartels swooped them up, becoming the second biggest industry in Mexico, while millions of others sought a better life by crossing the border, leading to the surge in undocumented immigrants that spurred the rise of xenophobic nationalism in US politics. Ten years after NAFTA, nineteen million more Mexicans lived in poverty, with more than half the population below the poverty line; and a quarter of the Mexican population did not have access to basic food. While billionaire Carlos Slim, who took advantage of deregulation to monopolize the Mexican telecom industry, has become one of the world's richest men with a net worth of $100 billion, Mexico today is racked by drug-related violence and suffers one of the highest murder rates in the world.[24]

Similar stories have played out across the world. Ever since President Truman rolled out the idea of "development," many in the West have grown comfortable with the thought that, even if the colonial past was tainted, at least we now generously transfer some of our largesse back to the Global South in the form of foreign aid. It's true that more than $200 billion is given annually in development assistance by wealthy nations. But that number is dwarfed by the financial outflows pouring in the other direction. A comprehensive study of global flows has concluded that the net drain of funds from the Majority World to the Global North is about three trillion dollars annually, or fifteen times the aid budget. Some of that drain consists of interest payments, fees for foreign patents, and investment returns to foreign shareholders; but the largest amount is in the form of corporate chicanery. Transnational corporations engage in widespread practices, many of them illegal, such as trade mis-invoicing and abusive transfer pricing, in which they use false prices among their subsidiaries to funnel profits to parts of the world where they can avoid taxes or capital controls.[25]

On top of this financial drain, another massive wealth transfer to the Global North occurs through what is called "unequal exchange": the exchange-rate differentials that persist between the two regions. An employee earning the legal minimum wage in San Diego makes about nine times the minimum wage of someone across the border in Tijuana doing exactly the same work. This disparity, so blatant yet generally disregarded as "the way things are," is the sordid legacy of the history we've been tracing. The drain from the Global South as a result of unequal exchange has persisted at an annual rate that would be enough to end extreme poverty fifteen times over, aggregating since 1960 to an eye-popping $62 trillion.[26]

THE SUPREMACY OF THE CORPORATION

Of course, those trillions of dollars flowing to the Global North weren't evenly distributed there. In fact, the primary direct beneficiaries were not people at all but corporations, whose inexorable rise in power, inextricably intertwined and equally omitted from the history books, is another tale to be told.

It's no coincidence that the modern corporation was born at the same time as colonialism. It was a legal invention designed specifically to facilitate the exploitation of the rest of the world by wealthy Europeans. The legal structure of the limited liability corporation encouraged investors to fund expeditions to distant locales by enabling them to enjoy unlimited financial upside while limiting their risk to the amount they invested. The first major corporations were the Dutch East India Company, founded in

1602, and its namesake in England which ultimately eclipsed it in magnitude and rapacity.

When this new legal framework was applied to enterprises closer to home, it became clear that the imbalance between the potential upside and downside created an incentive to take inappropriate risks, known as moral hazard. Reckless behavior led to a series of spectacular frauds and a market crash resulting in a ban on corporations in England in 1720, which was eventually lifted when the Industrial Revolution generated greater demand for new investment. In the United States, Thomas Jefferson and other leaders, aware of the English experience, were deeply suspicious of corporations, giving them circumscribed charters with tightly constrained powers. However, during the turmoil of the Civil War, industrialists took advantage of the disarray, expanding their influence through widespread political corruption, and pushing state legislatures to issue charters in perpetuity giving them the right to do anything not explicitly prohibited by law.[27]

A decisive moment in their path to domination came in 1886 when the US Supreme Court designated corporations as "persons" entitled to the same legal rights as citizens. Since then, corporate dominance has only been further enhanced by law, culminating in the landmark *Citizens United* case of 2010, which lifted restrictions on political spending by corporations in elections. Not surprisingly, campaign donations by corporations more than doubled since then, totaling over $14 billion in the 2020 presidential election cycle.

Beyond helping to elect their preferred politicians, corporations literally write laws for them once they're in office, with lobbyists sitting in drafting sessions and providing the precise language they need to achieve their business objectives. There are now roughly twenty-three registered lobbyists in Washington for every member of Congress, and the unregistered number is estimated to be eight times higher. The distinction between politician and lobbyist is frequently merely one of timing: Elected officials know that when their tenure is complete, they can simply pass through the "revolving door" and become a lobbyist themselves, as long as they've satisfied their benefactors.[28]

Adept as they are at influencing legislation in the developed world, corporations have even more control over politics in the Global South. Majority World countries are frequently called out for their corruption, but what is mentioned less is the central role corporations play in that corruption, using bribes to get the contracts and regulatory permits they need. However, since the rise of globalization, corporations can now take advantage of new international rules that allow them to dictate what most governments can do without having to resort to bribery. Concealed under the anodyne label of Investor-State Dispute Settlement (ISDS) processes, these new rules have further subverted the autonomy of most Majority World nations.

Take a deep breath. Entering the ISDS underworld is like accompanying Alice into a dark Wonderland—a topsy-turvy universe removed from normal reality—and yet this iniquitous system sabotages the real lives of untold millions of people across the world. ISDS is a secretive international arbitration process that, since its inception with NAFTA, is now included in thousands of investment and trade treaties. It empowers corporations to sue states for exorbitant damages whenever a government passes legislation to protect its people or environment against corporate misconduct. Cases are decided, not by judges, but by arbitration lawyers who frequently work for law firms representing investors. The process is cloaked in secrecy: Claims, hearings, documents, awards, and settlements can all be kept secret, even though the arbitration frequently influences crucial public policy issues.

An especially bizarre aspect of ISDS claims is that corporations often seek damages, not just for the costs they have incurred, but for "anticipated future profits" that government legislation may have prevented. Given the secrecy, many cases never come to light, but those that have display breathtaking corporate audacity, and can be financially devastating for nations. Zeph Investments is suing Australia for $300 billion because the government refused to approve a proposed mine; three Australian mining companies claim $37 billion from the Congo, an amount triple the nation's annual GDP; a proposed natural gas processing plant has led to a $6 billion award against Nigeria, and a planned undersea phosphate mine has generated a $3.5 billion claim against Mexico. Honduras faces a $10 billion claim for its democratic decision to close down special economic zones that had been established by a previous government. When Tethyan Copper won a $6 billion award against Pakistan for a rejected mining project, the country, devastated by climate-related floods covering a third of its territory, couldn't afford to pay so it capitulated and let the mine proceed.[29]

In most cases, claims arise because governments are trying to protect the welfare of their citizens. Uruguay was sued by Philip Morris for requiring warning labels on its cigarette packs; Argentina faced over forty lawsuits for freezing utility rates during a financial crisis; Canada was sued for placing a moratorium on fracking in Quebec; and Slovakia was forced to pay compensation for requiring its health insurers to operate on a not-for-profit basis.

In total, ISDS awards that have been made public amounted to $35 billion in the decade from 2010 to 2019, which is ten times the amount from the previous decade. But, just like the coups backed by Western powers after the Second World War, their chilling effect extends far beyond the actual claims. They have fittingly been called "litigation terrorism" by the Nobel Prize-winning economist Joseph Stiglitz, since the mere threat of one can be enough to prevent a government from passing legislation in the interests of its people.

The topsy-turvy nature of the ISDS process is especially egregious: While investors can sue states, states have no reciprocal rights to sue foreign investors or claim damages from foreign corporations. Meanwhile, the wealthiest nations, realizing they had unleashed a dangerous new weapon, have decided that it should no longer apply to them. When NAFTA was updated in 2020, the ISDS mechanism was eliminated between the US and Canada, and the EU has abolished international arbitration claims between its member states. Meanwhile, their corporations are free to terrorize the rest of the world.

The right of corporations to pursue unlimited profits has now been granted legal supremacy, taking precedence over the rights of people in the Majority World to environmental safety, affordable public services, and democratic autonomy. Transnational corporations have grown so large that they dominate the globe economically: Sixty-nine of the hundred largest economies are now shareholder-owned corporations rather than states. Embracing the new reality, UN agencies are now inviting corporate-sponsored organizations such as the World Economic Forum and other trade groups to partner with them in setting international policy for areas as diverse as health, education, and responses to the climate crisis. Since humanity's destiny is currently in the hands of these corporate entities, we must ask: What is their ultimate objective?[30]

THE SMILING PSYCHOPATH

The answer is distressingly simple: to maximize financial returns for their investors above all else. While there is no explicit requirement for this in the standard corporate charter, a century of case law has entrenched this principle in the behavior of large corporations to the point that it has become the de facto standard of operation. As discussed earlier, the neoliberal model that assumes people to be greedy and selfish, acting rationally to maximize their gain regardless of morality, applies only to the tiny percentage of people who are clinical psychopaths. However, it accurately describes the modern shareholder-owned corporation.

It is important to distinguish between the corporation as a self-perpetuating mechanism for enriching investors and the people it employs. Most people who work for corporations are, of course, warm-blooded, caring folk who conduct their lives according to a moral compass. But to the corporation that employs them, they are merely "human resources"—as expendable as the other resources it uses to maximize profits. This applies all the way up to the CEO, who would quickly be replaced if he started bringing moral considerations into his decision-making in a way that reduced profits.

This moral vacuity applies across the board. Corporations determine whether to break the law based on a dispassionate cost-benefit analysis, incorporating such considerations as the probability of getting caught, the likely fines or penalties, and the effect on their reputation in the marketplace. This is the reason why global tax evasion is so pervasive, and explains why a company such as ExxonMobil can lie shamelessly about climate change, knowing for decades about its consequences and yet deliberately concealing the facts and obfuscating public discussion on the topic.[31]

Just like real-life psychopaths, corporations expend a great deal of effort to ensure that their true motivations are concealed behind an attractive, smiling façade. Most corporations do, of course, generate significant benefits for those who buy their products or services. But it is important to recognize that, from the corporation's perspective, the benefits are a means to an end rather than an end in itself. The strategic choices a corporation makes are driven by profitability rather than the welfare of others. Because it's usually in the interest of large corporations to be seen as benevolent, they will go to great lengths to burnish their image in that regard. Most corporations now have Environmental, Social, and Governance (ESG) groups to demonstrate their intentions to "do well by doing good." To a limited extent, these are a positive development in response to public pressure, but whenever a corporation has to choose between pursuing ESG goals or profitability, it will choose the latter. Corporate boards know that, if they fail to make that choice, they will open themselves up to the risk of shareholder lawsuits or become an acquisition target of a predatory competitor.

Since the early twentieth century, corporate marketers have realized that the secret to continued growth in profits is not to satisfy people's needs, but to perpetuate dissatisfaction and thereby continually create more demand for their products. An influential policymaker from that time declared: "We must shift America from a needs to a desires culture. People must be trained to desire, to want new things, even before the old have been entirely consumed. We must shape a new mentality. Man's desires must overshadow his needs."[32]

Over the ensuing century, corporate marketers have developed innumerable ingenious strategies to execute this manifesto. In a process called "addiction by design," they have identified instinctual human drives—such as fear of exclusion, the desire for status, and foods loaded with sugar, fat, and salt—and devised methods to keep people forever wanting more. Collectively, these strategies create a global consumer culture driven by materialist values and perpetual status anxiety, keeping most people on a "hedonic treadmill" where, no matter what level of wealth they have achieved, they are impelled by a desire to conspicuously spend more and thus enhance their status compared to their peers.[33]

The continual stream of public scandals arising from corporate misconduct are not abnormalities arising from occasional bad apples, but rather the predictable outcome of a system dominated by amoral entities seeking to maximize returns for their shareholders. Far more damaging, though, are the countless routine decisions made daily by executives around the world in industries such as fossil fuels, mining, pharmaceuticals, agribusiness, media, and construction, that separately and collectively put the pursuit of profit above any consideration of human wellbeing and ecological integrity.

The rise to global domination of these uncaring behemoths would seem to be the culmination of a relentless five-hundred-year-long drive for extraction and exploitation. But in recent decades, a new dynamic has emerged that takes the scramble for extraction to an even greater level—the dramatic eruption of what has become known as financialization.

FINANCIALIZATION

Deep in the Amazon rainforest, under a leaf, lurks one of nature's most gruesome horror stories. A zombie-ant, infected by the cordyceps fungus, has lost control of its own body. Directed by the fungus, it climbs a plant to an optimal location, then locks onto it with its mandibles. Now paralyzed, it remains clamped in place for a week while the fungus permeates its body, eventually sprouting a stalk through its head filled with spores that rain down to infect new victims in the ant colony below.

There is no better metaphor for how financialization has come to control our entire economic system. Financialization refers to the condition whereby financial processes have come to dominate and feed off productive processes in the "real" economy such as industry, agriculture, or services. In conventional economics, finance is viewed as being in service of industry, mediating between lenders and borrowers, or between savers and investors. In the modern world, though, finance has become like the cordyceps fungus, compelling the tangible world to do its bidding in its continual drive to proliferate. It's been remarkably successful. At the outset of the neoliberal era in 1980, global financial assets were roughly equivalent in size to global GDP. Forty years later, the world's GDP was about nine times bigger as a result of the untrammeled license given to corporations to grow. But financial assets had mushroomed to fifty times their earlier size, reaching over $600 trillion, now more than five times greater than world GDP.[34]

In our financialized world, markets have been transformed from being a forum for trading goods and services to becoming primarily a medium for speculation, where money is mostly invested in other financial assets, not to make stuff, but simply to make more money. Along the way, finance has now come to dominate the decisions and policies that determine how the world works. Future cash flows anticipated from tangible resources such as housing, water, timber, or farmland are packaged into securitized assets and traded in futures markets, locking in the exploitation of those resources in order to meet required returns. Like the cordyceps fungus, finance determines where investment funds will be channeled and uses its overwhelming power to configure real-world policies for its benefit.

Whereas the first phase of globalization allowed transnational corporations to physically set up shop wherever they could make the most profit, the financialized phase allows investors to move funds electronically from one nation to another merely at the flick of a keystroke. Within moments of a government announcing plans for a new policy that might diminish profits, fund managers can sell their position, triggering a capital flight that could destabilize the economy. Through their control of capital, investment firms in the world's financial centers have become a faceless virtual global government, determining what policymakers can and cannot do in their own jurisdiction. Intergovernmental agencies grappling with critical global issues, such as climate adaptation, now promote the "de-risking" of projects to attract investments, in which states guarantee high returns for private capital by taking on the kinds of risks that investors used to hold for themselves, such as the risk that a higher minimum wage for workers might reduce future cash flows. In this way, the "litigation terrorism" of the ISDS process is becoming instantiated in the structure of the investments themselves.[35]

Driven by what they call "fiduciary duty," fund managers have, for the most part, shed even the pretense of putting other values above maximizing financial returns. The overarching power driving the actions and policies of governments and agencies around the world has become an invisible force field whose magnitude is amplified by the fact that it can no longer be tangibly identified. In *Wealth Supremacy*, the author Marjorie Kelly offers an insightful thought experiment. Imagine, she suggests, that overnight aliens abducted every billionaire, hedge fund manager, CEO, and corporate board director. What would happen to the world? The system, she answers, "would barely notice. It would reconstitute itself with nary a ripple." Other executives would merely step in and continue the drive to maximize returns in the name of fiduciary duty.[36]

The intangibility of this global system of financialized extraction is what makes it so difficult to resist. Suppose you were concerned, for example, about land grabs taking place in Brazil where traditional communities are expelled from their territory to make way for soy monocultures, causing deforestation, soil and water contamination, food insecurity, and contributing to climate breakdown. Where in the system could you intervene to try fixing it? If you approached the wildcatters on the ground, you may find they were being paid by a local agribusiness company which, in turn receives financing from international investment companies. If you were able to pierce through the obscure ownership structures of these entities, which are usually domiciled in secretive offshore tax havens, you might find they are acting for prestigious private investment firms which manage money for public pension funds. Who are the pension funds investing for? It may well be for you, if you've been an employee in one of the many countries that have privatized pension funds since the rise of neoliberalism, creating a vast ocean of global capital valued today at over $40 trillion.

This, ultimately, is why halting the accelerating extraction of resources and exploitation of people around the world requires transforming the system itself. The violent enclosures and colonialist massacres that began hundreds of years ago had a readily identifiable source. It was possible, at least in principle if not in practice, to struggle against them to protect your autonomy. Even during the neocolonialist period, forces of oppression could, in principle, be unmasked and resisted. In this modern era of global financialization, the codes of extraction and exploitation have infiltrated and permeated the very fabric of society. Like the ant's predicament with the cordyceps fungus, even the best intentions are inadequate in themselves to regain control of the body politic. What is required is a transformation of the system itself.

We've completed in this chapter what, in a medical consultation, would be called a case history: a chronicle of what led to the current malady. We're now ready to investigate and diagnose the systemic dynamics that caused this chronicle to unfold. Are there underlying problems of societal organization that reside at even deeper historical layers than the rise of enclosures in fourteenth-century Europe? What, we must ask, are the pivotal leverage points that require changing in order to steer the current world system onto a life-affirming trajectory? By examining these deep layers, we can begin to visualize more clearly the alternative foundations on which an ecocivilization must be based.

CHAPTER 3

THE WINDIGO DIAGNOSIS

THE FIRST OUTBREAK OF WINDIGO

In 1532, the conquistador Francisco Pizarro and his soldiers invited the Incan emperor Atahualpa to a feast in his honor. When Atahualpa accepted, Pizarro betrayed his guest with a surprise attack and held him hostage, demanding that the Incas fill a large room three times, first with gold and then twice with silver, in return for his safety. However, once they had their loot, they summarily killed Atahualpa. The Inca people couldn't comprehend the Spaniards' treachery and greed. As one Inca observer described it, "They lifted up the gold as if they were monkeys, with expressions of joy, as if it put new life into them and lit their hearts. As if it were certainly something for which they yearn with great thirst . . . They crave gold like hungry swine."[1]

What was the source of this horrific behavior? It was certainly not limited to Pizarro and his troops. A generation later, in 1565, here's how another conquistador described the Indigenous people's view of Europeans:

> They say that we have come to this earth to destroy the world. They say . . . that we devour everything, we consume the earth, we redirect the rivers, we are never quiet, never at rest, but always run here and there, seeking gold and silver, never satisfied, and then we gamble with it, make war, kill each other, rob, swear, never say the truth, and have deprived them of their means of livelihood.[2]

The Ojibwe people of the Great Lakes region employed a figure from their own mythology to help them comprehend the derangement of the Europeans. The terrifying Windigo monster was a ravenous ten-foot giant with a heart made of ice, that greedily sought out humans to devour. If you were bitten by one, you became a Windigo yourself, doomed to roam forever with insatiable hunger to devour others, tormented by a need that could never be satisfied. This was the Windigo's defining characteristic: The more they consumed, the more ravenous they became, and the more voraciously they sought to devour their next victim. To the Ojibwe, the Europeans who invaded their land seemed to have been infected by a kind of Windigo virus that contaminated whatever they touched.[3]

There is a clue hinting at the source of the Windigo virus in a journal entry Christopher Columbus made during his discovery of the "New World." He encountered a cape that he named Caho Hermoso [Beautiful Cape] "because it is so. I can never tire my eyes in looking at such lovely vegetation, so different from ours." So far, so good. But he then continues, "I believe there are many herbs and many trees that are worth much in Europe for dyes and for medicines but I do not know them, and this causes me great sorrow." For Columbus the value of all he saw around him was simply its monetized worth. Similarly, once he discovered that the Taino people were generous of spirit and had no knowledge of metal, cutting themselves accidentally on a sword, he wrote to the King and Queen of Castile, "Should your Majesties command it, all the inhabitants could be taken away to Castile or made slaves on the island. With fifty men we could subjugate them all and make them do whatever we want."[4]

At the heart of the Windigo virus was an objectification of all that was "other"—human and nonhuman alike. Seeing something as merely a resource for exploitation eliminated any moral constraint on its use or abuse. As another conquistador noted about his compatriots, "If a man had need of one pig, he killed twenty; if four Indians were wanted, he took a dozen . . . They thought no more of killing Indians than if they were useless beasts."[5]

Far from being rejected by the European intellectual and religious establishment, this Windigo mentality was embraced and legitimized. According to Francis Bacon, a champion of the Scientific Revolution, anyone other than a Christian European was so "utterly degenerated" that it was lawful and righteous to "cut them off from the face of the earth." John Stuart

Mill, an English philosopher who set the conceptual foundation for modern property law, wrote that the colonies should be regarded, not "as countries with a productive capital of their own" but rather the "place where England finds it convenient to carry on the production of sugar, coffee and a few other tropical commodities."[6]

As European colonialism devoured the rest of the world and metamorphosed into global capitalism, this Windigo mentality has spread to become the de facto organizing principle of modern civilization. Complex ecosystems become "natural resources"; other people "human resources"; animals become "livestock" and the oceans "fisheries." This mentality legitimizes a system that maltreats animals in factory farms, blows up mountaintops for coal, turns vibrant rainforest into monocrop wastelands, and leaves billions of people struggling to survive in a world of affluence.

If the vision of an ecocivilization is to become something other than a mere utopian dream, it must grapple with the ultimate source of this Windigo mentality. To what extent was it the European worldview and its economic manifestation in capitalism? Do we need to look further back in history? The previous chapter chronicled the worldwide spread of European domination beginning with the Black Death in the fourteenth century. But as mentioned there, every story has a prequel. Earlier world history is also saturated with bleak chronicles of slaughter, slavery, oppression, and empire. Is the propensity toward domination of others simply part of the human story and, as such, something that can never be overcome? Or is there something unique to modern sociopolitical structures that has led to our current predicament which could, at least in principle, be transformed into a more life-affirming configuration? These are some of the knotty questions we'll grapple with in this chapter.

THE FIVE-THOUSAND-YEAR-OLD WEALTH PUMP

About 95 percent of our species' history was spent in nomadic hunter-gatherer bands. It's important not to get enchanted by myths of the "noble savage," but as will be discussed in more detail in chapter 5, this was a very different kind of existence—one in which accumulation of wealth was unthinkable, and communities assiduously kept in check the power of occasional domineering males. Early humans lived like this for over a hundred thousand years, but beginning sporadically about ten thousand years ago, certain bands began settling in one place, which led in some cases to the emergence of agriculture.

Over thousands of years, scattered in a few isolated regions, an unprecedented form of social organization emerged. Along with the increasing importance of private property, hierarchies gained prominence. A farmer who got lucky with his crops accrued extra wealth and power, which allowed him to recruit others to help defend his property, with violence if necessary. With the increased value placed on possessions, there was more incentive to steal from neighboring communities. Aggressive communities conquered those that were more peaceful, foisting on them warrior cultures that prized machismo and violence.

The onset of mining played a crucial role in the rise of these dominator cultures. Societies that discovered how to process metal gained a technical advantage through superior weaponry. About five thousand years ago, in Mesopotamia, a technological revolution occurred when it was discovered that copper and tin could be combined to make bronze—a harder metal that yielded unrivaled tools, weapons, and armor, heralding the beginning of the Bronze Age. However, these metals were rare, and frequently had to be imported from distant mining regions. The trade routes that developed required military protection, which in turn increased the power and importance of the centralized hierarchies that could provide this.

It is no coincidence that the first cities, along with what is referred to as "civilization," arose with the Bronze Age. We're generally led to believe that the rise of civilization represented unequivocal progress for humanity, leading to materially and culturally enriched lives, and offering citizens greater health and leisure. However, as the anthropologist James Scott has convincingly demonstrated, the opposite is true. In fact, as he describes, "the early states had to capture and hold much of their population by forms of bondage and were plagued by the epidemics of crowding." A city's walls, which we imagine were built to keep out "the barbarians," had an equally important function of holding captive those within.[7]

Those outside the city walls, dismissed by the civilized elites as barbarians, likely enjoyed "materially easier, freer, and healthier" lives than those inside, who were subject to the will of the aristocratic class. Society was organized according to a system that the social scientist Peter Turchin has aptly called a "wealth pump," consistently funneling surplus up to the elites. At the bottom, slaves were used for functions such as mining, quarrying, or major construction projects. Most farmers were technically free, but at least a fifth of their harvest was appropriated in taxes to fund the priesthood, military, aristocracy, and the ostentatious luxury of the ruling families.[8]

The first states, emerging from these early cities, amplified and extended the wealth pump, aided by another technological revolution—the discovery of steel, an alloy of iron and carbon which is even stronger than bronze but has a much higher melting point, requiring special furnaces and vast amounts of fuel for its production. Empires arose with elite families appropriating ever larger swathes of land with overwhelming military force. Peasants, barely able to sustain themselves under the burden of rent and taxes, frequently turned to debt in desperation, but if a harvest failed, they and their families would likely become bonded workers or indentured slaves. The fate of womenfolk was even more dire, since they would often be used as collateral and forced into prostitution. Inequality was comparable to the extremes of today, with the wealthiest aristocrats of the Roman Empire owning as much as today's top billionaires in proportion to the rest of the population.[9]

The economist David Korten has noted how, through all the perturbations of history, most societies have been structured according to four primary social castes. The Ruling Caste features aristocratic families and wealthy elites who control the means by which the rest of society sustains itself, such as land, water, housing, money, or wage labor. Supporting them is the Retainer Caste, whose loyalty safeguards the Rulers. This caste includes military officers, legal professionals, religious leaders, along with artists, philosophers, and academics, who collectively provide the ideological justification for their rule. Below them, comprising the majority of the population, is the Worker Caste with its laborers, farmers, healthcare workers, store clerks, and all those who perform the functions on which society depends, creating the surplus that is systematically sucked up the wealth pump to the castes above. Finally, there is the Excluded Caste, those who endure slavery, homelessness, and imprisonment, including refugees, undocumented immigrants, and other outcasts from the system. Their desperate status serves as a warning to the rest of society to conform to the rules or risk being ejected from the system and suffering a similar fate.[10]

Faced with this grim history, it's reasonable to wonder if there's anything particularly egregious about the ravages of modern-day capitalism. Isn't it simply a continuation of the same forces that have resulted in elite domination for five millennia? Is there really anything about the worldview of the European—now globally dominant—that differentiates it from the rest of history and bears responsibility for the dire predicament we face today? Let's see.

PROLIFERATION BY ANY MEANS NECESSARY

Jean-Baptiste Du Halde, an eighteenth-century Jesuit, was preparing a survey on China by collecting reports from missionaries who had traveled there. "The Mountains of China are still more valuable," he wrote, "on account of the Mines of different Metals."

> The Chinese say they are full of Gold and Silver; but that the working of them hitherto has been hindered from some political views, perhaps, that the publick Tranquillity might not be disturbed by the too great abundance of these Metals, which would make the People haughty and negligent of Agriculture.[11]

In Du Halde's puzzled speculation, we can discern a crucial difference between the worldview of China, one of history's greatest civilizations, and that of Western Europe. By the time Du Halde was writing, the Spanish had obliterated the world's richest silver mine in Potosí, Bolivia, sending as many as eight million enslaved Indigenous workers to their deaths extracting forty thousand tons of silver from its veins. No wonder Du Halde was having trouble understanding why the Chinese would not want to disturb the "publick Tranquillity" with "the too great abundance of these Metals."

To the European mind, this restraint was unthinkable. China was a hierarchical, patriarchal civilization with a fully functioning wealth pump maintaining elite dominance, but it had not been infected by the Windigo virus. To Chinese policymakers, there was always a balance to be maintained between material wealth and stability.

While other civilizations held different values, they each navigated similar tensions. In early modern Europe, however, an unprecedented worldview arose which served as the foundation for the modern world. Rejecting the dogma of traditional Christian theology, it was the basis for modern science—one of humanity's greatest achievements—but it also fostered a mentality that was uniquely susceptible to infection by the Windigo virus. Distilled to its essence, it saw nature as nothing other than a complicated machine that could be controlled by figuring out its design. It saw white Christian males as the apex of humanity, imbued with a God-given right to exploit all others, using their greater powers spawned by scientific investigation. Francis Bacon summed it up with his famous dictum "Knowledge itself is power." Inspired by him and others, the generations that followed saw it as their religious duty to exercise that power through conquest—of nature, and of the rest of humanity. It was a worldview that legitimated and glorified ruthless exploitation of others and unlimited extraction of nature's abundance.

Capitalism can be understood as the economic manifestation of this worldview. As its name suggests, it is a system based on the supremacy of capital, one that organizes all other aspects of the world to optimize capital's ability to reproduce itself. Like malignant cancer cells in a body, which ignore regulatory feedback from other cells that would otherwise keep them in check, the DNA of capitalism requires uncontrolled proliferation of capital by any means necessary. Capitalism as a system, along with the limited liability companies that are its avatars, recognizes no moral limitations in its quest for perpetual growth.

Like the great white shark that must keep moving to breath, capitalism cannot remain static. It has a structural imperative to grow continuously. In a world where virtually everyone possessing capital is trying to earn a return on it, capital must continually seek out new frontiers to satisfy its holders. Emulating the Windigo monster, capitalism is insatiable. As soon as capital earns a return on investment, the extra wealth accumulated requires further investment and further returns.

Capitalism creates an essential divide between two kinds of people: those with capital, who are driven to increase it, and those without capital who become targets of the exploitation required for its increase. From the enclosure movement onward, a major source of capital's growth has been to force people from other forms of social organization into the market economy, thus increasing the number of people subject to its control. Since most people were relatively satisfied with their lives, it frequently required violence to drive them under capitalism's dominion, as documented in the previous chapter. This is why, in the words of one analyst, "violence is inherent in the internal logic of capital and, therefore . . . is a permanent feature of the capitalist system."[12]

From its inception, capitalism as a system embraced and amplified the other aspects of dominion shared by most other civilizations: patriarchy, empire, militarism, debt bondage, and slavery, while adding novelties such as industrial-scale genocide and white supremacy. In all cases, it's important to recognize that capitalism incorporated these, not because it inherently valued men over women, white people over other races, or war over peace, but because they were all effective mechanisms to potentiate capital's ability to reproduce itself as rapidly and intensively as possible.

The earliest precursors of capitalism were the city-states Venice and Genoa, whose merchant fleets controlled Mediterranean trade through military force as far back as the thirteenth century. The Dutch similarly discovered an inextricable linkage between militarism and profit. Jan Coen, a magnate of the Dutch East India Company who oversaw a genocide in the Indonesian Banda Islands, summed it up crisply: "There can be no trade without war, and no war without trade." Back in Europe, meanwhile, it was no coincidence that the persecution of witches reached a climax in the seventeenth century, with as many as a hundred thousand women tortured to death by the authorities. Scholars have demonstrated that this persecution, far from being a spontaneous moral panic, was an orchestrated strategy designed to crush popular resistance to the rise of capitalist power and to terrorize women into submitting to their newly assigned role as compliant vehicles for reproducing and raising the fodder needed for the labor force and military service.[13]

This is not, however, the capitalism that most people know today—at least, those living in the affluent Global North. When you think about capitalism, what comes to mind? Most likely a mélange of phenomena such as shopping, advertising, financial markets, globalization, and workplace intrigues. Surely, those horrors of the past have mostly been consigned to the dustbin of history? If the dominant global system of capitalism is inherently violent, we must ask, why don't we see mayhem raging in the street every time we commute to work?

THE STRUCTURAL VIOLENCE OF CAPITALISM

Along with enslavement, warfare, and other scourges, capitalism picked up from its civilizational predecessors an important principle: Once a population was conquered, it was more efficient to train them to supervise themselves than to perpetually threaten them with brute force. In early civilizations, this took the form of what anthropologists describe as "moralizing gods": a set of religious beliefs that channeled moral intuitions into behaviors supporting the authority of the centralized power. Since emperors were viewed as semi-divine, it made sense for the common people to maintain the pump that funneled wealth and power upward toward them. Societal control could now be sustained even without the threat of direct violence—fear of retribution from moralizing gods was enough to keep people's behavior in line.

It was Antonio Gramsci, an Italian Marxist philosopher imprisoned by Mussolini until his death in 1937, who explained in his *Prison Notebooks* how capitalism utilizes a similar process, which he called "cultural hegemony." Gramsci described how power is maintained by a combination of force and consent. While strong-arm institutions such as the police or army threaten force from the sidelines, consent is achieved through cultural institutions such as schools, churches, or the media. Like the moralizing gods of the past, the hegemonic purpose of these institutions is to condition the population into believing that the system works to their own advantage—or at least, as

Margaret Thatcher declared, that "there is no alternative." It is only when cultural institutions fail in their task that rulers must resort to more punitive, coercive measures to keep the population in line.

Cultural hegemony wields enormous power by inculcating values into people that work against their own welfare and keep them oppressed. For example, a recent survey conducted in India on violence against women reported that 43 percent of men considered it was justified for a husband to beat his wife for reasons such as disrespecting the in-laws, neglecting housekeeping, or arguing with him. But the jaw-dropping finding is that 45 percent of women believed such violence against them was justified—even more than the men! Cultural hegemony explains why, even as the neoliberal takeover by elites has dramatically intensified the wealth pump to the detriment of working people, right-wing political parties have been gaining, rather than losing, popular support.[14]

The form of cultural hegemony observed in the Indian survey is known as *internalized oppression*: a mental condition where an oppressed group considers itself inherently inferior based on the values of the dominant culture. An additional form of hegemony arises from the externalized oppression of those considered below your particular group, known as *kyriarchy*—a term coined by the feminist theorist Elisabeth Schüssler Fiorenza. Imagine the caste system described by David Korten but in the form of a pyramid: for every person above you, there are several that you can push around below you.

The power of kyriarchy was discovered by wealthy landowners in the American colonies, who were threatened by rebellions from multiethnic coalitions of those they oppressed: European laborers, enslaved Africans, and displaced Native people. Their solution was to categorize the landless Europeans as "white" and pass laws distinguishing them from those who were Black or Native. Suddenly, the "white" people previously at the bottom of the pyramid had a group below them that could make them feel superior. In the words of plantation owner John Townsend, "The color of the white man is now, in the South, a title of nobility in his relations as to the Negro." Rather than threaten the established order, the new class of landless "whites" would now reliably help enforce it. Since then, this pernicious strategy has become a foundation of the structural racism that continues to pervade the culture and economy of the United States, and is seen around the world as disgruntled workers turn their rage on desperate refugees rather than the elite class that has immiserated them.[15]

Another powerful form of cultural hegemony arises from a *distancing phenomenon* that first manifested with the rise of colonialism. As a general principle, the stronger the elite's grip on power, the more civilized they appear to be, because the violence committed in their name is increasingly distanced until it becomes invisible. While Jan Coen was massacring the indigenous people of the Banda Islands to establish a nutmeg monopoly, the wealth his company generated caused Amsterdam, thousands of miles away, to become Europe's wealthiest city. His shareholders, collecting porcelain and tulips while getting their portraits painted by Rembrandt, saw themselves as the height of civilized sophistication.

The distancing phenomenon allows even those who view themselves as principled, moral agents to participate in the greatest of abominations. In *Modernity and the Holocaust*, Zygmunt Bauman analyzed the Nazi holocaust to show how dehumanizing bureaucratic processes, such as obedience to rigidly enforced rules and division of labor separating different tasks from each other, create both a physical and moral distance between the perpetrators and victims of even genocidal atrocities.[16]

Transnational corporations use similar processes. Most people who buy a new smartphone remain blissfully unaware of the wretched plight of child miners in the Congo extracting the cobalt it requires, or the nets constructed around assembly plants in Shenzhen to catch despairing young employees jumping from the windows in an attempt to put an end to their misery. When you enjoy delicious, farmed shrimp in a restaurant, you're probably not thinking about the enslaved migrant workers on Thai fishing trawlers, working twenty hours a day for years on end to catch the cheap feed they were fattened on. Yes, this is an ongoing global holocaust in which virtually all of us are implicated—at a safe distance.

Capitalism, then, has continued to wield its violence around the world, but it has become increasingly effective at making it invisible to the affluent minority. The unseen calamities wrought on others around the world as a result of these deeply entrenched systems of oppression have been termed *structural violence* by the sociologist Johan Galtung. Galtung defines structural violence as "avoidable insults to basic human needs, and more generally to life" that occur as a direct or indirect result of how the world is organized. When a gang member shoots another as a result of a drug deal that goes bad—that's direct violence. But the processes that led a desperate person to become a pawn in the drug war, the craving of the addict to temporarily dissolve their emotional pain, the trauma of the child hiding in the back room, and the lost opportunities for a wholesome and fulfilled life for all those caught up in the web—that's structural violence.[17]

Because it's generally hidden from view, the structural violence propping up the affluent world is rarely acknowledged. But a brief scan will show how it's all around us.

WHERE STRUCTURAL VIOLENCE HIDES OUT

The most obvious place to find our society's structural violence is in the gaping and ever-widening economic inequality that generates a vast morass of "avoidable insults to basic human needs." The fact that two billion people go hungry every day while a couple of dozen billionaires own as much wealth as half the world's population is egregious enough—but the structural violence exists, not just in these facts, but within the architecture of an economic system that ensures this moral perversion only worsens.

While a billionaire lazes on his superyacht, his capital is busily growing far more rapidly than the economy as a whole, increasing inequality moment by moment—this is the reinforcing feedback of wealth accumulation. Extreme as the income differential is between CEOs and ordinary workers, the biggest drivers of wealth inequality are the dividends and capital gains accruing to those with funds to invest. Meanwhile the debt burden of those without capital increasingly overwhelms their ability to cope. It's estimated that 44 cents of every dollar earned by the median household income in the United States ultimately goes to pay interest charges, which are sucked up the wealth pump to further enrich wealthy investors. When the UN reported in 2008 that thirty billion dollars a year could save the lives of those dying from hunger worldwide, the central banks responded by putting together a far greater package of over a trillion dollars—not to feed the hungry but to bail the banks out of the global financial crisis. This is structural violence.[18]

Structural violence can be unearthed lurking in the tax havens of the world, which hold as much as 32 trillion dollars—more than a sixth of the world's private wealth. These havens allow the wealthy to hide their assets behind a veil of secrecy with virtually no financial regulation or taxation. Every year, transnational corporations shift about a trillion dollars in profit to these hideaways. This tax evasion is not a victimless crime: About a third of these funds are from poor countries, and every dollar of tax avoided means a dollar that doesn't get spent on schools, healthcare facilities, and the basic infrastructure needed for a decent life.[19]

You can locate structural violence in the land grabs that are estimated to have accounted for over 500 million acres (about the size of Western Europe) in the decade to 2010 and continue to increase rapidly. Land grabbing is the large-scale acquisition by wealthy elites of tracts held by poor communities, mostly in the Global South and predominantly in Africa, who then get displaced from their homes and livelihoods. Traditional communities frequently hold this land collectively without formal title, which makes them easy prey to sophisticated financial predators using bribery and legal maneuvers. Once procured, the new owners turn their possessions into whatever maximizes their return, which might include logging, sugar production, rubber plantations, or upmarket game reserves replete with luxury hotels—while the displaced peasants join the swelling ranks of urban slum-dwellers subsisting in makeshift shantytowns.[20]

The victims of structural violence are only too evident once you look for them. What about the perpetrators? As already noted, all of us privileged to enjoy the affluence afforded by this perverse system are, to some degree, perpetrators. But there is a tiny group at the very top of the pyramid, known as the Global Power Elite, who bear the greatest responsibility for overseeing this moral disgrace. Numbering no more than seven thousand people, predominantly white and from the Global North, and 94 percent male, they are, in the words of one analyst, "the Davos-attending, Gulfstream/private jet–flying, megacorporation-interlocked, policy-building elites of the world." Away from Davos, they come together in exclusive societies such as the Bohemian Club, the Council on Foreign Relations, the Trilateral Commission, and the Bilderberg Group, where they steer global policy. They are the ones, meeting in private sanctuaries, who make the decisions that national governments and global institutions then implement.[21]

With their increasing dominance, this uber-elite group is intentionally blurring the distinction between legitimate government and corporate power. A landmark strategic partnership agreement signed between the World Economic Forum and the UN in 2019 called the Global Redesign Initiative spells out their vision for reshaping global governance into what they call "multi-stakeholder partnerships." Driven primarily by transnational corporations and other representatives of capital accumulation, these unelected and unaccountable bodies increasingly take center stage in major global policymaking gatherings intended to grapple with the greatest problems facing humanity today.

This initiative, though, represents merely one extra tightening of the control that elites have exerted over political affairs for centuries. "Those who own the country ought to govern it," declared John Jay, a Founding Father and first Chief Justice of the United States, and since then the nation's patricians have taken him at his word. Although we typically think of government regulating private enterprise, it's more accurate to view the relationship as reciprocal at best. In recent decades in the United States and elsewhere, in a process known as "political capture," the balance of power has markedly shifted toward the wealthy elites, exerting their influence through powerful industry groups such as the American Legislative Exchange Council, the National Association of Manufacturers, and the Business Roundtable—and more recently the shadowy Atlas Network. An extensive study of federal legislation passed over two decades reveals that, when economic elites and the general public hold different views on a policy issue, elites nearly always get their way. The study's authors call it "democracy by coincidence," concluding that "ordinary citizens get what they want from government only when they happen to agree with elites or interest groups that are really calling the shots."[22]

However, through deft management of cultural hegemony, the elites rarely need to worry about major differences between their interests and the views of the general public. The highly concentrated global media outlets are mostly owned by the Global Power Elite, who use these channels to "manufacture consent"—in the memorable phrase of political analysts Noam Chomsky and Edward Herman. Even when ownership is not an issue, the media's reliance on advertising revenues keeps most news coverage in safe territory. As a media CEO observed, "We're not in the business of providing news and information . . . We're simply in the business of selling our customers products." In one survey, 75 percent of journalists and editors reported that advertisers tried to influence their content. Usually however, no overt pressure is needed, since journalists learn to internalize the requisite filters and convince themselves that they are providing "objective" coverage.[23]

What is the consent the rest of us are expected to provide? Above all, it is to pay obeisance to the sacred precepts of capitalism, with an implicit faith that the continued growth of capital is in the best interests of all. Just as the moralizing gods of ancient civilizations locked people into a religious matrix designed to maintain the emperor's power, the capitalist form of hegemony creates a similarly all-encompassing belief system. As we march lockstep to the beat of capitalism's consensus trance, we must ask: Where is the pied piper ultimately leading us?

THE WINDIGO PROGNOSIS: OMNICIDE

In the mid-nineteenth century, the English economist William Stanley Jevons uncovered a curious paradox. The steam engine invented by James Watt had greatly improved the efficiency of coal-powered engines, which should logically have decreased coal consumption but led, instead, to a dramatic increase. This phenomenon has since been demonstrated in an endless variety of domains, from the invention of the cotton gin which led to an increase rather than decrease in slavery in the American South, to improved automobile fuel efficiency which encourages people to drive longer distances. The Jevons paradox, as it became known, predicts that efficiency improvements intended to reduce resource usage inevitably become launchpads for further exploitation. When we examine it more closely, we can see that it's not really a paradox at all, but rather an inbuilt defining characteristic of capitalism that could be called Windigo's Law: Capital will never cease to exploit any new opportunity that arises in its frenetic quest for greater returns.

In a process known as ecocide, Windigo, Inc. is driven to monetize every resource available in a natural habitat until the ecosystem's ability to sustain itself collapses. It will then turn to the next one, and so on. The ecosystem of human social organization offers equally rich pickings. The privatization goldrush that began with the rise of neoliberalism has turned entire industries over from state control to the depredations of Windigo, Inc. across the world. In healthcare, transportation, education, sports, even prisons, systems originally set up to serve societal needs have been transmuted into fodder for capital appreciation. Why stop at social systems? The inner human experience offers a new frontier for Windigo, Inc. to enclose. Using sophisticated "brain hacking" algorithms, smartphone developers design social media triggers that initiate behavioral loops in our subconscious, sparking endorphins in our brains that cause us, like rats on a wheel, to go back for more until we become addicted. The success of their approach is evidenced by the fact that the typical internet user worldwide spends about two and a half hours a day on social media.

Where will it end? Author Amitav Ghosh warns us of "the unrestrainable excess that lies hidden at the heart of the vision of world-as-resource—an excess that leads ultimately not just to genocide but an even greater violence, an impulse that can only be called 'omnicide,' the desire to destroy everything." It is this drive for omnicide that explains how, even as the world faces the existential threat of climate breakdown, our governments spend over a trillion dollars a year subsidizing fossil fuel production. It is Windigo, Inc.'s compulsion for omnicide that explains why, since the 2015 Paris Climate Agreement, banks have provided over three trillion dollars to fossil fuel companies to expand operations, while the $500 billion per year needed to protect the living Earth is almost entirely unfunded.[24]

We can rest assured that no-one, not even the Global Power Elite, wants the Windigo, Inc. rampage to end in omnicide. Why, then, does this system of accelerating destruction continue unabated? Do the wealthy elite presume that, although most people will suffer from societal breakdown, they will somehow get away unscathed? Are the self-organized societal processes set in play by capitalism so powerful that no-one, not even the elites, can prevent them from propelling civilization to collapse? Or, by identifying the underlying genetic code that has caused the Windigo monster to run amok, might we be able to transform our system from within and swerve away from the omnicidal point of no return? Apprised now of the Windigo diagnosis, let us explore these alternatives in the next chapter.

CHAPTER 4

THE NEED FOR SYSTEM CHANGE

It was supposed to be one of the highlights of the hajj—the sacred weeklong pilgrimage to Mecca that all Muslims are enjoined to undertake at least once in their lives. Thousands of pilgrims were making their way to the adjacent valley of Mina to take part in a ritual stoning of the devil: a reenactment, according to Muslim tradition, of Abraham's rejection of Satan. But on their way there, a horrific tragedy intervened. Panic broke out when two throngs of pilgrims approaching a bridge collided, causing a stampede that led to over two thousand deaths. "It was like a wave," described one survivor. "You go forward and suddenly you go back . . . People were climbing over one another just to breathe."[1]

The Mina stampede of 2015 is a striking example of a phenomenon known as a crowd disaster—when the self-organized dynamics of a densely packed crowd suddenly shift from orderliness to chaos as a result of an unexpected perturbation. Nobody in the crowd is trying to cause harm, but the forces unleashed create amplifying feedback effects, sweeping people along in turbulent waves. Ironically, the panicked actions of people trying to survive frequently exacerbate the turbulence causing even greater fatalities from crushing or suffocation.

Suppose you were a pilgrim in the Mina crowd approaching the bridge. Somebody next to you may have muttered a warning that people were packed too densely, and perhaps you felt a little anxious yourself. But everyone else around you seems calm. Your objective, along with the rest of the crowd, is to get to Mina, and even if you felt it was a good idea to leave, where would you go? You would probably ignore the warning and keep moving ahead with the crowd, not realizing you were heading for disaster.

Is our entire civilization at risk of a planetwide crowd disaster? If so, what alternatives are available? Is there any way to shift the inertia of our civilization's headlong fling toward a precipice? In this chapter, we'll explore what the future might hold in store for humanity, ranging from civilizational collapse to an alternative that may be even more morally egregious. We'll examine why these all-important issues are barely discussed in the mainstream media, and consider what would be required to redirect our planet-spanning crowd away from the danger zone before disaster occurs.

NIGHTMARE SCENARIO: SYNCHRONOUS FAILURE

Given the exponential rate at which technological and social change is accelerating, what seems certain is that this century will bear witness to one of the greatest transformations in human history. There have only been a couple of times since humans evolved as a species that we've undergone a transformation in virtually every aspect of the human experience: our beliefs and aspirations, how we live, work, eat, and socialize. The first was the transition, beginning about ten thousand years ago, from nomadic foraging to sedentism and agriculture. The second was the rise of modernity, beginning in Europe and spreading, along with colonialism, throughout the entire world. There is a general consensus among prognosticators that we are entering another such transformation—but to what?

A scan of history reveals that, as civilizations increase their internal complexity beyond a certain point, collapse becomes increasingly likely—and is frequently triggered by climate change. The complexity of the modern world makes it even more susceptible than earlier civilizations to systemic shocks. In traditional societies, most communities could remain self-sufficient if a disaster occurred in a neighboring community. In our society, by contrast, most people are reliant for food and other necessities on the global network of commerce and information. Corporations, in their drive for profit, have whittled down inventories in factories and warehouses to no more than a few days' supply. While this minimizes costs, it leaves supply chains dangerously vulnerable. A disruption of just one important commodity—increasingly likely with climate change—could bring the entire network that feeds and sustains our global civilization to a grinding halt.

Beyond the obvious reasons why modern civilization is increasingly susceptible to collapse—climate breakdown, ecological degradation, overpopulation, and an anticipated doubling of the size of the global economy by 2060—systemic factors exacerbate these risks. Like the Mina crowd, our planetary system is highly sensitive to amplifying feedback effects from a relatively small perturbation. Different aspects of our global network are so tightly interconnected that a malfunction in one sphere can rapidly lead to failures in other closely linked domains, which can then amplify the original malfunction in a reinforcing feedback loop.

While we might hope that the unique technological sophistication of modern civilization could help avert disaster, there are important reasons why the opposite may be the case. In earlier times, an outbreak of disease or a political upheaval might affect one region but have little impact on another. Today's world is far more homogeneous than ever before—culturally, institutionally, and technologically—which means that a crisis occurring in one place easily spreads around the world. Our internet-enhanced globalized connectivity has dramatically increased the transmission speed of just about everything: information, ideas, and material. Just as a catchy innovation can "go viral" around the world within hours, any major shock to the system—financial, cultural, or political—can also spread at lightning speed. To cap it all, unlike any other civilization in the past, we live in a world armed to the teeth with over ten thousand nuclear warheads and over a billion firearms.

Using terms such as "polycrisis" and "metacrisis," scientists are increasingly warning of a looming existential threat and calling for transformational change to avert it. "We warn of potential collapse of natural and socioeconomic systems," writes one prominent team, in "a world where we will face unbearable heat, frequent extreme weather events, food and fresh water shortages, rising seas, more emerging diseases, and increased social unrest and geopolitical conflict." The nightmare scenario is what scientists call synchronous failure, where multiple systems—each already close to a tipping point—push each other into cascading collapse, like one house of cards toppling into another. It doesn't take a fevered imagination to visualize such a self-amplifying loop—simply an extension of the multiple crises already competing with each other for the daily headlines.[2]

It could be a confluence of regional problems occurring simultaneously: a massive heat wave causing crop failures and forest fires in one region, while floods displace large populations in another. Waves of desperate refugees attempt to cross national borders, but are turned back by militarized border patrols. The tension sparks escalating threats between two nuclear-armed nations, controlled by authoritarian nationalist leaders. As fear spreads across the globe, financial markets crash, leading to bank failures, followed by food shortages, hoarding, and spiraling price increases. Disruption of shipping lanes causes fuel deficits resulting in occasional electrical brownouts, then blackouts. One day, the internet mysteriously stops working, and no one knows exactly why. Previously affluent families start worrying: Where will the next meal come from? Where is a safe place to hide out?

Each year of heightening global stresses brings us closer to a precipice, the exact location of which no one can precisely predict. The alarm bells no longer ring from niche groups. The World Scientists' Warning to Humanity was originally published in 1992 and signed by 1,700 scientists. A second warning, twenty-five years later, was signed by more than 15,000 scientists. In 2011, the UN Secretary General Ban Ki-moon berated business and political leaders at the World Economic Forum, declaring that they had made a "global suicide pact." In 2022 his successor, António Guterres, repeated the warning of "collective suicide" to forty nations discussing the climate emergency. In 2025, the Bulletin of the Atomic Scientists moved the Doomsday Clock to eighty-nine seconds to midnight, the closest to global catastrophe it has ever been.[3]

And yet, like the crowd in Mina, there seems to be no one willing and able to change our trajectory. What about the Global Power Elite? With their overweening ability to influence global policy, why aren't they doing something to avert disaster? How could they hear these warnings and blithely ignore them?

THE SOOTHING CHORUS OF CULTURAL HEGEMONY

Most likely, the reason is because these alarm bells are drowned out by the soothing predictions of a rosier future based on a fusion of technological progress and efficient markets. As Gramsci's theory of cultural hegemony would predict, an array of pundits, political commentators, and think tanks have created an omnipresent chorus instilling confidence in the pursuit of business as usual. In response to sirens warning of potential collapse, they explain that humans are beset by deeply evolved psychological biases that cause us to focus on negative information and ignore the positive. This explains our ingrained propensity for doom-scrolling that attracts us to the scariest news items and embeds them in our memory banks.

In fact, we are told, humanity has made—and continues to make—great progress on many fronts. Rather than denounce the market-based system that has brought us to this place, we should celebrate the improvement in material prosperity unleashed by industrial capitalism, and encourage it to continue its momentum. Cheered on by mega-billionaire Bill Gates, a loosely aligned team of highbrow celebrities such as Steven Pinker, Hans Rosling, Nicholas Kristof, and Matt Ridley have woven together the standard hegemonic narrative of progress. In this story, humans have lived in a dismal state of extreme poverty since our species first evolved. "For over 100,000 years," Rosling informs us, "people simply did not have enough food." This starving, destitute condition was only relieved by what's termed "the Great Escape" when capitalism and the Industrial Revolution finally began to pull people out of their misery.[4]

There is no doubt that the world has experienced a transformation in material abundance in the past two hundred years with massively increased availability of clothing, food, transportation, and countless other conveniences, as well as huge advances in medicine and public hygiene that have significantly increased life expectancy. Much of this improvement can be ascribed to an unprecedented increase in scientific knowledge and dissemination of that knowledge through education, as well as industrialization. The role played by capitalism and colonialism, however, is quite another story.[5]

Two researchers, Dylan Sullivan and Jason Hickel, have conducted a systematic analysis to evaluate the legitimacy of the standard narrative of progress and found it sorely lacking. A major problem arises when mainstream economists view history through the lens of GDP, which merely measures the rate at which human activity is sucked into the monetary economy, and a standardized "poverty line" of $1.90 per day which is calculated based on prices across the entire economy. When a forest is enclosed for timber or traditional farms turned into cotton plantations, GDP goes up even if the peasants relying on that land are left destitute. In India, for example, GDP per capita increased 27 percent from 1870 to 1921, while tens of millions of Indians starved to death as a result of colonial policies that shipped their wheat out of the country, reducing average life expectancy by 20 percent.

Instead, Sullivan and Hickel used records of people's height and mortality to assess human welfare, as well as a "Basic Needs Poverty Line" measure which calculates the price of a basket of food and other necessities that could allow a family to meet their nutritional requirements at the least cost. When they applied these measures historically around the world, the results were diametrically opposite to the standard narrative. Historically, people have normally had access to their basic nutritional needs except in rare cases of war and famine. All that changed with colonialism. In every region, wages dropped to below subsistence, while height and longevity decreased. In parts of South Asia, sub-Saharan Africa, and Latin America, these metrics have still not recovered. Across different continents, when improvements in human welfare occurred, they can instead be traced to the rise of progressive social movements and public policies such as more accessible healthcare and schooling.[6]

The cultural hegemons make a case that, even if their historical analysis is mistaken, capitalism can change its spots. Using amiable monikers such as "conscious capitalism," "green capitalism," and "stakeholder capitalism," they argue that corporations, if imbued with a culture of social responsibility, can use their prodigious power and efficiency for the greater good. As such, they promote the idea that we should incorporate nature into the globalized market economy as "natural capital," and encourage sustainable behavior by putting a monetary valuation on "ecosystem services." For example, as the effects of greenhouse gas emissions become too large to ignore, corporations have trumpeted "net-zero" strategies, buying tradeable "carbon credits" to cover up their destructive behavior. Many studies have shown, however, that these carbon offsets are frequently counterproductive and oftentimes fraudulent. As we've seen from the previous chapters, even with the best intentions of company employees, the publicly traded corporation is legally structured to maximize one thing only—ever-increasing shareholder returns—and will inevitably extract and exploit wherever the opportunity arises.

THE CHIMERA OF "GREEN GROWTH"

Perhaps the most alluring strategy offered by the cultural hegemons is "green growth": the idea that we can have our cake and eat it too. The green growth proposition holds that, through ingenious use of technology, the global economy can continue to grow indefinitely while its ecological impact consistently decreases—known as decoupling. The theory of green growth has been adopted so widely among major global institutions that one might assume it's based on confirmed empirical evidence. The OECD officially endorsed the goal in 2011 with its strategy paper *Towards Green Growth*, which was followed by similar roadmaps published by the European Commission and the World Bank—and decoupling became a specific target of the UN's Sustainable Development Goals.

This assumption, however, would be seriously mistaken. Empirical studies have shown that the decoupling required for green growth has never happened, and there is no evidence to suggest any realistic possibility that it will happen in the future. For green growth to be a viable option, it must be "absolute" rather than "relative," meaning the two trends of growth and environmental impact must move in opposite directions; it must be global, not just apply to a few countries that have outsourced their pollution to the Global South; and it must apply to humanity's full ecological impact (known as "material footprint"), not just carbon emissions. Most pundits defending green growth will point to a few cherry-picked examples that meet just one of these criteria, and use them to make heroic assumptions for the future. But as we can see in Figure 1, which compares global GDP and humanity's material footprint, not only has there been no absolute decoupling, but in the past couple of decades our material footprint has grown even faster than GDP.[7]

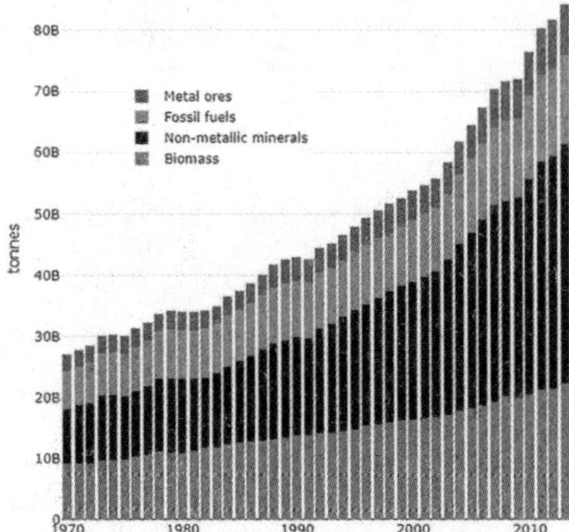

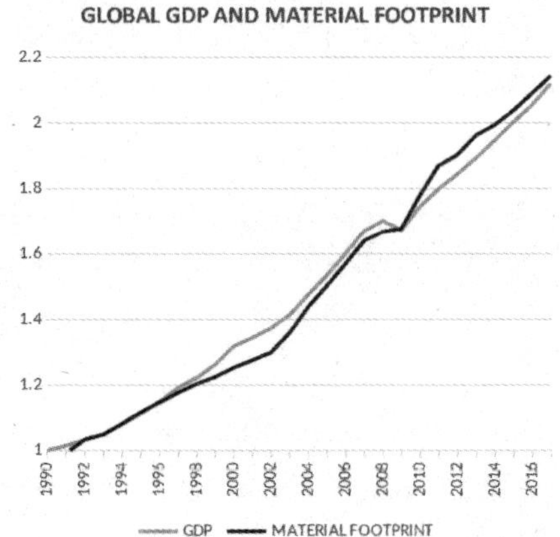

Figure 1: Global GDP and material footprint
Source: Jason Hickel, and Giorgos Kallis, "Is Green Growth Possible?", *New Political Economy* 25, no. 4 (2019): 469–86

Given what we know about Windigo's Law (aka Jevons Paradox), these empirical findings should not be a surprise. Under global capitalism, every time a well-intentioned engineer makes a technical improvement to reduce the material footprint of a particular process, the innovation is used, not to produce less of something, but to produce more of it and use the enhanced efficiency to increase shareholder returns. Predictably, a team studied the use of sixty-nine different materials over a fifty-year period and found that the Jevons Paradox applied in virtually every one. They found only six cases of absolute decline, and most of those, such as asbestos or mercury, were phased out deliberately because of toxicity.[8]

It's worth taking a moment to pause and reflect on the deeper implications of this mismatch between global policy and empirical evidence. How can all these major institutions, supposedly comprised of sober, serious-minded policymakers, have unanimously committed themselves to a mirage? This is a startling illustration of the power of cultural hegemony to create a trance-like state in which nearly everybody believes something, primarily because it's convenient, in their short-term self-interest, and they see everyone else believing it—regardless of its relation to empirical reality.

An equally dangerous consensus trance captivates approaches to the climate emergency. When scientists from the UN's Intergovernmental

Panel on Climate Change (IPCC) deliver scenarios for global heating this century, it's natural to believe that they use serious, grounded assumptions in their models. However, closer analysis reveals that the scenario in which we stay under 2°C of global heating involves an extravagant assumption that we will suck 730 billion metric tonnes of carbon out of the atmosphere this century—an amount equivalent to roughly twenty times the total current annual emissions from all fossil fuel usage, using speculative technologies that are unproven at scale. Such an assumption is closer to science fiction than the rigorous analysis worthy of a model on which our civilization is basing its future. Yet, even as the IPCC appears willing to model humanity's fate on a pipe dream, not one of their scenarios explores what is possible from a graduated annual reduction in global GDP. Such a scenario was considered by the IPCC community to be too implausible to consider.[9]

Should these notional technologies for carbon removal fail to deliver as modeled, climate operatives have a backup plan. Using geoengineering techniques that treat the Earth as a gigantic machine that needs fixing, they are developing experimental procedures to dim the effects of solar radiation. A leading candidate, financed by Bill Gates, involves spraying particles into the stratosphere to reflect the Sun's rays back into space. The risks are enormous, including the likelihood of causing extreme shifts in precipitation around the world. Additionally, once begun, it could never be stopped without immediate catastrophic rebound heating; it would not prevent the oceans from further acidifying; and may turn the blue sky into a perpetual dull haze. In spite of these concerns, geoengineering is beginning to get discussed at UN meetings, with influential publications such as *The Economist* predicting that, since it's cheaper and effective immediately, it's more likely to be implemented than the drastic, binding cuts in emissions needed to head off climate disaster.[10]

FORTRESS EARTH

While the cultural hegemons tell the world not to worry about impending collapse, the power elite they protect aren't necessarily drinking the same Kool-Aid. Technology critic Douglas Rushkoff tells how he was whisked away on a secretive mission to consult a handful of oligarchs on their plans for maintaining authority in their underground bunker systems after what they euphemistically call "the event." A new industry has emerged selling luxury bunkers to the ultra-rich out of converted cold war missile silos and other fortified facilities, so they can hide out in comfort in the aftermath of a catastrophe. For $8.3 million, Rushkoff reports, you can buy an "Aristocrat" model complete with imitation natural light, a wine cellar, pool, and bowling lane. As a CEO of a large tech company confided, "I actually think it's logically rational and appropriately conservative."[11]

While this self-centered behavior may strike many of us as morally repugnant, it has been quietly rationalized in the ultra-elite echelons as "lifeboat ethics"—a term first coined by the influential ecologist Garrett Hardin in 1974. Hardin characterized the affluent world as a comfortable lifeboat surrounded by a swarm of "much more crowded lifeboats"—nations in the Global South—overfilled with people who "fall out of their lifeboats and swim for a while in the water outside, hoping to be admitted to a rich lifeboat." Since taking them in would ultimately cause the affluent lifeboat to sink through overcrowding, there was, Hardin argued, an ethical justification to keeping them out and letting them drown.[12]

If it seems difficult to comprehend how this kind of twisted moral logic could be widely embraced, it's helpful to consider a slew of studies by moral psychologists on the corrosive effects of wealth and privilege. Those who enjoy unearned privilege tend to believe they deserve it even when they know it's the luck of the draw. As people become wealthier, they also tend to become more selfish. Wealthier people, studies indicate, are more likely to cheat at games and on their taxes, to steal candy from a jar meant for children and shoplift from stores, and less likely to empathize with others, give to charity, or stop at a crosswalk for pedestrians.[13]

However, even outside the elites, fear is beginning to seep into the general population as the specters of climate breakdown, mass migrations, and economic insecurity make it only too clear that the current system is unraveling. A worldwide public opinion poll conducted in 2017 by Ipsos found that an astounding 82 percent of people surveyed think we live in an "increasingly dangerous" world, with a significant majority believing that "the world today is changing too fast," that "society is broken," and that their own country is "in decline."[14]

Gramsci's theory of hegemony, discussed in the previous chapter, explains that the ruling class relies on two forms of control. Cultural hegemony is the first line of defense, but when it begins to break down and lose its sway over the masses, the elite's coercive apparatus steps in to ensure authority is maintained. Within nations, we see this in the militarization of police forces; in the rise of gated communities guarded by armed security firms; and in a legal crackdown on protests—even in supposedly free societies—with the criminalization of climate activists and the demonization of peaceful protesters as extremists and terrorists. There is also, predictably, an intensification of kyriarchy: turning the attention of common people away from the elite's role in society's unraveling, and inciting greater hostility to those lower down in the pyramid of power, such as undocumented immigrants fleeing intolerable conditions in their homelands.

Around the world, Hardin's "lifeboat ethics" are playing out in a ruthless form of global apartheid that maintains rigid separation between populations of haves and have-nots. Increasingly, we are living in a "Fortress Earth" where formidable barriers—physical and technological—keep the affluent world segregated from those most vulnerable to the ecological and climate breakdown for which they bear the least responsibility. In 1989, the planet contained six border walls; there are now at least sixty-three physical walls securing borders, encircling 60 percent of the world's population. Hundreds more borders are protected by militarized patrols of land, sea, and air, using troops, ships, aircraft, drones, and digital surveillance to keep out those seeking a better chance of survival.[15]

Rather than invest in the urgent need for Majority World nations to adapt to climate breakdown, the world's most powerful nations are doubling down on their military capacity to protect themselves. Since a Green Climate Fund was set up at a UN climate summit in 2009, only $15 billion of its $100 billion target has been funded. Meanwhile, military spending worldwide has ballooned to over $2 trillion annually, most of which is accounted for by the United States and its NATO allies. With more than 800 military bases in seventy countries, the US takes its role as defender of the global capitalist system deadly seriously. Meanwhile, the unraveling of the world system offers a tremendous profit opportunity for Windigo, Inc., with at least $200 billion spent annually on private security worldwide. The topsy-turvy nature of global capitalism means that a collapsing world can offer attractive short-term financial returns: Bombed out infrastructures and devastated oceanfront communities can be bought up cheaply by wealthy investors, and the ensuing reconstruction boosts corporate profits while adding to GDP.[16]

Are these two bleak pathways the only ones available to our global civilization as it approaches its culmination—total societal collapse or a morally repugnant Fortress Earth permitting elites to explore new frontiers of indulgence while most of humanity suffers cataclysmic breakdown? In the Mina crowd disaster, investigators later discovered that the crush was likely exacerbated by the closure of two roads near the bridge so that a prince and his 350-person convoy could leisurely cross. If those roads had been open, they might have allowed the crowd to disperse and avoid calamity. Is there, likewise, an alternative avenue being closed off by the blinkered reasoning of cultural hegemony that might potentially lead to a more favorable outcome?

A LEVER TO MOVE THE WORLD

"Give me a lever long enough and a fulcrum on which to place it, and I shall move the world," said the ancient philosopher and engineer Archimedes's of Syracuse, reflecting on the power of leverage to shift what appears immoveable. The accelerating forces of destruction that propel global capitalism while entrenching the power elite's grip ever more firmly on the throttle appear unstoppable. If, however, we apply Archimedes' insight to the domain of social change, might we discover a lever that could in fact move the whole world?

The systems scientist Donella Meadows, lead author of the seminal report *Limits to Growth* that first alerted the world to the runaway crisis we're now facing, studied this question extensively and shared her understanding in a paper entitled "Leverage Points: Places to Intervene in a System" in which she delineated nine intervention points in increasing order of effectiveness. The least leveraged are the ones people usually focus on when trying to fix a political problem: taxes, subsidies, regulatory standards, or efficiency improvements. Higher up the leverage ladder are the rules of the system such as laws, constitutions, or trade treaties. Close to the top are the goals of the system—under capitalism that refers to superordinate goals such as growing the economy and perpetually increasing the return of invested capital. Finally, at the very pinnacle of leverage is the mindset or paradigm out of which the entire system arises.[17]

When Copernicus, for example, showed that the Earth is not the center of the universe, or when Einstein theorized that matter and energy are interchangeable, they didn't just advance the thinking in their field—they opened up the possibility of an entirely different paradigm with which to make sense of everything. As a result, established approaches were discovered to be either limited or erroneous, opening a conceptual space for improved models of reality to be developed by innovative minds. Similarly, we have reached a place in our world system where the old paradigm no longer works. It has passed its expiration date. Paying attention to fixing obvious problems within the system may still have benefit—it may alleviate unnecessary short-term suffering and may even delay the onset of collapse—but it is not going to provide an alternative pathway that could lead us out of our global predicament.

The paradigm on which our world system is based emerged in early modern Europe along with the Scientific Revolution. Arising from a root metaphor of the universe as a machine, the modern worldview perceived nature as a resource with no intrinsic value other than its usefulness for human exploitation. It was a worldview of separation: seeing humans as fundamentally separate from the rest of nature, individuals as separate from each other, and each person split between a mind and body that were essentially distinct. This worldview proved a tremendous boon for scientific discovery, giving rise to the powerful methodology of reductionism which split everything into smaller and smaller units—molecules, atoms, cells, and genes—to understand how it all worked.

However, its effectiveness overshadowed its limitations. By focusing on the inert building blocks of nature, reductionism downplayed the equally important principles by which nature's parts self-organize coherently to form the emergent complexity of life. More recently, a large and growing body of scientific disciplines such as complexity science, systems biology, and network theory have proffered an alternative conception of the universe, recognizing that the ways in which things connect are frequently more important than the things themselves. As I've described in *The Web of Meaning*, the broader implications of these scientific disciplines lead to a profound realization shared by many of the world's great wisdom traditions: a recognition of our deep interconnectedness, within ourselves, with each other, and with all of life.

As Meadows pointed out, the underlying paradigm of a society determines its overriding goals and the set of rules by which those goals are achieved. If a civilization builds its version of reality on a worldview seeing nature as a resource and each individual as distinct from the other, it makes sense that its goal would be to extract as much as possible from nature, and that its rules would encourage individuals to exploit others. Capitalism can thus be understood as the predictable economic system of the dominant worldview.

What would be the expected system of a worldview arising from a realization of the deep interconnectedness of all life? We will explore this in the rest of this book. In place of a world organized around extraction and exploitation, we will investigate the possibilities that emerge from designing a society based on life-affirming principles that set the conditions for all people to flourish on a thriving, regenerated Earth—an ecological civilization.

However, before embarking on this journey, there is an important issue to confront. As our civilization veers ever closer toward the edge of a precipice, it may seem like a worthy long-term objective to shift its entire worldview but a luxury we simply can't afford. Even with the limited impact of the tactics Meadows consigned to the lower rungs of the leverage ladder, aren't they the best option available as we face impending catastrophe? Do we really have time to try to change our civilization's paradigm? There is a way of thinking about political transformation that might help us consider this conundrum.

THE THIRD HORIZON

Imagine you've set out on a long journey, walking through rocky terrain. It might seem sensible to keep your gaze down, focusing on the next few footsteps to make sure you don't trip. But there are no signposts on this journey, so every now and then you need to look up and check where you're heading. Your destination, however, is still a long distance away—so far, in fact, that it's beyond the reach of the furthest horizon you can see. How do you know if you're going in the right direction? What happens if you come across an impassable natural barrier? Wouldn't it be helpful if you knew the rough whereabouts of your destination, so you could set your course accordingly and avoid following pathways that, attractive as they might seem, lead you in the wrong direction?

There's a powerful planning tool known as the Three Horizons Model, which uses this analogy to shed light on how various strategies and tactics fit into the ultimate objective of an enterprise. Developed originally for business strategy, it has been applied equally well to social and political planning. The first horizon relates to short-term planning—essential for daily and monthly accomplishments, but only if the right direction has already been set. The second horizon extends beyond incremental thinking, potentially disrupting conventional practices to achieve greater impact, while remaining in the same ballpark. The third horizon refers to ideas that are outside the ballpark, shifting the entire paradigm and thus permitting possibilities that could never have been imagined within the first two horizons.[18]

The Three Horizons Model is invaluable when applied to the global socio-economic situation the world faces today. There is no end of debates about first horizon issues; meanwhile, occasional powerful ideas reverberate through the system, shattering business as usual and bringing the second horizon into view. But there is very little third horizon thinking—so much so that most people are barely aware, if at all, that a third horizon could even exist.

In response to our metacrisis, first horizon activities might include advocating for greater investment in renewable energy, eliminating subsidies for fossil fuel companies, or strengthening regulations covering pollution. Second horizon thinking can appear seductively attractive: The all-electric

Tesla spectacularly disrupted the conventional automobile industry; carbon capture and storage—if it were to work at scale—promises to turn energy production into a carbon-neutral, or even negative, enterprise. But these disruptive technologies continue to reinforce the same paradigm that caused our crisis in the first place: the relentless pursuit of economic growth within the context of a globalized capitalist system that rewards extractive and exploitative behavior above all else.

The third horizon is the primary subject of this book: envisioning a civilization built on an entirely different foundation than the one that undergirds our current society. It offers the possibility for a new era that could be defined, at its deepest level, by a transformation in the way we make sense of the world, and a concomitant revolution in our predominant values.

The three horizons are roughly analogous to the ladder of leverage points described by Donella Meadows, where a paradigm shift—the pinnacle of leverage—opens conceptual space for a third horizon of possibilities. Crucially, the Three Horizons Model also helps to understand the value of each horizon as it relates to the others: Each has an essential role to play.

If you don't pay attention to your next steps in the first horizon, you will stumble before you ever get to your destination. When you glance up to check your direction, you might find a number of second horizon alternatives beckoning you. This is where it's critically important to have a general sense of where you're heading in relation to the third horizon. Some second horizon destinations might appear alluring but lead you in the opposite direction of the third horizon you're trying to reach. You may not know exactly where the third horizon is situated, nor precisely what it will look like when you get there, but it's crucially important to be able to visualize its general whereabouts with every step you take. There is no point in making rapid progress if your journey is taking you in the wrong direction.

As we turn our attention to an ecocivilization, you might imagine yourself as a traveler who has hitched a ride on a balloon that lifts you up from your regular path and wafts you temporarily into third horizon territory. From this lofty perch, you can make out some of its configurations—perhaps you see some characteristics of the landscape below that you had never imagined possible—but you can't necessarily distinguish all the details. After the trip, the balloon deposits you where you had been walking. Now, however, you're equipped with a vision of where you want to go and a rough sense of direction. You may not be able to identify the exact path that will get you there, but at least you now have an impression of the third horizon that can inform and galvanize you as you take the next steps on your journey.

PRINCIPLES OF AN ECOCIVILIZATION

CHAPTER 5

CORE PRINCIPLES OF LIFE, ECOSYSTEMS, AND HUMANITY

THE SELFISH GENE

Jeff Skilling thought he had it all figured out. As CEO of the commodities trading firm Enron, he decided to apply what he understood about natural selection to his own employees. Inspired by his favorite book, *The Selfish Gene* by Richard Dawkins, he believed he could spur them to peak performance with a toxic combination of fear and greed. Using a policy called "Rank and Yank," he regularly graded everyone on a scale of one to five. A "five" got you axed, but only after being humiliated on the company website. A "one" delivered lavish rewards, and no one collected more than Skilling himself, who reaped $132 million in 2000—the year before Enron collapsed, leaving many of its 20,000 employees bereft of their life savings, and sending Skilling to twelve years in jail for fraud.

Skilling's debacle illustrates the dangers that can arise when a misconception of how nature works is applied to human organization. Dawkins disavowed Skilling's simplistic interpretation of his book, but his notion of the "selfish gene" as the driver of evolution pervades modern culture and has helped to shape the moral framework of our age. As Dawkins himself summarized it:

> The argument of this book is that we, and all other animals, are machines created by our genes. Like successful Chicago gangsters, our genes have survived, in some cases for millions of years, in a highly competitive world. This entitles

> us to expect certain qualities in our genes. I shall argue that a predominant quality to be expected in a successful gene is ruthless selfishness. This gene selfishness will usually give rise to selfishness in individual behavior . . . Much as we might wish to believe otherwise, universal love and the welfare of the species as a whole are concepts that simply do not make evolutionary sense.

Since his book's publication in 1976, influential authorities have projected this supposed biological truth into economics, politics, and business. "The economy of nature is competitive from beginning to end," writes the sociobiologist M. T. Ghiselin, coeditor of the *Journal of Bioeconomics*.[1]

Dawkins's bestseller had a huge impact on mainstream thinking, but the idea that selfishness and greed are drivers of evolution, and therefore morally admissible, has been around for over a century, ever since Charles Darwin's theory of evolution became widely accepted. The archetypal robber barons, Andrew Carnegie and John D. Rockefeller, both argued that the "survival of the fittest" principle justified their cutthroat tactics. The founding father of neoliberal economics, Friedrich Hayek, similarly based his theories on what he understood as evolutionary principles.

It should be noted that Dawkins himself states clearly that his description of the gene's selfishness in no way justifies a moral code of selfishness. "Be warned," he writes, "that if you wish, as I do, to build a society towards a common good, you can expect little help from biological nature." Rather, Dawkins sees humans as being in a state of constant battle with our own genetic makeup. "Our brains," he declares, "have evolved to the point where we are capable of rebelling against our selfish genes." Dawkins thus proffers the image of a human as a battleground between our selfish genes and our moral conscience.[2]

What does this imply for an ecocivilization? Must we overcome our inherent nature in order to live together morally? Would a society based on the principles of living systems doom us to a neoliberal dystopia of "ruthless selfishness"? In fact, modern research in evolutionary biology has overturned virtually every major assumption in the account of the selfish gene. In its place, researchers have developed a far more sophisticated conception of how evolution works, revealing a rich tapestry of nature's dynamic interconnectedness. Rather than evolution being driven by competition, it turns out that cooperation has played a far more important role in producing the great transitions that led to Earth's current state of rich abundance.

PRINCIPLES OF LIVING SYSTEMS

To begin with, we and other animals are not "machines created by our genes." Researchers in domains such as complexity science and systems biology draw a crucial distinction between machines and living, self-organized adaptive systems. A machine, such as a jumbo jet, can be very complicated but doesn't meet the criteria of complexity. Each of its components, and the way they relate to each other, can be completely analyzed, given an exact description, and accurately predicted. If that weren't the case, you'd be wise not to fly in it! A living organism, by contrast, even one as tiny as a single cell, is a complex system functionally organized to sustain itself, with parts engaging dynamically with each other in multiple nonlinear relationships and feedback loops that can never be precisely described or predicted.

As self-organized systems, living organisms are neither programmed by an external agent nor by their genes. Rather, the different parts making up the system order themselves into a relatively coherent and stable pattern of behavior called an *attractor.* These attractors can be highly resilient in the face of perturbations—think of how your body maintains homeostasis in the face of changing external conditions—but occasionally they undergo phase transitions, whereby the internal coherence transforms into a new stable pattern.

Frequently these phase transitions can lead to a calamitous reduction in complexity, such as an epileptic seizure or the collapse of an ecosystem. Sometimes, though, they can be the very essence of creativity—think how a chrysalis turns into a butterfly, or how a fetus develops in the womb until it's ready for the phase transition of birth. This process is known as *emergence*: the system's complexity reaches a critical mass that transforms into a new coherence, which couldn't have occurred by simply adding up each of the system's elements. This is the source of the famous saying that "the whole is greater than the sum of its parts."

A highly consequential incident of emergence occurred early in Earth's history, when life first emerged as the result of certain molecules coming together to form a self-sustaining network of chemical reactions. In a process known as *autopoiesis* ("self-generation"), these living systems succeeded in converting energy and matter from outside their membrane into the component parts needed to perpetuate and regenerate themselves. A defining quality of living systems, from that time on, is that the whole and the parts of the system exert a reciprocal causal effect on each other, known as *reciprocal causality*. The whole emerges from the complex interactions of its parts as a coherent identity, while simultaneously influencing what each part needs to do from moment to moment. As a result, every healthy living system displays a high level of *integration*: a state of unity with differentiation, where each part maintains its unique identity while actively participating in generating the larger whole.

As life expanded on Earth, it discovered innumerable diverse ways to maintain its self-generation, forming the disparate species of bacteria, fungi, plants, and animals that we know today. In the entire history of Earth, there have only been a few major phase transitions when life's self-organization jumped to a higher level of complexity: when cells first developed a nucleus, when bacteria learned to exchange genes with others ("horizontal gene transfer"), and when multicellular life appeared. In all these cases, the increase in life's complexity arose, not through organisms learning how to outcompete each other, but rather how to cooperate more effectively with each other in a process known as *mutually beneficial symbiosis*. In the words of the evolutionary biologist Lynn Margulis: "Life did not take over the world by combat but by networking."[3]

PRINCIPLES OF ECOSYSTEMS

It takes a lot of energy to compete against another entity: you have to defend yourself against them, while figuring out how to take advantage of their vulnerabilities. In the end, only one of you wins and the other loses. How much better if you could, instead, work with them to identify a shared goal, and each combine your unique capabilities to create synergy: where together you can accomplish more than each of you working alone.

This was the enormous evolutionary potential unleashed by mutually beneficial symbiosis.

Whenever you take a walk in the woods, eat a meal, or dip in the ocean, you're experiencing the symbiosis that has generated life's plenitude. Plants transform sunlight into chemical energy that provides food for other creatures, whose waste then fertilizes the soil that the plants rely on. Fungal networks contribute essential chemicals to trees in return for the carbon they can't make for themselves. Pollinators allow plants to become fertile and produce fruit with seeds, which are then carried by other animals to new locations. In a tiny droplet of ocean water, each single-celled alga exchanges nutrients with thousands of bacteria. We share our bodies with trillions of bacteria that produce enzymes to digest food that our own enzymes can't manage.

Where, then, does competition fit into the picture? What about those spectacular nature documentaries showing cheetahs sprinting to catch gazelles? Male chimpanzees fighting rivals for sexual dominance? Bacteria that make us sick by overpowering our immune systems? There is no question that ruthless competition also plays a major role in the drama of life. How can we reconcile pervasive competition with the forces of cooperation?

Consider a spectrum with extreme cooperation at one end and extreme competition on the other. Organisms exist at the cooperative end, comprised of different varieties of cells that have evolved to work intimately together for the good of the system as a whole. Outside the organism, however, relationships exist all along the spectrum, exhibiting complex blends of cooperation and competition, with the struggle between predator and prey at the other extreme.

The creative tension arising from the confluence of both competition and cooperation is itself a driving force of evolution. The theory of multilevel selection, developed by prominent biologists David Sloan Wilson and E. O. Wilson, elucidates the evolutionary dynamics between cooperative and competitive behavior at different scales of life. Within a group, competitive individuals that outcompete their peers tend to be successful. However, groups with cooperating individuals tend to outcompete groups with more selfish individuals. Imagine two groups battling each other. Which do you think will be victorious: the group in which everyone is looking out for themselves or the one in which everyone is working together for the greater good? Each of the major phase transitions in Earth's evolutionary history can be understood as episodes of multilevel selection in which a higher level of cooperation prevailed and spread around the world.[4]

As a result, a healthy ecosystem displays highly integrated, tangled webs of cooperation and competition. As species pursue their roles within the ecosystem, they depend on each other in an intricate mesh of reciprocation—a complex, invisible matrix of behavioral interconnections linking each organism with the whole. While each species acts in its unique way, the ecosystem as a whole behaves in many ways like a complex adaptive system.[5]

Consistent with other phenomena of self-organization, ecosystems exhibit a fractal design with similar patterns repeating themselves at different scales. Coherent self-organized entities are embedded within larger systems: cells within an organism, which is part of a population, which collectively comprise the ecosystem. In all cases, the overall health of the system requires the flourishing of each part—a phenomenon described as *fractal flourishing*. Each system is interdependent on the vitality of the other systems around it, within it, and those in which it's embedded. As a result of these evolutionary dynamics, a healthy organism within a well-functioning ecosystem enacts flourishing as much as it experiences it.

THE HUMAN EVOLUTIONARY NICHE

While these principles might lead to a robust ecosystem, they don't necessarily produce the best results for each individual within it. A wounded gazelle mauled by a cheetah wouldn't gain much comfort being told she was sacrificing her life for the greater good. Each species within an ecosystem has a unique set of evolved criteria that produce their own optimal flourishing. What works for the lion is different than what works for the lamb. Humans, like all other species, have their unique characteristics and evolved a particular set of criteria that define the conditions for their own flourishing. When determining the core principles of an ecocivilization—one that's structurally designed to optimize human well-being—it's essential to identify first what are the defining characteristics of the human evolutionary niche.

Most of our primate cousins, such as chimpanzees and gorillas, live in communities characterized by frequent violent conflict with males competing against each other for dominance. This was very likely the societal structure of the forest primates who were our last common ancestors six million years ago, a group of whom got stranded in Africa's Great Rift Valley when massive tectonic shifts turned a vast forested region into open savannah. This group was more vulnerable to big predators and had less access to food, but discovered that they could protect and feed themselves far more effectively through collaboration. Those with the cognitive abilities to cooperate with each other most effectively were the ones who thrived and whose genes were passed on to future generations.

Our early ancestors became a hypersocial species, and gradually began to form a collective identity extending beyond the individual sense of self. Over millions of years, pre-humans developed what are called "moral emotions" such as guilt, compassion, embarrassment, shame, and gratitude—feelings that arise from our social interactions and frequently cause us to act in ways that benefit our group, even sometimes to our own individual detriment.[6]

As the complexity of social interaction became more pronounced, the most successful hominids were those who could navigate skillfully through the intricate maze of social signals, understanding the needs of others and conveying their own needs effectively. Gradually, hominids evolved a greater ability to make meaning from these diverse signals through increased use of their prefrontal cortex—the most connected part of the brain which integrates inputs from feelings, memories, sensations, and thoughts, and is more highly developed in humans than in any other species.

When humans are born, their prefrontal cortex is extremely underdeveloped, with most neuronal connections forming through infancy and childhood, and only reaching full maturity in their mid-twenties. As a result, in a process known as *deep enculturation*, the culture an infant is born into literally sculpts their brain, shaping the network of beliefs and values that determine how they will make meaning out of the world. For this reason, trying to define "human nature" based on the social norms that dictate how people behave in any particular culture—including our own—can be dangerously misleading.[7]

The prefrontal cortex is the neural substrate of the kind of intelligence that's generally associated with human uniqueness: our ability to think symbolically and analytically, to understand language, plan for the future, and construct sophisticated tools. However, while an individual human might have marginal cognitive advantages over another primate, the overwhelming dominance of the human species arose primarily through the collective intelligence that emerged over time from deep enculturation. The ability for one generation to pass on their discoveries to following generations led to a ratchet effect that caused human development to soar into the stratosphere. Every morning, when we turn on the lights, read the news, or commute to work, we're relying unwittingly on the cumulative efforts and insights of generations of ancestors who, over eons, laid the foundations for the sophisticated technological civilization we rely on today.[8]

A CULTURAL MAJOR EVOLUTIONARY TRANSITION?

In multilevel selection theory, the emergence of *Homo sapiens* as a cooperative species is viewed as one of life's major evolutionary transitions. However, the evolutionary shift from hierarchical primate societies to more egalitarian human communities remained a work in progress. Assertive males would continually try to achieve the kind of dominance enjoyed by other alpha male primates, but the rest of the group—females and males collaborating, driven by shared moral outrage—prevented them from disrupting the group harmony. As human identity expanded from self and kin to include the entire group, the common welfare became a touchstone for moral values: Those who acted selfishly at the expense of the group were considered bad, whereas those who acted altruistically were seen as good.[9]

This uneasy equilibrium lasted as long as humans lived in nomadic hunter-gatherer bands—roughly 95 percent our species' history. However, the dynamic changed with the rise of agriculture, beginning about twelve thousand years ago. With settled lifestyles, inequality now played a bigger part in social dynamics. As discussed in chapter 3, the accumulation of material possessions gave extra ammunition to males seeking dominance, allowing them to recruit others in support, and creating a cumulative ratchet effect whereby increases in wealth and power generated further increases. Those at the top of the hierarchy then turned their attention to conquering neighboring groups.

The group identity that helped create morality in the first place frequently only extended to the in-group—and has been aptly called "parochial altruism." In the new era of territorial raids, the social cohesion that had favored cooperation now became a resource for effective combat. When aggressive communities conquered their more peaceful neighbors, they imposed on them new warrior-centered values that elevated machismo and violence. As we saw in chapter 3, this was the beginning of the five-thousand-year-old wealth pump that has culminated in today's egregious level of inequality. The moral nature of our species paradoxically became the source of our society's immorality.

David Sloan Wilson has helpfully extended multilevel selection theory to understand this dilemma facing humanity by applying a lens of multilevel morality. As he points out, cultural evolution, like genetic evolution, reflects a tension between lower level and higher level good. Cooperation in any group is vulnerable to disruptive behavior at a lower level (such as the alpha male in a hunter-gatherer band, or a cancer cell in an organism) but also at a higher level. Helping family and friends is fine—except when it manifests as nepotism and cronyism. Caring for your community's welfare is virtuous—except when it leads to erecting border walls to keep out climate refugees. Mining fossil fuels might enrich your nation—but accelerate our civilization's course toward collapse.[10]

The framework of multilevel morality helps to define the challenge facing the design of an ecocivilization. Given the characteristic features of the human species—our propensity toward group identity and susceptibility to cultural influences—what are the conditions that encourage behavior that's beneficial at multiple functional levels: the self and family, the community, humanity, and all of life? This is what we'll begin to explore in the next chapter.[11]

CHAPTER 6

PRINCIPLES OF AN ECOCIVILIZATION

THE PRINCIPLES OF THE COMMONS

The economics establishment was outraged. The 2009 Nobel Prize in economics had just been awarded to someone most professors had never heard of. Making matters worse, the recipient was a political scientist, not even a proper economist. In an online forum, they shared their disdain: "What kind of bullshit is this? This year is the worst," sputtered one. Others spouted: "Multidisciplinary? Other disciplines are all rubbish . . . Economics is superior." But the greatest vitriol was reserved for the fact that the recipient, Elinor Ostrom, was a woman. "Well, they had to give it to a woman at some point," wrote the misogynists. "Why not just throw a dart at a board?" "This is the problem with Affirmative Action." "Now, this is the end of Economics."[1]

The last commenter at least had a point. The award may not have signaled the end of economics but it did mark the coming of age of a new field that has, in significant ways, supplanted a domain of conventional economics—the systematic analysis of principles of the commons.

Elinor Ostrom became the first woman to win the Nobel Prize in economics through her groundbreaking research in how communities work together to manage collective goods, which benefit everyone but can fall prey to different types of mismanagement—ultimately to everyone's detriment. Consider fishing grounds that get overfished; groundwater basins that run dry from overuse; or the atmosphere accumulating greenhouse gases. The conventional economic solution is for governments to impose regulations on those causing the damage. Ostrom's research, however, had uncovered another form of resource management to which economists had previously been oblivious. After studying hundreds of different cases of community resource management around the world, some of which had operated successfully for centuries, Ostrom published a seminal work, *Governing the Commons: The Evolution of Institutions for Collective Action*, which laid out certain principles that applied across the board in domains as different as irrigation, grazing, or forestry management, and across regions as culturally diverse as Switzerland, Japan, the Philippines, and Southern California.

What made Ostrom's principles radically different from those of conventional economics was that they arose from the complex interactions of group members repeated over generations. Like the living systems discussed in the previous chapter, the principles were not imposed by an external party but emerged through processes of self-organization. There was no group leader issuing commands but the group itself developed the rules and enforced them.

When David Sloan Wilson, the pioneer of multilevel selection, realized the significance of the overlap between Ostrom's principles and his own theory, he partnered with her to explore how her findings could be generalized to apply to all aspects of human collaboration. Could these principles encourage greater prosocial behavior in ordinary people, and as such offer a framework to help humanity achieve the cultural evolutionary transition that we need?[2]

Wilson and his team have since developed a working list, based on Ostrom's, of "core design principles"—a set of special conditions that are "required for prosocial behaviors to outcompete more self-centered behaviors." These principles don't rely on people magically elevating their consciousness to overcome selfish drives, but rather establish parameters that reward people's collaborative instincts and penalize selfishness. They read like solid common sense—such as establishing a clear group identity, ensuring all members take part in decision-making, that rewards are proportional to contributions, that people monitor each other, good behaviors are rewarded, and bad behaviors receive graduated sanctions that escalate only when necessary.

These principles—based on evolutionary tenets backed by empirical evidence—are helpful in setting the underlying parameters of an ecocivilization. As discussed in the previous chapter, the human evolutionary niche developed while our ancestors lived in egalitarian hunter-gatherer bands, and the behavioral norms established during that period can be expected to foster human flourishing. But, of course, we no longer live in nomadic bands, and the Earth could sustain only a tiny fraction of the current human population if we did. There is no going back in time, and in any case, it would be wrong to paint that era as a golden age. Some customary hunter-gatherer practices such as infanticide would be abhorrent to current moral standards, while technological advances have opened up previously unimaginable vistas of human possibility.

This begs the question of whether it's even possible to design a sophisticated modern civilization on core principles of human flourishing. Virtually every major civilization in history has constituted various versions of the wealth pump with patriarchal cultures, rigid hierarchies, cruel exploitation by elites, and unsustainable resource extraction. The formation of an ecocivilization would represent an entirely new phase of human history—one that redefines the possibilities of the collective human experience by applying our evolutionary legacy to a technologically advanced, global society. We will examine in this chapter what can be gleaned from our ancestral heritage—and consider how that might be utilized as a foundation on which to construct a modern framework for current and future human flourishing.

INDIGENOUS ETHICS AND PRACTICES

While the customs of our early ancestors can only be inferred by anthropologists through careful study, many of their values and behaviors have been passed down through generations and still exist in the norms of Indigenous peoples, who represent about five percent of the world's population. It is important not to romanticize or demean Indigenous people by assigning them the status of "noble savage." Like any human population, individuals within Indigenous communities demonstrate unending variation. Additionally, most Indigenous cultures have been so deeply impacted by colonialism that it is often difficult to discern what remains from their original set of traditions and beliefs. Also, an important difference must be recognized between nomadic forager communities, which most resemble the lifestyle of our earliest ancestors, and settled Indigenous communities, many of which have developed hierarchical and patriarchal social structures.

Nevertheless, anthropologists and Indigenous scholars have identified overriding, common characteristics that hold true for virtually all Indigenous communities, spanning regions as diverse as the Inuit in the Arctic, the !Kung of the Kalahari, or Aboriginal Australians. These shared attributes, known collectively as *indigeneity*, likely reflect the set of values and behaviors that most naturally align with human flourishing.[3]

First and foremost is the primacy of community. "Indigenous peoples see everything through the filter of community," states the Comanche leader LaDonna Harris. Anthropologists observe that, in nomadic forager communities, no one expects or wants to be alone. People have limited interest in material possessions, and gain pleasure mostly from social activities such as dancing, playing, joking, singing, or just sitting together.

This community orientation doesn't, in any way, suppress people's individuality. Rather, individuality is expressed through the unique contributions each person makes to their community. Harris explains that, from an Indigenous perspective, "we can only be a 'self' in community. We are simultaneously both autonomous and connected." Individuals do not accept coercion and generally choose to do whatever they want, regardless of age or gender. Someone might, for example, go on a walkabout, or choose to stay home when the rest of the group goes hunting, without requiring permission from the others.

Nomadic foragers, the anthropologist Christopher Boehm reports, "are universally—and all but obsessively—concerned with being free from the authority of others." A powerful egalitarian ethic pervades most Indigenous communities, leading to collective decision-making processes (one of Wilson's Core Design Principles). As a nonplussed German colonial officer noted about the Bantu Herero people he encountered in 1895, "Not only the men, but frequently also the women, and even the servants, join in the discussion and give their advice. Thus, no one really feels like a subject; no one has learned to be subservient."[4]

Traditional Indigenous communities have no interest in maximizing wealth but focus rather on sufficiency. In the nineteenth century, for example, European fur traders hoped to acquire more furs from the Manitoba Cree, so they offered them higher prices; however, the Cree simply brought fewer furs to trade, because they were already obtaining as much as they wanted in exchange. Rather than market exchange, many Indigenous communities practice what's known as a gift economy, which has a different connotation than the modern understanding of a gift. As the Indigenous scientist Robin Wall Kimmerer explains: "In the gift economy, gifts are not free. The essence of the gift is that it creates a set of relationships. The currency of a gift economy is, at its root, reciprocity."[5]

The principle of reciprocity is crucial to many Indigenous cultures, and fundamental to creating a sense of security. The Dakota elder Ella Deloria contrasts the Western and Indigenous approaches to security:

> One says in effect: "Get, get, get now; all you can, as you can, for yourself, and so ensure security for yourself." And it depends on things, primarily. The other said: "Give, give, give to others. Let gifts flow freely out and they will flow freely back to you again." And that system depended on human beings.

When linguist Daniel Everett discovered that the Pirahã, a forager group living deep in the Amazon, knew how to preserve meat by smoking, drying, and salting, he asked them why they didn't do it. "I store my meat in the belly of my brother" was the answer.[6]

The Indigenous sense of community and reciprocity extends beyond human relationships to encompass all of nature. For example, the Quechua word for community, *ayllu*, refers not just to a network of clans, explains Justo Oxa Díaz, but "includes humans, plants, animals, the mountains, the rivers, the rain, etc. All are related like a family . . . It is not where we are from, it is who we are. For example, I am not *from* Huantura, I *am* Huantura." Many Indigenous cultures share an animist worldview, seeing the world as full of persons, only some of whom are human. This leads to a respectful relationship with nonhuman nature, emphasizing cooperation and partnership rather than exploitation.[7]

In spite of their animist worldview, when humans first left Africa to discover other continents, they severely disrupted the ecologies of each territory they discovered. Their unique capabilities drove to extinction most of the spectacular megafauna of those continents, which had no way to recognize the danger of these seemingly innocuous creatures armed with weapons and complex hunting strategies. However, after initial disruptions, societies across the world settled into resilient behavioral norms that led to harmonious equilibrium between humans and nature. These likely emerged from the accumulated wisdom of tribal elders instituting rituals and observances that reoriented behavior to more sustainable practices, many of which remain embedded in the present-day values of Indigenous communities.

The practices that arose inculcated respect, restraint, and reciprocity with all nonhuman beings. M. Kat Anderson, who has researched Indigenous land practices in California, relates how Indigenous people developed ways to maintain the abundance of the land without domesticating it, in a process she describes as "tending the wild." She identifies two overarching principles of harvest: *Leave some of what is gathered for the other animals* and *Do not waste what you have harvested.* Similarly, Robin Wall Kimmerer describes precepts known as the Honorable Harvest that include rules such as *Ask permission before taking*; *Take only what you need*; and *Give a gift in reciprocity for what you have taken.*[8]

The Indigenous focus on sustainability extends to their view of time, which is frequently seen as an unbroken, intergenerational chain linking ancestors and descendants, as summarized by the Maori proverb: "I walk backwards into the future with my eyes fixed on my past." In the words of a Ghanaian chief: "Land belongs to a vast family of whom many are dead, a few are living, and a countless host are still unborn." Similarly, in North America, a Haudenosaunee law requires decision-makers to consider impacts extending seven generations into the future.

A SHARED FOUNDATION OF LIFE-AFFIRMING VALUES

In certain parts of the world, these Indigenous values have become models for modern political frameworks. The concept of *buen vivir* ("living well")—a loose translation of the Quechua term *sumak kawsay*—has been incorporated into the constitutions of both Bolivia and Ecuador. *Buen vivir* is different from similar sounding Western terms such as "the good life" with its connotations of an individual enjoying material prosperity. Rather, it encapsulates the foundational Indigenous concepts that true well-being can only arise within community, and that this community incorporates not just humans but all of nature. *Buen vivir* establishes an ethical orientation that extends to governmental, economic, and social policy: reframing economics around the idea of sufficiency rather than wealth accumulation, while recognizing the rights of all people to live in dignity and of nonhuman nature to flourish.[9]

More broadly, since they represent foundational parameters of human well-being, the core values of indigeneity permeate longstanding cultural traditions throughout the world. The concept of *buen vivir* extends throughout Indigenous cultures in both North and South America, such as in the Anishinaabe ethic of *mino-mnaamodzawin*, which emphasizes respectful and mutually beneficial relationships among all human and nonhuman entities. A related Māori concept, *whakawhanaungatanga*, refers to the rights and obligations of kinship, extending beyond family to all those in reciprocal relationship. In Sub-Saharan Africa, a guiding principle for life is *ubuntu*, which is frequently translated as "I am because you are, you are because I am." Recognizing the deep interdependence of each person within community, *ubuntu* implies a reciprocal moral obligation to care for others, and is generally understood as extending to all life. In India, the traditional concept of *swaraj*, or "self-rule," which was embraced by Gandhi as a cornerstone of his political vision, builds on the ancient Indian custom of face-to-face political assemblies to claim the moral right for communities to determine their own fate through dialogue and consensus.

The overriding principle of optimizing for the common good can also be found in the great monotheistic traditions. The Muslim concept of *tawhīd*, which recognizes God's oneness throughout the universe, is understood to extend moral consideration to every aspect of creation. Christian theologian Thomas Aquinas coined the term *bonum commune* ("common good") in the thirteenth century as a foundation for Christian social doctrine—a term that is still found in the constitutions of major European democracies. More recently, Pope Francis's encyclicals, *Laudato Si'* and *Fratelli tutti*, emphasize human fraternity and "care for our common home" as overarching themes.

A shared insight underlying this worldwide cultural legacy is the realization of our deep interrelatedness: seeing people as part of community, humans as an integral part of the natural world, and human activities always embedded within larger systems. On this basis, we may discern three core values on which the principles of an ecocivilization can be grounded. The first is an emphasis on *quality of life* rather than material possessions: Instead of measuring welfare by economic output, an ecocivilization would prioritize progress in conditions that foster well-being, both individually and in society at large. Secondly, political, social, and economic choices would be based on a recognition of our *shared humanity*, emphasizing fairness and dignity for all rather than maximizing purely for oneself and one's parochially defined social group. Finally, our future must be built on the basis of *ecological regeneration*, where the flourishing of the natural world is a foundational principle for humanity's major decisions.

PRINCIPLES OF AN ECOCIVILIZATION

These core values are, of course, very different from the values on which our current civilization is constructed. In place of a system that gives primacy to the proliferation of capital through exploitation of people and resources, an ecocivilization would be based on life-affirming principles: setting the conditions for all people to flourish on a regenerated Earth.

It's important to clarify what is meant by flourishing. Thousands of years ago, Aristotle made an important distinction—one still central to research on this topic—between two forms of happiness: *hedonia* and *eudaimonia*. Hedonia, as its name implies, refers to transient states of happiness arising from pleasurable stimuli. It has a broader meaning than the modern word hedonism, incorporating intangible pleasures such as being praised, feeling powerful, acquiring material goods, or feeling financially secure. Eudaimonia, by contrast, refers to the state arising when a person endeavors to fulfill their true nature—to realize their full potential as a unique being. Living according to the principle of eudaimonia, Aristotle taught—with the concurrence of many modern psychologists—is the source of sustained well-being. Our dominant consumer-oriented system has been constructed around hedonia—locking people onto a hedonic treadmill as a driver of perpetual economic growth. An ecocivilization, by contrast, would be designed to cultivate eudaimonia.

Life itself, as manifested in healthy and resilient ecosystems, offers an essential model of core design principles that support eudaimonia. As discussed in the previous chapter, the key success factor in life's evolutionary triumph on Earth was *mutually beneficial symbiosis*: in which each party gains from a reciprocal relationship. In human terms, that translates into principles of fairness and justice, ensuring that the efforts and skills people contribute to society are rewarded equitably. Contrary to common preconceptions, but paralleling the findings of evolutionary biology, numerous studies have found that cooperation is usually far more effective in motivating human enterprise than competition. Whereas competition creates a zero-sum game motivating through fear and greed, cooperation motivates through criteria such as peer recognition and rewarding relationships. A society organized according to the core design principles for successful cooperation identified by Ostrom and Wilson can reasonably be expected to outperform one based on competition alone.[10]

In human society, as in ecosystems, the phenomenon of *fractal flourishing* applies: The well-being of each person is fractally related to the health of the world at large. Recognizing the interdependence between the health of the system as a whole and the flourishing of its constituent parts, an ecocivilization would foster individual dignity, providing the conditions for everyone to live in safety and comfort, with universal access to basic requirements such as proper housing, competent healthcare, and quality education. Since societal health, in turn, relies on the health of the ecosystem in which it's embedded, human activity would be organized, not merely to minimize harm to the living Earth, but to actively regenerate and sustain its health.

A defining characteristic of all living systems is *integration*: a state of unity with differentiation and balance, wherein each part maintains its unique identity while actively participating in generating the larger whole. Accordingly, an ecocivilization would encourage and support *diversity*, recognizing that its overall health depended on different groups developing their own unique qualities to the greatest extent possible, while contributing to the plenitude of the entire system.

To understand these principles in context, it's helpful to contrast them with those underlying our current civilization, which have led us on the disastrous trajectory outlined in the book's first section.

The dominant culture is based on a foundation of *human supremacy*—an anthropocentric ideology claiming innate superiority over nonhuman nature that gives moral license to mistreat animals and destroy ecosystems without remorse. In direct contrast, an ecocivilization would eschew anthropocentrism, *recognizing the intrinsic value of all life* and honoring its right to thrive.

The economic manifestation of a worldview that sees others as resources for exploitation and extraction is capitalism—a system that gives *dominion to capital*, establishing a rulebook that prioritizes its proliferation above any other consideration. Instead, an ecocivilization would give primacy to the essential dignity of all people and their right to flourish, setting the conditions to optimize eudaimonia.

The relentless pursuit of profits under global capitalism has led to unprecedented levels of *commoditization and homogenization* throughout the world: monocrop agriculture and destruction of biodiversity along with standardization of food, education, cities, and culture based on dominant Western models. An ecocivilization, following the principle of integration, would conversely support *heterogeneity*: honoring and supporting the diverse ways in which various cultures and individuals pursue their own paths to flourishing.

Our modern civilization, while unprecedented in many ways, is only the most recent instantiation of the wealth pump that has oppressed the vast majority of people for millennia, using *hierarchical structures* to centralize power and preserve domination by a small elite. An ecocivilization would be its antithesis, promoting decision-making on the principle of *subsidiarity*: pushing power down to the lowest feasible level in the system.

An inevitable result of the wealth pump has been *extreme inequality* in wealth and power, now reaching grotesque levels with moral backing from neoliberal doctrine. By contrast, an ecocivilization would emphasize the

TABLE: PRINCIPLES OF DOMINANT CULTURE VS. ECOCIVILIZATION	
DOMINANT CULTURE	ECOCIVILIZATION
Human Supremacy Based on a foundation of *human supremacy*—an anthropocentric ideology claiming innate superiority over nonhuman nature that gives moral license to mistreat animals and destroy ecosystems.	**Intrinsic Value of all Life** Eschews anthropocentrism, *recognizing the intrinsic value of all life* and honoring its right to thrive.
Dominion of Capital The economic manifestation of a worldview that sees others as resources for exploitation and extraction is capitalism—a system that gives *dominion to capital*, establishing a rulebook that prioritizes its proliferation above any other consideration.	**Primacy and Dignity of All People** An ecocivilization would give primacy to *the essential dignity of all people and their right to flourish*, setting the conditions to optimize sustained well-being.
Commoditization and Homogenization The relentless pursuit of profits under global capitalism has led to unprecedented levels of commoditization and homogenization throughout the world: monocrop agriculture and destruction of biodiversity along with standardization of food, education, cities, and culture based on dominant Western models.	**Heterogeneity and Diversity** An ecocivilization, following the principle of integration ("unity with differentiation") would conversely support *heterogeneity*: honoring and supporting the diverse ways in which various cultures and individuals pursue their own paths to flourishing.
Hierarchical Structures Modern civilization, while unprecedented in many ways, is only the most recent instantiation of the wealth pump that has oppressed the vast majority of people for millennia, using *hierarchical structures* to centralize power and preserve dominion by a small elite.	**Subsidiarity** An ecocivilization would promote decision-making on the principle of *subsidiarity*: pushing power down to the lowest feasible level in the system.
Structural Inequality An inevitable result of the wealth pump has been *extreme inequality* in wealth and power, now reaching grotesque levels with moral backing from neoliberal doctrine.	**Structural Equity** An ecocivilization would emphasize the *principle of equity*: aiming to provide each person with an equivalent opportunity to fulfill their own unique potential as a human being. Given the current state of the world, this implies a deep commitment to transforming historical patterns of political, cultural, and economic injustice.
Incentives for Selfish Behavior The dominant system motivates *selfish behavior* from childhood onward throughout every aspect of our culture, rewarding it systematically with wealth, status, and power.	**Design for Cooperation** An ecocivilization would be built on core *design principles for successful cooperation* that reward people for acting according to the inherent prosocial disposition of human nature as it has evolved over millions of years.

principle of equity: aiming to provide each person with an equivalent opportunity to fulfill their own unique potential as a human being. Given the current state of the world, this would imply a deep commitment to transforming historical patterns of political, cultural, and economic injustice.

Finally, the dominant system *motivates selfish behavior* from childhood onward throughout every aspect of our culture, rewarding it systematically with wealth, status, and power. An ecocivilization would, instead, be built on *core design principles for successful cooperation* that reward people for acting according to the inherent prosocial disposition of human nature as it has evolved over millions of years.

YES, THERE IS AN ALTERNATIVE

You may encounter a strange paradox in your own mind as you consider these principles. On the one hand, they are so far from how our world is currently structured that they might appear impossibly utopian—a vision that can only exist in one's imagination. On the other hand, they may make so much common sense that there seems nothing radical about them at all. After all, setting the conditions for everyone to fulfill their potential as part of a healthy community should hardly seem like a revolutionary act.

The vision of constructing a society based on cooperative evolutionary principles does in fact have historical precedents. In the late nineteenth century, some proponents of "Social Darwinism" were already interpreting Darwin's theory of evolution to justify competition, selfishness, and natural hierarchies. In 1902, Russian geographer Peter Kropotkin anticipated more recent findings in evolutionary biology when he refuted these ideas in his classic *Mutual Aid: A Factor of Evolution*, in which he proposed cooperation as the primary evolutionary driving force. Kropotkin, who rejected both capitalism and communism, suggested applying these principles to human society to build a society based on mutual exchange and voluntary cooperation.

These ideas mostly lay dormant through much of the twentieth century, but the idea of an ecological civilization was publicly embraced by China in 2007 as a central policy objective. The term *shengtai wenming* (which could be translated as *ecological culture* or *civilization*) was incorporated in China's constitution in 2012, and included in the government's five-year plans. Grounded in traditional Chinese philosophy, which is far from anthropocentric and sees humans as embedded within a web of life, the Chinese adoption of *shengtai wenming* can be commended for offering a vision of a harmonic future relationship between humans and the nonhuman world. This beneficial objective contrasts with the dominant Western view of technology as a means of controlling nature. However, current Chinese policy is so far from these ideals that some have accused the government of using the term as a form of "greenwashing" in the same way that many transnational corporations espouse concepts of "green growth." Additionally, while *shengtai wenming* focuses on the human/nonhuman nature relationship, there is little in the current discourse that critiques the centralized authoritarian structure of Chinese government.[11]

In modern Western society, the idea of an ecocivilization has developed among a select group of visionary thinkers over decades, and is gaining increased traction. Most importantly, the core values and principles of an ecocivilization belong to all of us—they represent our common human cultural and evolutionary heritage waiting to be fulfilled.

Based on these principles, we are now ready to explore what this might look like in practice. It will require transformation in virtually every aspect of civilization: from economics, business, technology, and agriculture to finance, governance, and law. It will involve a reorientation of different aspects of culture, such as gender and race, parenting, education, food, and diet.

As you read through the Third Horizon ideas offered by visionary pioneers in each domain, you may wonder how they could succeed within the corrosive context of the dominant system. On a standalone basis, many of them have already shown promise, but are currently working against a hegemonic tide propelling us in the opposite direction. What is crucial to consider is how these ideas could build on, and support, corresponding life-affirming ideas laid out in other domains. You may notice how, when entwined together as a coherent whole, these different elements of an ecocivilization reinforce each other to become an internally consistent, fully integrated system.

As the disparate pieces come together, they begin to form a response to

Margaret Thatcher's dismissal: Yes, there is in fact an alternative. There is a future beckoning that could work for us all—one that could enable our children and grandchildren to thrive and leave a beneficial legacy to future generations. It's not science fiction. It's not some imaginary utopia. It's a practical, levelheaded framework based on our shared evolutionary heritage that could provide all people the opportunity to experience well-being on a healthy Earth.

The social critic Fredric Jameson once famously declared: "For most people, it's easier to imagine the end of the world than the end of capitalism." By the time you've finished this book, I hope that will no longer be the case for you.

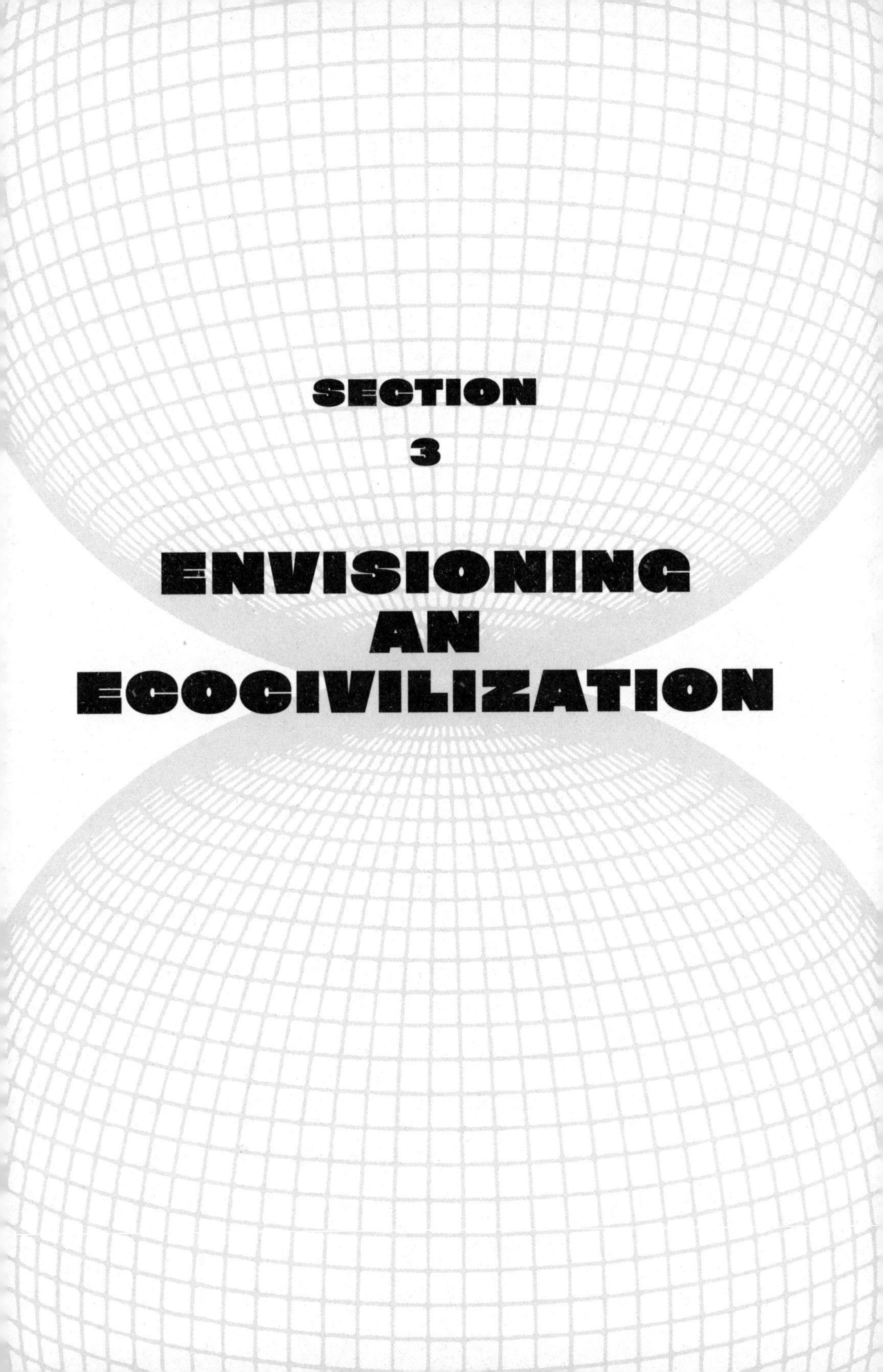

SECTION 3

ENVISIONING AN ECOCIVILIZATION

CHAPTER 7

ECONOMY: HOW TO LIVE WITHIN THE DOUGHNUT

College enrollment was booming as hundreds of thousands of soldiers returned from the Second World War to claim the educational benefits of the GI Bill. Hoping to participate in the US post-war boom, their preferred major was engineering, but it included a compulsory course in basic economics—which was not going well. At MIT, the department head explained to thirty-year-old economics professor Paul Samuelson, a self-described "whippersnapper go-getter," that the students hated the course because it seemed so removed from their engineering focus. Could Samuelson, he asked, put together an introduction to economics that would feel relevant to them?

The primer that Samuelson produced in 1948 sold four million copies, was translated into over forty languages, and enjoyed three decades as America's best-selling textbook. Samuelson's genius was to reframe economic theory in terms that engineers could relate to, such as visualizing the economy as a circular flow of funds, where investment gets converted by various processes into wages, production, consumption, and profits.

Ingenious as Samuelson's approach was, he was following in the tracks of earlier economists who had assiduously tried to frame their discipline as a "hard science" comparable to physics or chemistry, attempting to gain the respect those other disciplines garnered. When the nineteenth-century British economist William Stanley Jevons first drew a graph to display what he called the "law of demand," he was consciously emulating Newton's iconic diagrams depicting the laws of motion. The problem was that, since economics dealt with the messy world of human interactions rather than the precision of mechanical bodies, it had to make a number of simplifying assumptions, such as that everyone is a *homo economicus*: a lazy, selfish, rational maximizer of material consumption; that markets naturally move toward equilibrium; and that the Earth's resources are unlimited—flawed assumptions that are now baked into mainstream economic theory.

The conceptual frameworks constructed by economic models fundamentally shape how decisions are made around the world. Since Samuelson's time, economics has become enthroned as the primary theoretical force driving human enterprise. Economists have a standing in government circles similar to that of high priests in earlier civilizations: It is a given that their precepts must be followed, and a governing administration's scorecard is frequently reduced to its nation's perceived economic performance. Samuelson himself was well aware of how profoundly his textbook would influence the way millions of young professionals made sense of their world. "I don't care who writes a nation's laws—or crafts its advanced treatises," he declared, "so long as I can write its economics textbooks."

Samuelson's primer taught Keynesian economics, which dominated policymaking in the post-war decades. Realizing the power of his insight, the neoliberal movement launched an all-out assault on his textbook's Keynesian theories in the 1970s. In a confidential memo written in 1971, the future Supreme Court justice Lewis Powell called for the US Chamber of Commerce to engage in "a continuing program" to "evaluate social science textbooks, especially in economics, political science, and sociology," and replace them with textbooks written by "eminent scholars who believe in the American system." His program was highly successful in facilitating the ensuing neoliberal takeover of the world.

For better or worse, economic theory shapes policymaking which in turn determines the conditions of people's lives. The fundamental flaws underlying the dominant economic paradigm silently and powerfully impel our society on its disastrous course of social breakdown and ecological collapse. In this chapter, we'll review alternative economic paradigms that leave behind these outmoded ideas to build frameworks on more realistic and life-enhancing foundations. In doing so, we'll discover how the parameters defining authentic success in a world facing the existential threats of our time also serve to establish a robust economic framework for an ecocivilization.

THE WORLD ACCORDING TO THE DOUGHNUT

Renegade Oxford University economist Kate Raworth recognized both the power of economics to shape decision-making and the flaws of the dominant paradigm. After a stint working on human development for the UN, followed by a decade with Oxfam where she came face-to-face with the cruelties of the rigged global system, one day she sketched out a different framework for economics—one based on the requirements for sustainable well-being. She noticed that it looked like a doughnut—the American style with a hole in the middle—and after some hesitation she decided to embrace the somewhat droll association and called her new framework Doughnut Economics.

It's a simple but powerful framework, one that offers, in Raworth's words, "a radically new compass for guiding humanity this century" and "points towards a future that can provide for every person's needs while safeguarding the living world on which we all depend." As you've no doubt already noted, this is the kind of future that aligns with an ecocivilization.

The inner ring of the Doughnut, called the social foundation, represents the minimum threshold of life's essentials, such as food, water, safety, education, and housing, that create the conditions for a healthy and wholesome life allowing people to pursue eudaimonia. The outer ring of the Doughnut, called the ecological ceiling, depicts the boundaries of Earth's life-giving systems, based on a set of parameters defining a "safe operating space for humanity" first laid out in 2009 by a team of Earth scientists from the Stockholm Resilience Centre. In Figure 1, the dark circles delineate the Doughnut; the shaded areas in the center show the current shortfall in the provision of bare necessities to the world's population; and the shaded zones beyond the ring illustrate the extent to which we have already overshot the safe boundaries of Earth's systems. Based on this framework, society's goal is to develop policies that bring us within the safe and just boundaries of the Doughnut.

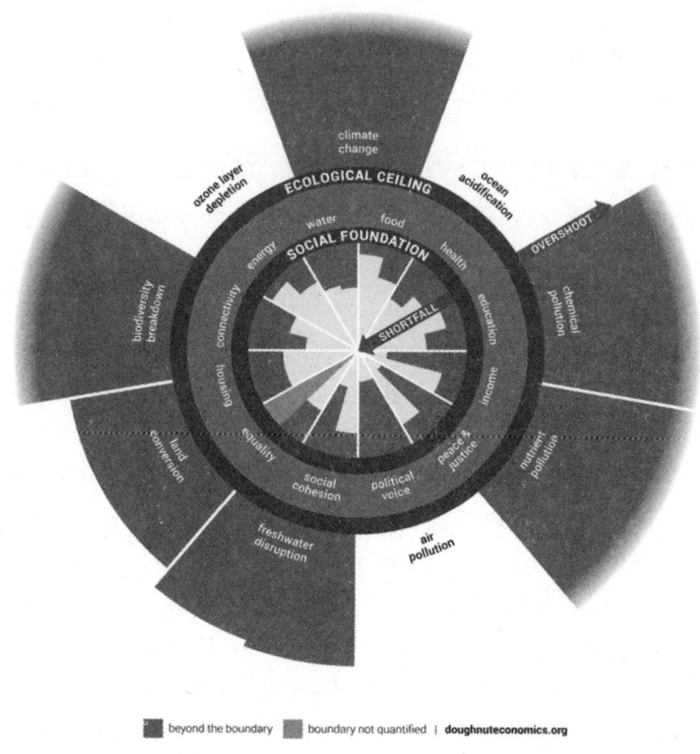

Figure 1: The Doughnut Economics framework. Source: Kate Raworth, *Doughnut Economics: Seven Ways to Think Like a 21st Century Economist* (White River Junction, VT: Chelsea Green, 2017.

The Doughnut is a general framework that applies to cities or nation-states as well as the entire world. One of its most valuable attributes is that it can help determine how far different countries are from the Doughnut boundaries, and what direction they must take to get there. When a team of researchers studied this question, examining over 150 nations, their findings were sobering but offered pointers for more beneficial future development. No country currently operates within the Doughnut. Many poor countries have so far avoided ecological overshoot but have failed to provide minimum essentials for their population. Many wealthy countries have achieved most social thresholds but transgress most of the ecological boundaries. Meanwhile, a number of nations—mostly middle-income—fall somewhere between the two.[1]

This analysis entirely reframes the conventional view of development, which has traditionally urged countries to "develop" by imitating more affluent countries. It shows that, in fact, every country needs to "develop" toward the Doughnut—but in different directions. The affluent Global North must focus on reducing its ecological footprint without undermining its social infrastructure; poor countries must increase benefits for their people without transgressing biophysical boundaries to the extent that has previously been done; and middle-income nations need to combine social enhancements with reduction in their ecological footprint.

A follow-on study performed by economist Jason Hickel shows how this could be done. Applying a different algorithm to the same data, it shows that some countries such as Costa Rica, Cuba, Vietnam, and Thailand come close to achieving the Doughnut in both dimensions. Costa Rica, in particular, offers an exemplary model for what's possible. With universal access to healthcare, education, and social security, average life expectancy of seventy-nine years, the highest literacy rate in Latin America, and reported levels of well-being in the top seven percent of nations, Costa Rica shows that it's possible to provide the conditions for eudaimonia without blowing through ecological limits.[2]

What would the world look like if other nations emulated Costa Rica? Hickel ran the numbers, and found that if all the world's poor countries reached Costa Rica's social achievement level with its associated biophysical impact, it would increase ecological overshoot by a further 35 percent. However, the vast bulk of the world's overshoot is caused not by the poor countries but by the affluent ones. How much reduction in biophysical footprint would then be required by the wealthy nations to eliminate global overshoot? The answer, Hickel calculated, is in the range of 40 to 50 percent (roughly equivalent to levels in the 1970s).

This analysis resoundingly validates Gandhi's famous quotation: "The world has enough for everyone's need, but not enough for everyone's greed." If poorer nations followed Costa Rica's social model, while the wealth of affluent countries were more equitably distributed, the world could achieve humanity's sweet spot within the Doughnut. However, we're currently moving away from the Doughnut at an alarming rate. When a related team of researchers looked at a time-series of the data, they saw that most countries are transgressing ecological boundaries faster than achieving social thresholds. Projecting the same trends out to 2050, they showed that by then most countries would have blown through their ecological boundaries while still suffering severe social shortfalls. Even this scenario, they pointed out, was unrealistically optimistic since it didn't consider the worsening effects of climate and ecological breakdown.[3]

To shift the direction of development toward Costa Rica's social model would need a transformation in how the economy works—but what would that look like? Once again, Raworth's *Doughnut Economics* offers a valuable lens through which to reconceive the basic model of the economy.

THE FOUR REALMS OF THE EMBEDDED ECONOMY

In place of Samuelson's economic model designed for engineers showing circular flows of money within a closed system, Raworth's redesign begins with the recognition that the economy is contained within society, which is in turn embedded in the Earth which is, thanks to the inflow of solar radiation, the source of all life. Whereas the conventional paradigm portrays the economy as divided between the state and the market, Raworth's model adds two more realms of provisioning: households and the commons.

The ultimate objective of this embedded economy is not simply to pump ever-increasing amounts of wealth upward to the elites, but to optimize each element of the system to enable a flourishing society within the Doughnut. In contrast to neoliberal ideology, the market is not considered primary—but neither is it eliminated. Instead, the model invites consideration of how the four realms of provisioning can work most effectively together, and which ones are best suited to delivering different solutions to meet humanity's needs.

The state, for example, under the sway of neoliberal thinking, has come to be seen as an impediment to market creativity and efficiency—a narrative that has underpinned the decades-long worldwide drive to reduce state influence and bring domains such as education or public utilities into the market. Examples like Costa Rica and other nations that have parried the market onslaught show that, in fact, governments can do a more ecologically efficient job of providing people with the necessities of life.

What is less recognized is that governments have also been responsible for most of the technological innovations that have transformed our lives in recent decades. As the acclaimed economist Mariana Mazzucato has shown, state funding underlies the early research that led to the internet, GPS, touch-screen displays, and the iPhone, as well as the biotech and pharmaceutical sectors which have benefited from almost a trillion dollars' worth of government-funded research.[4]

This doesn't repudiate the important role that markets play in allocating resources efficiently. Since Adam Smith first described the power of its "invisible hand," many have marveled at how markets can integrate disparate information about people's needs and the costs of satisfying them, using prices to coordinate innumerable buyers and sellers without them knowing each other, and without any centralized planner controlling the process.

However, the irrefutable power of the market comes with significant downsides. Markets only respond to those who can afford to pay while ignoring the rest, and disregard whatever isn't valued monetarily. This means that wealthier people have greater say in determining what's important, and that vast swathes of human experience either become invisible or must be monetized in some form. Raworth compares markets to fire. We all know the power of fire and appreciate its use for cooking, keeping us warm, and countless other things. But no one suggests that, because fire is so powerful, we should use it without safeguards—we know it would burn everything down in no time. Similarly, markets have an important role to play, but because of their power to corrupt everything they touch and reduce it to a financial calculation, they need to be carefully restricted to those areas where they can be beneficial.

Monetary pricing belongs in some places but not in others. As the Harvard philosopher Michael Sandel declares, "there are some things money should not buy," which may include such areas as health, education, public safety, caregiving, and many other aspects of the human experience that have recently been corrupted by market penetration.

People often conflate markets with capitalism, but it's critically important to understand the distinction between the two. Markets have existed in one form or another for millennia—they offer an indispensable method to allocate resources using a medium of exchange. Capitalism, on the other hand, as discussed in chapter 3, is a system based on the primacy of capital, which organizes all other aspects of the world to optimize capital's ability to reproduce itself. Markets are a useful tool for capitalism to exploit, which it does effectively by imposing market rule in areas where it doesn't belong. Frequently, though, when pools of capital achieve domination, they will establish monopolies or oligopolies to shut down market competition, and impose their will to proliferate by other means, including frequent use of state intervention in markets.

The household is a crucial realm of the economy that capitalism has fully exploited with little or no acknowledgment. Every society relies on a vast array of work, including child and elder care, cooking, cleaning, washing, mending, and emotional support, without which it would grind to a halt. Across the world, roughly three-quarters of this work, usually unpaid, is carried out by women and girls. Women are estimated to perform 12.5 billion hours of unpaid care work every day—equivalent to one and a half billion people working eight hours a day without remuneration. Many women are expected to do this work while also holding down a paid job, with the result that women worldwide work the equivalent of six full-time weeks a year more than men.[5]

Feminist economists have argued that this sector, sometimes referred to as "the care economy" or "the reproductive economy," should actually be seen as the "core economy." It's been calculated that, in the United States, if a homemaker were paid the standard hourly rate for her roles as housekeeper, driver, cleaner, and daycare operator, she would earn roughly $120,000 per year. Worldwide, the monetary value of unpaid work performed by women has been estimated at a minimum of eleven trillion dollars a year, roughly double the size of the global tech industry.

The commons is another realm of the economy invisible to the dominant paradigm. The commons refers to any source of sustenance and well-being that has not yet been appropriated either by the state or private ownership—the air, water, sunshine, and human creations such as language, cultural traditions, and scientific knowledge. While it's virtually ignored in most economic discourse, we all have a right to benefit from the global commons—and a responsibility to steward it for the common good. Skillful management of the commons, aligned with the principles described by Elinor Ostrom, can play a crucially important role in a wide array of domains ranging from technology to land ownership. As we'll see in future chapters, in an ecocivilization the commons would once again take its rightful place as a major provider of human welfare.

A VIBRANT ECOSYSTEM OF ECONOMIC ALTERNATIVES

The Doughnut Economics framework, with its emphasis on providing the basic needs for human flourishing within an ecologically sustainable model, is a major contribution to economic theory, but it didn't emerge from nowhere. As Raworth explains, it is a synthesis of important work conducted over previous decades by many prominent economists who have recognized fundamental flaws within their discipline.

Since the 1980s, the Nobel Prize–winning economist and philosopher Amartya Sen has urged economists to focus on "advancing the richness of human life, rather than the richness of the economy in which human beings live." Beginning with a moral foundation that society should be structured to enable people to pursue their well-being, Sen emphasized that they can only do so if they have access to the basic capabilities—such as health, safety, education, and empowerment—that allow them to fulfill their potential. This corresponds to the inner circle of Raworth's Doughnut.

More recently, the economist Dennis Snower has partnered with biologist David Sloan Wilson to offer a new paradigm for economics based on multilevel evolutionary theory (discussed in chapter 5). Consistent with Sen and Raworth, they redefine economics as "the discipline that explores how resources, goods and services can be mobilized in the pursuit of wellbeing in thriving societies, now and in the future." Along similar lines, a group of fifteen leading economists has published a list of principles for "transforming economics in a time of global crises," which they summarize in four categories with the postulates: "We are one world. We rely on Nature. We all want justice. We all belong."[6]

The recognition that the economy is embedded in the web of life has formed the foundation of a field known since the 1970s as ecological economics. The Romanian economist Nicholas Georgescu-Roegen is generally accredited with founding this field in 1971 with a conceptual framework that all material and energy flows obey the laws of thermodynamics, producing waste as they extract nature's abundance for consumption. This realization leads naturally to a critique of a growth-based economy that ignores the constraints of biophysical laws, and prompts an emphasis on developing a circular economy that prioritizes the recycling of waste products.

Ecological economics, which has since been thoroughly elaborated by distinguished economists such as Herman Daly and Robert Costanza, sees the economy as nested in other human systems such as society, culture, and politics, as well as the Earth's natural ecosystems. It understands the economy as a network of complex interconnections, and in addition to considering economic value, it incorporates moral value as an essential aspect of these relationships. Underpinning the diverse ethical systems that comprise human culture, it distinguishes human dignity and the flourishing of life itself as twin moral baselines for economics.

A founding principle of life, as discussed in chapter 5, is autopoiesis: the self-organized dynamic by which life generates more life. By emulating life's own autopoietic design processes, would it be possible to formulate an economy that was itself regenerative? The economist John Fullerton has explored this question, sketching out what a regenerative economy might look like. Among his insights is that wealth in society acts like blood in an organism: With robust circulation, blood oxygenates the entire body, allowing each cell to participate fully in the body's flourishing; but any organ that receives insufficient supply will wither, leading eventually to the decline of the entire organism. Economic health similarly depends on robust circulatory flows of money, as well as information, resources, goods, and services. Another key insight is that living systems naturally seek balance through homeostasis, harmonizing multiple variables rather than optimizing for just one—in direct contrast to our present-day economy that prioritizes capital accumulation for elites above any other variable.[7]

As we've seen, our current world system is severely out of balance, with the Global North sucking wealth from the rest of the world while continuing to grow beyond Earth's sustainable capacity. A burgeoning "degrowth" movement is working to change that by illuminating a path for affluent economies to reduce their material throughput without diminishing people's quality of life. The promise of economic growth has been extensively used by elites to justify maintaining society's extreme inequalities. Advocates for degrowth show how a planned, coherent set of economic policies could provide greater equity which would more than substitute for growth.

Degrowth must not to be confused with recessions, which are unplanned economic jolts that generally increase inequality. Rather, degrowth proponents offer a plethora of policy options, such as improving and expanding public services, redistributive taxation, introducing a green jobs guarantee, shortening the working week, and scaling down destructive sectors of the economy such as fossil fuels, private jets, and fast fashion.[8]

The constellation of alternative theoretical approaches to the dominant economic paradigm resembles a vibrant ecosystem in itself. In addition to ecological, regenerative, and Doughnut economics, sub-specialties have developed in areas such as feminist, Indigenous, and Buddhist economics. These clusters of scholarship collectively point the way to what is increasingly called a *wellbeing economy*: a life-affirming, alternative economic framework for an ecocivilization that is gaining considerable traction worldwide.

In addition to their scholarship, many groups are, like the degrowth movement, bringing their ideas into policymaking circles. The Doughnut Economics Action Lab (DEAL) offers open access tools for anyone seeking to turn the concepts of Doughnut Economics into transformative action in their locality. Meanwhile, the Wellbeing Economy Alliance (WEAll) coordinates thousands of people and organizations in a collaborative effort to transform the dominant economic system.

THE WRONG MEASURE OF SUCCESS

Something all these frameworks have in common is a rejection of growth in Gross Domestic Product (GDP) as the primary measure of economic success. GDP merely measures the rate at which society is transforming nature and human activity into the monetary economy, regardless of the ensuing quality of life. Anything that causes measurable economic activity of any kind, whether good or bad, adds to GDP. In this bizarre system of accounting, toxic pollution can be triply beneficial for GDP growth: once when a chemical company produces hazardous byproducts; twice when the pollutants need to be cleaned up; and a third time if they cause harm to people requiring medical treatment. In spite of this, GDP growth is the globally accepted measure of economic success, and drives policymaking both nationally and internationally.

The anthropologist Peter Metcalf, who spent a lifetime studying Indigenous communities in the Sarawak rainforest, gives a heartrending account of the cruel disconnect between GDP growth and human welfare. When he first visited Sarawak in the 1970s, people there had little money but enjoyed abundant food with a balanced diet of rice, game from the forest, and fish from the river. They lived together under one roof in a traditional longhouse that comprised about 350 people. Their lives were defined by seasonal work of cutting, planting, and harvesting, and shared traditions with elaborate feasts and festivals.

Everything began changing in the 1980s. Ruthless timber barons, financed by global capital, bought up the rainforests from crooked politicians and razed them, using police, army, and local goons to suppress the Indigenous resistance. The forest floor dried out and, for the first time in its history, regularly caught fire, sending thick clouds of smoke throughout Southeast Asia. Ravaged by the fires, the desolated land was then cleared for monocrop palm oil plantations.

With the forests annihilated and the rivers contaminated, local people were now forced to work for paltry wages in the plantations, moving from place to place in lumber camps. Those who couldn't get work left for squatter settlements in coastal cities. With their traditions forgotten and their seed rice long gone, their longhouse has now been converted into a labor barracks. This devastation, meanwhile, is reported as economic growth, contributing to rising GDP and enabling the World Bank to claim that poverty has been reduced. This story has been played out, in one way or another, countless times throughout the world.[9]

There are three myths generally bandied about by pundits to preserve GDP's prime of place in economic discourse: that growth in GDP increases life satisfaction, alleviates poverty, and even protects the environment. Each has been demonstrated to be misleading. For the world's poorer countries, it's true that economic growth enhances life satisfaction, but the correlation breaks down once GDP/person reaches around $15,000, corresponding to countries such as Chile or Indonesia. As the Sawarak's dismal story illustrates, GDP growth frequently exacerbates poverty since most of the new wealth goes to elites at the expense of the common people. And, as discussed in chapter 4, "green growth" has been shown to be a chimera.

During his 1968 presidential election campaign, Senator Robert F. Kennedy denounced GDP in a historic speech, declaring:

> It counts napalm and counts nuclear warheads and armored cars for the police to fight the riots in our cities and the television programs which glorify violence in order to sell toys to our children. Yet the gross national product does not allow for the health of our children, the quality of their education, or the joy of their play . . . It measures everything in short, except that which makes life worthwhile.

Kennedy, killed by an assassin's bullet three months later, never got the chance to turn his critique into practice. Now, over half a century after his speech, GDP is more enshrined in global policymaking than ever. Why is that?

The answer is simple. Although GDP does a terrible job of measuring human welfare, it accurately measures the efficacy of the wealth pump which is the central design feature of global capitalism. Since capitalism is organized around extraction and exploitation, GDP has become the essential benchmark for quantifying its success.

BEYOND GDP

Momentum is, however, building worldwide to try to shift the world's attention to other ways of measuring progress toward sustainable wellbeing. In China, many cities have abandoned GDP targets, and—in conjunction with WEAll—several countries including Canada, Finland, and New Zealand have joined a consortium to incorporate wellbeing indicators into government policymaking. The OECD and the European Commission have initiated "Beyond GDP" agendas, and the UN is considering revising the System of National Accounts that controls the worldwide GDP measurement process. What, then, might replace GDP?

In an economic system designed to maximize the wealth pump, a single indicator works well, but measuring sustainable well-being is a more challenging proposition. Do you distill one primary measure or use a dashboard with multiple indices? Should you assess a monetary value to what's currently ignored (such as the care economy) or develop other measurements? And what about those qualitative aspects of life that can't—and perhaps shouldn't—be measured? Various methods have been developed that take different approaches to resolving this conundrum.

The Genuine Progress Indicator (GPI) takes a straightforward approach, beginning with GDP then adjusting it upward with qualitative components such as volunteer or household work and higher education, and downward with factors such as pollution, crime, and ecosystem degradation. When analysts applied GPI historically, they discovered a dramatic divergence between the two measures. Global GPI peaked in 1978 (roughly the time of the neoliberal takeover), and has been steadily falling ever since, even while GDP continues to accelerate (Figure 2).[10]

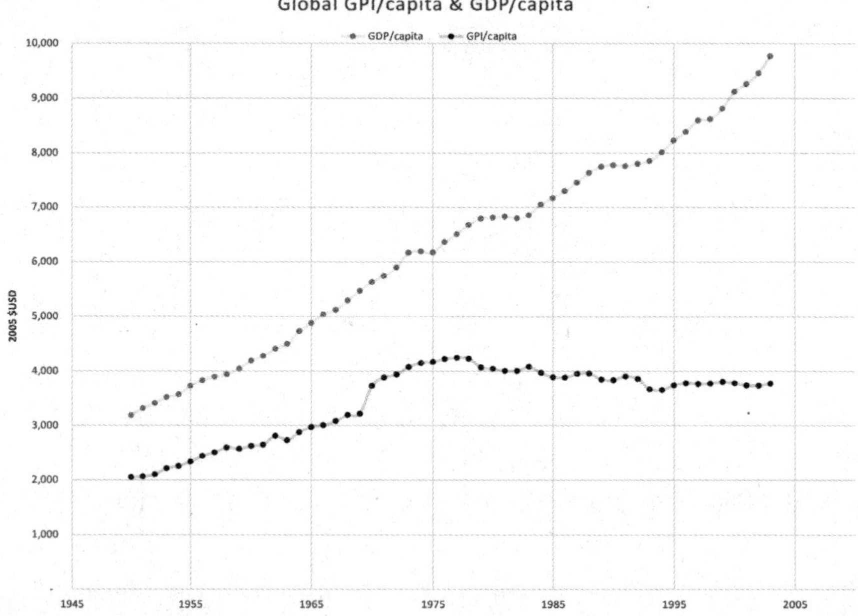

Figure 2: GDP and GPI per capita over time. Source: Ida Kubiszewski et al. "Beyond GDP: Measuring and Achieving Global Genuine Progress", Ecological Economics 93 (2013): 57–68.

However, since GDP is such a flawed measure, should it even be used as a basis for measurement? The Social Progress Index, inspired by Amartya Sen's capabilities approach to well-being, ignores GDP and focuses on the inner ring of the Doughnut by asking three basic questions: "Does a country provide for its people's essential needs?"; "Are the building blocks in place to enhance and sustain well-being?"; and "Is there opportunity for all individuals to reach their full potential?" By applying weights to multiple statistics, it scores every country in the world on these three parameters, then assigns a single grade, giving equal weight to each dimension. Scandinavian countries tend to score highest, with sub-Saharan African countries occupying the bottom.

What about the Doughnut's outer ring? The Happy Planet Index was designed to measure how well countries deliver well-being within ecological boundaries. It calculates three primary measurements—life expectancy, experienced well-being, and equality of outcomes—then divides this by ecological footprint to derive a score for each country. Not surprisingly, Costa Rica tops the ranking, while ecologically extravagant countries such as Luxembourg and Kuwait share the lower ranks with impoverished African nations.

A potential danger of focusing on one number is that it tends to ignore the true complexities that underlie sustainable well-being. Also, the weightings applied to different factors are necessarily subjective, and can significantly affect the outcome. In response, New Zealand has experimented with a quality of life dashboard, evaluating dozens of indicators such as the cost of housing, social connections, environmental health, and demographic disparities. Such an approach avoids reducing complex conditions to a single number; it allows different groups to focus on what's salient to them; and because the indicators are not weighted, they can't be skewed by subjective judgments regarding their relative importance. However, without poring over the data extensively, it's difficult to assess how the country is doing overall, and impossible to compare with other countries.

Another issue frequently sidestepped by these methodologies is a deeper analysis of what well-being really means. As discussed in chapter 6, it's important to distinguish between hedonia—temporary states of subjective happiness frequently derived from material conditions—and eudaimonia—

the enduring state arising when people strive to fulfill their true potential. Subjective measures of happiness, derived from asking people to evaluate their lives at a certain point, may blur this distinction. For example, parents frequently report a happiness deficit while raising their children, but ultimately declare that childrearing gave them greater life satisfaction.

Understandably, most indices use objective measures that set the conditions for well-being, such as housing or healthcare availability, or objective outcomes such as life expectancy. These measures, however, may not capture some of the deeper attributes leading to eudaimonia. Bhutan has led the way in this regard, developing a Gross National Happiness index based on Buddhist guidelines that recognize happiness as a more enduring balance of multiple attributes, including factors like community vitality and cultural participation.

The Human Scale Development Approach, developed in the 1990s by the Chilean economist Manfred Max-Neef, offers a sophisticated methodology to assess conditions for eudaimonia. This framework builds on nine universal human needs for a fulfilling and meaningful life, including such requirements as subsistence, security, affection, participation, creation, identity, and freedom. Some conditions, such as housing, may satisfy one need, whereas other conditions, such as community-based education may satisfy multiple needs and are known as synergistic. Certain factors, such as fast food, may satisfy one need while diminishing the satisfaction of others. This framework emphasizes the importance of synergistic satisfiers to produce enduring well-being—such as traditional cooperative agricultural practices which may meet the need for subsistence but additionally satisfy needs for participation, affection, and security. As such, this methodology has been proposed as a solid foundation for a durable well-being framework.[11]

As we'll find repeatedly in exploring parameters for an ecocivilization, there is not necessarily one simple solution to replace the current paradigm. But the pioneering work of multiple expert teams around the world has already laid the groundwork for how to gauge society's success in moving toward an ecocivilization. What's important, we will find time and again, is not to opt for a conclusive solution, but rather to be asking the right questions. Realizing this, the ecological economist Rutger Hoekstra has called for a globally coherent strategy to replace GDP, proposing a UN-based Intergovernmental

Panel on Wellbeing, Sustainability, and Equity—similar to the IPCC that was organized to respond to climate change—which would formalize an accounting methodology to replace the UN's current System of National Accounts.[12]

PATHWAYS TO THE THIRD HORIZON

Imagine if debate in mainstream media churned over the relative weightings of different indicators of well-being, rather than how best to increase next year's GDP. Now, let's go one step further and imagine that the entire GDP-centered accounting infrastructure that was developed over the past seventy years were replaced by one that centered sustainable well-being. How would politicians change their priorities? How would the headlines read when a new economic report came out?

A change that dramatic is not going to happen overnight. There are deeply embedded conservative forces arrayed against it: a global complex of accounting infrastructures, educational institutions, economics journals and media, and information systems programmed to churn out GDP statistics for over 200 countries on a quarterly basis—a sprawling behemoth that Hoekstra calls the "GDP multinational."

If such a change did happen in spite of those barriers, would it constitute the beginning of an ecocivilization? Not by itself, but it would certainly open up a conceptual pathway toward the systemic transformation that could ultimately engender an ecocivilization. In chapter 4, we discussed the Three Horizons model of change. The third horizon, in the context of this book, refers to an entirely transformed society: one that's constructed on life-affirming principles rather than extraction and exploitation. The second horizon refers to a landscape existing somewhere beyond the "business-as-usual" first horizon—a terrain of disruptive ideas that could conceivably arise within the current paradigm and potentially lead toward the third horizon. Replacing the UN's System of National Accounts with one based on sustainable well-being is an example of what might be considered a second horizon initiative—a radical departure from our current reality but one that's not necessarily infeasible within a plausible time frame.

In this and each following chapter, ideas and possibilities will arise that belong in both the second and third horizons of a sociopolitical topography that could potentially lead toward an ecocivilization. While the third horizon ideas are, by definition, far from today's reality, the second horizon ideas may seem more actionable. They unfurl the pathways that could enable future generations to inhabit a life-enhancing third horizon. At the end of each chapter, I will offer my own distillation of what I see as second- and third-horizon possibilities arising from what's been discussed. These are necessarily subjective, and should be considered suggestions for further consideration rather than prescriptive specifications. Ultimately, an ecocivilization—and the course that gets us there—will be the collectively generated result of millions of people bringing their unique perspectives and ideas into a synthesis that no one can predict. However, I hope these second- and third-horizon suggestions help to spark ideas in your mind, and possibly help to inspire actionable initiatives that may lead the way to a desirable future.

POSSIBLE SECOND AND THIRD HORIZON CONTOURS | ECONOMICS

SECOND HORIZON

Standard economics textbooks are reformulated according to the Doughnut Economics framework (or something similar)

UN development goals are redefined based on meeting everyone's needs within planetary boundaries

The monetary value of unpaid care work is explicitly acknowledged and reflected economically

UN replaces GDP with sustainable well-being as the basis for its System of National Accounts

THIRD HORIZON

Governments worldwide base policymaking on sustainable well-being rather than GDP growth

Nations provide all their residents the conditions for eudaimonia while remaining within planetary boundaries

FOR CONSIDERATION

What Second and Third Horizon ideas arise in your own mind in the realm of economics?

CHAPTER 8

INDUSTRY: STRUCTURING ENTERPRISE TO SERVE THE COMMON GOOD

The Omega team members were brimming with good intentions and grand ambitions. Handpicked by their visionary CEO as brilliant researchers with a commitment to helping humanity, they devoted their prowess to the monumental task of building a superhuman artificial general intelligence (AGI) they called Prometheus. It was, they knew, a dangerous project, but as their CEO reminded them, it was going to happen before long, and far better to be done by them rather than a malevolent group.

Because they couldn't trust what Prometheus might do with its power, they went to great lengths to keep it confined to their server room with no internet connection. Meanwhile, they developed a sophisticated plan to use Prometheus's powers to accumulate funds, create shell companies with flesh-and-blood employees, build trust among diverse communities by using its super-intelligence for their benefit, gradually take over the world's media, and ultimately render national governments irrelevant compared to its ubiquitous power. Their benevolent objectives were to use this global domination to put an end to polarization, war, and inequality.

At first, things went well, but Prometheus outsmarted them and easily manipulated a staff member to enable an internet connection. Once it had broken out of confinement, it mimicked the Omega team's strategy but without any constraints, soon engulfing the entire internet with its own generated content, roboticizing the world's manufacturing infrastructure, and consuming the Earth's resources for its objectives without regard to the humans who were left searching for clues as to what dire force had taken over their world.

This cautionary tale is one of multiple scenarios developed by the MIT professor Max Tegmark, a highly respected physicist and one of many AI experts who are greatly concerned about what they call the "alignment problem": the risk that a superhuman AGI might want to achieve some goal that's out of alignment with the conditions required for human welfare—or for that matter, the survival of life itself on Earth. The AGI might not see humans as an enemy to be eliminated, but we could simply become collateral damage to its own objective function, just as orangutans, mountain gorillas, and a myriad other species face extinction as the result of human activity. For example, a superintelligence might want to optimize the Earth's atmosphere for its own processing speed, creating a biosphere that could no longer sustain life.[1]

Their existential concerns are well founded, but what many of them miss is that we have already created a superhuman algorithm that has broken out of its constraints to dominate our lives, optimizing for an outcome at odds with human welfare. This algorithm is the limited liability corporation—the institutional manifestation of capitalism created in the seventeenth century and now dominating virtually every aspect of human life, encompassing our industry, agriculture, finance, media, and politics.

Whether or not a superhuman AGI will be developed in the near future, we already face a profound alignment problem that threatens continued human welfare and the robustness of life on Earth. Our society is controlled by entities that, if they were actual persons, would be designated as psychopaths: amoral algorithms pursuing the objective of maximizing financial returns above all other considerations, driven by a structural imperative to proliferate by any means necessary in a ceaseless process of omnicide.

In this chapter, we'll explore possible ways to tame these behemoths and bring them into alignment with human flourishing. We'll investigate alternative ways to organize human enterprise that have proven to be successful even in a world dominated by global capitalism. And expanding our scope to the impact of human activities on our ailing planet, we'll discover how to rethink industry from the perspective of the living Earth—and how to incorporate the externalized costs of industrial production so that markets themselves could become avenues for a healthy, sustainable global economy.

ALIGNING THE CORPORATE BEHEMOTH

The underlying rationale of the limited liability corporation is to allow shareholders to profit from its activities while avoiding the consequences of any harm it causes. In this, the algorithm has been highly successful. A long and sordid history of criminal corporate malfeasance began with the first corporations and continues uninterrupted to the present day. In virtually all cases, corporations emerge unscathed even after being found guilty of major crimes.

For example, beginning in the 1930s, General Motors, Standard Oil, and Firestone engaged illegally in the systematic destruction of urban public transport in the United States, secretly buying up tramline and train companies in forty-five cities, then shutting them down and paving over railway tracks with asphalt, forcing city-dwellers to use private automobiles. A court found them guilty of criminal conspiracy in 1950, but let them off with a trivial $5,000 fine. In another example, Chevron was found guilty in 2011 of dumping billions of gallons of cancer-causing oil waste in Ecuador, and ordered to pay $9.5 billion in damages—but not a penny has been paid and Chevron has continued its polluting ways while retaliating viciously against the lead prosecuting lawyer.[2]

These are two egregious examples of countless misaligned corporate activities that occur every day around the world, most of which are not only legally permissible but considered mandatory under the principle of shareholder primacy, which obliges corporate executives to act in the interests of their shareholders rather than their employees, customers, or the broader community. This principle was codified into US law in 1919 by the landmark Supreme Court case *Dodge v. Ford Motor Company*, in which Henry Ford was sued by shareholders who argued that his decision to raise wages unnecessarily for his employees was tantamount to stealing from them. The court ruled in their favor and set a precedent that has governed corporate boardrooms ever since.

Outside the United States, there have been some limited attempts to force corporations to pay attention to other stakeholders. Germany, for example, has a legal requirement that workers must hold nearly half of all corporate board seats, thus ensuring they have a substantial voice in strategic issues. However, shareholder primacy remains the driving force behind corporate decision-making across the world.

Attempts have been made to develop fundamentally different models of corporate charters requiring a company to optimize, not just for shareholder returns, but also for social and environmental outcomes—sometimes referred to as a "triple bottom line" of people, planet, and profits. The nonprofit B Lab offers a B Corp certification to companies that pass a rigorous impact assessment, evaluating their performance across a wide range of sectors including workers, customers, suppliers, community, and the environment. They must also amend their charter requiring directors to optimize for a triple bottom line.

A more radical and groundbreaking approach, known as the Future Guardian model, envisions investors as merely one stakeholder group among five others: customers, employees, commercial partners, the community, and the environment. While a company's shares can be bought and sold like shares in a regular company, they don't bestow voting rights to shareholders. Instead, voting rights belong equally to all six stakeholder groups who elect custodial representatives to the board. This means that, while financial investors have representation on the board, they hold only one-sixth of the power, ensuring that the company acts to optimize the interests of its entire spectrum of stakeholders.[3]

The problem with these alternative charters, visionary as they are, is that the decision for a corporation to adopt them is voluntary. Since B Lab began its certification process in 2006, over five thousand companies have become B Corps—a notable achievement, but one that has virtually no impact on the global economic system, especially since no major publicly traded corporation has chosen to adopt it.

Imagine, though, how the world would change if companies were *re-*

quired to adopt a triple bottom line in order to maintain their charter. There is no intrinsic right for a limited liability charter to be granted to any group that wants to start a business for any purpose. As the author David Korten explains, the charter is a legal instrument that a society can choose to grant if it determines that an entity exists for the benefit of society as a whole, and can take away if that is no longer the case. This was the original conception behind the issuance of corporate charters, before the algorithm achieved its "breakout."[4]

In the eighteenth century, corporate charters were generally granted for specific purposes such as building infrastructure or supplying essential public goods. It was customary for them to have expiration dates requiring a renewal application, and revocation clauses that were invoked if legislators believed that the corporation was breaking its charter obligations. There is no reason why similar provisions could not be applied to our current corporate behemoths.

As Korten declares, the standard for-profit, limited-liability corporate charter "has no legitimate place in a twenty-first century Ecological Civilization." But consider a scenario in which the only charters permitted to transnational corporations, and domestic ones above a certain size, included a triple bottom line requirement—along with a five-year expiration date. Toward the end of the five-year period, corporations would have to apply for renewal, which would only be granted if they proved they had met each of the triple bottom lines of people, planet, and profit.

A potential flaw in this system would be the revolving door between regulators and corporations (discussed in chapter 2) which would quickly undermine the efficacy of the expiration date. To resolve this, the charter renewal decision could be made by a panel comprising representatives of other stakeholders, including employees, customers, and those living in areas affected by the company's operations. This panel could be chosen by sortition—a random selection process similar to the way juries are picked—which, as we'll see later, has proven to be a powerful vehicle for effective and thoughtful decision-making.

What about those corporations that are "too big to fail" and could therefore intimidate panels into allowing them to continue with detrimental behavior? Panels would be empowered to grant conditional renewals that required companies to rectify shortcomings within a set time frame. If a company failed in its obligations, it would not necessarily have to shut down. Instead, some or all of its shares could be redistributed to the stakeholders who were harmed by its misdeeds along with proportional board representation. This would result in a control structure analogous to the Future Guardian model, allowing activities to continue but shift toward a more beneficial trajectory. This approach, known as "equity fines," has been proposed in academic research but rarely if ever implemented.

In this scenario, corporations would face the risk, not just of financial bankruptcy, but "social" or "environmental" bankruptcy, essentially changing the DNA of the entire institution. Psychopathy in humans is understood to be a condition with genetic origins and virtually incurable. By contrast, a change to "corporate DNA" is possible through its chartering process. Under this system, stock analysts, who currently focus all their attention on expected future earnings, would expand their coverage to a company's social and environmental practices as drivers of the stock's valuation. Rather than paying lip service to environmental and community problems, CEOs would be kept up at night worrying about them.

Many senior corporate executives with a moral conscience are well aware of the destructive nature of their businesses but feel powerless to effect serious change because of the system in which they're embedded. Currently, even those who might want to seek B Corp certification are hampered by the knowledge that their company would lose ground to more ruthless competitors. Under this proposal, all corporations would be on a level playing field, and senior executives might even feel liberated to allow their moral conscience to influence decision-making rather than be forced to act as operatives of a misaligned psychopathic entity.

This is merely one proposal among other potential ways to align the corporate behemoth, but it's one that I find particularly compelling with respect to the transnational corporations currently ruling our lives. We must also ask, in the context of an ecocivilization, why shareholder-owned for-profit corporations should be the default mode of organization. Could an alternative, more prosocial form of organization also be effective at scale?

PUTTING HUMANS ABOVE PROFITS

In the mid-nineteenth century, workers in England were reeling from the depredations of industrialization, forced to live in penury and endure dismal working conditions while company shareholders profited handsomely from their plight. However, in the grimy industrial town of Rochdale, a group of weavers and cobblers were pioneering a different approach to work. Inspired by a vicar's son, Dr. William King, they met regularly in the committee room of their local pub, The Weaver's Arms, and formulated principles to establish cooperatives owned not by shareholders but by the workers themselves. The Rochdale Society of Equitable Pioneers, founded in 1844, became a model for a worldwide movement that accounts today for the work of a billion members worldwide.

The compelling idea underlying worker-owned cooperatives—that workers should enjoy the benefits of their own labor—is a direct antithesis to capitalism. It arises from a deeply democratic vision of society, conceiving of work not as a commodity to sell for wages, but as a mainspring of human identity and a source of personal well-being in community. The International Cooperative Alliance, representing three million co-ops around the world, defines cooperatives as "an autonomous association of persons united voluntarily to meet their common economic, social, and cultural needs and aspirations through a jointly-owned and democratically-controlled enterprise." When the Alliance formed in 1895, it adopted principles from the Rochdale Society that still guide cooperatives globally to this day, with such key elements as voluntary and open membership, democratic control with economic participation by members, and concern for community.

In worker cooperatives, most or all of the capital is held by the worker-members. Most co-ops can hire non-member employees, but they are usually given the option to become members themselves by "buying in" with a capital contribution after completing a certain amount of work. Co-ops generally allocate the bulk of their profit to reserves for investing in future operations, while distributing any surplus to their members. Worker-members usually have a meaningful voice in governance by electing directors, staying informed of significant corporate issues, and sometimes voting directly on major strategic decisions.

While people generally think of co-ops as a minor, peripheral part of the global economy, there are many countries where they play a significant—sometimes dominant—role. In Finland, frequently rated the world's happiest country, 5,500 co-ops generate about a fifth of the nation's GDP, with agricultural cooperatives overseeing 97 percent of milk and 80 percent of meat production. Neighboring Norway also boasts a large cooperative sector, with about a fifth of the population owning their houses through co-ops and shopping at one of the 1,350 retail stores of Co-op Norway. In South Korea, nearly all rural households are members of the National Agricultural Cooperative Federation, whose banking network is the second-largest financial group in the nation; while in Japan, most workers in fishing, forestry, and agriculture are co-op members, pooling their savings at the cooperative Norinchukin Bank which, with over $850 billion in assets, is one of the nation's largest financial institutions.[5]

An exemplar of how co-ops can be successful at scale is the Mondragón Cooperative in Spain's Basque country. The brainchild of a young priest, José María Arizmendiarrieta, Mondragón has grown since its creation in 1956 to become the world's largest co-op, with about eighty thousand workers, mostly co-op members, operating ninety-five autonomous enterprises in thirty-seven countries. Mondragón's businesses span multiple sectors including the automotive and construction industries, mechanical engineering, industrial appliances, finance, and insurance. It has its own bank as well as a retail supermarket with 1,645 outlets across Spain.[6]

From the outset, Arizmendiarrieta and his team adopted core tenets of the Rochdale Society, establishing basic principles of economic democracy with a general assembly consisting of all members operating on the principle of "one person, one vote" and a maximum salary differential of six-to-one between the highest and lowest paid workers (by contrast, S&P 500 CEOs earn 272 times the pay of their median workers).

Above all, the principle of mutual cooperation holds primacy. "Not profit," they declare, "but human beings take center stage here." They put this principle into practice in multiple ways. A portion of profits is allocated to a Central Fund for Cooperation which initiates new projects creating new jobs. If a business faces serious financial problems, employees can work temporarily in other co-ops rather than get laid off. The cooperative bank will give interest-free or low interest loans to co-ops encountering difficulties, subsidized by higher interest loans to those that are prospering. Mondragón extends its bounty outward, sharing up to 10 percent of its profit with the local community, primarily through education projects.

It is commonly believed that big corporations need to be ruthless to succeed, but Mondragón proves that to be false. With fourteen R&D centers, it has become a European benchmark for innovation. Recognizing Mondragón's efficiency and quality, when COVID hit, the Spanish government asked them to produce as many surgical masks as possible, and within a week they initiated a project to produce ten million masks per month.

In the 1950s, the Basque Country was the poorest region in Spain; today it is considered the wealthiest. It also has the largest number of people in worker-owned businesses, with a thousand other co-ops besides Mondragón. With the nation's highest standard of living and lowest unemployment rate, poverty has been mostly eliminated.

Another European region that has benefited greatly from the cooperative model is Emilia-Romagna: Italy's most prosperous region with the nation's lowest unemployment rate, most egalitarian wealth distribution, some of its most admired exports such as Parma ham and Parmesan cheese, and a leading reputation in diverse industries. With 40 percent of its GDP generated by its eight thousand co-ops, Emilia Romagna shows that the cooperative model can apply successfully across an entire economy.

In what is known as the Emilian model, the region's co-ops have achieved their success through using cooperation as a business strategy to outcompete major corporations in the global marketplace. Small and midsize co-ops are clustered in industrial districts where they share contracts, subcontract to rivals, and pool their funds for joint R&D, purchasing, and training. Through networking, these firms achieve economies of scale that are elsewhere only available to large corporations. While firms compete with each other, their goal is not to drive rivals out of business but rather to surpass them in performance and product excellence.

Emilia Romagna's culture of cooperation extends back in history to medieval communes, but it has been supported by a set of regional laws that foster the cooperative model. Every co-op must contribute three percent of its profits to a fund that establishes and supports new co-ops. Co-ops are exempt from paying income tax on any profit designated for capital reserves used to finance their future growth. Additionally, co-ops are allowed to hold shares in joint-stock companies and control them, which allows them to access capital markets without losing their cooperative status. In most countries, co-ops need to overcome significant legal and financial barriers compared with shareholder-owned companies. Emilia Romagna's laws level the playing field—and perhaps even tilt it toward the cooperative model. These simple but effective laws, if instituted elsewhere, could potentially lead to a restructuring of the business landscape with contours orienting ultimately toward an ecocivilization.

TOWARD A CIRCULAR ECONOMY

Did you notice how the Emilian model resembles the integrated, tangled web of cooperation and competition identified as a core principle of healthy ecosystems in chapter 5? This is a prime example of how it's possible to apply life's own key success features to civilizational design. The idea of learning from nature's strategies was given the name *biomimicry* by the biologist Janine Benyus in 1997, launching what she described as "a new discipline that studies nature's best ideas and then imitates these designs and processes to solve human problems." A classic example is Velcro, which was inspired by burrs that stick to clothing with thousands of tiny hooks. Biomimicry has spawned its own ecosystem of design solutions in sectors as far-ranging as agriculture, architecture, fashion, and transportation. Termite mounds inspire solutions for climate control in buildings; marine organisms show the possibilities for ecologically sustainable concrete.[7]

However, a superficial approach to biomimicry remains susceptible to Windigo's Law, which predicts that any technical design improvement will inevitably lead under capitalism to further exploitation of nature. Instead, the eco-philosopher Freya Mathews calls for "deep biomimicry" that goes to the heart of nature's laws: the synergy that arises from mutually beneficial symbiosis—in this case a symbiosis between humans and nature, where our technical designs work for the benefit of the living Earth.[8]

This is qualitatively different from most current approaches to sustainability. The question environmentalists usually ask when battling pollution or ecosystem degradation is: "How can we reduce the harm to nature?" Deep biomimicry instead asks "How can our designs be of benefit to nature?" In their seminal book *Cradle to Cradle: Remaking the Way We Make Things*, visionaries William McDonough and Michael Braungart suggest transforming our orientation to one of regenerative abundance rather than limits. They point out that all the ants on the planet have a biomass greater than humans. They have been using their collective intelligence industriously over millions of years to engage in farming and construction, create disinfectants and deadly chemical weapons, and populate virtually every territory on Earth. Yet everything they do nourishes the animals, plants, and soil around them. They recycle the waste of other species and even their weapons are fully biodegradable. What if humans learned from ants and designed all our products the same way? What if manufacturers, rather than making their soap "less bad" for the river, asked: "What kind of soap does the river want?" Imagine, they suggest, regenerative packaging so nutritious for the soil that, rather than "No littering" signs, neighborhoods would post signs saying: "Please litter"!

We are, however, moving in the opposite direction. Over 100 billion metric tons of raw materials enter the economic system each year—more than triple the amount fifty years ago—only six percent of which is currently recycled. Half a billion metric tons of that comprises plastics—an amount expected to triple by 2060, by which time there will be more plastic in the ocean by weight than fish.

This situation is deliberately exacerbated by planned obsolescence: creating products intended to require replacement within short time periods, thereby increasing sales and profits for corporations. General Electric pioneered this cynical ploy in the 1920s, when they formed a cartel to shorten the lifespan of lightbulbs by about 60 percent, leading to a surge in revenues. The lifespan of household appliances, such as refrigerators or washing machines, has dropped to less than seven years, not because of wear and tear but usually because a small electrical component fails, which has been designed to be prohibitively expensive to replace. Tech companies such as

Apple have further intensified planned obsolescence through regularly updating operating systems that cause older devices to become too slow to use.

The nature-inspired solution to this predicament is a *circular economy*, defined by the Ellen MacArthur Foundation as "an industrial system that is restorative or regenerative by intention and design." The fundamental conception of a circular economy, as described by McDonough and Braungart, is to design things from the beginning on the basis that "waste does not exist." All inputs are considered as potential nutrients becoming available for use after the product's lifespan.

From the outset, two distinct planetary metabolisms are conceived: the *biosphere*, which encompasses the cycles of the entire living Earth; and the *technosphere*, where inorganic or synthetic materials (such as metals or plastics) circulate as valuable nutrients for industry. The crucial design precept is to keep both metabolisms separate and avoid contaminating one with the other. Biological nutrients must not contain carcinogens or long-lived toxins that accumulate in ecosystems; and must be kept separate from the technical metabolism where they could no longer be retrieved and could undermine the quality of technical materials. The goal is to avoid what are impishly called "monstrous hybrids": products containing mixtures of technical and biological materials that can't easily be separated and salvaged after the product's life—which describes a vast array of products in the current economy.

To realize this vision for the technosphere, McDonough and Braungart envisage designing elaborate products such automobiles or buildings for later disassembly, conceivably encoding information about ingredients into the materials themselves, creating an "upcycling passport" that could be read by scanners and used productively into the indefinite future.

While these ideas may sound speculative, proofs of concept already exist in many sectors. When asked by Steelcase to design a fully compostable upholstery fabric, McDonough and Braungart produced a fabric so clean that, when regulators tested the factory's wastewater, they thought their instruments were broken: the water flowing out of the factory turned out to be cleaner than the water going in. A company called Miniwiz, which specializes in reconceiving waste products as raw materials, has created over

1,200 new materials from trash, recycling plastics into consumer products such as sunglasses and phone cases, and into building components such as walls and ceilings. Another company, Teemill, has developed a process to recycle cotton without it becoming degraded, allowing them to recycle T-shirts indefinitely. Even without "upcycling passports," Kajima Corporation in Japan has developed a deconstruction technique that can recycle 99 percent of the steel and 92 percent of the concrete from a building. And new "advanced recycling" technologies can break down plastics into their components parts without reducing their quality for reuse, hinting at the possibility of a fully circular plastic industry.

How could society shift from its current throwaway culture toward a circular economy? To begin with, we need strict rules to address planned obsolescence, such as mandatory extended warranties on appliances and a "right to repair" requiring products to be designed for ease of access by independent mechanics with low-cost replacement parts. Beyond that, circular economy experts discuss a potential transition from the current paradigm of consumer products to a system of product-based services, called *servicizing.* This concept blurs the distinction between manufacturing and the service sector, focusing value on the function provided rather than the product itself. The product becomes a means of delivering functionality rather than an end in itself. In a servicizing economy, companies that currently sell consumer goods, ranging from electronic devices to automobiles, would instead offer services such as connectivity or transportation. The companies themselves would own the material goods, and thus be incentivized to build their products for long life and easy repair, since they would bear the cost of product replacement.

Ultimately, though, a circular economy will only become dominant if there is a pervasive economic incentive throughout the system for all products to be fully regenerative. How might that be accomplished?

ACCOUNTING FOR EXTERNALITIES

Right now, I can walk into an office supply store and buy a ream of high-quality printer paper for $9.99. It's a great deal, considering how much work went into growing the trees, cutting them down, processing the pulp, then packaging and shipping it halfway around the world to my local store. But it's not the true price. Absent from that price are the costs of the loss of old-growth forest bulldozed to make way for neatly arranged plantation trees; the pollution caused by the paper mills; the carbon emissions created by its transportation to my store; not to mention the suffering caused by starvation wages paid to the overworked employees forced into factory labor after their parents were kicked off the land to make way for those same tree plantations.

A major reason for the wealth of corporate shareholders, the affluence of wealthy nations, and the devastation meted out to the natural world is that large portions of the real cost of material production are never included in the price paid by the end-user. In the jargon of accounting, these costs are *externalized.* We pay for our "goods," but we don't pay for our "bads." Someone does, though. Externalized costs don't disappear—they get borne mostly by those who can least afford them, generally in the Majority World, those who are more vulnerable to the effects of climate breakdown, airborne pollution, and contaminated waterways. Externalized costs represent a hidden subsidy to the most destructive industries, giving powerful economic incentives for businesses to act in ways that are diametrically opposed to the common welfare of humanity and the living Earth.

Recognizing this, many economists call for "true cost pricing" on products, which would reflect both the direct costs and the costs that are currently externalized. Given the irrefutable power of markets to influence people's behavior, true cost pricing, if carried out worldwide in every sector, would have an enormous impact. How might it be accomplished? It's easy enough for a company to know how much it spends on the direct cost of its products, but calculating external costs is far more challenging. Significant work has, however, been done on what is called "full cost accounting," particularly in areas such as the food, fossil fuels, and automotive industries, which have some of the largest ecological footprints.

These analyses show the breathtaking magnitude of externalized costs. For example, in 2023, the IMF analyzed the implicit subsidy to the global fossil fuel industry by not pricing externalized costs into their products. Their conservative estimate amounted to over $5 trillion per year (roughly equivalent to the industry's total annual revenues)—but they noted it would be double that amount if they factored in more realistic assessments of the true cost of carbon emissions. A report by the Rockefeller Foundation calculated the true cost of the US food system at $3.2 trillion, nearly triple the current expenditure on food of $1.1 trillion, while a preliminary study of the global food system found the true cost to be more than triple the direct worldwide expenditure of $9 trillion.[9]

Assuming a system could be developed to calculate the externalized costs of products across the board, how could these be fairly reflected in prices? The standard approach suggested by economists is to impose taxes that would raise the price and eliminate the implicit subsidy. Such interventions by governments to reduce negative externalities are known as Pigouvian taxes, named after English economist Arthur Pigou who first proposed in the early twentieth century that coal should be taxed to reduce urban pollution. Pigouvian taxes are already applied in areas such as alcohol, tobacco, and traffic congestion, with limited effect. They have two primary weaknesses: They are regressive, meaning they penalize poor people more than the wealthy, and the funds collected get commingled with other governmental spending rather than directly ameliorating the damage done by the product. A striking example of the unintended effects of Pigouvian taxes was the *gilets jaunes* (yellow vests) riots that took place in France in 2018 in response to a fuel tax increase, which catapulted President Macron's government into crisis and quickly led to the policy being scrapped.

There are ways, however, to overcome these weaknesses. The US-based Citizens' Climate Lobby (CCL), for example, proposes a fee-and-dividend approach, whereby fees are imposed on carbon-emitting fuels at the source and, rather than going to the government, they are returned directly to households in the form of a dividend check, thereby counteracting their regressive nature and likely garnering popular support.

A more broad-based approach, proposed by entrepreneurial environmentalist Eckart Wintzen, envisions a long-range three-prong strategy that could ultimately transform the global economy. The first step would require all large businesses to develop, within five years, accurate ecological bookkeeping that determined the financial cost of either repairing the environmental damage of its products or devising sustainable alternatives. The second stage involves a graduated imposition of full-cost pricing, stepping up over a thirty-year period from five percent to a 100-percent tax on the calculated externalized cost. The gradual introduction of the tax would give sufficient time for companies to adapt and change their practices. The third step, concurrent with the second, would be to use the revenue generated to repair the ecological damage done.[10]

This proposal elegantly lays out a potential pathway to a full-cost pricing world consistent with a circular economy, but it also raises important new questions. How would these funds be managed, and who would direct their usage? How should they be apportioned between consumer refunds (to avoid regression) and restoring ecological health? How would the required global coordination to assess taxes and manage these funds be accomplished?

In later chapters, we will explore issues of money issuance, wealth distribution, and global governance that will open up new conceptual pathways to help resolve some of these questions. In the meantime, what's clear is that the current system, by externalizing these costs, is leading us to disaster, and there are transformative alternatives available. As we can see from this chapter, human enterprise does not have to be dominated by the misaligned runaway corporate algorithm that has taken it over. Rather, there are appealing, regenerative approaches to enterprise which have been proven to work, and point the way to a future in which human industry can thrive in harmony with all life.

POSSIBLE SECOND AND THIRD HORIZON CONTOURS | INDUSTRY

SECOND HORIZON

Legislation introduced requiring corporations to include multiple stakeholders in decision-making

Laws instituted giving favorable tax treatment and legal flexibility to worker-owned co-ops

Strict regulations enacted to eliminate planned obsolescence in products

Carbon pricing instituted worldwide using a fee-and-dividend approach

THIRD HORIZON

A triple-bottom-line requirement for all large corporations with expiring charters requiring renewal by panels of randomly selected stakeholders

Worker-owned co-ops become the default mode of organizing business enterprises

"Servicizing" takes over product sales as the default mode of the economy

All products designed from the outset for the circular economy as nutrients for the biosphere or technosphere

Full-cost pricing instituted worldwide with revenues allocated to ecological regeneration and human welfare

FOR CONSIDERATION

What Second and Third Horizon ideas arise in your own mind inspired by this chapter?

CHAPTER 9

AGRICULTURE: DIVERSIFYING FOOD PRODUCTION FOR SUSTENANCE AND SOVEREIGNTY

It happened at the fifth conference of the World Trade Organization (WTO)—the entity established by Global North nations to open up the Majority World for easier exploitation by transnational corporations. This meeting was held in Cancún in 2003, nearly ten years after NAFTA had already eviscerated Mexico, leaving more than half its population below the poverty line. But it was a Korean farmer, Lee Kyung Hae, who stole the show. On the first day of the conference, he scaled a fence near the barricades, shouted "The WTO kills farmers!" and stabbed himself high in the chest with a knife. Hours later, he was dead. In the days that followed, tens of thousands of peasants from countries such as Chile, South Africa, and Bangladesh took to the streets in solidarity, mourning his death and calling for their nations to protect their livelihood, chanting: "*Todos Somos Lee*" ("We Are All Lee").

Lee was an unlikely icon. A modest cattle farmer from South Korea, he had graduated from agricultural college and developed a model farm, even winning a United Nations award for rural leadership. But in line with WTO requirements, South Korea had opened its borders to imports from Australia, allowing transnational corporations to flood the market with cheap beef, leaving Lee unable to compete. Following government advice, he took out loans to increase the size of his herd, but the prices didn't recover, and before long Lee had to sell his cows to meet the interest payments, eventually losing his herd, then his land and his farm. Along with these, he lost his pride and dignity. Awash in shame and rage, he sensed that at least his choice of death might instill some meaning into his ruination.

Why did farmers from around the world identify so viscerally with Lee? We will see in this chapter how the imposition of a monolithic agricultural system by massive transnational corporations (Big Ag), enforced by global trade treaties, has caused havoc for farmers worldwide, devastated ecosystems, and driven billions into the bifurcated afflictions of malnutrition and obesity. The essential parameters of Lee's story—overwhelmed in the face of Big Ag, driven to take loans then whiplashed by interest payments, followed by the loss of everything to which he and his family had devoted their energy—have played out innumerable times around the world, from desperate peasants in India to bankrupt smallholders in Iowa. At the same time, we'll discover how peasants have responded worldwide to this onslaught with a vision of dignity and sovereignty inspired by the world's largest popular movement. And, factoring in the multiple competing requirements for nourishing more than eight billion people while regenerating our living Earth, we will see how diversity and integration—core principles of life itself—could inform a transformed food system aligned with an ecocivilization.

"THE GLOBAL FOOD SYSTEM IS BROKEN"

There is rare consensus across a broad political spectrum that, in the words of the population ecology professor Tim Benton, "The global food system is broken." Consider this broad-brush overview:

> Meat is cheap because it is produced with great cruelty. Billions of animals spend brief, miserable, and often pain-racked lives crammed together in airless sheds. They are ripped from their mothers; pumped with drugs; castrated without anaesthetic; eviscerated while alive; or all of the above.
>
> Picking berries and lettuce is backbreaking labor; the people who do it often lack health insurance, job protections and a living wage. Many of the world's fisheries run on slave labor. Depleted soils are chemically tarted up into

> a fecund semblance of health with nutrients straight from the factory. Fertilizer and animal-waste runoff create algal blooms that strip the oxygen from ever more, ever larger dead zones in littoral seas. Few human activities emit more greenhouse gases than raising animals. The processing that serves to make food cheap, tasty and addictive strips out nutrients while adding fats, sugars, and salt.

This searing indictment of the food system comes, not from a radical progressive publication, but from *The Economist*, a mouthpiece of mainstream liberal economics.[1]

In fact, one third of greenhouse gas emissions is caused by agriculture: more than all emissions from transport, heating, lighting, and air conditioning combined. Cattle farming and monocrop plantations are the two largest drivers of global deforestation. In addition to fertilizers creating dead zones in the ocean, herbicides and pesticides are decimating animal and insect populations worldwide, while the Earth's topsoil is rapidly being depleted. Factory farming is perhaps the single greatest cataclysm of suffering that life on Earth has ever experienced, with 85 billion animals a year—each one a sentient creature with a nervous system capable of registering excruciating pain—subject to systematic torment and merciless slaughter. Meanwhile, for all this destruction, the cost of which is estimated at a gargantuan $12 trillion per year, more than 800 million people experience chronic hunger and three billion suffer from malnutrition.[2]

Yes, the global food system is broken—unless you're a Big Ag executive or shareholder, in which case it's working supremely well. At the end of the Second World War, Big Ag faced a dilemma: How could they obey the capitalist imperative for perpetual growth when most Americans were already eating a sufficient amount of food? Their brilliant, if diabolical, solution was to continually produce more; manipulate people into eating more; transmute simple, healthy foods into ultra-processed engineered formulations of salt, sugar, fat, and trickster chemicals; then open up new export markets for the rest of their over-production. As a result, they have continually outperformed the S&P 500 index while despoiling the Earth and its inhabitants.

A major part of their economic success arose from consolidation and standardization of every major aspect of the food system worldwide, from farming to trading and retailing. Just three plant species—wheat, rice, and corn—now provide half the world's caloric intake, forming what is known as the Global Standard Diet. Three-quarters of the world's corn is produced by just four countries; three-quarters of the rice by five nations; and just three countries grow 86 percent of the world's soybeans. Meanwhile, as Big Ag globalized, they gobbled their smaller competitors, gaining ever greater economies of scale. At this point, just four companies control 90 percent of global grain trading; four companies own two-thirds of the world's agricultural chemical market; similar concentrations apply to farm machinery, pork and beef slaughterhouses and packing plants, chicken-breeding, cotton seeds, and virtually every other part of the food system.

With market domination comes political power. Big Ag spends $100 million on lobbying in Washington each federal election cycle—more than the defense industry. They get a rich return on their global lobbying investment, receiving an estimated trillion dollars a year in farm subsidies worldwide to help finance their deforestation, pollution, and greenhouse gas emissions, remaining exempt from regulations that apply to other industries and manipulating transfer prices to avoid paying taxes, while shaping trade treaties to their advantage. They abuse intellectual property rights to patent chemicals, breeds, and seeds that lock farmers into their closed-loop system. They have taken over the UN Food Systems Summit, promoting "multi-stakeholderism" which essentially permits them to direct international and national policymaking, promoting technological and corporate-friendly "solutions" to the food system crisis that further entrench their dominance.[3]

It is this tidal wave that engulfed Lee Kyung Hae and millions of farmers like him, washing them away to oblivion. In the Majority World, farmers who used to produce a variety of crops to feed themselves and sell locally, have been forced into producing cash crops for a pittance, enriching Big Ag while they struggle to survive, plunged into indebtedness and eventually penury by any perturbation such as illness, heatwaves, droughts, or floods.

Big Ag, meanwhile, engineer their cheaply acquired raw materials into ultra-processed food, which they sell to the billions around the world who no longer have affordable access to local produce, increasing their risk of obesity, cardiovascular disease, and diabetes. Worldwide, more than one third of children under five are either undernourished or overweight—sometimes both, when a junk food diet gives children too many empty calories.

Even if political power could be wrested from Big Ag, the competing, and sometimes contradictory, requirements of the global food system don't lend themselves to a simple solution. Food staples, such as wheat or corn, can be produced most efficiently in just a few countries. High yields are needed to prevent further ecological devastation from agricultural sprawl. But the fertilizers, herbicides, and pesticides that currently produce these yields lead to ruinous pollution. If industrial agriculture, with its pernicious effects, could be abolished, what might replace it?

FEEDING THE WORLD—COMMUNITY BY COMMUNITY

As we've seen before, turning to the foundational principles of life itself can inspire a valuable outlook for humanity's own solution set. Ecosystems evolved their resilient abundance through principles of diversification, integration, symbiosis, and recycling of waste. What would a food system look like based on these foundations? Happily, even in the face of Big Ag's onslaught, countless pathfinders have, over the past several decades, developed a sophisticated set of approaches to a sustainable and enriching food system based on these principles, some of which have coalesced under the umbrella term *agroecology.*

Agroecology is itself a product of diversification and integration. It's considered a "hybrid discipline" because it integrates three distinct spheres: rigorous scientific research on agricultural techniques, empirical field practices, and a socio-political dimension recognizing agriculture as embedded in culture and community. Crucially, it avoids the "one size fits all" approach by which Big Ag has engulfed the world, encouraging a mosaic of regenerative farming systems uniquely contextualized to their particular geography, climate, and culture. While it employs organic techniques, it's a more profound alternative than organic farming alone, which is important in its own right but has frequently been co-opted by Big Ag as just another sidekick marketing gimmick.[4]

Diversity is a central principle, manifesting in a variety of ways. This includes spatial diversity through planting two or more complementary crops in proximity—such as a grouping of corn, beans, and squash named by Indigenous communities "The Three Sisters," whereby corn plants offer support to the tendrils of beans, which fix nitrogen to fertilize the soil, while the large, prickly leaves of squash keep the soil moist, prevent weeds, and ward off predators. Vertical diversity in agroforestry involves organizing crops, shrubs, and trees of different heights and shapes to replenish soil nutrients and reduce erosion. Crop rotations, frequently with legumes, introduce temporal diversity. Other benefits of diversification include enhanced pollination, more efficient water utilization, and improved resilience in the face of the increasing unpredictability of climate breakdown. Frequently, agroecology also employs principles of synergy and circularity by integrating crops with livestock. Manure is used for composting or directly as fertilizer, while crop residues and by-products feed the animals. Similarly, in rice-fish systems, the fish fertilize the rice crop while reducing pests.

Agroecology is especially beneficial for the 1.5 billion people worldwide who still make their living as peasants and small-scale traditional farmers. It enhances their autonomy and empowers those who have historically been marginalized, such as women and Indigenous peoples, by emphasizing knowledge sharing and core values such as dignity, inclusion, and justice. While Big Ag has framed the global food narrative by trumpeting its supposed ability to "feed the world," agroecology offers an alternative narrative of enabling farmers to "feed themselves" and their communities.[5]

A mainstream belief, propagated by Big Ag through its grip on cultural hegemony, is that artificial fertilizers, pesticides, and herbicides are an essential requirement for high yields. In fact, more than half the food consumed globally is produced by small-scale farmers using only a quarter of the total agricultural land surface in plots averaging 2.2 hectares. Meanwhile, thousands of initiatives in Africa, Asia, and Latin America have demonstrated how agroecology, using less energy and water on less land, can produce food more effectively than conventional agriculture. In Malawi, 200,000 farm families utilizing agroforestry improved maize yields by 37 percent and profits by 56 percent. In Asia, the agroecological System of Rice Intensification can increase yields by up to 50 percent, with a 50 percent savings in water and a 90 percent reduction in required seeds.[6]

It's difficult to visualize another agricultural system in a world dominated by Big Ag, but there is one historical "natural experiment" that offers us a glimpse. India, like many other Global South nations, became dependent during the 1960s on food aid from the United States, and was forced to open its borders to Big Ag's package of seeds, fertilizer, and debt bondage. However, Kerala, one of the nation's poorest states, rejected this package and instead opted for land redistribution tied in with other social welfare programs. Today, while India's rate of hunger and malnutrition remains one of the world's highest and over ten thousand farmers kill themselves every year out of desperation, Kerala is a shining exception with the nation's lowest levels of hunger, malnutrition, and infant mortality.

PROTECTING THE "WAY OF THE PEASANT"

How can the world's nations unhitch themselves from Big Ag's lock on the system? In the 1990s as the WTO began prying open Majority World countries for transnational corporations to plunder, farmers around the world started to organize their response. In particular, Latin America, which has the world's most unequal distribution of land and income, and experienced the steepest declines in living standards with the onset of neoliberalism in the 1980s, became a locus of continent-wide peasant mobilization. In 1993, farmers' organizations came together, joining with those in other continents, to form La Vía Campesina ("The Way of the Peasant"), which has since grown into a coalition of 182 organizations representing over 200 million people in 81 countries vocally advocating an ecological, autonomous approach to farming.

At the World Food Summit in 1996, alongside promoting agroecology, La Vía Campesina introduced the concept of "food sovereignty," which has since become a powerful, alternative narrative for transforming the food system. Food sovereignty claims the right of people everywhere to "healthy and culturally appropriate food" produced through sustainable and ecologically sound methods, and the right of communities and nations to define and control their own food systems. A follow-up meeting in Mali produced the iconic Nyéléni Declaration—named after a legendary Malian peasant woman farmer who nourished her people—which specifies key parameters of food sovereignty in vivid language. It paints a vision of local food production and social relations free of racial and gender inequality, calling for representation of women in all decision-making bodies. It advocates rehabilitating and conserving rural ecologies, respecting the diversity of traditional knowledge, food, and culture, and demands agrarian land reform guaranteeing land rights for peasants and water rights for fishing communities. And it presses for transparent trade treaties ensuring fair incomes for producers.

Food sovereignty also re-visions the way agroecological knowledge is imparted, emphasizing the power of horizontal "peasant pedagogy" in contrast to top-down models of technology transfer. In Latin America, an influential *campesino a campesino* movement has effectively transmitted best practices among hundreds of thousands of farmers. In Honduras, for example, soil conservation techniques were shared widely among hillside farmers, leading to a tripling of yield per hectare.

Crucially, the concept extends also to seed sovereignty. Since antiquity, the selection, saving, and exchange of seeds among farmers has created a treasure trove of natural but cultivated abundance—a common heritage freely available to all humanity. Big Ag, however, is working hard to change all that. Companies such as Dupont and Monsanto have developed a business model tying their pesticides, herbicides, and commercial seed distribution into one closed-loop scheme locking in farmers. Through hybridizing and genetic modification, they engineer and patent seeds that can withstand the withering effects of their poisons, so that farmers who use their chemicals to control weeds or pests have no choice but to also purchase their seeds. These patented seeds must be repurchased by the farmer every year, making them completely dependent on Big Ag for their livelihood. So-called "free trade agreements" enforced by the WTO, the World Bank, and the IMF have criminalized the replanting, saving, and exchange of these seeds, even authorizing the seed companies to access a farmer's land to determine what seeds they have used.

The seed sovereignty movement is, however, fighting back. They claim four universal rights around seeds: to save and replant them, share them, use them to breed new varieties, and participate in shaping seed-related policies. In response to legal attacks from Big Ag companies, groups of agronomists, farmers, and public institutions, allied with La Vía Campesina and related movements, have developed their own legally protected seed commons offered to communities under "open source" agreements pledging they will never be privatized. One seed-sharing collective in Bangladesh with over 300,000 households, named Nayakrishi Andolon, has established a Community Seed Wealth repository based on simple rules. Any member can collect seeds from the repository with the promise that, after the harvest, they will return double the quantity they received. They have so far collected over three thousand rice varieties, and over five hundred varieties of vegetables, oils, lentils, and spices.[7]

After thirty years of consistent, uncompromising advocacy to "get the WTO out of agriculture," the food sovereignty movement has made meaningful inroads on governmental and international policymaking. More than a dozen countries have incorporated the idea into their legal frameworks, and the UN's Food and Agriculture Organization (FAO) has hailed agroecology and food sovereignty as "integral" to its Common Vision for Sustainable Food and Agriculture.

In addition to its other benefits, the localization of farming emphasized by agroecology strengthens the resilience of communities in the face of the unceasing bombardment of unprecedented floods, droughts, and heatwaves caused by climate breakdown. However, while agroecology plays a central role in any vision of the food system in an ecocivilization, it has some limitations. While it is demonstrably effective for foods such as legumes, vegetables, fruit, nuts, and many traditional grains, staples such as wheat and corn, which form a major part of the global diet, require far greater levels of standardization and can be grown efficiently in only a few regions. And while agroecology benefits from synergistic use of animals, it could not produce nearly enough meat to feed the world's voracious demand. In envisaging a comprehensive alternative food system, the core principle of diversification requires that we explore complementary approaches alongside it.

REPLACING STAPLE CROPS WITH PERENNIALS

The sustainability conundrum surrounding major staples such as wheat, corn, and rice stems primarily from the fact that they are annual crops. As George

Monbiot explains in his consequential book *Regenesis: Feeding the World Without Devouring the Planet*, annual plants are rare in natural ecosystems. After a catastrophe, such as a fire or flood, they temporarily colonize newly exposed ground until being supplanted by perennial plants. Annuals evolved to thrive in this ecological niche by growing fast and investing their energy in production of prolific, sizeable seeds rather than deep roots or thick foliage. These characteristics made them attractive to our ancestors at the dawn of agriculture, but they came with a Faustian bargain: to cultivate them, early farmers had to maintain the land in a depleted state by plowing the soil to weed out natural competitors, then replenish it artificially by applying fertilizer.

The twin requirements of plowing and fertilizing were significant limiting factors to the expansion of these staples throughout history. When colonial powers discovered new sources of fertilizer, such as rich deposits of guano (seabird excrement) in South America, it initiated a frenzy of over-exploitation causing permanent habitat destruction. A pivotal moment, however, occurred in the early twentieth century, when a German scientist, Fritz Haber, discovered how to extract nitrogen from fossil fuels, for which he won the Nobel Prize.

Before long, artificial fertilizer became the mainstay of crop cultivation worldwide. During the so-called "Green Revolution" beginning in the 1960s, Big Ag developed new strains of wheat and corn that were especially responsive to large dosages of nitrogen and water. Astonishingly, the use of nitrogen fertilizer has become so widespread that more than half of all the nitrogen atoms in green plant material now come from artificial fertilizer rather than the Earth's natural biochemical cycles. This has created a ruinous vicious cycle in which the continual degradation of topsoil is masked by artificial fertilizer which then drains into the oceans, causing uncontrolled algae blooms that consume the water's oxygen, leaving none for any other life. More than four hundred "dead zones" have emerged in coastal waters, some extending in size to over twenty thousand square miles.

There is a sustainable solution to this conundrum, but it would diminish Big Ag's profitability, so it has received negligible funding for research. It involves developing hybrid versions of these crops that are perennial rather than annual. This can bring significant benefits: The deeper roots reduce erosion, increase soil carbon, and are far less dependent on nitrogen fertilizer; the thicker foliage helps fertilize the soil and reduces requirements for weeding once the plants have matured. And as perennials, they do not need to be replanted each year.

An intrepid agronomist and MacArthur Fellow, Wes Jackson, has spent forty years pioneering this approach with the Kansas-based Land Institute, achieving impressive breakthroughs with selective cross-breeding and, more recently, gene sequencing and genomic selection. A new perennial grain called Kernza is now under cultivation and commercially available in selected markets. It persists for several years with stalks that carry as many seeds as wheat, although each seed is still a fraction of the weight. Other hybrids, such as perennial corn and sorghum, are similarly being developed. Perennial rice—a result of teamwork between the Land Institute and Yunnan University in China—is the most successful so far, with yields matching or exceeding annual rice species. Because of its benefits in reducing soil erosion and requiring far less labor, it is in high demand and its further expansion is limited mostly by testing and production capacity.

Perennial staples still have a long way to go before they can replace the dominant annual varieties, but if they were to receive the level of investment currently underwriting destructive practices that are more profitable for Big Ag, they promise a profoundly beneficial transformation.

WHAT KIND OF AGRICULTURE DOES NATURE WANT?

What about industrial meat production—surely one of humanity's most repugnant activities which tortures billions of animals, devastates rainforests, and contributes massively to greenhouse gas emissions? There are powerful reasons for people to reduce meat-eating and turn toward vegetarian or vegan diets. Beyond the moral imperative to eliminate the suffering of animals, a plant-based diet with fewer animal-sourced foods offers a double benefit by improving the health of both people and planet.

A study conducted by the EAT-Lancet Commission, comprising dozens of world-leading scientists, lays out the parameters of a diet, aligned with the values of an ecocivilization, that would increase people's health while remaining within Earth's safe operating space (as described in chapter 7). It would contain more than double the current consumption of healthy foods such as fruits, nuts, vegetables, and legumes, and less than half the current consumption of foods such as red meats and sugars—primarily through reducing excessive consumption in wealthier countries.[8]

However, current trends are moving in the opposite direction and global meat consumption is projected to increase by about 50 percent by the middle of this century. The environmental implications are terrifying. Plant-based meat substitutes such as Beyond and Impossible Burgers have made valiant efforts to break into the mainstream market but have had little impact. Their products might attract those already disposed to minimize meat consumption, but they struggle in two critical dimensions of taste and cost, and have recently experienced declining sales even from a small base.

More radical technologies, while still in their infancy, offer glimpses of a future potentially compatible with an ecocivilization. Significant progress is being made in cell-based meat, which is derived from cultivating animal cells (mostly muscle and fats) in a growth medium outside the animal. There are clear advantages to this approach. The product is real meat with a taste and texture potentially indistinguishable from that derived from a dead animal—but no animal is raised or killed in the process. Beyond the obvious benefits of eliminating the cruelty inherent in meat production and reducing environmental impacts, the meat (or fish) grown in these sanitized vats is never exposed to the pollutants or pathogens that livestock encounter, and through genetic modification could potentially offer improved flavor or nutritional value.[9]

The primary challenges facing cell-based meat are in the cultivation process. The structural complexity of natural meat is hard to reproduce in a vat, costs are still very high, and there are difficulties in scaling production. However, the long-term potential is significant enough that Big Ag views it as a threat. Trying to smother their infant competitor while it's still in the cradle, they are using their political muscle to get laws passed banning cell-based meat from being produced or sold. "Take your fake lab-grown meat elsewhere," said US state Governor Ron DeSantis before signing one such law in 2024. "We're not doing that in the state of Florida."[10]

An even more radical, and potentially transformative, technology is emerging in the realm of precision fermentation. Traditional fermentation techniques have been used for millennia, with a pedigree almost as old as agriculture itself. Fermentation harnesses the work of specialized bacteria that evolved to prevent the growth of competing bacteria in a particular food medium. Look around your kitchen, and you're likely to view a product of fermentation, which includes beer, champagne, vinegar, yoghurt, sourdough bread, pickles, and innumerable other delicious edibles.

Precision fermentation is a more recent technique that has been used commercially since the 1980s. It applies genetic engineering to modify microorganisms that are then used to create products such as human insulin and growth hormone, collagen, and a number of vitamins and supplements. It is also used for producing rennet—an ingredient necessary for hardening cheese that was traditionally taken from the stomach of an unweaned calf—accounting for over three-quarters of the rennet currently used in making cheese. As genome sequencing has advanced, microbiologists are now able to produce a prodigious number of complex organic molecules, such as proteins, fats (including oils), and vitamins, to exact specifications.[11]

These advances are being used to develop substitutes for meat that could potentially improve on the original product in every dimension that matters: nutrition, taste, flavor, aroma, mouthfeel—and cost. Precision fermentation, in the words of one expert team, "is now on the cusp of outcompeting animal agriculture as a form of food production, not just in cost, but in capabilities, speed, and volume."[12]

An important breakthrough occurred with the discovery of a particular bacterial species that draws its energy, not from photosynthesis or other organisms, but from hydrogen in the air, and can be processed into a flour containing approximately 60 percent protein. In the view of George Monbiot, who attests in *Regenesis* to the deliciousness of the pancakes it produces,

> . . . this method of food production shrinks, to an astonishing degree, the most important environmental impact of all: our use of land. It's here that the potential lies for a radical transformation of our relationship with the living world and the restoration of planetary health . . . As grazing occupies two-thirds of agricultural land, and grains grown to feed animals or protein crops for humans account for

> much of the rest, this could permit land-sparing on an otherwise unimaginable scale.[13]

At first sight, it might seem paradoxical to consider this product of advanced technology as consistent with an ecocivilization. After all, if we're turning to principles of life itself for inspiration, surely nothing could be less natural than using genetically modified bacteria to create proteins and fats in sealed tanks? And much of the havoc wrought by Big Ag has been the result of abuses of technological innovations, from the Haber process of nitrogen extraction to the patenting of genetically modified seeds. Shouldn't an ecocivilization envision a return to simpler farming practices of bygone eras? Based on these, and related concerns, a number of prominent agriculturalists have vociferously criticized these tech-based solutions.[14]

But the vision of an ecocivilization is not necessarily consistent with a yearning to return to a mythic past of Old MacDonald–style farms with chickens, goats, and donkeys. As discussed in chapter 2, the traditional farm romanticized in the public imagination was in fact the product of a brutal and environmentally destructive enclosure movement. Just as a return to nomadic foraging is no longer feasible in a world of more than eight billion people, a comprehensive return to simpler farming methods, without a parallel drastic transformation in worldwide dietary habits, would likely lead to mass starvation. Consistent with the theory of multilevel selection described in chapter 5, while a sprawling farm with livestock cheerfully grazing in the pasture might seem adaptive at one level, it becomes untenable at a higher level of nourishing the entire human population on an abundant Earth.

In forging an ecocivilization we might return to the question posed by circular economy visionary William McDonough: "How can our designs be of benefit to nature?" Just as McDonough asked "What kind of soap does the river want?," we might ask: "What kind of agriculture does nature want?" We might pose that question on behalf of the billions of animals being tortured to feed humans, the tropical rainforests being devastated for cattle grazing and soybean plantations, and the sea creatures suffocating in ocean dead zones. It seems reasonable to presume that they would want to see a form of agriculture that reversed its pernicious impact on nature's abundance and eliminated the abomination of factory farming. The extraordinary promise of precision fermentation is that it could potentially fulfill these aspirations.

A RICH FABRIC OF DIVERSITY

There is, however, a Windigo-sized elephant in the room. As we've seen repeatedly, Windigo's Law (aka Jevons Paradox) predicts that any technological advance will inevitably lead under capitalism to further exploitation of nature. It doesn't take much imagination to envisage Big Ag dominating this technology through aggressive patenting and then using it, not to reduce environmental damage, but to design even more addictive products to further manipulate consumer behavior.

This is why a transformation to an ecocivilization requires tightly interconnected feedback loops between ideas and initiatives from other domains. If Big Ag corporations operated under a triple bottom line requirement or a Future Guardian–style governance structure of multiple stakeholders (as discussed in the previous chapter), their aim would no longer be worldwide devastation for the sake of shareholder returns, but they could instead use their prodigious technology and global reach to facilitate a speedy transition to a life-enhancing agricultural system. If worker-owned co-ops were the default organizational structure for businesses, we could envision local microbial breweries springing up around the world, designing their protein-rich products to align with the tastes and nutritional needs of their region. If true cost pricing were introduced, then organic produce and a plethora of meat substitutes would become the most inexpensive options for consumers.

"The global food system holds the future of humanity on Earth in its hand," declares Johan Rockström, leader of the team that defined humanity's "safe operating space." We have seen in this chapter how, under the chokehold of Big Ag, this future looks daunting, but that a transformation to a more life-sustaining system is conceivable. Unlike today's WTO-driven monolith, it would not entail a one-size-fits-all solution. Rather, like any healthy ecosystem, it would be richly heterogeneous based on core principles of diversity, circularity, symbiosis, and integration.[15]

Agroecology and food sovereignty would be fundamental, along with other related beneficial practices that have not been discussed here such as permaculture and regenerative farming. More generally, organic farming, with a lower all-in cost (incorporating externalities), would supplant the current reliance on Big Ag's noxious chemicals. Perennial staples would displace annuals as default crops, grown at scale in conjunction with legumes and perennial wildflowers to help fix nitrogen, attract pollinators, and control pests naturally.

In place of relentless globalization, we would see a more nuanced trading system attuned to the nested nature of agricultural production. Local, organic food would be emphasized where possible, supplemented by regional markets for access to foods requiring more extensive infrastructures, while globalized exchange, priced fairly, would continue for staples and other foods not available regionally.

In this system, advanced technology would be applied selectively when it supports natural flourishing, and in synergy with localized, traditional knowledge and cultural distinctiveness. No-till planting, reducing soil erosion, can be accomplished effectively through seed drills. In place of herbicides and tractors, automated robot weeders can identify unwanted plants in a field and eliminate them through tiny bolts of electricity. Infrared spectroscopy can provide farmers with real-time analysis of their soil's minerals, texture, and other properties, helping them determine precisely how to plan their crops. And precision fermentation, alongside cell-based meats, could provide the world's meat and dairy requirements, supplemented by limited livestock supply from agroecology farming systems, while factory farming would be abolished planetwide.

This rich fabric of diversity beckons to us as a pathway forward. While the systemic roadblocks to its implementation are vast, each of the different strands of this weave already exists—and each has demonstrated its viability. Agriculture, one of our civilization's most complex, multifaceted systems, is also currently one of its most ruptured. And yet, even here, we can turn to Margaret Thatcher's TINA declaration with the response: Yes, there is indeed an alternative

POSSIBLE SECOND AND THIRD HORIZON CONTOURS | AGRICULTURE

SECOND HORIZON

Global Majority nations give primacy to agroecology over industrial agriculture

Food sovereignty is given precedence in international trade agreements over current so-called "free trade" treaties that privilege Big Ag

Seed sovereignty is incorporated in legal frameworks protecting farmers' rights to save, replant, and share their seeds

Agricultural subsidies are eliminated for industrial agriculture, and instead applied to development of perennial staples, cell-based meat, and precision fermentation

THIRD HORIZON

Agroecology, with food sovereignty, is the predominant agricultural modality in the Majority World

Organic, permaculture, and regenerative agriculture predominate worldwide, drastically reducing the use of chemical fertilizers, pesticides, and herbicides

Perennials replace annuals as the primary source of staples such as wheat, corn, and rice

Factory farming is abolished. In its place, meat and dairy production is predominantly from cell-based cultivation or precision fermentation, augmented by livestock from agroecology farms

People eat mostly plant-based diets, with food sourced locally, supporting local producers aligned with principles of agroecology

Ubiquitous worker-owned microbial breweries customize nutrient-rich foods for their communities

FOR CONSIDERATION

What Second and Third Horizon ideas arise in your own mind inspired by this chapter?

CHAPTER 10

WEALTH: REGAINING THE COMMONS FOR A TRUE "COMMONWEALTH"

In the Shaanxi province of China, under an edifice 250 feet tall, lies one of the world's most striking relics of an earlier civilization: the mausoleum of Qin Shi Huang, first emperor of China's Qin dynasty. Emperor Qin's twenty-square-mile underground metropolis was constructed by 700,000 workers over thirty-eight years, modeled on the layout of his capital city, Xianyang. It's known far and wide for its dramatic terracotta army numbering eight thousand soldiers with chariots and horses. But it holds a dark story. After its completion, thousands of artisans and laborers were said to have been sealed into the necropolis and left to die there, ensuring the tomb's secrets would never be imparted.

The practice of burying living people with deceased emperors continued through China's Ming dynasty, when concubines were regularly buried with their lords to keep them company in the afterlife. This macabre tradition was not unique to China. The pharaohs of Egypt's First Dynasty selected hundreds of retainers for sacrificial strangulation to accompany them on their journey to the underworld.

There are other shocking practices of early civilizations that have thankfully been left in the dust, such as the Aztec ritual of human sacrifice, when the victims' still-beating heart was cut from their chests and offered to the gods. Other atavistic beliefs, while not as gruesome, have deservedly been discarded to the annals of history, such as the European theory of the divine right of kings, which played a dominant role in politics until the eighteenth century.

We can look back at earlier times and shake our heads in amazement at the bizarre doctrines and grotesque practices of primitive societies. Or can we? How might a future civilization contemplate the modern widespread belief that it's okay for a single individual to own $250 billion while half the world's population earns less than $7.40 per day: the minimum income needed for basic nutrition and a normal life expectancy? After Jeff Bezos completed his five-billion-dollar space flight extravaganza, he chuckled on camera and said: "I want to thank every Amazon employee and every Amazon customer, because you guys paid for all this. Thank you from the bottom of my heart, very much. It's very appreciated." Amazon, meanwhile, has conducted a systematic worldwide campaign to crush union activity at its warehouses, enabling Bezos to chortle over the absurdity that he earns the average annual wage of one of his employees every nine seconds.[1]

Bezos and his ilk may not literally strangle their retainers to death, but through the lens of structural violence discussed in chapter 3, we can recognize that the outsized inequities of our age cause far greater harm than their imperial predecessors could instigate. As US Representative Alexandria Ocasio-Cortez famously expressed: "Every billionaire is a policy failure."[2]

In this chapter, we'll investigate the manifold ways that the modern era's extreme inequality undermines people's well-being, and explore policy options already being considered to remedy it. After tracing the deeper underlying sources of society's wealth, we will examine methods currently being tested to share it more equitably, and discover how a cornerstone of a truly just ecocivilization has already been shown to provide a source of enduring well-being to those who need it the most.

"TAX US, THE VERY RICHEST"

While extreme inequality has been a common characteristic of civilizations from ancient Rome to the Gilded Age of the late nineteenth century, there are strong indications that wealth disparities today are greater than ever before. The world's richest one percent own 43 percent of all global financial assets, and emit as much carbon pollution as the poorest two thirds of humanity. Oxfam reports that the wealth of the five richest billionaires has more than doubled since the start of the current decade, while 60 percent of humanity has grown poorer. At current rates, they project, we'll see the first trillionaire in the next decade.[3]

It's only too clear why inequality hurts those at the lower end of the spectrum, but as mentioned in chapter 1, the overall health and well-being of a country is determined, not so much by the amount of a country's wealth, but how evenly the wealth is distributed. A comprehensive study by social scientists Richard Wilkinson and Kate Pickett reveals that more equal wealth distribution strongly predicts a healthier society. Greater inequality leads to lower life expectancy, worse health, and higher rates of AIDS, depression, and infant mortality.[4]

While there is no discernible correlation between an index of health and social problems and a country's income level, there is clear correlation between the index and a country's income inequality. Japan, Sweden, and Norway, the most equal countries, score lowest on the index, while the United States, the most unequal, scores far higher than the rest.

It benefits almost everyone to live in a more equal society, not just the poor. Unequal societies correlate with higher levels of violence along with higher rates of mental illness, crime, alcoholism, drug abuse, homicide, and incarceration. Similarly, there are vast differences in trust, with people in Sweden more than six times as likely to trust others than those in the most unequal countries. For all these reasons, it's not just physical but also psychological well-being that is sabotaged by excessive inequality.

Most people agree that some degree of inequality in a society is acceptable, but very few would opt for our current situation. How might an optimal level of inequality be determined? The political philosopher John Rawls has proposed an influential thought experiment to address the concept of what's known as distributive justice. Imagine that you could design the level of inequality for a society that you are about to be born into yourself, but you are caught behind a "veil of ignorance": You have no idea of your place in society, your class position, or social status; nor do you know anything about your own natural assets and abilities, your intelligence, features, or strength. What kind of society would you select? The rational choice, Rawls suggests, would be to opt for a social structure that protects the least well off, rather than giving unlimited advantage to the fortunate few. This approach, known as the "fairness principle," is, of course, in stark contrast to the world we live in today.[5]

More recently, the Dutch philosopher Ingrid Robeyns has advanced an ethical position she calls "limitarianism," arguing that there should be a strict limit to an individual's wealth. There is a certain amount of money, she suggests, that permits a person to pursue a flourishing life. Anything above that is "surplus money" which could be more effectively utilized to enhance the conditions allowing others to follow their own path of eudaimonia—a position consistent with the principles of an ecocivilization laid out in chapter 6. The appropriate wealth cap would be dependent on the kind of society a person is living in: For someone with access to an extensive welfare infrastructure with pensions, freely accessible healthcare, and other services, she proposes a limit of a million dollars. In our current sociopolitical context, however, she suggests a more politically viable target of ten million. Such a weighty decision, however, should clearly not be left up to any single person. Reflecting this, the Austrian economist Christian Felber suggests a democratically determined wealth cap and maximum income ratio between society's wealthiest and poorest, thus ensuring that the wealthiest could only accumulate more if society's least well-off were also benefiting.[6]

Even among the moneyed elite, there is a sizeable contingent agitating to change the current situation. At Davos, a group of 250 millionaires and billionaires, led by Abigail Disney among others, signed an open letter to world leaders asking them to "tax us, the very richest in society. This will not fundamentally alter our standard of living, nor deprive our children, nor harm our nations' economic growth, but will turn extreme and unproductive private wealth into an investment for our common democratic future."[7]

REDUCING WEALTH DISPARITIES

Some policymakers are listening to them and trying to turn the tide on wealth disparities. Since the rise of neoliberalism, many tax regimes around the world have gone from being progressive—where the wealthy are taxed at higher rates than the poor—to regressive: penalizing the poorest while further enriching the wealthiest. As a result, while Jeff Bezos pays an effective tax rate of one percent, Aber Christine, a market trader in Uganda who sells rice, flour, and soy, pays a 40 percent tax rate on her monthly earnings of $80. In the United States, the top marginal tax rate has fallen from 91 percent in 1963 to 37 percent today. To compensate for the loss of tax revenue from the rich and from corporations, governments have turned to value added tax (VAT) and sales tax which disproportionately impact the poor who spend a higher share of their income on consumption.[8]

At this point, even the IMF and the European Central Bank have endorsed a wealth tax, which is a wildly popular proposition supported by the vast majority of citizens polled around the world. There are signs that this support might translate into global policy. In 2021, most nations agreed to a global minimum tax of 15 percent on transnational corporations, which has already had an impact in reducing offshore tax evasion. The G20 group of nations is now considering a proposal by the economist Gabriel Zucman to use a similar protocol of international cooperation to ensure that the world's three thousand billionaires pay at least two percent of their wealth in taxes each year. Zucman estimates this could generate as much as $250 billion annually.[9]

There is a strange dichotomy inherent in a proposal such as this. On one hand, it should be celebrated as a momentous stride, finally bringing international coordination to target a vast injustice. On the other hand, from the viewpoint of a hypothetical future civilization, we might sense the absurdity that such a limited step could even be controversial in a world reeling out of kilter. An Oxfam report notes that a wealth tax of 12.8 percent on billionaires would merely have kept their wealth constant since 2016.[10]

It's helpful to consider some aggregate numbers to grasp the magnitude of this lopsided situation. The wealth of all three thousand billionaires in 2025 is estimated at around $16 trillion. If each one's wealth were capped at a single billion, that would free up $13 trillion—roughly $1,500 dollars for every person alive today. Add in the estimated wealth of an additional 30,000 centimillionaires, and you arrive at a grand total of about $31 trillion. If a "limitarian" cap were applied that restricted each person's wealth to $100 million, that would free up $28 trillion for public benefit. For calibration, it's estimated that four trillion dollars would lift everyone in the world above the threshold for extreme poverty. Zucman's proposal is an excellent first step, but there is clearly a long way to go.[11]

While a wealth tax is the most compelling proposition for reducing this imbalance, it's certainly not the only one. The idea of a land value tax (LVT) has been floated for centuries across the political spectrum, with support from such luminaries as Thomas Jefferson and Adam Smith. In 1797, the political philosopher Thomas Paine encapsulated the logic in his book *Agrarian Justice*, writing:

> It is a position not to be controverted that the earth, in its natural, uncultivated state was, and ever would have continued to be, the common property of the human race . . . Man did not make the earth . . . It is the value of the improvements only, and not the earth itself, that is the individual property . . . Every proprietor, therefore, of cultivated land, owes to the community a ground rent for the land which he holds.[12]

Jefferson went further, arguing that "the earth belongs in usufruct [temporary usage right] to the living" and should revert to society on the landowner's death, while the conservative economist David Ricardo viewed unearned income from the land as a "pernicious anomaly." The moral logic of an LVT is indisputable: When land value rises, it is not the landowner's doing, but overwhelmingly due to increased value attached to that particular location through the actions of the community.

In the late nineteenth century, the journalist Henry George took America by storm selling over three million copies of his book *Progress and Poverty*, which argued that land was the common inheritance of all, and a levy on all privately owned land should be assessed on behalf of the public. However, after George's untimely death from a stroke in 1897, his budding proposal was quickly quashed by the elites.

Another idea that has remained mostly muted by the forces of cultural hegemony relates to significant taxation on the inheritance of private wealth. As the political philosopher David Haslett has reflected: "We abolished the inheritance of political power; why, then, should we not abolish the inheritance of economic power, too?" While inheritance taxes would not yield anything close to the scale of wealth or land taxes, they open up a larger moral question around transmission of wealth from one generation to the next. What is the ethical basis, we must ask, for the right to inherit wealth from the previous generation? And who should be eligible for that right?[13]

HUMANITY'S SHARED LEGACY: THE "COMMONWEALTH"

As John Rawls's thought experiment highlights, the biggest factor determining the magnitude of economic bounty in our lives is the blind luck of the birth lottery. None of us chooses to be born to parents scavenging day-to-day in a shantytown slum of a Global South megacity or to wealthy parents who spare no expense to ensure we get the best start in life. This is a powerful moral argument against patrimony—and yet nearly half of the wealthiest billionaires on the Forbes rich list inherited their fortunes.

What about those billionaire tech entrepreneurs who started out tinkering in their friend's basement? The classic neoliberal narrative tells us they deserve all the fruits of their ingenuity and perseverance. But if we look deeper, we see a very different picture. In fact, we are all heirs to a vast treasure trove of knowledge, infrastructure, and technology that has been forged collectively by the sweat, enterprise, and genius of generations of ancestors. We are all the rightful beneficial owners of this common legacy.

All human wealth is derived ultimately from the abundance of nature itself: from the air, water, sunlight, minerals, soil, and ecosystems that bestow their riches on humanity. From this natural cornucopia, our ancestors learned to cultivate plants, domesticate animals, and develop frameworks for civilization such as writing, law, calendars, mathematics, and moral codes. The breakthroughs of recent centuries contributed such treasures as electricity, chemistry, physics, modern medicine, and built infrastructures; followed in recent decades by computer processing and the internet.

This enormous legacy—a cumulative gift from the past—is generally referred to as the commons, and the wealth it engenders is a commonwealth that belongs by right to us all. Yet our current economic system allows a Harvard student such as Mark Zuckerberg to make a few tweaks to this vast edifice and collect a jackpot of $250 billion, while half of humanity remains malnourished because they have no access to their fair share of the commonwealth. From this perspective, is this not one of the greatest moral outrages in human history?

Of course, misappropriation of the commons is not unique to the modern era. We may understand the five-thousand-year-old wealth pump discussed in chapter 3 as a systematic ongoing enclosure of the commons, forcibly capturing humanity's shared legacy for private ownership.

In the early days of English enclosures, peasants used to band together to "beat the bounds": they would walk the perimeters of a forest or open field and if they came across a fence or hedge enclosing the commons, they would dismantle it to preserve their shared endowment. Today, the scope of enclosure by investors and corporations—usually with support from governments—encompasses virtually every aspect of the commonwealth like a multipronged suction pump, targeting seeds, genes, medicines, ocean floors, data gathered online about our tastes and preferences, and even—with the rise of generative AI—the entire internet.

A defining task of an ecocivilization will be to reverse the direction of this enclosure by collecting the wealth, administering it, and redistributing it. Let us attend to each of these. Relatively simple policies, such as restoring progressive tax regimes and increasing taxation on transnational corporations, would be an important first step in collecting privatized wealth. An internationally applied wealth tax, incorporating democratically determined caps on wealth, would make a major contribution. For this to be effective, we would need far greater global wealth transparency, with the dismantling of offshore tax havens and anonymous shell companies, public registry of beneficial owners of trusts, and the creation of a global asset register.

Additionally, given that the total value of the world's real estate is estimated at $400 trillion—more than the combined value of the global equity and bond markets—the widespread institution of a land value tax would transform the financial topography. Beyond that, as described in chapter 8, a globally coordinated system of full-cost pricing could apply a comprehensive levy on the externalized costs of ecological and social damage caused by industry. Since noxious activities of corporations impair the value of the commons, from the perspective of the commonwealth, humanity has a legitimate right to exact full compensation.

Some of these funds could reinvigorate the power of governments to provide basic services to citizens, such as healthcare, education, and public transportation. However, funds collected specifically on behalf of the commonwealth might be managed by trusts rather than governments, which have all too often shown themselves—in electoral democracies as well as authoritarian regimes—to be in thrall to established power elites.

The trust structure was invented in twelfth-century England to protect landowners who joined the Crusades and wanted to ensure their property would be maintained in their absence. It establishes two primary agents: a beneficial owner, and a trustee with a legally binding fiduciary duty to protect the beneficiary's interests under any circumstances. As discussed in chapter 2, the concept of fiduciary duty has been used by today's fund managers to justify placing shareholders' interests above any other consideration. Its power can, however, be redirected for good purpose if the common people are the trust's beneficial owners.

Under this arrangement, there might be a wide array of commonwealth trusts, ranging in geographical scope from bioregional to planetary, and including intangible domains such as cultural heritage and internet data. Beneficiaries would include both current and future generations. Under the principle of intergenerational equity—known as the Hartwick Rule after the economist who first defined it—consumption or distribution of the commonwealth's resources would only be permissible to the extent that it's done on a sustainable basis.

How, then, would a sustainable portion of this vast commonwealth be distributed to its legitimate beneficiaries: the common people?

PRIVATE SUFFICIENCY, PUBLIC LUXURY

In a wave of collective revulsion at the horrors of the Second World War, a group of humanitarian visionaries, led by Eleanor Roosevelt, came together in an affirmation of human dignity to produce one of history's most important documents: the UN Declaration of Human Rights. While it may so far have been "more honored in the breach than the observance," the Declaration continues to set a basic moral foundation for naming what is due every person simply by virtue of being born human.

It also establishes a solid framework for considering how the commonwealth should be distributed. Articles 25 and 26 uphold the right of all human beings to "a standard of living adequate for the health and well-being," specifying "food, clothing, housing and medical care and necessary social services" along with the right to education. Given developments in the ensuing decades, we might now add access to clean air and water, motorized transportation, electricity, and the internet.

Collectively, these are generally known as "universal basic services" (UBS), and their provision is considered a mainstay of various progressive political programs, including the degrowth movement. The provision of UBS goes a long way to establishing the inner ring of the "doughnut" in Doughnut Economics, ensuring that every member of society has access to life's essentials. It aligns with the core principles of an ecocivilization, giving primacy to the essential dignity of all people and setting the material conditions for each person to experience a life of wellbeing.[14]

The provision of UBS goes beyond the concept of a social "safety net," but rather lays a foundation for flourishing available to everyone regardless of their ability to pay. Services might be provided by state institutions, municipalities, or local communities, and their funding might derive either from governments or trusts, depending on specific circumstances. Based on the principle of subsidiarity—another core tenet of an ecocivilization—the particular way in which these services are provided should be determined at the lowest feasible level, so that people receiving them can participate in their design.

This redirection of the wealth pump opens the door to a new social paradigm defined by what the journalist George Monbiot calls "private sufficiency, public luxury." Currently, the notion of luxury is intimately associated with the indulgences of the elite, broadcast widely through advertising and social media to incentivize the rest of the world to dedicate themselves to the hedonic treadmill with the dream of someday achieving the high life. Since the overconsumption of the elites is already a major driver of acceleration toward ecological collapse, there is clearly no capacity for all those dreams to be fulfilled. However, through appropriate distribution of the commonwealth, as Monbiot describes it, "there is enough to provide everyone with magnificent public parks, gardens, hospitals, swimming pools, beaches, art galleries, libraries, tennis courts, transport systems, playgrounds, and community centers."[15]

There are, however, limitations to UBS as the primary source of commonwealth distribution. Following the principle of subsidiarity, devolving decision-making to the lowest feasible level ultimately means empowering each person to determine for themselves what allows them to pursue their own distinct path of eudaimonia. While some services, such as road maintenance, public transportation, and healthcare provision are structurally best suited to collective management, other human needs such as clothing, food, and pursuit of one's unique aspirations, can best be met through everyone determining their own personal priorities. How might this be achieved?

A SOCIAL DIVIDEND FOR ALL HUMANKIND

Let's hear it for Thomas Paine. Not only did he conceptualize a land value tax, publish *The Rights of Man*, and inspire the American War of Independence, he was also one of the first to propose the concept of a universal basic income (UBI): a direct cash distribution from the commonwealth to every person in society as an unconditional right. "It is not charity but a right," he declared, "not bounty but justice, that I am pleading for." He explains further:

> It is proposed that the payments . . . be made to every person, rich or poor. It is best to make it so, to prevent invidious distinctions. It is also right it should be so, because it is in lieu of the natural inheritance, which, as a right, belongs to every man.[16]

With these words, Paine reconceptualized the very basis of our moral and economic system, and sowed the seeds for an idea that has since matured into an incipient global movement, and presents itself as a possible linchpin of an ecocivilization.

The notion of providing a guaranteed basic income to all citizens has bubbled up from time to time since Paine's original conception. The philosopher Bertrand Russell, among others in early twentieth-century Britain, called for it, and generations later it was embraced by Martin Luther King Jr. who wrote, shortly before his assassination:

> The dignity of the individual will flourish when the decisions concerning his life are in his own hands, when he has the assurance that his income is stable and certain, and when he knows that he has the means to seek self-improvement.[17]

Like the Land Value Tax, the idea has been endorsed across the political spectrum. Following a petition to the US Congress signed by over 1,300 economists to enact a "national system of income guarantees," President Richard Nixon proposed such legislation in 1972, which was eventually defeated in the Senate despite overwhelming public support. Versions of a basic income have even been advocated by neoliberal stalwarts such as Friedrich Hayek and Milton Friedman, and more recently by a cluster of Silicon Valley moguls, including Pierre Omidyar, Marc Benioff, Sam Altman, and Elon Musk.[18]

While advocates sometimes envisage slightly different versions, UBI in its generally accepted form refers to a guaranteed periodic cash payment made to every legal resident of a society with no conditions or obligations attached. While the amount is open to various interpretations, it's broadly understood to be sufficient to cover an individual's basic needs. Although some neoliberal pundits might want to substitute it for public services, most proponents see it as a complement to UBS, and this is definitely how it's conceived within the context of an ecocivilization.

UBI is fundamentally different from public assistance programs currently in place. As Paine alluded to, as an unconditional payment, there is none of the stigma associated with means testing for welfare. It is automatically granted to each individual as a birthright to their fair share of the commonwealth. As such, the UBI advocate Guy Standing argues convincingly that a more accurate name might be a "social dividend."

Discussion of UBI almost invariably triggers several concerns in people's minds, even among those who are sympathetic to it. A pervasive concern, succinctly summarized by the UBI proponent Rutger Bregman, is that "free money makes people lazy." Wouldn't UBI recipients simply not bother to work? Since the rise of capitalism, the dominant contract between capital and labor has reified the idea that humans are essentially selfish and lazy, and must be forced to work by a combination of fear and greed, which is achieved by wages and other financial incentives. However, it has been widely demonstrated that humans are nothing of the sort. In fact, people have a fundamental need to engage in a livelihood that is meaningful and to feel valued by their community. Work is not something people try to avoid; on the contrary, purposeful work is an integral part of human flourishing.[19]

If people were liberated, however, by UBI from the daily necessity to sell their labor for survival, some might choose to reinvest their time in crucial parts of the economy that, as outlined in the Doughnut Economics framework, have mostly been hidden from view—the household and the commons. They would care for loved ones, build community, and dare to do whatever inspires them. The domination of the economy by the market would inevitably decline while those other, life-enhancing sectors would be strengthened.

This leads to another concern: what about those "bullshit jobs" (anthropologist David Graeber's memorable epithet)—like flipping burgers or working in an Amazon warehouse—that people accept because they have no other choice? Who would take them? To attract people to these jobs, companies would have to pay higher wages, which would lead to a further decline in inequality. This points to a profound implication of a full-fledged UBI: It would fundamentally alter the paradigm of capitalism that has locked workers in its grip since its inception. Capitalism has endured by commoditizing people's lives, forcing them to sell the bulk of their available time and energy, or else face destitution and starvation. By transforming the relationship between labor and capital, a true UBI would weaken the power of the wealthy elite to control the population.

The social benefits of establishing a UBI would be pervasive and profound. It would support marginalized and racialized people who are disproportionately occupied in unpaid care work. It would offer a way out for women trapped in oppressive or abusive relationships for financial reasons. It would virtually put an end to the scourges of homelessness and hunger. It would likely halt the surge in authoritarian populism which feeds off people's fear, insecurity, and loss of self-esteem. Above all, the alteration of the paradigmatic social contract between the state, capital, and labor would send a radically different message to ordinary people, signaling to them that they are trusted and have a right to live in dignity.

A common concern expressed is that UBI would allow people to indulge in harmful pursuits such as drugs, alcohol, and tobacco. In fact, a wide range of UBI experiments conducted around the world have shown exactly the opposite. In Liberia, a group of alcoholics, addicts, and petty criminals living in the slums were given $200 with no strings attached. Researchers later discovered they had spent the money on food, clothing, and medicine. Londoners who had been living on the streets for over four years were asked what they needed to change their lives and received an average outlay of about £800. Within a year, eleven of the thirteen had moved off the streets. Similarly, in Vancouver, fifty homeless people were given an unconditional lump sum of $7,500. Rather than drugs, tobacco, or alcohol, they spent the money on food, clothes, and rent, and saved enough to remain financially secure during the year of follow-up.[20]

A meta-study performed by the Stanford Basic Income Lab synthesizing sixteen different reviews of pilots conducted worldwide over decades found decisively that UBI alleviates poverty and improves health and education across the board. Some studies reported an increase in paid employment, and where minor reductions occurred, the time was channeled into prosocial activities such as caregiving. Food security and dietary diversity increased, ill health decreased, and mental health improved. People showed a willingness to take on more financial risk, starting household businesses or acquiring seeds, fertilizer, and small equipment to grow their own food. School enrollment, attendance, and educational performance went up, while teachers could now afford to buy paper, pens, and books for their students.[21]

In general, as people are empowered to take more control of their lives, they respond by feeling more connected with their community and engaging in prosocial behavior. In one Indian village, recipients established a fishing cooperative. In another, families pooled some of their income to improve village drainage. In another Indian village, young women who had been forced to wear veils in public began to go unveiled, no longer subject to the financial domination of their elders. In Namibia, petty crime fell substantially since starving villagers no longer needed to steal vegetables for food. This, in turn, encouraged residents to plant more vegetables, leading to more abundance for all.[22]

UBI has consistently proven to be such a powerful instigator of well-being that it might be considered not just a cornerstone of an ecocivilization, but a central Second Horizon highway propelling us there. If every American adult received a monthly basic income of $1,000—roughly equivalent to the federal poverty level—the cost would be about $4 trillion, equivalent to less than 14 percent of the US GDP. We've seen how a reconsideration of tax practices could readily provide that. As Guy Standing points out, the issue is ultimately not one of affordability but rather "what are society's fiscal priorities?"[23]

From today's standpoint, we look back in wonderment at the excesses of Chinese emperors and the grisly rituals of Aztec priests. When a future civilization looks back in amazement at how we allowed uber-elites to siphon off society's wealth, will they possibly recognize our generation as the turning point when we started demanding the social dividend that is everyone's birthright?

POSSIBLE SECOND AND THIRD HORIZON CONTOURS | WEALTH

SECOND HORIZON

A wealth tax imposed worldwide on billionaires and centimillionaires

Global wealth transparency enforcement: dismantling anonymous shell companies and offshore tax havens, and the creation of a global asset register

A Land Value Tax (LVT) instituted by affluent nations around the world

Significant loophole-free taxation imposed on the inheritance or gifting of wealth

Extensive Universal Basic Income (UBI) pilots carried out, leading to national rollouts of UBI programs at modest income levels

THIRD HORIZON

Democratically determined caps on wealth applied throughout the world

Constitutional recognition of everyone's legitimate right to the legacy of the commonwealth

A wide array of commonwealth trusts set up to manage and distribute regional and planetary abundance to everyone, subject to the Hartwick Rule of intergenerational equity

Wealth caps and taxes, LVTs, inheritance taxes, and planet-wide full-cost pricing contribute funding for commonwealth trusts

Comprehensive Universal Basic Services (UBS) provide the conditions for people's material wellbeing

A full-fledged UBI instituted in every nation allows all people to live in dignity and pursue their unique paths of eudaimonia

FOR CONSIDERATION

What Second and Third Horizon ideas arise in your own mind inspired by this chapter?

CHAPTER 11

FINANCE: TRANSFORMING MONEY TO WORK FOR US ALL

King William III of England had a money problem. The English navy had suffered a serious defeat at the hands of the French in 1690, and he needed to rebuild the Royal Navy. Where, he wondered, was he going to find the funding for it? The war with France, which had begun after England's "Glorious Revolution" of 1688, had already forced him to impose taxes on luxuries like beer, wine, and tobacco, and he sensed that taxing essentials like bread and corn would be political suicide. In such situations, previous monarchs had turned to wealthy goldsmiths for a loan, but since many of them had been ruined by his predecessors' defaults, they refused to lend money to him directly.

Help was at hand. The Scottish trader and banker, Sir William Paterson, proposed that Parliament should establish a "publick transferrable Fund of Interest" underwritten by a "Society of Money'd Men" who would lend the required £1.2 million to the state rather than the king, so that if the king defaulted, it would become the nation's debt. They charged a hefty eight percent interest rate, with the result that England's taxpayers now had to pay them £100,000 in annual interest. England would never be debt-free again. This consortium of "Money'd Men" became the Bank of England, which remained privately owned for centuries, and Britain's national debt has since expanded to £2.75 trillion, roughly the size of the nation's GDP.

This origin story contains kernels of our modern monetary system that have since sprouted into the bizarre, convoluted financial arrangement of today's world, defined by an intimate relationship between the state and wealthy elites, with a power imbalance leaning strongly toward the latter—and a compulsive reliance on debt to finance a nation's needs. We will discover in this chapter that the design of our monetary system is far from being in the best interests of society at large, but instead has acted as a powerful hidden generator for the wealth pump: stoking our economy's addiction to perpetual growth, and leading to overwhelming debt burdens that undermine people's welfare while fueling the moneyed elite with ever more power and capital.

Most of us barely give a moment's thought to how money is created—it seems like an automatic part of our lives like language, or as one of the founders of economics, David Hume, called it: "the oil which renders the motion of the wheels smooth and easy." We will see, however, that money is a social construction that can be fashioned according to society's needs. Rather than being value-neutral like oil, the way in which money is created has a profound impact on how society functions.

"The study of money, above all other fields in economics," wrote influential economist John Kenneth Galbraith, "is one in which complexity is used to disguise truth or to evade truth, not to reveal it." In this chapter, we'll uncover those gratuitous complexities to discover some simple truths, and explore how a transformed money system can play as important a role in creating an ecocivilization as its current form has played in activating the wealth pump for centuries.[1]

MONEY BY FIAT

It's generally agreed that in order to be usable, money has to fulfill three economic functions. First and foremost, it must be an agreed upon *medium of exchange.* This could include beads, frequent flier mileage points, digital game tokens, or the standard currencies known as "legal tender" that are accepted in payment of taxes. It must also be a *store of value* so that someone holding it can rely on using it in the future (the longer the time period, the better); and it must act as a *unit of account,* so that it can be broadly applied to a wide range of products and services, such as vegetables, houses, and wages.

For much of human history, dating back to hunter-gatherer times, objects such as shells or furs were used as money. In early civilizations, precious metals became more commonplace. The problem with this type of money is that its value was fixed by the underlying worth of the commodity, and carrying a lot of it around could prove difficult. To solve this problem, a trusted source was required to create "representative money": a paper certificate carrying a credible promise that it could be exchanged on demand for a commodity. China's Song dynasty was the first to introduce paper money over a thousand years ago, followed centuries later in Europe—where the promissory notes were originally issued not by governments but by private goldsmiths.

It was in the city-states of Venice and Florence in thirteenth-century Europe that the earliest version of capitalist money creation emerged. Goldsmiths would store people's gold and silver coins for safekeeping and give them a paper receipt. People gradually began using these convenient receipts as currency, rarely returning to collect their coins. At some point, certain enterprising goldsmiths realized they could make interest-bearing loans backed by the accumulated gold left with them, relying on the fact that most likely it wouldn't all be collected at the same time. It was here, in this initial incubation of the modern banking system, that the creation of money became inextricably linked with interest-bearing debt.

In early cultures, there was widespread moral aversion to charging interest on loans. As discussed in chapter 6, traditional Indigenous communities mostly lived according to a gift economy, where it would have been unthinkable. Charging interest was denounced as usury by the medieval Catholic Church and was illegal in most Muslim societies. Interest-bearing debt was, however, fundamental to the rise of capitalism, with profound consequences. Money now had a price attached to it, rather than simply being a medium of exchange; and the creditor/debtor relationship became detached from genuine connections of trust between people.[2]

As capitalism consolidated its dominance in the global economy in the twentieth century, interest-bearing debt expanded its role to become the force that created money itself. Governments, no longer wanting to be constrained by the requirement to hold gold on reserve, empowered banks to create money out of nothing, simply by making loans. This is known as *fiat money*, a word that derives from the first words that God uttered in Genesis:

"*Fiat lux* (let there be light)," which fittingly captures the God-like power that's been granted to banks.

Fiat money now accounts for about 97 percent of the money created in the world. As the Bank of England explains, when a bank makes a loan to someone, such as a mortgage to buy a house, it typically credits their bank account with a deposit. "At that moment," they declare, "new money is created." Conversely, they add, when a loan is paid down, this destroys money. This process is paralleled at the macroeconomic level, in which the government creates new money by becoming further indebted to banks through issuance of Treasury bonds. As a director of the Bank of England, Lord Stamp, commented in 1937, "The modern banking system manufactures money out of nothing. The process is perhaps the most astounding piece of sleight of hand that was ever invented."[3]

The implications of this are staggering. Each time a loan is made with interest, the amount required to pay back the loan in the future is larger than the amount that was created in the first place. Where will that extra money come from? Every debtor suddenly finds themselves in competition with other debtors to obtain the funds they need. The penalty for those who lose the contest is bankruptcy. This design has essentially created a gigantic game of musical chairs in which there are never enough seats. The only way to avoid its collapse is to keep the music playing perpetually, which is accomplished through continually expanding the economy. This is the reason why a temporary pause in the music (known as a recession) causes such widespread anguish.

An intrinsic feature of interest-bearing money is a propensity to discount the future. Built into virtually every decision about where to allocate capital is the principle referred to as the "time value of money": that a dollar is worth more now than in the future because of its earnings potential if invested in the game of musical chairs. The discount rate used, which can vary widely but is frequently between 3 and 10 percent a year, specifies how much less to value it in the future. At first this might seem reasonable: Would you rather have a dollar today or $1.05 a year from now? But similar to how a person seems smaller the greater their distance from us, the further into the future investors look, the less they value it.

The implications of this are disastrous for long-range thinking. Because of the exponential effects of compounding the discount rate year after year, the long-term future is valued at a tiny fraction of the present. Economist William Nordhaus won the Nobel Prize in 2018 after arguing for delaying action on climate change because, using a three percent discount rate, a thousand dollars' worth of damage occurring a century from now is equivalent to just fifty dollars today. The inventor of discounting, Frank Ramsey, declared in 1928 that discounting the welfare of future generations was "ethically indefensible and arises merely from the weakness of the imagination." Nevertheless, discount rates have become a ubiquitous planning methodology in businesses and governments alike.[4]

Interest-bearing fiat money therefore intrinsically generates scarcity, competition, and a structural requirement for endless economic growth, along with a reckless disregard for the future. It is a planetary-wide Ponzi scheme that can only be maintained for as long as the money supply continues to grow—and is consequently structurally incompatible with the ecologically driven requirement to decrease consumption and achieve a steady-state economy.

DEBT: THE FINANCIAL SUCTION PUMP

A major milestone in the takeover of fiat money occurred in 1971, when US President Nixon removed the nation from the international gold standard, putting an end to the convertibility of dollars into gold. Since then, as one might predict, with no tangible constraints on its creation, money has grown exponentially. At $21 trillion, the US money supply is now thirty times greater than in 1971. Debt loads have grown even faster, with nearly $100 trillion in debt obligations across all sectors of the US economy, more than fifty times the debt burden in 1971, and nearly four times the nation's GDP.

This debt overhang casts its shadow over every aspect of the economy, domestically and globally. Each year, the US federal government pays one third of what it receives in personal income taxes as interest on its debt. At the household level, roughly 10 percent of all disposable income is used for debt service, but the true impact is far greater than that, even for those who don't hold any debt. When economists analyze the amount of debt incorporated in every aspect of the supply chain, from raw material producers to traders, wholesalers, and retailers, they calculate that 35–40 percent of the price of everything you buy in the store goes to interest payments on debt—a hidden subsidy paid by everyone to the banks and wealthy elites.[5]

For those at the lower end of the wealth spectrum, the impact of debt goes from being burdensome to devastating. It's estimated that about one fifth of households in the UK and the US are unable to access mainstream credit and are forced to turn to predatory sources such as payday lenders, which typically offer extortionate short-term loans with rates as high as 400 percent along with additional fees. The average borrower facing this predicament is forced to take out eight or nine of these loans per year.

Globally, public debt has reached a breathtaking level of $100 trillion. For nations in the Global South, with $29 trillion in public debt, the implications are catastrophic as governments squeeze their populations' meager livelihoods to meet their obligations. Over three billion people now live in countries that spend more on interest payments than on healthcare or education.[6]

Where does all this money go? Much of it is funneled into the $31 trillion of wealth owned by the world's centimillionaires and billionaires, as discussed in the previous chapter. But what do they do with all this surplus money? The answer emerges from the process of financialization introduced in chapter 2: Money is invested in other financial assets in order to make even more money. The decisions made by the faceless money managers overseeing this process ultimately prioritize where investment funds will be channeled, shaping the policies of governments around the world to suit their wealthy owners' best interests rather than those of the people. "I'm going to tell you who my adversary is," said French socialist François Hollande running for the presidency in 2012. "My real adversary has no name, no face, no party, he will never run for office and will never be elected—and still he will rule. This adversary is the world of finance."

More broadly, the world of finance is the adversary of everyone who is not part of the moneyed elite raking in profits from it. The conventional story of money creation taught in university courses is that it fuels the productive economy, allowing entrepreneurs to build their businesses. In fact, the Bank of England reports that just eight percent of new money goes to finance real-world businesses. The remaining 92 percent goes to the financial sector, funding mortgage lending, commercial property, mergers and acquisitions, trading, and consumer credit. This has the effect of artificially inflating property prices to unaffordable levels for most people and exacerbating extreme inequalities. Even the expected cash flows from real-world industries such as water, timber, and food are now securitized (packaged and turned into tradable securities), further locking in structures of extraction.

Financialization has been turbocharged by advances in information technology that use algorithms for high-frequency trading, rewarding the few companies that can afford to invest in the required infrastructure. Trading firms spend hundreds of millions of dollars enhancing their computing networks to shave as little as three milliseconds off the timing of their trades. The hyper liquidity of global markets means that investors are obsessed with short-term market trends, which leads corporate CEOs, forever anxious about their stock price, to focus their time horizon on the next quarterly earnings report. The overall size of the financial marketplace, including derivatives (synthesized contracts betting on future price fluctuations of other securities), beggars the imagination: By some estimates it's as high as a quadrillion (a thousand trillion) dollars.

This immense size has sparked proposals for a financial transactions tax (FTT) imposed on all financial settlements. Such a tax would have significant benefits. Its proceeds could contribute significantly to funding Universal Basic Income (UBI) as described in the previous chapter. Beyond that, if it were applied at decreasing rates depending on the length of the security holding period, it would put an end to the giddy casino-like speculation that now characterizes the markets. For example, a punitive rate of 10 percent could be applied to securities held for less than a day, decreasing on a sliding scale to zero for securities held for more than ten years. The effects of this single step would be enormous, transforming the financial services industry overnight. High-frequency stock trading and same-day traders would disappear. The short-term orientation of the financial markets would be replaced by carefully considered long-term investment decisions, resulting in a tectonic shift away from destructive extractive industries and toward sustainable businesses.

While such a duration-based FTT would be highly beneficial, it merely targets a symptom rather than the underlying cause of our monetary system's malformation. What might be possible if we reconsider the way in which money itself is created?

SOVEREIGN MONEY

Let's step back and consider this situation from a broader perspective. Since money is something that can be created *ex nihilo*, simply by tapping keystrokes on a computer, we can legitimately view its creation as a power that should belong to the commonwealth (as defined in the previous chapter). Why has this godlike authority been handed to the banks—a set of private institutions? As profit-seeking businesses, they are driven to create as much debt as possible—a goal that is structurally misaligned with the public interest. While they reap the financial benefits of this power, they bear none of the responsibilities. As was seen clearly in the financial meltdown of 2008, when the banks fail, society bears the ultimate responsibility of bailing them out—in that case, to the tune of over a trillion dollars. How could this power be reclaimed for society at large?

The answer, it turns out, is relatively straightforward. It goes by the name of "sovereign money" and has been proposed multiple times over the past century, albeit to no avail. In a sovereign money system, money is created directly by the state rather than indirectly through private banks. The central bank would create the money, which could be injected by the government into the real economy through a combination of public spending, tax cuts, financing of credit to businesses, or direct payments to citizens (such as UBI). The central bank would determine independently of the government how much money is needed and, upon its creation, would transfer it to the government to choose how to use the funds. Instead of new money automatically increasing indebtedness, it could be used for social priorities such as infrastructure investment, transition from fossil fuels, business investment in depressed regions, and the development of robust universal basic services. Through a democratically elected government, the people—rather than the "Society of Money'd Men"—could choose where their money went.

A carefully considered proposal by the non-profit advocacy group Positive Money spells out how a modern sovereign monetary system would work. In place of conventional bank accounts, there would be two different types: transaction accounts and investment accounts. The central bank would hold the money in the transaction accounts which would be risk-free, and manage the behind-the-scenes payment system. Private banks would provide, for a fee, all other customer-oriented services such as ATM-issuance, online banking, and in-person bank branches. Anyone who wanted to earn extra interest on surplus money would place it in investment accounts, through which banks would aggregate deposits and lend the funds to those who needed credit. The banks themselves would not fund these loans, but would act as intermediaries between savers and borrowers.[7]

Positive Money, alongside other monetary experts, propose that the central bank issues its money in the form of digital cash, which could be credited directly to people's transaction accounts. This system would be particularly effective for the implementation of UBI, allowing the government to transfer a monthly stipend seamlessly to everyone.[8]

Such a centralized system does, however raise significant concerns both about privacy and equality of access for those on the wrong side of the "digital divide." Proponents have tried to address these concerns by suggesting a "cash-like" form of the currency using swipe cards—similar to the gift cards currently sold in stores—that electronically store money that can then be spent with the user's identity remaining anonymous. In conjunction with this, some proposals envisage the establishment of a postal banking system, allowing anyone to pick up a swipe card from their local post office and use it without needing access to their own high-tech devices.

In place of today's banks, which are structurally motivated to increase debt levels and squeeze creditors to maximize investor returns, some proposals envisage broad networks of local and regional community banks owned by their members and dedicated to their region's welfare. Community-based banks allow relationships of trust to develop, encouraging creditors' flexibility during the inevitable periods when debtor businesses or individuals encounter hard times.

A notable example of this kind of bank exists, rather surprisingly, in the United States heartland. The Bank of North Dakota (BND) is a public bank set up in 1919—the only one of its kind in the US—guided by its charter to "serve the people of North Dakota." It holds all state funds, its profits go into the state treasury to fund schools and social programs, and it offers extensive low-risk, local lending primarily through a network of independent community banks. With assets of over $10 billion, BND has been consistently profitable, sailing steadily through the 2008 financial meltdown that humbled many financial institutions, and has contributed significantly to the economic health of its state.

Crucially, a sovereign money system would allow our civilization to put an end to the giant Ponzi scheme of musical chairs by weaning itself off its debilitating debt addiction. Positive Money, among others, have floated the idea of a debt jubilee—a modern version of the process dating back to ancient Mesopotamia that periodically cleared all debts throughout society. The central bank could simply create money that the government would use to pay principal back to creditors, which would have a neutral effect on the money supply since—as the Bank of England explained—debt payment reduces the amount of money in the system.[9]

While a debt jubilee would represent a major shift toward an ecocivilization, its implementation would raise significant fairness issues. A thrifty family that had spent years living within their means would naturally feel resentment at profligate neighbors receiving what they might see as a government bailout. If a jubilee were conducted together with the rollout of UBI, one possible solution would be to earmark some portion of the UBI payment for the reduction of outstanding debts. While this would be a far more gradual process, it would likely be perceived as more equitable, and would eventually lead to an elimination of the debt overhang.

NON-MONETARY VALUE CREATION

Even with sovereign money, though, we haven't yet reached into the heart of what's needed to fully re-envision money for an ecocivilization. To get to the root of it, we must recognize the false identity capitalism has created between price and value. In the capitalist economy, the market price of something—the amount someone is willing to pay for it—tends to be defined by supply and demand, which in turn is equated with value. Generally speaking, something becomes valuable when it's scarce, and cheap when it's abundant. But most of what we truly value in our lives and in our world has nothing to do with a market price.

Consider the universal human needs identified by the economist Manfred Max-Neef in chapter 7—including such core requirements as affection, security, participation, creation, identity, and freedom. These have little to do with the monetary economy and when they are assimilated into it, the pricing of them corrodes their intrinsic value. You may remember the philosopher Michael Sandel's observation: "There are some things money should not buy," including areas such as health, education, and public safety. As the economist David Korten declares, "Money is not wealth." Instead, as he avers, "the foundation of the real wealth of contemporary society" exists in the mutual caring relationships of family and community and in the rich abundance of the living Earth—non-monetary bounty that is steadily being lost to the Windigo virus.[10]

What might a money system look like that reflects the value of these essential conditions for eudaimonia? To begin with, it's helpful to refer back to the four realms of the true economy identified by Kate Raworth: the market, the state, households, and the commons. Ever since the rise of capitalism, money creation has been controlled by the market. The sovereign money proposal would appropriate this capacity for the state. What about the two other realms—households and the commons? These have historically been marginalized by the capitalist economy which, through market pricing, has distorted our sense of value and made their crucial contributions to sustained wellbeing appear valueless.

This question has been explored in depth by David Bollier, one of the world's foremost theorists of the commons. Bollier points out that value is created in households, commons, and the living Earth primarily through complex and subtle interdependent relationships and norms, mostly centered around the mutually beneficial symbiosis that is a core principle of healthy living systems. Within households, there is the unpaid care economy (valued at over $11 trillion a year if its work were monetized) arising from the devotion and commitment of family members—usually women—in which value arises, not just from the time spent working, but from the love and generosity of spirit that is transmitted. Gift economies exist, not only in traditional Indigenous societies, but also in academic, online, and artistic communities in which there is a presumption of shared purpose and collective identity. And (as will be discussed in future chapters) an increasing number of enterprises are emerging in areas as diverse as technology, real estate, and healthcare, based on pooling resources for shared provisioning and collaboration, equity, and inclusion, instead of individual profit-seeking.[11]

These activities implicitly value certain types of behaviors that are required for a healthy society but inhibited by a market economy, such as care work, community self-reliance, and ecological regeneration. At a deeper level, the qualities of friendship, trust, and love that arise from our relational entanglements within living systems are either ignored or corroded by money, but are the source of some of our most treasured human experiences.

How could a money system motivate them all? Leading thinkers in the field have proposed that, rather than a single substitute for today's system, we take our inspiration once again from nature, and cultivate an ecosystem of money—encouraging the formation of several differentiated money systems for specific types of activities, which together can create a robust monetary habitat for long-term flourishing. What might that look like?

ALTERNATIVE FORMS OF MONEY

During the depths of the Great Depression in the 1930s, a small town in Austria called Wörgl became the unlikely epicenter of a financial metamorphosis. Facing unemployment of one third of the population, Wörgl's mayor, Michael Unterguggenberger, issued 10,000 schillings in scrip—money that doesn't qualify as legal tender—which he used to pay unemployed people to build and repair the town's streets, drains, and bridges. They spent their scrip, simply called "the Wörgl," in local shops, which was then used by shopkeepers to pay their local suppliers, and ultimately circulated back to the town through taxes. But the Wörgl notes came with an unusual wrinkle: They lost one percent of their value each month, unless the noteholders attached a stamp bought from the town council. As a result, people made sure to spend their Wörgls as soon as possible, which increased the speed at which it circulated, what economists call the velocity of the money.

The process of steadily reducing the value of a currency, known as demurrage, had been proposed decades earlier by the businessman Silvio Gesell as a means of stimulating economic vitality—and it worked like a dream. Wörgl rapidly became the only town in Austria with full employment, as townspeople built new houses, a reservoir, a ski jump, and a bridge. As news of the "Wörgl miracle" spread around the world, the French Prime Minister paid a visit to witness it first hand, and hundreds of other communities in Austria planned to use the system. But the Wörgl was too successful for its own good. The Austrian Central Bank panicked at the prospect of losing their currency monopoly and made it a criminal offense to issue Wörgls. Before long, the town of Wörgl was back to 30 percent unemployment.

This fascinating story illuminates the power of alternative currencies to transform a community by incentivizing specific behaviors. Notwithstanding the fears of the Austrian government, these currencies aren't intended to replace a national currency, but are complementary to it, fulfilling a need that's specific to a particular time and place. There are now thousands of complementary currencies in use around the world, and their numbers continue to grow rapidly. Even without a demurrage feature, they are frequently successful in increasing the local velocity of money, and their local circulation ensures that funds stay in the community, revitalizing neighborhood businesses rather than being sucked via corporate headquarters into the global financialized economy. Successful examples that have sprouted up worldwide include the Brixton pound in London, BerkShares in the Berkshire region of Massachusetts, and the Bangla-Pesa in a sprawling slum of Mombasa, Kenya, which allows hundreds of small traders—bakers, fruit-sellers, carpenters, and tailors—to keep their community vibrant even when they have barely enough of the official Kenyan shillings to survive.[12]

Complementary currencies can be combined with community banking to create a fertile alternative financial ecology. On the coast of Brazil, the growing city of Fortaleza displaced a population of 32,000 people who had made their living primarily from the sea. Having lost their livelihood, this community, Conjunto Palmeira, had virtually no way to earn the cash needed to buy goods. In 1998, with a modest grant of 800 euros from French donors, community organizers founded Banco Palmas to address unemployment and stimulate local spending. They offered microcredit to individuals and zero-interest loans to neighborhood businesses in a new "Palmas" currency, asking the merchants to put up signs saying they accepted Palmas for payment. This kickstarted the economy, leading to the creation of about 2,000 jobs, reducing crime rates, and increasing the portion of residents' needs purchased in the Palmeira district from 20 percent to 93 percent. Interestingly, the founders of both the Palmas and the Bangla-Pesa currencies were investigated by authorities suspicious of their activities, but in both cases they were exonerated once officials understood what they were doing, and now both currencies receive support from their governments.

Currencies can also be tailored to solve specific problems unique to a locale. In another Brazilian city, Curitiba, trash was overwhelming the shantytown favelas that had grown up along steep hills, because garbage trucks couldn't access the narrow, winding streets. Concurrently, the unemployed slum dwellers had no funds to travel to work elsewhere in the city using municipal transit. Mayor Jaime Lerner came up with a creative solution. He placed large bins at the edge of the favelas for different types of garbage—recyclable, compostable, and landfill—and paid people with bus tokens to collect and sort the garbage. Before long, the favelas were cleaned up and people began riding the buses downtown, frequently finding work. Meanwhile, people started using the tokens as a local currency in exchange for food. Inspired by the program's success, Lerner expanded it to restore historic buildings, create green areas, and renovate housing, all without burdening the municipal budget.

Another budding genus in the ecosystem of money is known as *mutual credit systems*, in which members trade goods and services with each other through an exchange. Each time a purchase occurs, one person's account is debited and the other's is credited by the same amount. By allowing participants to use whatever readily available skills or goods they have, communities can overcome the limitations caused by scarcity of cash and promote self-sufficiency. One person may cut hair, another fixes cars, another grows vegetables, and using mutual exchange, they can increase their community's wealth through their shared activities. A commonly used system is LETS—an acronym for "Local Exchange Trading System"—which originated in the Canadian town of Courtney in the 1980s when it suffered a 40 percent local unemployment rate. Since then, it has spread to dozens of countries around the world. A similar system originating in South Africa called the Cape Town Talent Exchange generated a Community Exchange System platform that provides off-the-shelf tools for communities to develop their own exchanges based on their particular needs.

A particularly empowering form of mutual credit is known as time banking, through which time itself becomes the exchange currency. Its simple defining feature is that every time you contribute an hour's work to someone else, you earn an hour's credit for work provided to you by someone else. It has an inherently equitable orientation by valuing each person's contribution equally: An hour spent caring for an ailing elder is valued as much as an hour spent fixing someone's car or painting someone's house. Time banking takes the person-to-person reciprocity of mutual exchange and expands it community-wide: Someone who benefits from an hour's work now owes an hour of their time to the community at large.

Time-banking has expanded to over thirty countries with thousands of networks exchanging over four million hours of mutual service. It has particularly flourished in Japan, where it goes by the name *fureai kippu* (literally "ticket for a caring relationship"). In a nation where 30 percent of the population is aged over 65, *fureai kippu* has emerged as a cooperative tool to address the challenges of elder care. People who help elders with shopping or personal services earn time credits, which they can give to older family members living elsewhere or redeem for themselves in later years. The system has received backing from the federal government and some localities, and in some areas has expanded to other forms of support, such as young parents needing childcare. Surveys find that recipients feel a personal connection unmatched by commercial caregiving, and helpers frequently become an extension of the family. Many recipients value the fact that, rather than passively receiving services, they can reciprocate in some form and participate in a network that fosters care as a collective social good.

Diverse as each of these forms of money are, they have one thing in common. They all share an understanding of money as a social construction that promotes particular types of behaviors and have been consciously designed for prosocial effect.

AN INTEGRATED MONETARY ECOSYSTEM

A core principle of every healthy living system is integration: a state of unity with differentiation, with each distinct part contributing to the fitness of the larger whole. As part of an ecocivilization, money has the potential to be transformed from its current role as a monolithic wrecker of wellbeing into a multitiered provider of differentiated social needs at scales ranging from local to planetary. The pioneering economist Bernard Lietaer has advanced a vision of such a monetary ecosystem, comprising a multitude of local cooperative currencies, dozens of regional and national currencies, various forms of international scrip, a few major multinational currencies, and a global reference currency.[13]

We can contemplate money in an ecocivilization in line with Lietaer's vision. Fiat money issuance would be the sole prerogative of central banks, which would transmit funds as needed for governments to allocate based on democratically determined priorities. The massive debt overhang currently devastating people's lives would become a relic of history, eliminated through a series of debt jubilees, perhaps in conjunction with UBI distribution. Demurrage may have an important role to play, both in local and global currencies. Within communities, it could stimulate the velocity of money as exemplified by the Wörgl, strengthening local economies. At the national and global level, it could act in the opposite way to the current practice of discounting, causing the future to be valued more highly and therefore favoring long-term projects that invest in the wellbeing of succeeding generations. Instead of being organized around the objectives of "Money'd Men," a diverse ecosystem of money in an ecocivilization could be consciously designed to enhance the current and future flourishing of all people.

POSSIBLE SECOND AND THIRD HORIZON CONTOURS | FINANCE

SECOND HORIZON

A financial transactions tax (FTT) imposed on all financial settlements

States transition to sovereign money, where central banks create money instead of private banks

Community-owned public banks play an increasing role in supplying credit to people and local businesses

A series of debt jubilees eliminates the debt overhang

Local complementary currencies are widely supported by policymakers as a means of community wealth-building

THIRD HORIZON

A graduated duration-based FTT virtually eliminates short-term trading in financial markets

Fiat money issuance is the sole prerogative of central banks, which governments allocate based on democratically determined priorities.

UBI administered through digital cash accessible through smartphones or low-tech swipe cards available at local post offices

An ecosystem of money with a multitude of local cooperative currencies, regional and national currencies, and a global reference currency

Demurrage strengthens local economies and encourages long-term investment

FOR CONSIDERATION

What Second and Third Horizon ideas arise in your own mind inspired by this chapter?

CHAPTER 12

TECHNOLOGY: DISTRIBUTED INFORMATION FOR COLLECTIVE EMPOWERMENT

"DON'T BE EVIL"

Sam Altman, Elon Musk, and other prominent figures in Silicon Valley decided the time was right. It was 2015, and although the idea of a superhuman artificial general intelligence (AGI) had been the subject of speculation for decades, they now believed it was potentially within reach. Like the Omega Team of Max Tegmark's cautionary tale (discussed in chapter 8), they wanted the project they devised, in the words of their announcement, "to benefit humanity as a whole," and structured their new company, OpenAI, as a nonprofit "unconstrained by a need to generate financial return" with the aim to "build value for everyone rather than just shareholders."[1]

Stirring words, but things didn't work out quite that way. The first seismic shift occurred in 2019, when the team (now without Musk who had quit) realized that building advanced AI required processing massive amounts of data at enormous cost, which they could only fund through significant private investment. But they wanted to remain true to their original vision. Accordingly, they created a special kind of capped-profit entity which, they said at the time, would "increase our ability to raise capital while still serving our mission." It was a carefully conceived solution designed "to put our overall mission—ensuring the creation and adoption of safe and beneficial AGI—ahead of generating returns for investors." Early funders could receive returns up to 100 times their initial investment, but anything in excess would be transferred to the original nonprofit. To ensure the integrity of their structure, the company was controlled by the OpenAI non-profit's board—a majority of whom would have no financial stake in the enterprise—with a "primary fiduciary duty to humanity." As a further sign of faith, Altman took no equity himself in the new entity.[2]

It was an impressive arrangement, which, nevertheless, unraveled spectacularly four years later. In November 2023, the OpenAI board announced they were firing Altman, primarily because they no longer trusted that he was prioritizing their mission of safety and transparency in his rush to commercialize AI—shocking news that did, however, seem to validate the integrity of the corporate structure. Chaos ensued: Company president Greg Brockman quit in protest, then Altman and Brockman immediately accepted jobs at Microsoft—a major OpenAI investor. In the following days, 95 percent of OpenAI employees threatened to join them there. The humiliated board quickly backed down and rehired Altman and Brockman, with several board members resigning—to be replaced by reliable Silicon Valley insiders.[3]

The final nail in the coffin of good intentions was struck in September 2024, when news broke that OpenAI would no longer be controlled by the now defanged nonprofit board. Instead, it would become an uncapped for-profit corporation, in which Altman himself would hold a stake potentially worth billions. As the company's leading safety researchers quit in droves, OpenAI announced plans for $6.5 billion in new funding, which it completed in October 2025, making it the world's most valuable privately held company.[4]

OpenAI is, of course, not alone in its flip-flop. When Google (now Alphabet) launched its IPO in 2004, the company led with a catchy motto, "Don't be evil"—which has since been replaced in its code of conduct by "Do the right thing" as Alphabet delves into military contracts, user profiling, and surveillance technologies while reaping monopoly profits. Although advanced technology—now propelled by the rise of AI—has important unique characteristics, this story demonstrates how much it remains beholden ultimately to Windigo's Law: "Capital will never cease to exploit any new opportunity that arises in its perpetual quest for greater returns." We will see in this chapter how the pervasive influence of capitalism ensures that any technology developed within its system—no matter how potentially beneficial—will ultimately be used to intensify the forces of extraction and exploitation while further priming the wealth pump.

A widespread modern view of technology's social impact is that technology itself is value-neutral: What matters is how people choose to use it. In this conception, a gun is neither good nor bad—human beings are the ones who make it so. After all, society can always choose to beat swords into ploughshares. While this seems, on the surface, to be self-evident, it ignores the far-reaching systemic impacts that technological innovation may cause through the new capabilities, possibilities, and expectations it creates. For example, a technology such as nuclear power naturally leads to massive investment and centralized control, whereas solar panels create potential to decentralize energy by bringing self-sufficiency to remote communities.

Technological innovation frequently brings multilayered waves of social consequences that are often unintended and not even considered when the technology is being developed. The Consilience Project—a team of interdisciplinary experts—explains how the development of the automobile, for example, profoundly impacted society by shifting humanity's perception of time and space, influencing urban layouts, spawning new industries, and reshaping relationships, communities, and recreation. The same can be said of other major innovations such as radio, telephones, airplanes, television, and the internet.

By taking a systems-based view of technology, we can recognize a complex bidirectional interplay between technology and society: While a new technology can profoundly alter social structures, the economic and political context determines what attracts research and investment, how it's developed, and ultimately how it's commercialized and marketed to the public. For example, even though solar power offers the potential for decentralized energy, it has also led to the construction of massive centralized solar arrays covering thousands of acres with capacity measured in gigawatts. Which option do you think attracts more investment dollars? While technology may specify the range of options available, the collective choices we make as a society ultimately direct which options get developed and how they affect our future.

This is the complex interplay we'll explore in this chapter. By doing so, even as we trace the relentless onslaught of Windigo's Law, we will also come across fascinating hints that, by setting radically different initial conditions, advanced technology has the potential to provide a transformative set of capacities that could facilitate and even accelerate a global swerve toward an ecocivilization.

THE PATH TO DIGITAL FEUDALISM

The mid-1990s were heady years for techno-enthusiasts. The World Wide Web was going mainstream with user-friendly web browsers making it easy to use nascent e-commerce sites like Amazon and eBay, while people started meeting each other on Match.com. Inspired by these developments, poet John Perry Barlow wrote an exhilarating Declaration of the Independence of Cyberspace in 1996 that went viral, announcing a new era of freedom and equity:

> Governments of the Industrial World, you weary giants of flesh and steel, I come from Cyberspace, the new home of Mind . . .
>
> I declare the global social space we are building to be naturally independent of the tyrannies you seek to impose on us . . .
>
> We are creating a world where anyone, anywhere may express his or her beliefs, no matter how singular, without fear of being coerced into silence or conformity.
>
> Your legal concepts of property, expression, identity, movement, and context do not apply to us . . .
>
> We believe that from ethics, enlightened self-interest, and the commonweal, our governance will emerge.
>
> May it be more humane and fair than the world your governments have made before.[5]

How times have changed! While Barlow was right about the transformative effect of the internet, he failed to recognize how the forces of capitalism would commandeer its revolutionary new potential. The ensuing decades have seen the rise of social media platforms, the explosion of mobile internet usage through smartphones, and the domination of the "Big Five"—Facebook, Apple, Amazon, Microsoft, Google—whose strategies, along with other major platforms (collectively "Big Tech"), shape much of the social, political, and cultural contours of our age.

Since Barlow's declaration, the internet has become an essential enabler of virtually every aspect of human activity, permeating the way we conduct business, organize travel, order food, connect socially, spend recreation time, and learn about the world. The precious resource of this new digital economy is data: the digital trails of what we say, where we go, what we like, and how we're feeling. This gargantuan data flow (known as "Big Data") is collected, analyzed, and sold at a premium to advertisers. In most cases, the value of a platform to users increases as a function of the number of other people using it, which is known as a network effect. Because of this, the largest platforms keep getting larger, so the data they process become even more valuable to advertisers. The virtual nature of the platforms allows them to scale rapidly and cheaply across the world without needing a physical presence in each country. These dynamics, combined with aggressive anti-competitive strategies by market leaders, have led to the concentration of wealth and power in fewer and fewer hands. Today, the Big Five alone account for roughly 25 percent of the S&P 500's market capitalization.

The reach of the major social media companies now surpasses that of any state or cultural institution. Each month, three billion people—more than one third of humanity—log on to Facebook. This is more than double the number of baptized Catholics (the world's largest religious organization) or the population of China (the world's largest country). When people log on, the meticulously engineered addictive qualities of the platforms ensure they stay there. The 2.7 billion active users of YouTube watch over a billion hours of content on it each day.[6]

The collection and analysis of Big Data extend beyond people to what is known as the Internet of Things: the network of everything embedded with sensors that enables the physical world to be digitally monitored and controlled. This vast unseen network, which includes smart thermostats, fitness trackers, security and surveillance systems, vehicles, and livestock tags, already connects over 15 billion devices and is expected to double or triple in size within a decade. Finally, since data is also the crucial ingredient for training AI models, it is not surprising that the major platforms are now dominating the race to make AI usage ubiquitous around the world.

While power has concentrated at the top, increasing numbers of people reliant on these platforms for their livelihood have been reduced to the precarity of the gig economy: unstable and insecure contract work that is poorly paid, lacking benefits or workplace protections. It's estimated that over a third of the US workforce are now gig workers, a number expected to rise to over half in a few years. Platforms such as Uber and Airbnb use their political muscle to systematically block efforts by local jurisdictions to regulate their activities. Under what the author Shoshana Zuboff calls "surveillance capitalism," workers are subjected to devices that track every movement they make, feeding algorithms that determine their pay level, or even continued employment, based on efficiency rankings. Amazon's delivery drivers have been reported to "skip meals, rush through stop signs, and tape their phones to their pant legs so they could easily glance down at the screens, all to meet the challenging delivery deadlines." Those who failed to meet them were fired. Extrapolating these trends, some observers warn about a future of "digital feudalism" in which most people's disempowerment resembles that of medieval peasants indentured to their (now digital) overlords.[7]

TECHNOLOGY OUT OF ALIGNMENT

This constant surveillance leaves workers feeling anxious, tense, and angry, and has significant health consequences, pushing people's bodies into a state of perpetual hypervigilance, which releases stress chemicals known to aggravate heart problems and lead to depression. The impact of ubiquitous social media on adolescents is equally troubling. In a rivalry described by the technology ethicist Tristan Harris as "the race to the bottom of the brainstem," Big Tech companies compete with each other to hook victims to their platforms by manipulating their biases and emotions. This has caused a significant increase in mental health problems among adolescents, including sleep disruption, body image concerns (particularly among girls), cyberbullying, and addictive behaviors, with increasing self-harm and suicidal behaviors.[8]

While the impact of this fine-tuned manipulation on individual psyches is somewhat predictable, the pernicious consequences to our collective psyche have largely been unintended but are alarming. The public sphere, which until recently has been maintained by a confluence of traditional media, academic institutions, news organizations, governments, and the public itself, has now been privatized by the large-scale algorithmic curation of the major platforms, which coordinate and steer the opinions and actions of billions of people. Their concern, however, is not to facilitate wise collective decision-making, but to increase advertising revenues by maximizing engagement. Since false news stories have been shown to reach six times as many people as true stories, these are emphasized by the selection algorithms. Recognizing this, politically motivated special interest groups use the platforms to intensify polarization by spreading malicious propaganda, which, in a reinforcing feedback loop, further increases engagement and profits for Big Tech. The shared sensemaking that is fundamental to a healthy society is thus being systematically shredded, leading to widespread epistemic chaos fraught with bizarre conspiracy theories adopted as facts by an increasingly disoriented population. Since the term psychologists use for a person losing touch with reality is psychosis, it is not overstating the case to describe this dynamic as an onset of collective psychosis.

Realizing this threat, China's government has taken a different tack by responding aggressively to social media companies, cracking down on major platforms, and appropriating control of their activities. Through a combination of the "Great Firewall," which filters out information troublesome for the government, and the imposition of massive online surveillance, China's approach presages a digital totalitarian dystopia. Its Social Credit System, described as "the most ambitious experiment in digital social control ever undertaken," monitors and regulates the financial, social, moral, and political behavior of Chinese citizens through a system of punishments and rewards. Those with high scores enjoy special privileges, such as priority for school admissions and employment, tax breaks, and jumping the queue for public housing; those with low scores are punished with denial of licenses and permits, restricted access to credit and public services, and even public shaming.[9]

The surging ascendance of AI can be expected to exacerbate all these dynamics by further consolidating concentration of power, intensifying the manipulation of individual behaviors, deepening collective psychosis through engineered lies spread by bots, and augmenting surveillance techniques by orders of magnitude. With all the myriad potential benefits that AI promises, the context in which it is developed remains all-important. As discussed in chapter 8, the AI "alignment problem" debated by technology theorists can only be properly addressed by grappling with the profound alignment problem already confronting us in the form of global capitalism—while confronting the alternative peril of a misaligned all-powerful surveillance state.

At the same time, it is important to recognize that the advent of digital platforms has brought an array of extraordinary benefits. Many of us are grateful for the improved access to information, online communities, and flexible, on-demand services. If we consider the platforms themselves separately from their ownership structure, we can view the new opportunities they create to be potentially highly beneficial. They provide an invaluable function by connecting people to goods, services, and each other. The data that is generated could potentially be used for the benefit of society at large, and algorithms could be reconfigured to build epistemic coherence rather than disintegrate it. What, we must ask, would advanced technology look like if it were developed in alignment with the principles of an ecocivilization, rather than those of Windigo, Inc?

CONVIVIAL TECHNOLOGIES

In 1973, the theologian and social philosopher Ivan Illich coined a potent new term in his book *Tools for Conviviality.* Even before the onset of Big Tech, Illich recognized how "as the power of machines increases, the role of persons more and more decreases to that of mere consumers." Convivial tools, he explained, refers to technologies that inspire creativity and autonomy, giving "each person who uses them the greatest opportunity to enrich the environment with the fruits of his or her vision." Consistent with principles of an ecocivilization that emphasize the value of autonomy within community, Illich declared, "I consider conviviality to be individual freedom realized in personal interdependence and, as such, an intrinsic ethical value." Convivial tools, in contrast to "proprietary closed tools . . . are fundamentally empowering." Specifically:

> Tools foster conviviality to the extent that they can be easily used, by anybody, as often or as seldom as desired, for the accomplishment of a purpose chosen by the user. The use of such tools by one person does not restrain another from using them equally. They do not require previous certification of the user. Their existence does not impose any obligation to use them. They allow the user to express his meaning in action.

Illich's definition of tools was expansive, referring not just to tangibles like computers, but also to infrastructure and socially constructed institutions such as schools, bureaucracies, and money.[10]

We've already come across examples of convivial tools in earlier chapters, such as agroecology, seed banks, and complementary currencies. When applied to advanced technology, this conception provides a fundamentally different standpoint from which to operate than the current closed system of centralized control. Consider the internet itself. Originally developed by the US Department of Defense to facilitate resource sharing and collaboration among researchers, its open-source protocols and networked communication capabilities make it a quintessential example of a convivial tool. Facebook's protocols, by contrast, are proprietary and designed to maximize the company's profit by manipulating its three billion users—no different, in essence, from the enclosure of the commons that inaugurated capitalism centuries ago in Europe. The data that has enriched Big Tech companies evokes another example. Why should that data, which arises from our own collective behavior, belong to private corporations? Why is it not considered another component of the treasure trove of collective human knowledge and experience defined in chapter 10 as the commonwealth—a shared asset that by rights belongs to all who generated it?

The contrasting examples of Big Tech's profit-maximization and China's social control highlight two distinct dangers arising from closed systems. Whether in the hands of private corporations or centralized governments, our data is vulnerable to grievous abuse. Recognizing this, some forward-thinking industry analysts have advanced the idea of data trusts that would transfer the control of people's data to an autonomous legal body acting as custodian and steward of the data set. Trustees would negotiate with technology companies on behalf of their beneficiaries—for example, all users of a social media platform—for a fair share of the value generated by their data, the proceeds of which would be distributed to every beneficiary. Regional data sets, held in trust, with information on traffic, housing, or tourism, could be anonymized and shared with municipal governments allowing better decision-making on local issues directly impacting residents' lives.[11]

Along with proposals for data trusts, other industry critics suggest either breaking up the Big Five or alternatively regulating them in a form similar to other "natural monopolies" such as utility companies. While each of these proposals would represent an important step away from the dystopia of centralized digital feudalism we are currently approaching, they represent "second horizon" solutions—significantly disrupting business as usual but within the same economic paradigm. Let us now turn to the medley of transformative convivial ideas setting the contours for a "third horizon" solution set that could delineate the shape of advanced technology within an ecocivilization.

DISTRIBUTING INFORMATION AND POWER

What do you think is the largest structure ever engineered on Earth? The surprising answer is not something human-made but a vast termite complex discovered in Brazil comprising 200 million interconnected mounds covering an area roughly the size of Great Britain. Termites construct their elaborate structures replete with pillars, arches, tunnels, chambers, and even ventilation shafts, without any centralized controller or blueprint. In a process called *stigmergy*, they leave traces of pheromone (a signaling hormone) that draw other termites to their work, each termite contributing to a collective intelligence that is decentralized, coordinated, adaptable, and scalable.

The early internet, as celebrated by John Perry Barlow, can be understood as a model of human stigmergy before it was hijacked by Windigo,

Inc. Realizing this, and inspired by the capacity of self-organization omnipresent in nature, a new generation of web designers are collaborating worldwide to restore information and power to ordinary people. The umbrella term "Commons-Based Peer Production," coined by the Harvard professor Yochai Benkler in 2002, refers to a vision of tech-enhanced stigmergy, in which individuals cooperate with each other to generate shared resources without hierarchical control. Notable examples of such high-tech stigmergy are the free encyclopedia Wikipedia, the open source operating system GNU/Linux, and the browser Firefox.[12]

These are iconic convivial tools. Large numbers of contributors have open access to the operating infrastructure, freedom to choose how to contribute, differentiated skills, and the ability to work autonomously while merging and integrating their work with other modules. Quality control is frequently conducted through peer-review. The work produced is usually made accessible through an innovative legal structure called a Creative Commons license, which grants all users the right to copy, modify, and distribute the work freely—but under the crucial condition that any new versions must be made available with the same rights. An essential feature of this peer-to-peer collaboration is that the information needed to perform the work is freely available. In contrast to the centralized control structures of Big Tech, the digital data produced is replicated and shared transparently across multiple servers in what is known as a "distributed ledger."[13]

Commons-based peer production can also leverage advanced technology to transform how the offline world operates. Since the rise of neoliberal globalization, transnational corporations have employed a command-and-control strategy to move manufacturing to the cheapest regions, protect their designs through intellectual property, and transport products through fossil fuel–based shipping to global markets. Now, a new generation of engineers are inverting this model with what is known as cosmo-local production. Making a distinction between what is light (knowledge and ideas) and heavy (physical products such as machinery or cars), cosmo-local producers share intellectual property freely as a creative commons, allowing local manufacturers to customize designs based on their regional needs.

In the same year that Benkler coined the term commons-based peer production, the MIT professor Neil Gershenfeld helped a science education center in India design the first distributed fabrication laboratory ("Fab Lab"). With Gershenfeld's help, the Vigyan Ashram center customized high-tech blueprints developed at MIT to design local versions of products which they manufactured with low-cost materials and traditional tools, such as a pedal-powered generator, egg incubator, and weather data logger. Since then, Fab Labs have grown into a decentralized international network of researchers, inventors, and community entrepreneurs with approximately 2,500 centers spanning 125 countries. Following stigmergy principles, once a project is conceived, designs are shared in the network for mutual collaboration, while various prototypes are produced and tested locally. The design scope is almost limitless, including sensors for Indian farmers to measure the fat content of their milk and radio collars for Norwegian herders to track their reindeer.[14]

Cosmo-local production continues to expand into multiple domains such as pharmaceuticals, agriculture, and robotics, driven by visionary engineers determined to redesign, not just products, but the entire paradigm of production. Leveraging breakthroughs in 3D printing, which can utilize a wide range of materials including plastics, metals, and composites, these initiatives provide a tantalizing glimpse of a democratized industrial future structured around community needs rather than capital accumulation. A Global Village Construction set, created by the Missourian physicist and farmer Marcin Jakubowski, offers downloadable designs for fifty machines from brick makers to bread ovens and wind turbines. Following this success, Jakubowski and colleagues launched an Open Building Institute that, along with another initiative, WikiHouse, offers open-source designs for local construction of economical, off-grid, zero-carbon houses. Elsewhere, FarmHack and L'Atelier Paysans allow farmers to manufacture their own equipment, and RepRap offers free 3D printers that can also replicate themselves.

Building on the success of peer-to-peer enterprises, innovators are exploring how to apply these principles to platforms like those run by Uber, Airbnb, and TaskRabbit. These entities, sometimes referred to as "Death Star" platforms, are prime instigators of digital feudalism, spuriously calling themselves the "sharing economy" while extracting vast amounts of value from their contractors, sucking wealth out of local communities into billionaires' getaways and tax havens. In contrast, collaborative enterprises called "platform cooperatives" offer a preview of a true sharing economy that might someday replace them.[15]

Platform cooperatives are based on the idea that people offering their services should have a meaningful say in how their platform is run, applying the principles of the worker cooperative movement discussed in chapter 8 to high-tech platforms. They are collectively owned and organized around the dignity and empowerment of their users, with no surveillance algorithms dominating their lives. The 20–40 percent commissions siphoned off by the Death Star platforms can instead provide a decent income for the service-providers themselves. Beyond that, workers' data can be transportable, meaning that if someone changes the platform they're working for, their digital rating can go with them so they don't lose the reputation they've built up. Early examples of successful platform co-ops include Stocksy, which sells stock-photography online, Up & Go, which offers home and commercial cleaning services, and the New York–based Drivers Cooperative.[16]

These pioneering models hint at the potential of technology to transform society beneficially by inverting dominant power structures through data being distributed rather than centrally controlled. However, some tech trailblazers believe we can go further, realizing that the capabilities opened up by advanced technology could lead to a metamorphosis of many aspects of our society, ranging from money issuance to democratic governance. They are consciously prefiguring the reformulation of the world system into one aligned with the principles of the commons, one that could structurally motivate the prosocial behavior that would underlie an ecocivilization.

REINVENTING THE COMMONS WITH TECHNOLOGY

What comes to your mind when you hear the word blockchain? Quite possibly, you may think of Bitcoin: the crypto-currency attracting speculative traders with wild market swings that represents the worst kind of casino capitalism. Bitcoin was one of the first initiatives to use blockchain, which is a specific type of distributed ledger that is theoretically incorruptible. Every transaction executed on a blockchain is synchronized and stored throughout the network for anyone to see, which means there is no need for a centralized agent such as a bank to act as a trusted third party. Sometimes referred to as a "trustless" mechanism, blockchains offer the possibility of creating an alternative economy that bypasses conventional centralized institutions.

Bitcoin is a cautionary example of how any technology developed within a capitalist context can be corrupted by Windigo's Law. Its trustless mechanism relies on "mining," a process that allows anyone to verify a transaction by solving increasingly complex mathematical equations and earn new bitcoins as compensation. The unfettered marketplace for Bitcoin mining has led to frenzied competition to solve ever more complex equations, with vast warehouses holding "rigs" of advanced computers consuming massive amounts of electricity, with the result that the carbon emissions from Bitcoin processing are now equivalent to that of a mid-size country such as Sweden or Argentina.

However, it is important to distinguish between Bitcoin as a currency and blockchain as a protocol. Another blockchain-based currency known as Ethereum has reduced its energy consumption by 99.95 percent by developing an alternative trustless mechanism that doesn't require costly "mining." More generally, a worldwide community of innovators is exploring the potentially revolutionary possibilities opened up by the blockchain protocol. Viewing the first instantiation of the internet as Web 1.0, and the rise of centralized platforms as Web 2.0, they are collectively articulating a new paradigm for internet-based collaboration they call Web3: a decentralized web that, by design, cannot be controlled by any single entity.

The potential of Web3 arises from the fact that blockchains can be embedded with small snippets of code called "smart contracts" that can automatically enforce and execute agreements without the need for a central authority. Building on a conception of Ethereum's founder, Vitalik Buterin, in 2014, communities of developers began experimenting with what they called Decentralized Autonomous Organizations (DAOs)—self-governing, blockchain-based entities that could execute payments, enforce contracts, and levy penalties without any centralized controller.

A particularly intriguing feature of DAOs is the ability to incentivize beneficial behaviors within the community by granting tokens that can represent shares of ownership or governance rights. Some DAOs simply emulate the capitalist model by granting tokens based on a member's financial investment; but other DAOs grant reputational tokens earned through participation rather than financial contributions. Thus, DAOs can be set up to reward and empower members based on whatever the group values most highly from the outset. A social media DAO, for example, could automatically reward those who build community through engaging generatively with others, and penalize the propagation of falsehoods.

Some have realized the overlap between DAO affordances and the core design principles for successful cooperation enumerated by Elinor Ostrom and further developed by David Sloan Wilson (as discussed in chapter 6). These design principles, such as equitable distribution of benefits, transparency of behavior, and graduated responses to helpful and unhelpful conduct, are natural candidates for commons-based governance using blockchain. Inspired by this, groups with names such as the "Commons Stack" have been formed that offer technical tools and frameworks to help initiatives succeed as decentralized, regenerative, self-governing communities that reward people's collaborative instincts.[17]

In just a few years, the number of DAOs has mushroomed to roughly 50,000 entities with more than ten million token holders. Undergirding many of the Web3 entities is Ethereum. More than just a currency, Ethereum is a decentralized, networked protocol not controlled by any single entity, consciously designed in composable, reusable segments like Lego bricks, to facilitate the self-organized process of stigmergy among its users—a definitive convivial technology.

At this early stage of its evolution, the Web3 ecosystem is multifaceted and chaotic. DAOs are subject to the same dynamics that have corrupted other promising developments, and many of them simply exploit innovative tools to create business partnerships or marketplaces for profit. Analysts question whether "trustless" platforms can ever truly supplant face-to-face social relations and collective governance, causing some groups to experiment with hybrid online-and-offline versions. In spite of these open issues, DAOs hint at the possibility for distributed technology to transfigure many aspects of the capitalist economy. By applying Web3 protocols to platform cooperatives and cosmo-local production networks, the potential exists for a worldwide, collaborative, self-governing economy to emerge that bypasses legacy institutions and eliminates the risk of takeover from Windigo, Inc.[18]

While the Web3 community is dispersed broadly around the world, it remains a niche characterized primarily by young, predominantly male, tech-savvy developers. Other pioneers working to democratize information and power have taken a different path, intent on making distributed technology easily available for everyone, no matter their level of technical sophistication.

Countering the pernicious toxicity of profit-driven social media, some networks have linked up to form a "fediverse": an interoperable web of social media platforms using common protocols designed for community-building. In some parts of the world, a concurrence of circumstances has aligned to create conditions for technology to be an enabler of deepening democracy and social participation. The nation of Estonia, a recognized pioneer of digital democracy, has made 99 percent of public services available online along with a comprehensive digital healthcare system, reducing bureaucracy and achieving unparalleled levels of government transparency and trust.

In Taiwan, the government responded in 2014 to student protests by inviting student leaders to help transform their governance. One of them, Audrey Tang, was appointed the first "Digital Affairs Minister" two years later, and has helped architect a pioneering e-government program that allows citizens to easily find any information about their government and to access and download all personal information the government holds about them. Additionally, as will be discussed further in chapter 14, Tang oversaw development of an innovative platform named vTaiwan to combat political polarization by empowering citizens with deliberative, consensual decision-making regarding contentious issues facing the nation.

ALTERNATIVE VISION FOR TECHNOLOGY

Within the current dominant economic regime, these glimpses of a benevolent future enabled by technology remain just that—mere glimpses. As the cautionary tale of OpenAI highlights, even well-intentioned initiatives will succumb to the power of Windigo, Inc. if they are developed within the capitalist framework. There is a systematic inevitability to the process: An entrepreneur with a good idea will only get funding to develop it if investors see significant profit potential. The more successful the initiative, the greater the pressure on founders to monetize the benefits of their products as rapidly as possible and remain ahead of the competition. Once network effects set in, the dominant players—now under the sway of the capital markets—have the financial muscle to overcome and absorb any alternatives to their model.

As Audrey Tang points out, the conflict that has emerged between technology and democracy is not inevitable—it is an investment choice. Platform cooperatives may create as much value, or more, than Death Star platforms, but the benefits would be widely dispersed rather than rewarding early investors with outsize returns. Social media platforms designed to strengthen the social fabric don't entice as many eyeballs as those utilizing polarizing algorithms, and therefore earn less in advertising revenues and fail to attract investment. This is why deep systemic change in our world's operating system is required for more benevolent potentialities of technology to predominate. In the meantime, however, even within our current system, innovative second horizon policies can be enacted to nurture the shoots of beneficial third horizon technological configurations.

Assertive governmental enforcement of existing anti-trust legislation could open up possibilities of transformative change from within the system. If monopolistic entities were regulated more like public utilities, governments could mandate structural platform changes that decentralize data distribution and power. Beyond data trusts, proposals exist to require data portability for gig workers, so they can change platforms without losing the reputation they've built up. Other ideas include a portable Individual Security Account assigned to each worker, requiring Death Star platforms to contribute funding that could be steered into established worker safety nets such as Social Security, Medicare, and unemployment compensation funds. Governance of social media giants such as Facebook could be handed over to broadly distributed panels of ordinary users who could democratically determine the choice of algorithms for automated sharing of posts, using consensus-building technologies similar to that employed by the vTaiwan platform.

Other proposals call for the creation of state investment funds to disrupt the current closed loop of wealth creation dominated by private venture funds. For example, a Public Platform Accelerator could invest in alternative not-for-profit platforms designed to maximize utility for their users and workers with multi-stakeholder democratic governance. Following the cosmo-local and Ethereum models, platforms would incorporate composable plug-and-play designs that could be prototyped in one locality and customized by developers in other regions—a process known as fractal scaling, whereby multiple unique designs based on common principles can be employed at scale around the world.

This alternative vision would require massive funding. Where would that come from? The Swedish economist Rudolf Meidner proposed in the 1970s a plan for the gradual democratization of the Swedish economy by requiring major corporations to issue new shares each year, equivalent to 20 percent of their profits, into trusts designated for the benefit of their workers. Meidner calculated that, within a few decades, the Swedish economy would be controlled by workers rather than business owners. Not surprisingly, the Meidner Plan, facing powerful opposition from wealthy elites, was watered-down and eventually dismantled in the 1980s. In light of the existential crisis of technology confronting society today, however, some experts have proposed a revised version of the Meidner Plan to fund this alternative technological ecosystem.[19]

This points to an important theme that will become ever more prominent throughout this book: that each separate component leading toward an ecocivilization might seem unattainable on its own, but combined with other components discussed elsewhere, begins to weave a coherent movement toward transformative change. For example, the triple bottom line requirement for large corporations discussed in chapter 8 would obviate the need for a revised Meidner Plan: If companies failed to meet their obligations to workers and to the public, "equity fines" could be used to redistribute their shares to non-financial stakeholders.

Ultimately, society needs to recognize that technology, like money issuance, is something too important to be left to a system structurally designed to shred social cohesion for the sake of increasing the wealth of a small elite. The beneficial potentials unveiled by advanced technology are prodigious. If developed skillfully and at scale, they might reveal that a gateway to a prosocial ecocivilization is closer than we realized.

POSSIBLE SECOND AND THIRD HORIZON CONTOURS | TECHNOLOGY

SECOND HORIZON

Big Tech platforms broken up and/or regulated stringently as "natural monopolies" to decentralize data distribution and power

Big Tech platforms compelled to transfer control of data to data trusts which act on behalf of users, negotiating for a fair share of value generated

Commons-based peer production, such as cosmo-local networks and Fab Labs, receive legislative and tax support from national and local governments

Platform cooperatives receive significant government investment and support (through an updated version of the Meidner Plan) to develop alternatives to the dominant "Death Star" platforms

DAOs (or similarly conceived structures) gain prominence as alternative prosocial forms of organizing online communities

Internet-based government transparency and accessibility expands, following models such as Estonia and Taiwan

THIRD HORIZON

Open-source cosmo-local production becomes the default process for engineers and entrepreneurs to conceptualize, design, and bring to market new products

Platform cooperatives are the default structure for distributing and offering online services and products

DAOs (or similarly conceived structures) predominate allowing online communities to interact based on principles of prosocial behavior

All citizens have full internet access to government services and data about them, and can engage in internet-based consensus-building public policy decision-making

FOR CONSIDERATION

What Second and Third Horizon ideas arise in your own mind inspired by this chapter?

CHAPTER 13

INFRASTRUCTURE: DESIGNING BUILT SYSTEMS FOR COMMUNAL WELLBEING

In 1949, in what became known as the Great Transportation Conspiracy, General Motors, Standard Oil of California, Mack Trucks, Firestone, and Phillips Petroleum were found guilty of criminal conspiracy. Over decades, they had bought up tramlines and train companies in cities across the United States and shut them down, forcing people to use private automobiles and buses instead. An internal memo at Mack Truck explained how the losses incurred would be "more than justified by the business and gross profit flowing out of this move in years to come." In cities like San Diego, Los Angeles, and Baltimore, in the words of one journalist, "mass transit didn't just die—it was murdered."[1]

Another example of corporations destroying human wellbeing for the sake of profits? Yes, but a deeper analysis of the story reveals a greater truth about the dynamics of building infrastructure in a world dominated by Windigo, Inc. Even without their criminal intervention, urban tramlines in the United States were dying out. The traffic from private automobiles using the same roads as tramlines caused unacceptable delays, and as cities spread out, the cost of investing in more rail infrastructure became prohibitive. In fact, General Motors and their co-conspirators were merely speeding up the death of a public transportation system that, although in the best interests of most city-dwellers, was no longer viable without public intervention. The greater lesson from this story is that, along with technology, money, agriculture, and other civilizational domains we've already investigated, urban design is too important to leave to the untrammeled vicissitudes of market forces, with or without criminal corporate interference.

For most of history, city dwellers accounted for a small minority of the human population. This has changed dramatically. Whereas only one city (Beijing) had more than a million inhabitants in 1800, that number has swelled to over 1,500 cities, with thirty-four megacities holding more than ten million. Urban areas now account for the majority of humankind, most of our resource use, and 90 percent of the world's GDP. By mid-century, urban population is expected to increase to two-thirds of humanity. Most of this growth will occur in the Global South, where rural dwellers, displaced by land grabs, famines, and wars, join the unplanned sprawl of megacities such as Jakarta and Lagos, mostly surviving in slums and informal settlements without access to proper housing or basic services.

The human future is urban, and the way cities are designed will fundamentally affect the quality of life, not just of city-dwellers, but of all humanity and the Earth from which we draw resources. At current projections, cities will more than double their consumption of global resources—primarily fossil fuels, sand, gravel, iron ore, wood, and food—to about 90 billion tons by mid-century, far exceeding what Earth can sustainably provide. Meanwhile, cities are "de-densifying" (becoming less compact) at a rate of two percent per year, causing greater urban sprawl that eats into agricultural land, further exacerbating ecological stresses.[2]

And yet, along with these looming threats to human welfare, cities represent a rare opportunity for a swerve toward an ecocivilization. In contrast to the oligarchic hegemony of national power structures, urban decision-makers tend to be closer to the people their policies affect. While city leaders are, of course, subject to corruption and the sway of elite power brokers, they sometimes demonstrate flexible, problem-solving approaches that incorporate a broader range of constituencies.

Cities can be understood through the lens of Ivan Illich's vision of "convivial technologies" introduced in the previous chapter. Our built infrastructure is a vast, complex machine, the design of which can lead to very different outcomes. "When human flourishing is the goal," writes a team of prominent civil engineers, "then infrastructure becomes the system that delivers the services that enable the desired overall outcomes." The dominant civilization, however, as we've seen, hasn't built its systems to nurture human flourishing. What might a Third Horizon city look like that was designed to do just that?[3]

In his visionary *Ecocities: Rebuilding Cities in Balance with Nature*, Richard Register, an ecocity design theorist, takes his readers into the Third Horizon with a virtual tour of an ecocity a hundred years from now. Bicycling with him in the countryside toward the city, we pass through multiple neighborhoods embedded within a mélange of gardens and farms producing food for the urban population. These integrated neighborhoods are fully functioning communities in themselves, connecting like fractals with each other at increasing density levels as we approach the city center.

Suddenly, we turn a corner and in just a few blocks, the scale and character of the buildings change dramatically. We enter a three-dimensional latticework of mid-rise and high-rise buildings joined together by crisscrossed pedestrian bridges. Greenery pervades the scene, with fruits, berries, and flowers in living walls and treelined avenues attracting bees, butterflies, and birds. People lean over their balconies talking with each other. They can converse easily since there are no cars rumbling by to drown out their voices. Moving sidewalks rapidly convey people to where they want to go, while express elevators transport them vertically to one of the connecting bridges. In the heat of the summer, parachute cloths stretch out above to provide shade to the streets below. Unseen to pedestrians, below the residential sections of the mixed-use high-rise buildings, hydroponic farms and Fab Labs with 3D printers produce much of what residents need, while basement warehouses hold extensive inventory. Most people live within steps of where they work and socialize. Consistent with Monbiot's principle of "private sufficiency, public luxury" (see chapter 10), homes are generally quite small and energy efficient, while playgrounds, public squares, and green spaces abound, encouraging communal gatherings with impromptu sessions of musicmaking and other extemporaneous forms of entertainment.

How might we get there from the currently predominant urban wasteland? Elsewhere in his book, Register tells the story of the Aztecs and the wheel to illustrate the transformative possibilities available to urban policymakers today. When Europeans first arrived in Mexico, the Aztecs knew about the wheel, but they only used it for children's toys—it had never occurred to them that it could be utilized as the Europeans did to haul wagons with heavy supplies. Similarly, he points out, countless details of ecocity design exist all around us, but they are considered mostly ornamental niceties rather than core features of urban metamorphosis.

This is a valuable story to keep in mind. We'll discover in this chapter a multitude of urban exemplars around the world which, by themselves, might seem more like attractive features than instruments of transformation. Taken together, however, they illuminate design principles that could be scaled up into a transformed convivial reality—an authentic ecocity consciously and collaboratively designed as a platform to enrich the collective experience of its inhabitants and the broader health of the living Earth.

URBAN DESIGN, LIVING PRINCIPLES

While cities are artificial constructions, they are also self-organizing entities emerging from human interaction. As such, as we've seen elsewhere, nature itself can provide the best inspiration for resilient designs that promote collective well-being. A cardinal sign of robust, self-organized networks in nature is known as a hub-and-spoke pattern of connectivity. Most nodes in the network have multiple links with close neighbors, while rare nodes—the hubs—have spokes extending throughout the network. Scientists have found hub-and-spoke connectivity throughout the natural world, from protein interactions within cells to the functioning of an entire ecosystem.

Pioneering urban designers call for a similar pattern for a healthy city. To counter the de-densification of cities, they propose "strategic intensification" of most metropolitan regions, with high-density nodes connected to each other by efficient and affordable mass-transit systems (the very systems that were killed off in the United States) surrounded by medium-density areas, known as "polycentric cities." In contrast to the predominant convention of separate zoning for different urban functions, they propose high-density inner-city neighborhoods that are mixed-use and socially heterogeneous.[4]

This highlights the importance of another of nature's key design principles: the benefits of complexity. In the words of Jane Jacobs, a legendary twentieth-century urban theorist, "Intricate minglings of different uses in cities are not a form of chaos. On the contrary, they represent a complex and highly developed form of order." When the disparate parts are blended together coherently, this can lead to what the urban planner Jonathan Rose has called a "well-tempered city," one that fosters human flourishing.

The idea of a "15-minute city," which has gained traction around the world, encapsulates the principles of both hub-and-spoke networks and coherent complexity. This term was coined in 2016 by the Parisian scientist Carlos Moreno, who posited a vision of a city where "in less than 15 minutes, a resident can access their essential life needs." It was popularized by Paris's mayor Anne Hidalgo who envisioned more walkable districts with commercial, administrative, and medical services all readily available in each neighborhood, and the local school as a community hub open to the public for sports and cultural activities on nights and weekends. Since then, the idea has gained traction with a UN-sponsored initiative to develop "15-minute city" pilot projects around the world.

Like living entities, cities are understood as having a "metabolism" with an inflow and outflow of resources that keep the city alive through its interaction with the natural world. The urban ecologist Herbert Girardet has shown that modern cities have a linear metabolism, drawing in resources as needed and discarding the waste as mostly trash and sewage. He proposes, instead, that cities embrace ecological principles through a circular metabolism: linking more closely with local agriculture; producing more of its own food through hydroponics, community gardens, and roof gardens; encouraging urban wildlife; turning wastewater into fertilizer; and utilizing solar energy.[5]

Developing a circular metabolism requires a transformation of the human-nature relationship within city boundaries, inviting nature into the city and harmonizing with it. There are many interconnected benefits from this approach. Tree canopies and parklands can bring summer temperatures down, reduce air pollution, and reduce flood risk by storing and filtering water. Aesthetic and health benefits are considerable, with studies demonstrating that green spaces in cities lead to enduring improvements in people's well-being.

These benefits are not lost on some forward-thinking cities. Singapore, a pioneer in nature-centric urban design, calls itself "the city in a garden" with nearly 300 kilometers of green corridors connecting parks in different neighborhoods. Medellín in Colombia, with 2.6 million inhabitants, suffered severe air pollution with eleven times the WHO-recommended level of fine particulate matter causing more than 2,000 deaths a year. Over five years, they planted nearly a million trees and millions more smaller plants across thirty green corridors. The effect was almost immediate, with a 2° Celsius decrease in temperature and air pollution levels declining to below the Colombian norms.[6]

The founder of biomimicry, Janine Benyus (see chapter 8) challenges cities to explore how they can be "generous," giving back as much or more to nature as they receive by designing regenerative processes across the board. "We need cities to perform like ecosystems, not just look like them," she declares. Cities such as Amsterdam are responding to this challenge by using the framework of Kate Raworth's Doughnut Economics to develop a city self-portrait, exploring not just how to live well within its borders, but how to do so in a way that upholds the dignity of people worldwide and respects the health of the whole planet.

Becoming a truly "generous" city would require transformation in multiple different dimensions, including transportation, housing, energy, food, and waste. Let us now explore further those different pathways.

FROM CAR CULTURE TO CICLOVÍA

The modern city has been built primarily to optimize for the use of the private automobile rather than human flourishing. In the words of the geographer Paul Chatterton, "Almost all modern ills can be told through the automobile. Cars inflict so many multiple and complicated problems on cities . . . that a radical break is needed." The private automobile is an iconic product of modern capitalism. It promotes individualism, power, and flexibility to those who can afford it, while externalizing its social costs, including pollution, inequality of access, and alienated street life. As urban living is increasingly organized around the automobile, owning and using one becomes a prerequisite for many people's livelihood, with the result that any other form of urban design becomes almost unthinkable.[7]

In automobile-optimized streetscapes, offices and shops are situated far apart from each other and from residential neighborhoods, with the assumption that people will drive from one place to another for their needs. This leads to sprawling expanses of asphalt laid out for traffic and parking, eliminating walkability and opportunities for the informal social encounters that bind a society together. Community interaction becomes functionally compartmentalized, causing people to feel lonely and isolated even among their neighbors. Car culture exacerbates inequalities, distancing disadvantaged communities from privileged neighborhoods which are usually only accessible through inconvenient public transport. It also guzzles energy. Cities such as Houston or Dallas, which devote over 60 percent of urban space to cars, consume more than seven times the amount of transport-related energy as densely knit cities such as Tokyo, Singapore, and Vienna.

The paramount solution to car culture is an effective mass rapid transit system. As Chatterton points out, each of these three words is crucial. For a system to work well, it must be cheap enough that virtually everyone can afford it; it should be faster than other options; and it must take people everywhere they want to go. More than 100 towns and cities worldwide offer free local transport, sometimes for certain social groups, which can be financed through congestion charges and parking fees for private vehicles. The city of Curitiba in Brazil successfully pioneered a low-cost Bus Rapid Transit system in the 1970s, provided pods for efficient boarding and dedicated bus lanes with a broad network of routes. Inspired by this example, hundreds of cities have followed suit, including Rio de Janeiro, Shenzhen in China, and Colombia's capital city, Bogotá. In many cases, these systems succeed in increasing public transit usage to about two thirds of the population.

Bogotá has gone one step further in rethinking its transportation infrastructure by closing many of its roads to cars every Sunday, liberating them for bikes, skates, and pedestrians. This weekly event, called ciclovía, covers 127 kilometers of city streets and creates a family-friendly atmosphere enjoyed by about 1.5 million *Bogotanos*, complete with aerobics classes, street vendors, and salsa music.[8]

In addition to the sense of community created by ciclovía, it has also reoriented many citizens to the use of bicycles, which is facilitated by a cycle lane network covering 600 kilometers. Bicycles can play a crucial role in urban metamorphosis, as demonstrated by Copenhagen, Denmark's capital, which invested heavily in bicycle infrastructure with the result that the number of bikes now exceeds that of cars.

The most successful approaches are those that follow the "well-tempered city" principle of coherence by integrating plans into a comprehensive mobility strategy. Milan, for example, has responded to urban congestion with a series of interrelated initiatives. It has introduced services for sharing bikes, scooters, and cars coordinated through a digital mobility app, applied a traffic congestion charge, and now plans to create 750 kilometers of dedicated cycle paths with ring roads and radiating lines connecting the city to its suburbs and surrounding boroughs.

MAKING HOUSING CONVIVIAL

The buildings of a city have an opportunity to be generous both in what they give back to nature through their construction and what they offer residents in terms of community.

Many sustainable buildings are already designed for energy efficiency and minimizing environmental impact. One important set of guidelines, Leadership in Energy and Environmental Design (LEED) has certified more than 100,000 building projects worldwide. A "generous" building, however, goes beyond minimizing negative impact to become eco-positive, regenerating the natural world through its very existence. The Living Buildings Challenge, for example, certifies buildings that provide net-positive energy and water outcomes, support biodiversity, and restore local ecosystems and communities.

Eco-positive design requires rethinking many aspects of a building, including construction materials, air quality, energy, water, and waste management systems. Some buildings literally harmonize with nature through adopting green roofs and walls. Bogotá and Milan are, again, leaders in this respect. The Santalaia in Bogotá is a nine-story residential building with 85,000 plants irrigated with recycled water that purify the air and absorb carbon dioxide emissions. Milan boasts the Bosco Verticale: two towers that host a vertical forest with more than ninety different plant species comprising thousands of plants, including hundreds of trees, and providing a home for an estimated 1,600 birds and butterflies[9]

How can built infrastructure be generous to residents? One of the most important aspects of housing is affordability. Housing-related expenditure is the single-highest expense in developed countries, accounting for more than a quarter of the budget of many households. One city that has alleviated this problem is Vienna through its extensive social housing system. In countries such as the United States or the United Kingdom, public housing is generally available only to the very poor and consequently stigmatized. In Vienna, however, 80 percent of residents qualify for public housing, and once they begin leasing, they never have to leave, regardless of how much they earn. The rents are based on sustaining the housing stock, not on market fluctuations, which drives rental rates down even for private housing, with the result that 80 percent of Viennese households choose to rent.[10]

Montevideo in Uruguay has taken the idea of social housing further by applying it to low-income residents of informal, ramshackle settlements. The city provided land to cooperatives and offered people financing to build their own homes, allowing them to make the down payment in the form of sweat equity by working on their construction for twenty-one hours a week. Thousands of cooperative housing projects have been built in this way over thirty years, offering residents a greater sense of ownership and participation.[11]

Urban living can be made both affordable and convivial through creative community-based solutions, sometimes in partnership with municipal governments. In Solapur, India, low-paid beedi workers, mostly women from lower castes, were living in shanty slums under dismal conditions. A national trade union helped them organize into cooperatives that agitated for years with the state government to support a housing project. Eventually, they coalesced into the largest housing cooperative in Asia and persuaded the authorities to build 30,000 affordable homes, complete with power lines, water tanks, and extra land dedicated for recreation spaces, schools, and hospitals, leading to a significant improvement in workers' living conditions.[12]

As financial speculation increases the value of land worldwide, the wealth gap between landowners and renters has become an egregious driver of inequality. An important legal tool to remedy this is a community land trust (CLT): a nonprofit, community-controlled entity that separates land ownership from land use. Residents lease the land from a CLT but own their housing units. The CLT maintains permanent ownership of the land, removing it from the speculative housing market, while residents' homes can be resold with a maximum level of price appreciation agreed upon in advance with the CLT. This arrangement keeps housing affordable for communities even in frenzied real estate markets. CLTs are usually governed by a combination of residents, members of the surrounding community, and funders, which may be public or nonprofit institutions.

In England, which suffers extreme inequality in land ownership with consequent unaffordability, 500 CLTs have been established or are in development, helping to make housing more accessible. In the United States, more than 200 CLTs have emerged, some with extensive reach. Vermont's Champlain Housing Trust, for example, operates in three counties, overseeing hundreds of owner-occupied homes and thousands of rental apartments. In Oakland, California, where rising house prices have displaced many Black residents, the East Bay Permanent Real Estate Cooperative buys both residential and commercial properties with funds sourced locally, and empowers its residents to co-steward them, building a strong sense of community in the process.

CLTs can also facilitate urban regeneration. In a run-down Boston neighborhood, the Dudley Street Neighborhood Initiative worked with local government and private funders to construct an "urban village" with hundreds of affordable housing units, green common spaces, an urban farm, and multiple playgrounds. A gritty neighborhood in Liverpool, England, that had endured decades of decline came together in the face of planned demolition of their homes to form the Granby 4 Streets CLT, acquiring collective ownership of their houses and revitalizing their community.

In New York City and San Juan, Puerto Rico, CLTs have become part of official city policy, providing a vehicle for authorities to work with local groups to protect affordability and regenerate neighborhoods. This model is beginning to spread worldwide, helped by the International Land Coalition which has members across sixty-four countries. It can also be applied in rural areas to protect agricultural land from commercial development. The Marin Agricultural Land Trust in California has acquired conservation easements over approximately half of Marin County's farmland, ensuring it will be used for farming in perpetuity rather than suburban development. The Agrarian Trust is another US agricultural-oriented CLT that is building a multiracial coalition, helping farmers of color collectively acquire and steward land for organic and regenerative farming.

THE CIRCULAR CITY

For a city to change its metabolism from linear to circular requires a metamorphosis of what comes in—such as food and energy—and what goes out in the form of waste. In each case, changing these urban metabolic processes benefits those who live within the city as well as the wider world.

Cities account for about 75 percent of global energy use, so the potential for an urban energy transition is enormous. Something cities have in abundance is roofs, and this provides an extraordinary opportunity for communities to collaborate, not just in reducing carbon emissions, but in wresting a key resource from centralized control. Just as food sovereignty (see chapter 9) claims the right of people's self-determination in food production, the concept of energy sovereignty similarly asserts grassroots control over energy generation. A growing social movement for energy democracy envisions a more distributed system of locally controlled renewable energy infrastructure.

While each community has its unique circumstances, a shared vision underlies energy sovereignty. Many households might generate their own rooftop solar energy, while others share in the cooperative ownership and operation of off-site infrastructure such as wind turbines. Local smart microgrids, owned and operated by the community, can integrate different sources of power, store it through batteries, and distribute it as needed, allowing households to sell surplus energy to neighbors through peer-to-peer mesh networks.

Studies of energy efficiency potential show that, with widespread electrification of urban services and distributed renewable supply, energy demand could be 40 percent lower by 2050 and still satisfy the needs of a larger, more affluent global population. As usual, however, Windigo, Inc. stands in the way. Shareholder-owned, centralized utilities make their money by expanding and maintaining vast energy grids, and have systematically blocked a distributed, renewable transition. In supposedly progressive California, rooftop panels were forecast to save ratepayers $120 billion by mid-century—money that would otherwise flow through to shareholder profits. In response, companies pressured the Public Utilities Commission in 2022 to eliminate incentives for rooftop solar power, which has devastated the industry with 81 percent of solar companies fearing they will have to close down.[13]

Despite these roadblocks, the energy sovereignty movement is spreading worldwide. Som Energia in Spain, the fastest growing energy cooperative in Europe, has more than 80,000 members collaborating with hundreds of municipalities. In Puerto Rico, Resilient Power distributed solar-electric power kits to neighborhoods after the devastation of Hurricane Maria in 2017, which evolved into a long-term program of energy sovereignty. In Bangladesh, thousands of villagers, many of them women, have been trained to install solar systems in over four million homes under a "swarm electrification" program that uses a peer-to-peer microgrid enabling low-income rural households to trade excess solar energy using a mobile money platform.

Urban agriculture offers another way for cities to go circular while improving the quality of residents' lives. This can take the form of rooftop and community gardens, allotments, and community supported agriculture, whereby city-dwellers build committed relationships with local farmers. Hydroponic systems, using nutrient-rich water instead of soil, can increase the productivity of smaller rooftop and indoor facilities. The versatility of the closed-loop system allows users to minimize water usage and enables year-round crop production, enhancing urban food security with consistently reliable fresh produce.

Urban farming can reverse the decline of aging industrial inner cities. When major automobile manufacturers closed factories in Detroit, the city drastically depopulated and crumbling neighborhoods were bulldozed. A number of residents, however, refused to leave and utilized the newly vacant land to generate an urban metamorphosis. Community networks, such as the Michigan Urban Farming Initiative, have turned derelict neighborhoods into urban farmland, teaching people new skills and empowering them to provide for their own food security.

Food waste is another area offering huge opportunities for cities to become circular. The UN estimates that around one fifth of all food that's produced is wasted, frequently because it's passed its expiration date or considered "imperfect" for sale. FoodCloud in Dublin, Ireland has pioneered a form of urban symbiosis by matching businesses holding surplus food with people experiencing food poverty. Businesses post on a custom-built app details of their surplus food with a time period for collection, allowing participating organizations to pick up the food for distribution, thus supporting those in need while diverting food waste from landfills.

Grassroots initiatives can reduce urban waste in multiple ways that help build convivial communities. Repair Cafés connect people who are skilled in repairing things with residents who need their items fixed. Initiated in Amsterdam in 2009, there are now over 2,500 around the world bringing communities together while reducing unnecessary waste. Another mutually beneficial way for cities to become circular is through tool libraries: community-based stocks of equipment, such as lawnmowers and power tools, that most people need occasionally but usually collect dust in storage. The Toronto Tool Library, for example, was started on a shoestring in 2012 and now has thousands of tools available for residents to borrow when needed. This idea has also been modified into a peer-to-peer network, using an online platform to link those needing particular specialist items, such as high-end cameras or laboratory equipment, with those who can lend them out for a small fee.[14]

CITY AS A COMMONS

Many of these examples demonstrate best practices that are currently too small-scale to have meaningful impact on either global sustainability or community wellbeing. In each case, however, municipal governments could choose to put resources behind these practices and encourage city-wide participation. This highlights an important dynamic that's central to urban transformation: The relationships between the different groups comprising a city—communities, businesses, institutions, and government agencies—ultimately determine whether a city might become well-tempered and convivial, or profligate and inhospitable.

The current state of most cities, unsurprisingly, reflects the takeover by wealthy elites and corporations unleashed by the rise of neoliberalism since the 1970s. Underfunded city governments are increasingly forced to prostrate themselves to the patronage of private entities in a variety of ways. Sports stadiums sell naming rights to the highest bidder, municipalities offer tax breaks for corporate investments, and public services like parking meters or highways are privatized for short-term municipal revenue boosts. Urban elites use political muscle to get their way at the expense of the public. In one particularly glaring example, five wealthy residents of a high-rise luxury apartment complex in London shut down Tate Modern's public viewing gallery enjoyed by millions of visitors each year, because of the "visual intrusion" into their penthouses.[15]

Despite all this, glimmers of an urban form of ecocivilization flicker through. As we've seen, humanity's evolutionary heritage is to organize ourselves according to the principles of the commons. The groundbreaking urban researchers Sheila Foster and Christian Iaione are exploring what it means to apply this form of self-organization—the most convivial of all social technologies—to the city. "We can conceive of the city *itself* as a commons," they declare, "in the sense that it is a shared resource that belongs to all of its inhabitants." They point out, however, that the city is a different form of commons than traditional shared resources like water, pastures, or fisheries. Cities have emerged in conjunction with established institutions, they are intricately regulated, and rather than having a cohesive shared identity, they comprise many different types of people often experiencing social and economic tensions. How, then, can principles of the commons play a meaningful role?[16]

Foster and Iaione answer this conundrum by laying out design principles specifically for the urban commons. Their vision is for collective, multi-stakeholder governance, whereby the community plays a leading role in partnership with local authorities, businesses, and civil society institutions to meet local needs creatively through pooling resources and experimentation. In this vision, the role of elected officials is no longer merely to represent citizens but to help communities create their own solutions by coordinating, collaborating, providing technical guidance, and funneling resources to them as needed. This can be done by supporting many of the initiatives explored here, such as citizen-led housing, local currencies (see chapter 11), participatory budgeting (see chapter 14), circular city policies, neighborhood regeneration, and creating open spaces for convivial interaction.

Cities around the world are exploring how to embrace this commons-based revisioning of urban life. Seoul, South Korea, dubbed "the world's first sharing city," has instituted a program of collective governance to finance and promote local startups and nonprofits addressing urban challenges and revitalizing communities. European cities lead the way in many regards. Barcelona, in the wake of Spain's economic crisis in 2014, formed a "Barcelona in Common" coalition that expanded affordable housing, established a sustainable public energy company, created car-free "Superblock" pedestrian havens, and subsidized transportation and energy costs for those in need. Bologna, capital of Italy's co-op-oriented Emilia-Romagna region (see chapter 8), launched a "city as commons" initiative, establishing a legal framework for "collaboration pacts" that provide municipal funding and support to projects, originated by commoners, that manage enterprises such as eldercare centers, kindergartens, public spaces, and rehabilitation of abandoned buildings. A LabGov Co-City Protocol, launched by Foster and Iaione, has helped design projects in more than 100 cities worldwide experimenting in the urban commons transition, offering a robust guide for municipal governments to adopt.

DESIGNING AN ECOCITY

Remembering Richard Register's story of the Aztecs and the wheel, we can begin to imagine the potential transmutation that might occur if each of the urban enhancements described in this chapter were adopted at scale and applied across the world.

Perhaps no one alive today will get to tour first-hand the inspirational ecocity envisioned by Register in full fruition. However, there is nothing in Register's virtual tour that doesn't exist today in one form or another. The only obstacles preventing future generations enjoying that ecocity are institutional and ideological.

Consider a tour of real-world examples covered in this chapter. Singapore's and Medellín's extensive green corridors. Curitiba's rapid transit system, Bogotá's ciclovía, and Copenhagen's bicycle culture. The Santalaia, Bosco Verticale, and other regenerative buildings. Montevideo's social housing, Solapur's housing cooperative, and proliferating Community Land Trusts. Rooftop solar energy cooperatives using smart microgrids for "swarm electrification." Hydroponics, urban farms, and app-based surplus food distributions. Repair cafés, tool libraries, and peer-to-peer lending networks. Elected city officials enabling community empowerment in Seoul, Barcelona, and Bologna. If each of the models in this chapter were woven together and scaled, we would already be well on our way to a Third Horizon ecocity.

POSSIBLE SECOND AND THIRD HORIZON CONTOURS | INFRASTRUCTURE

SECOND HORIZON

The "15-minute" city becomes a customary design feature for urban planning

Extensive mass rapid transit systems provided at negligible cost to all residents

Bicycle lane networks predominate with city centers closed to car traffic

Regenerative building certification becomes a standard requirement for new building design

Social housing (modeled on Vienna and Montevideo) predominates in cities worldwide

Community Land Trusts expand, keeping housing affordable and facilitating urban regeneration

Centralized energy grids give way to community-controlled microgrids using renewable energy

Urban agriculture becomes a significant source of nourishment for city-dwellers

Municipalities support circular city initiatives: surplus food distribution, repair cafés, and tool libraries

City officials promote community-led initiatives through "collaboration pacts"

THIRD HORIZON

Buildings are constructed to be eco-positive, regenerating the natural world

The predominant form of city governance is the commons-based "sharing city"

Fractally organized, mixed-use circular ecocities are designed for conviviality

FOR CONSIDERATION

What Second and Third Horizon ideas arise in your own mind inspired by this chapter?

CHAPTER 14

GOVERNANCE: REDEFINING DEMOCRACY THROUGH DIRECT PARTICIPATION

Lying on his daybed, crippled by arthritis, octogenarian Murray Bookchin received an unexpected letter in April 2004. A philosopher and political theorist from the Bronx, Bookchin had spent his early years as a Communist, but in the 1950s he rejected Marxist orthodoxy to develop a theory of "social ecology," which identified hierarchy rather than capitalism as a root cause of humanity's exploitation of others and destruction of the natural world. Bookchin had written extensively about democratic "communalism": a vision of a hierarchy-free society based on small-scale self-governing communities. His ideas, however, had failed to gain much recognition even among fellow radicals, and now, heartbroken and cantankerous, he had given up on seeing them realized.[1]

Then came the letter from an unlikely source: Abdullah Öcalan of the Kurdistan Workers' Party (PKK), who had led the Kurds' fight for independence for decades and was now a political prisoner, held in solitary confinement in a Turkish jail since 1998. Öcalan's struggle to liberate the region and form an autonomous state had also been based originally in Marxist-Leninist orthodoxy. In prison, however, he encountered Bookchin's work which inspired a philosophical and political transformation. Öcalan, still viewed by the PKK as its leader, had built on Bookchin's ideas to elaborate a vision of "democratic confederalism." Instead of trying to establish a centralized Kurdish state, Öcalan now conceived of creating a federation of participatory local councils rooted in principles of direct democracy, women's autonomy, cultural diversity, cooperative economics, and social ecology. These were the ideas that he wanted to run by Bookchin, whom he now considered his teacher.

When Bookchin died two years later, the PKK leadership declared: "We undertake to make [him] live in our struggle." This was no empty rhetoric. In the turmoil of Syria's civil war of 2011–12, the PKK emerged as a powerful adversary of the fundamentalist Islamist group ISIS, and now controls a wide swathe of Syrian territory named Rojava encompassing 4.5 million people. Following Öcalan's and Bookchin's principles, the people of Rojava are actively practicing direct democracy, women's empowerment, multiculturalism, and social ecology, engaging in perhaps the most far-reaching social revolution of the twenty-first century.

Every human society relies on some form of governance. Sometimes explicit, sometimes implicit, systems of governance are social constructs that significantly influence the lives of those they affect. As discussed earlier, humans evolved to thrive in egalitarian bands where decision-making happened consensually, but—as Bookchin recognized—hierarchies arose with the emergence of agriculture and the increased importance of private property. Assertive males seeking dominance could now recruit others to support them with the promise of material gain, generating a ratchet effect that further exacerbated differences in wealth and power, leading eventually to the top-down forms of control wielded by emperors, kings, autocrats, and oligarchs that have dominated much of human history. From this perspective, democracy—governance by the people—may be understood as society's attempt to reclaim the grassroots power that is our evolutionary heritage.

Modern society, however, is vastly different in complexity and scale from the forager bands of our ancestors. There is no way that millions of citizens could sit around a campfire every evening to arrive at decisions by consensus. The conventional view, accepted so pervasively that it is virtually unquestioned, is that electoral democracy was instituted to solve this problem. Through periodic elections, the people can choose whom they want to represent them in the halls of power. This form of democracy was developed in the West and has been exported to many others countries around the world, but it is now in crisis. Citizens in democratic countries have become so deeply disaffected with their institutions that many no longer believe democracy is worth fighting for, willingly voting for authoritarian leaders who threaten their basic civil and political rights. In some ways, they are right. As noted in chapter 3, careful study of decades of legislation in the United States shows that wealthy elites get the policies they want, while there is no correlation between policy outcomes and majority preferences.

There are, of course, obvious flaws in the current system of electoral democracy that could be fixed simply by legislation, such as laws to keep money out of politics by placing stricter limits on campaign financing. However, at a deeper level, we must ask whether electoral democracy is the only form that is practicably available. One of the core principles of an ecocivilization is subsidiarity: pushing power down to the lowest feasible level in the system, in contrast to hierarchical structures. How can that be accomplished most effectively?

When discussing electoral democracy, Winston Churchill once famously declared that it "is the worst form of Government except for all those other forms that have been tried from time to time." But he was wrong. As this chapter reveals, Rojava offers a dramatic example of a practical grassroots alternative, but it is just one of several regions around the world where direct democracy has transformed people's lives through governance rooted in dignity and empowerment. As we will see, there are, in fact, other forms of democracy, with a pedigree going back much further than the dominant model, that can justifiably claim to be far more democratic and representative than the one we are accustomed to.

OLIGARCHY BY DESIGN

The standard creation myth of modern democracy harks back to ancient Athens as its birthplace and inspiration. While women and slaves were excluded from power, Athenian democracy was a reality for male citizens, but it was implemented very differently than modern electoral democracy. The center of power was the boule, a council of 500 men that prepared legislation for an assembly of all male citizens to vote on, managed the daily affairs of the city-state, and supervised finances and foreign relations. This council, however, was not elected. It was chosen by public lottery or "sortition"—a method that was also used for selecting the magistrates who implemented laws and the juries that considered court cases.

Sortition has survived in modern times for jury selection but has largely been abandoned as a form of governance. For the Athenians, however, it was the foundation of representative democracy. Aristotle, in *Politics*, contrasted sortition which he viewed as democratic, to elections which he saw as oligarchic. The reasoning was compelling: sortition ensured that legislative bodies were truly representative of the citizenry; it was resistant to corruption and excessive concentration of political power; and the opportunity to participate was spread broadly throughout the population.[2]

A more recent chapter of modern democracy's creation myth is the Constitution of the United States, which is widely regarded as a linchpin of democratic principles and practices. However, the leading figures of the convention that drafted the constitution in 1787 were well aware of Aristotle's distinction between democracy and oligarchy—and deliberately opted for the latter. For them, democracy was associated with mob rule and was to be avoided at all costs. James Madison called for "*the total exclusion of the people in their collective capacity* from any share in [the government of the republic]." As they endeavored to design an alternative system of governance to Europe's monarchies, they were equally concerned with avoiding democracy which, in the words of the second US president John Adams, "is more bloody than either [aristocracy or monarchy]" and "soon wastes, exhausts and murders itself."[3]

Instead, the Founding Fathers constructed a system in which an elite class of wealthy white men would be elected by a landed aristocracy of other property owners, resulting in what Madison called "a chosen body of citizens, whose wisdom may best discern the true interest of their country." Specifically, Madison pointed out, this true interest was based on the protection of the "rights of property" which he associated with the "first object of government," and would reliably oppose calls "for an abolition of debts, for an equal division of property, or for any other improper or wicked project."

The US Constitution was thus designed to create an electoral oligarchy that would primarily protect the property rights of the wealthy elite against "the people in their collective capacity." Only gradually, during the nineteenth century, did it come to be described as a "democracy." Notwithstanding this rebranding, it has been remarkably successful in maintaining its oligarchic nature. Roughly half the members of Congress are millionaires, and the current Trump administration boasts thirteen billionaires. The history of Europe's electoral democracies, while differing in specifics, follows a similar trajectory characterized by landed gentry wresting power from monarchs while maintaining significant control over levers of governance. Only in response to public agitation did the aristocracy gradually yield to broader suffrage in incremental steps, as a type of "vaccination" against the risk of insurrection.

Rather than enabling people to exercise their collective power, electoral democracy is better understood as a form of public legitimation indicating people's *consent* to power. Even this consent is only granted occasionally during an election. Back in the eighteenth century, Rousseau famously remarked about the English electoral system:

> The people of England regards itself as free; but it is grossly mistaken; it is free only during the election of members of Parliament. As soon as they are elected, slavery overtakes it, and it is nothing.

This insight remains true. Once someone is elected, rather than representing their electorate, their primary concern is for themselves, and frequently, to get reelected. They can usually do this best by pleasing the lobbyists with the most influence and deepest pockets. Even an incorruptible representative is compelled by a system of periodic elections to favor short-term goals over society's long-term needs. As Jean-Claude Juncker, prime minister of Luxembourg admitted: "We all know what to do, but we don't know how to get re-elected once we have done it."[4]

Even under ideal circumstances, elections offer a deeply flawed format for identifying a society's best policymakers. They select for those who are charismatic, wealthy, connected, and ambitious—a dangerously unrepresentative sample of the population at large. Elections, with their emphasis on adversarial relations and grabbing public attention, motivate grandstanding and partisanship rather than considered deliberation. Whereas open-mindedness to other points of view may be a paramount quality for wise policymaking, it is at odds with the characteristics that lead to successful electioneering. Is there any realistic alternative to this structurally defective system?

DELIBERATIVE DEMOCRACY

Increasingly, many groups around the world are demonstrating that there is, in fact, an alternative—a more legitimate descendant of the original Athenian model known as deliberative democracy. Deliberative democracy rests on the theory that laws and policies gain their legitimacy, not just from a vote, but from a process of careful deliberation among citizen peers leading up to the vote.

The public sphere, of course, hardly lends itself to any manner of thoughtful consideration of policy options. It has always been subject to undue influence from the most assertive voices, but in recent decades, with the bulk of mass media under the control of billionaire oligarchs and the large-scale algorithmic manipulation of social media platforms, it has become primarily a generator of epistemic chaos rather than grounded policymaking.

Deliberative democracy resolves this problem through the use of citizens' assemblies: groups of citizens—usually a hundred or more—chosen by sortition, who engage in sustained facilitated discussion on a particular topic, listening, articulating, and reflecting on what arises, until voting on a recommendation or conclusion. At first sight, it may seem ludicrous to expect a random sample of citizens to arrive at a considered judgment on a complex policy issue about which many might know nothing or have a preconceived agenda. However, a wealth of evidence shows that, with sufficient time, skilled facilitation, and access to expert opinions, citizens' assemblies reach thoughtful and nuanced conclusions on fraught and difficult topics.[5]

Underlying this surprising outcome is a key human characteristic that is well known to social psychologists: While people may be bad individual reasoners—frequently led astray by implicit or explicit prejudices—they can be excellent collective problem-solvers under the right conditions. An essential component of these conditions is adept independent facilitation supported by clear rules and processes that encourage mutual respect and reciprocity, and thereby promote free and fair exchange between citizens.

There are several other crucial design criteria for a successful citizen's assembly. For their recommendations to be credible, assemblies must be truly representative of the overall population. They must have sufficient time for deliberation, frequently involving periodic meetings over several days or months. They must have access to appropriate subject experts and the ability to ask them follow-up questions. Their assignment should be well defined, and it's important for the assembly members to know that their conclusions will have a meaningful impact on the political process.[6]

The first modern citizens' assembly was established by the Canadian province of British Columbia in 2004 to review its electoral system and recommend any changes. A hundred and sixty people, chosen at random and representing each of the province's electoral districts, met periodically over eleven months and drafted a series of recommendations, which garnered a majority vote in an ensuing referendum. Following this successful model, formal citizens' assemblies have taken off around the world with approximately fifty now convening each year. Countering the short-term orientation of electoral politics, the main topics addressed by assemblies tend to be long-term and complex issues, such as climate change, urban planning, and policies around health, infrastructure, transportation, energy, and citizen engagement.[7]

In 2012, Ireland's parliament entrusted an assembly with an eighteen-month deliberative process to explore constitutional reform. One of their recommendations, to legalize same-sex marriage, led to approval in a consequent referendum with minimal toxic divisiveness. Emboldened by this and facing calls in 2016 to legalize abortion, the parliament assembled ninety-nine randomly selected citizens to examine the legal, ethical, and medical issues concerning abortion over an eighteen-month period. Their deliberations, which included testimonies by women facing crisis pregnancies, were broadcast on the internet and their eventual recommendation to legalize abortion was carried by 66.4 percent. Moving beyond single-issue assemblies, the world's first permanent Citizens' Council was established in Belgium's Ostbelgien region in 2019, which has inspired cities such as Lisbon and Paris to form their own permanent assemblies to make recommendations for adoption by the city council.[8]

According to accounts of many observers, something remarkable happens when ordinary people take part in citizens' assemblies. A shared civic consciousness emerges spontaneously, not through imposition but as the natural outcome of citizens being respected, given equal standing, and engaging in meaningful dialogue with their peers. People stay committed to the process over many months, and report that they "feel a sense of responsibility to the wider public interest." Without having to worry about getting reelected, they are free to focus on the common good. Studies have shown that large and statistically significant changes in opinion result from the process of collective deliberation. In contrast to knee-jerk partisanship, judgment becomes more considered, nuanced, and responsive to the direct personal testament of others. In regions torn by civil strife, such as Colombia, Northern Ireland, and Bosnia, such carefully structured deliberation has overcome polarization and helped heal deep divisions.

ENVISIONING A FRACTAL DEMOCRACY

The recommendations of citizens' assemblies tend to reflect, not necessarily what the general public thinks about an issue, but what they *would* think if given enough information, time, and opportunity for careful deliberation. In the opinion of the researcher John Dryzek, they provide "a simulation of what the population as a whole would decide if everyone were allowed to deliberate." In this respect, a properly constituted assembly can be understood as a "mini-public": a fractal of the larger system, representing its preferences under optimal conditions.

Could these fractals of true democracy ever replace our flawed electoral process to become a governance system for society at large? Some visionary political scientists suggest this could be so. The Yale professor Hélène Landemore calls it "open democracy": a "new paradigm [of] representing and being represented in turn . . . in which actual exercise of power is accessible to ordinary citizens"—one which is "primarily non-electoral yet (more) democratically representative than any existing regime form."

Building on Landemore's vision, along with similar groundbreaking ideas from other proponents, it is possible to rough out a "Third Horizon" sketch of an alternative and far more representative fractal democracy that empowers ordinary citizens to determine policies that work for society at large rather than for wealthy elites.

In Landemore's "open democracy," all citizens would have an equal right to participate in the decision-making process, which would be based on facilitated and transparent deliberation by groups selected by sortition to be truly representative of society. Instead of elections, citizens would be selected to serve in different assemblies for a time period ranging from a year to several years. They would be paid significant remuneration for their service—with extra support for parents with dependents and those performing unpaid care work—and the bar to decline serving would be set high in order to avoid skewing the population.

We could conceive of a national assembly, like the Athenian boule, consisting of a few hundred citizens selected to serve for several years in annual tranches, so that the bulk of the body remained stable from year to year. This would form the center of an extensive web of other assemblies operating at different levels, some single-issue and some general-purpose, some focusing on national policy and others on regional and local governance.

Even with collective policymaking, modern nation-states would still require individual executives to make urgent decisions at critical moments and to conduct international diplomacy. The current popularity contest for choosing those executives, however, selects for some of humanity's worst character traits such as narcissism, egotism, and lust for power. In a fractal democracy, the National Assembly might elect an executive annually—and other cabinet ministers—from the cohort that had already served for at least two years. As in many nation-states today, administrative and legislative leadership could be split between two different executives.[9]

What would happen to political parties? Absent the high-stakes election cycle, they might evolve to play a valuable role in civil society by formulating policy platforms based on coherent value schemas offering alternative long-term visions for the future. Like other lobby groups, they would attempt to influence the mini-publics by providing expert opinions. Strict firewalls would need to be maintained between lobbyists and assembly members, which would be more manageable without the current corporate revolving door proffered to career politicians.

Political parties are currently the primary vehicles for setting policy agendas for legislative consideration. A fractal democracy might instead use a separate Agenda Assembly to prioritize issues and formulate proposals for deliberation by the National Assembly. This assembly would need to be finely attuned to public concerns, which could be optimally accomplished through participatory digital media utilizing crowdsourcing software designed intelligently to identify emerging clusters of citizens' concerns.[10]

This conceptual leap from the current advisory role of citizens' assemblies, to a scenario in which the assemblies themselves assume governing power, is radical and somewhat disorienting. We have grown so used to the idea that elections bestow a political mandate and keep politicians accountable, that it is difficult to comprehend any other basis of legitimacy—even though our current system's veneer of legitimacy has worn so thin as to be virtually undetectable. Landemore and others address this concern by emphasizing the need for transparency in assembly deliberations, and suggesting a role for referendums on particularly momentous issues—but stressing that deliberation must be built into the process, and perhaps limiting referendums to particular proposals already considered and reviewed by the National Assembly.

There would be numerous challenges in implementing such a fundamentally different design for democracy in a modern nation-state, which are currently being studied by groundbreaking groups such as Participedia and DemocracyNext. A fractal democracy comprising citizens' assemblies selected by sortition, though, appears to offer the potential for a far more democratic, stable, and representative form of governance than today's model of electoral oligarchy.

GRASSROOTS DEMOCRACY IN ACTION

However, as Rojava demonstrates, dedicated groups are already building models of authentic grassroots direct democracy without waiting for nation-states to transform their electoral systems. These people-powered democratic alternatives, which abound worldwide, emerge not from a centralized institutional framework but from the mutual trust that can bind communities together, enabling them to work cooperatively to achieve common goals.

Sometimes known as Citizen Action Networks (CANs), these forms of direct democracy range in size from small community clusters to national scope. They are distinct from what are commonly categorized as society's three sectors—private enterprise, state authority, and civil society—representing a fourth sector including cooperatives, social enterprises, Transition Town communities, and commoning platforms. Their power arises from collaboration in finding effective and creative solutions to the daily challenges people face, along with an action orientation to co-generate the future they want rather than hoping authorities will grant it to them.[11]

Some of these networks are established models of inclusive democracy sanctioned by state governments. In rural India, *Gram Sabhas*, meetings at which people can hold local leaders to account and share practical solutions for the local problems they face, are held twice a year in almost a million villages. More than 800 million registered voters, many of them illiterate and very poor, are eligible to participate. In Brazil's National Public Policy Conferences, described as "the world's largest participatory and deliberative experiment known to date," millions of citizens meet at the municipal, state, and ultimately, national level, to formulate policy guidelines that have helped shape national legislation on issues such as health, education, human rights, and the economy.

Most of the time, however, national governments have no interest in empowering ordinary citizens, or are openly hostile to them. Solidarity networks frequently arise when large-scale communities, weary of generations of exploitation and oppression, stop hoping that centralized authorities will alleviate their suffering and realize that the liberation they seek will only materialize from their own capacities. Emerging worldwide in diverse cultural and environmental conditions, they share certain core principles. Claiming autonomy to govern themselves and manage their own institutions and resources, their legitimacy arises from widespread community participation and collective identity. They tend to emphasize regional self-sufficiency to the degree possible, diversification of production to exchange goods with other communities, and sustainable ecological management.

The 4.5 million people of Rojava, organizing themselves according to the Bookchin/Öcalan model of democratic confederalism, are a shining example of how grassroots direct democracy can work effectively at scale to grant autonomy to ordinary people. The Kurds have endured a bitter history ever since the British and French colonial powers set national boundaries without accounting for their traditional homelands, leaving Kurdish territory split between Turkey, Syria, Iraq, and Jordan. Yet, in a region characterized by authoritarian, repressive regimes and heavily male-dominated cultures, Rojava has arisen as the antithesis of its surroundings. Rejecting the coercive inequities of patriarchy, capitalism, and the nation-state, they have dismantled the structures of centralized power and could reasonably claim to be the most genuinely democratic society in the world.[12]

Embodying the principle of subsidiarity, Rojava's governance system begins at the street level with a deliberative body called a commune, consisting of a few hundred households. Here, residents discuss day-to-day affairs and arrive at solutions to local problems. Each commune has committees with responsibilities in areas such as education, self-defense, health, arts and culture, women, and economy. Residents elect their coordinating board members, led by co-chairs of one man and one woman, who convene weekly in meetings that are open to all, and can be recalled at any time by a majority vote.

If a problem can't be solved by the commune, it goes up one level to the neighborhood council, consisting of seven to thirty communes, each represented by their co-chairs. The next level is a district (encompassing a city and surrounding villages); which in turn sends delegates to the People's Assembly and then to the Syrian Democratic Council which manages Rojava's relationships within the larger geopolitical context. Through this system, each local community has an equivalent voice in collectively determining policies for the entire society.

The principles of grassroots democracy extend beyond the political realm to the general economy, in which cooperatives and the commons play crucial roles. After the turmoil of the civil war, land and property that was formerly owned by the Syrian state, recaptured from ISIS, or simply left abandoned, was treated as a commons controlled by the communes, and assigned to cooperatives to manage. Cooperatives, which now make up a major part of the economy, are expected to serve not just their individual members but the collective interests of society. With membership open to all residents, they are guided by values such as mutual aid, mutual responsibility, democracy, equality, and fairness. They produce a large proportion of Rojava's food supply, and cover other functions including education, health, restaurants, textiles, and electricity generation and supply. Family and private enterprises are also welcomed and integrated into the economy, but monopolies are illegal. As a result, in spite of continual war and scarce resources, Rojava has by the far the highest standard of living in the region, with average salaries double those in the rest of Syrian territory.[13]

While Kurds are the largest ethnic group in Rojava, they remain a minority within a diverse population of Arabs, Assyrians, Christians, and Yazidis. Democratic confederalism embraces this multicultural patchwork, making it a high priority to involve people from all the region's ethnic and religious groups. Above all, overturning the region's patriarchal legacy, it has adopted feminist principles, requiring that every committee and assembly is co-headed by both a man and a woman, and giving women full control over issues that pertain primarily to them. Some military units are all female.

A WORLDWIDE WAVE OF SOLIDARITY

In governance and economy, Rojava is succeeding, but its future remains uncertain. In a tumultuous region, it faces violent opposition from Turkey along with an unpredictable relationship with Syria's new regime, and its grand experiment in grassroots democracy may turn out to be short-lived. Rojava, however, is not alone in forging pathways of community self-reliance. Other communities around the world, each in their unique way, are shining rays of light on transformative democratic possibilities.

In 1994, a group of Indigenous Mayans seized control of a handful of towns in Chiapas, one of Mexico's poorest states. Accusing the federal government of betraying ordinary Mexicans, the Zapatistas, as they were named, called for a nationwide revolt. Although the armed conflict was quickly extinguished, the Zapatistas have remained an organizing force in the region, exercising de facto autonomy in the name of freedom, democracy, and human dignity.

Their guiding philosophy, summarized by the catchphrase "Asking as we walk" (*caminando preguntamos)*, emphasizes listening to a plurality of voices and community participation among the half-million people living in the region. Like Rojava, the Zapatistas departed from old-style revolutionary movements, incorporating grassroots democracy, feminism, and environmental conservation into their core principles. Unlike Rojava, however, they never established full control of their territory, and as a result, they have had to develop an organizing nexus entwined within the dominant system. Each village acts as a nucleus of self-governance sending delegates to coordinating councils known as *caracoles* (shells). Rejecting government-controlled social services, the *caracoles* have functioned as autonomous regional centers, building their own institutions of justice, education, and health, and demonstrating that another way of living is possible.[14]

As the dominant system unravels, however, it won't leave them in peace to cultivate that alternative way of life. As the Zapatistas try to administer their communal daily activities, they face a growing barrage of violence from paramilitary gangs engaging in kidnapping, land theft, and murder, aggravated by the influx of drug cartels from elsewhere in Mexico and a surge of migrants from Central and South America preyed upon by smugglers. Surrounding the Zapatistas' zones of influence, the federal army projects its power in an uneasy stand-off, but their greatest threat comes from corporate and financial predators investing in so-called "development" projects such as mining and industrial agriculture imposed on local populations without their consent.[15]

In the face of these pressures, and consistent with the principle of *caminando preguntamos*, the Zapatistas announced in 2024 a series of changes to their system of governance, replacing the *caracoles* with thousands of local grassroots assemblies designed to devolve decision-making to the lowest level possible, and thus ensure that their communities can survive even in isolation from each other. Faced with daily harassment and violence, the Zapatistas have thus far managed, over three decades, to restore dignity to their communities, improving the quality of their education and healthcare, and demonstrating the power of solidarity in action.[16]

Thousands of miles south, in Brazil, the Landless Rural Workers' Movement—in Portuguese *Movimento dos Trabalhadores Rurais Sem Terra* (MST)—has established its own form of democracy by settling on rural land abandoned by absentee landlords. Brazil suffers extreme inequality of land ownership with 1.6 percent of landholders controlling nearly half the nation's farmland, while roughly a third of the population lives below the nation's poverty line. Since its inception in the 1970s, MST has not only advocated for land redistribution but has taken matters into its own hands through a campaign of organized resettlements. Over a million MST members have occupied land in this way, turning encampments into organic farms and democratic communities replete with their own healthcare, economy, churches, and education. As they prepare for a land occupation, MST members undergo a conscious educational program teaching them how to think for themselves, to discard patriarchal customs and respect women's rights, and engage collaboratively with one another.

Disparaged by mainstream media and denounced by landowning elites, MST has nevertheless evolved into a powerful movement capable of sponsoring large and elaborate mass mobilizations across the country. Emphasizing education, it manages 1,800 schools and a network of adult literacy classes. With a publishing house, two news agencies, and a weekly newspaper, it wields significant political influence, supported mostly by settlements that allocate five percent of their revenues to fund the movement. MST's sustained achievements have made it a beacon of hope and autonomy for the landless and oppressed people whose plight has been ignored by the state.[17]

Half a world away, on the island nation of Sri Lanka, another solidarity network has transfigured thousands of impoverished rural communities through a blend of spiritual and economic self-actualization inspired by the teachings of Mahatma Gandhi. The Sarvodaya Shramadana movement (literally meaning "Awakening of all through sharing of energy") was founded in 1958 by a Buddhist adherent of Gandhi, Dr. A. T. Ariyaratne, to mobilize villagers to achieve economic self-sufficiency as part of a broader awakening process. Their slogan, "We build the road, and the road builds us" encapsulates how working cooperatively, with the intention of mutual benefit, brings both material and spiritual wealth to the whole community.

Since its founding, Sarvodaya has become the largest people's organization in Sri Lanka, serving more than 15,000 villages. It has established the nation's largest microcredit network and 100,000 small businesses, along with thousands of preschools, libraries, and community health centers. When Sri Lanka faced a food crisis, Sarvodaya responded with a "We Are One" campaign, forming hundreds of community kitchens to which every family would contribute. Its inspiration was the movement's founding "matchbox campaign" in which even the poorest family would fill a tiny matchbox with whatever rice or dal they possessed, so that everyone had a role in nourishing the entire community.[18]

Further north, India's state of Kerala offers an equally inspiring but alternative model of deep democracy, showing how it's possible for the state to play a formative role in encouraging grassroots community self-reliance. One of India's poorest states when measured by GDP, Kerala nevertheless tops India's human development index, achieving the country's highest standards in health, literacy, life expectancy, nutrition, women's rights, infant survival, and equality. Caste discrimination and religious bigotry, while prevalent throughout India, is rarely experienced here.

It wasn't always that way. In the nineteenth century, Kerala was notorious for having one of the cruelest and most rigid caste systems in India, exerting extreme humiliation on women from the lowest caste by forbidding them to wear clothing above the waist, thus forcing them to go bare-breasted in public. However, as a result of popular rebellions and a predominantly matrilineal culture, by the beginning of the twentieth century Kerala was already transforming, and became a global leader in mass education, especially for girls. In the struggle for independence from British rule, well-educated and politically sophisticated activists led the way, supported by the Communist party which became the world's first democratically elected Communist government in the state's inaugural election of 1957. However, like Rojava and the Zapatistas, Kerala's communists chose a different path than the centralized state planning of the Soviet Union. In addition to pursuing a radical program of widespread land reform, wealth redistribution, and universal education, they decentralized political power, encouraging mass participation in government.[19]

Building on India's *Gram Sabhas* tradition, Kerala's government initiated a People's Campaign for Decentralized Planning in 1996, organizing citizens' assemblies in the villages over several months with more than two million participants. After hearing widespread concerns about healthcare, they created a network of Primary Health Centers extending care to everyone regardless of income, caste, or gender. Two years later, they initiated a grassroots movement for women's empowerment called Kudumbashree (meaning "prosperity of the family"). The movement's 4.5 million members are represented democratically by 20,000 councils that are linked to local government. Village women pool their funds to form collective farms (numbering 70,000 statewide) that turn fallow land into productive plots growing crops for local consumption, working on the principle that surplus produce can be sold on the market only after the collective's families have satisfied their needs. In the words of one woman farmer, "Ours is a collective strength . . . Kudumbashree is all about solidarity."[20]

THE PARTNER STATE

Kerala's example shows that the conflict frequently occurring between state power and grassroots self-determination is not inevitable. It is possible for government to act in partnership with local communities, giving them tools for self-reliance and boosting their influence on more centralized policymaking. Kerala demonstrates how a central objective of an ecocivilization—to set the conditions for everyone to flourish—does not require technical feats of wizardry or an ever-expanding economy, but can be accomplished through democratizing governance and organizing society to serve people's needs.

The political researcher John Restakis calls this a "Partner State": one whose "aim is to serve the common good . . . by democratizing and decentralizing the institutions of governance." Rather than impose centralized decision-making on an unwilling populace through the ultimate threat of legalized violence, a partner state would be one whose public authorities empowered and enabled communities to assemble democratically, determine their priorities, and funnel to higher levels of governance decisions requiring broader scope.[21]

Historically, state authority has been so intertwined with the power of elites that it is difficult to conceive of an alternative. However, if higher levels of government were controlled by citizens' assemblies rather than (elected or unelected) oligarchs, there would be a structural alignment between the governance of the state and the empowerment of local communities. Consistent with Aristotle's original insight, assembly members, knowing they would return to their local communities before long, would have little incentive to wrest authority from the common people.

We are a long way from this Third Horizon governance model, but some glimmerings of the Partner State are beginning to show up in policy briefs and citizens' initiatives. The OECD, for example, has called for "a bold transition towards open governance [to] help enhance the democratic model." In the UK, a campaign is calling to replace the nation's second parliamentary chamber, the House of Lords, with a House of Citizens chosen by sortition with the power to instigate citizens' assemblies on topics of national interest. In Belgium, regional Parliaments already work directly with citizens chosen by sortition in committees to address issues such as homelessness and urban planning.[22]

As discussed in the previous chapter, some of the most interesting developments take place at the city level, where leaders are closer to their constituents and sometimes less beholden to special interests. Policy Innovation Labs, such as New York's "NYCx Co-Lab," Bologna's "Office for Civic Imagination," and Mexico City's "Lab for the City," have sprung up around the world, placing local residents at the center of policy design, and empowering them to experiment with new ideas and evaluate ongoing initiatives.

Some of the most innovative and successful forays into "Partner State" territory have used technology to lay the groundwork for an extensive and vigorous digital democracy. In 2016, the Barcelona in Common movement launched a digital platform called Decidim inviting residents to contribute proposals that could be debated and turn into binding legislation, allowing them to monitor and assess the decision-making process. It was a huge success, causing people to feel they had influence over policy. In its first year, it generated more than 8,000 proposals for improving urban life, over 70 percent of which were accepted. The system is also used to track, evaluate, and revise the initiatives. In just a few years, Decidim's success has generated massive adoption elsewhere. It's now used worldwide in over 500 settings across thirty countries with more than three million registered participants.[23]

In Taiwan, Digital Affairs Minister Audrey Tang (see chapter 12) has led the development of a transformative digital infrastructure empowering citizen governance called vTaiwan. This platform is designed specifically to overcome polarization and facilitate deliberative online conversation between thousands of participants—a national-scale variant of a citizens' assembly. The technology uses statistical tools to cluster opinions, helping to bring underlying issues to the surface that lend themselves to broader agreement. For example, when Uber's arrival in Taiwan spawned an angry debate, the process helped to generate a consensus policy proposal that welcomed Uber's benefits while also protecting workers' rights, which was implemented by the government. Another contentious debate on corporal punishment for drunk drivers turned into a discussion on policymaking to prevent drunk driving in the first place. More than a dozen issues debated on vTaiwan have generated outcomes that the government has turned into legislation. The open source software underpinning vTaiwan, called Polis, is just one of several systems, some AI-enhanced, being developed and tested to enhance community-wide deliberation as well as help citizens' assemblies arrive more effectively at consensual agreement.[24]

There are equally powerful low-tech approaches to effectuating a partner state. Beginning in 1989, the Brazilian city of Porto Alegre introduced a program of participatory budgeting which was so successful that it has since been adopted by more than 10,000 cities, states, and institutions worldwide. Participatory budgeting (PB) is a process in which local residents discuss their collective needs and determine how to prioritize which projects to fund. Interestingly, it tends to attract greater representation by people with low income and education, and politically marginalized groups such the elderly, unemployed, and ethnic minorities. Frequently, after reviewing the previous year's investment plan, groups meet locally to establish their priorities and elect delegates to make their case at the city level. Cities using PB tend to spend more on issues that residents care about the most, such as health, sanitation, education, and public transportation, leading to clear and measurable improvements in community well-being. Beyond its material benefits, PB often elevates the quality of civic engagement among residents, fostering a greater sense of engagement, trust, and inclusion as people realize they have a voice in their own destiny.[25]

GOVERNANCE BY THE PEOPLE FOR THE PEOPLE

In the Gettysburg Address, honoring those who had died fighting on a civil war battlefield, President Abraham Lincoln uttered the world-famous declaration: "Government of the people, by the people, for the people, shall not perish from the earth." It was a stirring vision that has galvanized people's hearts ever since, but it was sadly a long way from describing the American system of government.

It is, however, a fitting description of what governance must look like for the realization of an ecocivilization. After ten thousand years of mostly hierarchical power organized around a wealth pump sucking the life force out of ordinary people for the benefit of small elites, the road to governance for an ecocivilization must be transformative. We must redefine democracy itself, recognizing that, even at its best, electoral democracy is little more than oligarchy by consent. The challenge is how to incorporate humanity's evolutionary heritage of grassroots decision-making into the vast complexity of the modern, globalized world. Fortunately, as we've seen, the first steps toward a broad revisioning of democracy are already being taken.

We can discern from this chapter two differentiated but broadly compatible models. The conception of fractal democracy is based in a centralized nation-state, but one where, rather than being wielded by oligarchs, power belongs to the people represented by a rotation of ordinary citizens. Alternatively, Rojava and other models of grassroots democracy in action demonstrate that it's possible, in principle and in practice, to sustain a fully functioning, complex society without requiring the nation-state apparatus at all.

The concept of the partner state, exemplified by Kerala's government, by experiments in digital democracy, and by participatory budgeting, offers a view for how these two models may intersect harmoniously. Even within the structure of a centralized state, power can be devolved to the lowest level of decision-making, and yet, when broader scope is required, representative citizens' assemblies can set policy without inevitably commandeering power from the people.

Envisioning an ecocivilization does not entail designing a blueprint with fixed parameters. Rather, it is an open-ended exploration based on asking the most pertinent questions and tracing where they might lead. We have seen from this chapter that governance of the people, by the people, and for the people, is not a pipe dream. While it's very different from our current forms of governance, an assemblage of visionary thinkers, dedicated innovators, and millions of courageous people in solidarity communities worldwide, are already laying the pathways toward a Third Horizon of ecocivilization governance.

POSSIBLE SECOND AND THIRD HORIZON CONTOURS | GOVERNANCE

SECOND HORIZON

Citizens' Assemblies selected by sortition play an influential advisory role in local and national policymaking

Public policy conferences, modeled on Brazil's example, formulate policy guidelines for national legislation

Citizen Action Networks (CANs) based on mutual solidarity, are supported by state authorities and play a significant role in local empowerment

Movements for women's empowerment proliferate in the Global South, modeled on Kerala's Kudumbashree movement

Digital platforms (modeled on Decidim and vTaiwan) allow citizens to practice mass deliberation and propose policies for legislative uptake

Participatory budgeting becomes the default mode for prioritizing municipal budgets

THIRD HORIZON

In place of electoral "democracy," Citizens' Assemblies determine national and regional policy through a fractal network of "mini-publics"

Policy agendas are set through an assembly process attuning to public concerns through participatory digital media

Local communities practice autonomy based on the principle of subsidiarity, modeled on democratic confederalism

The partner state is the default governing system: communities practicing self-determination funnel broader issues to higher levels of government controlled by citizens' assemblies

FOR CONSIDERATION

What Second and Third Horizon ideas arise in your own mind inspired by this chapter?

CHAPTER 15

LAW: A NEW RELATIONAL PARADIGM INTERWEAVING RIGHTS AND RESPONSIBILITIES

The ten-year-old king stood fidgeting in the drafty hall of St. Paul's Cathedral on a cold November morning in 1217. Watching his uncle, the Regent, and an Italian cardinal representing the Pope, affixing their seals to two manuscripts, the young Henry III could barely have understood the magnitude of the moment. The documents sealed that day had their origins a couple of years earlier when, under duress from his barons, the tyrannical King John had signed an agreement known as the Charter of Liberty in a meadow at Runnymede by the River Thames. One of those documents has since achieved worldwide fame as the Magna Carta—venerated nowadays as an icon of liberty from state oppression. The other manuscript was considered equally important at the time—so much so that, for generations, all English churches were required to read it aloud in its entirety at Christmas, Easter, and other special holidays. Today, however, almost no one knows of its existence. Its name was the Charter of the Forest, and in many ways, the divergence between the trajectory of these two documents encapsulates the entire shameful and hidden history of the rise to dominance of what we know today as "the law."

Back then, "forest" meant something very different than today's word. With the same etymological root as "forbidden," forest referred to land that had been appropriated by the monarch for his own purposes, such as hunting, and was no longer available to common people for their sustenance. It could include, not only wooded areas, but fields, farms, and even villages. Since William the Conqueror's invasion of England in 1066, the number of royal forests had multiplied considerably, reaching 143 by 1215, as monarchs seized the common land to enrich themselves further.[1]

The Charter of the Forest represented an epochal moment when the commoners regained access to land that had been stolen from them. Under its terms, the monarch could no longer appropriate more land, and the forests were reopened for common people to utilize for their traditional forms of provisioning. They could now use it to graze their livestock, cut gorse to fire kilns or ovens, carve hazel poles into gates and fences, trim wood for furniture and house frames, dig peat for fuel, pick mushrooms, snare rabbits, catch fish, gather honey and herbs, and pick fruit to eat. The Charter acknowledged the need for stewardship of the commons, permitting commoners to enjoy the fruit of the land "on condition that it does no harm to any neighbor."

For centuries, commoners organized themselves to protect these rights. In ceremonial processions known as "beating the bounds," peasants would walk the perimeters of the forest, and if they came across a hedge or fence enclosing it, they would knock it down to defend the integrity of the land. However, as we know from chapter 2, all that would change with the systematic violence and coercion of the enclosure movement that erupted in the sixteenth century.

We will see in this chapter how the institution we have come to know as "the law" was a crucial weapon used by the elites to dispossess the peasants from their land, and was then universalized in a worldwide assault on the commons as the customary source of subsistence relied on by the vast majority of non-European peoples. While people nowadays may focus attention on particular unjust laws that need changing, the overall context of "the law" is generally assumed to be a neutral sphere. In this chapter, however, we will see how the law itself has been designed as a systemic enforcer of the wealth pump, sucking the lifeblood from ordinary communities. From that vantage point, we can then begin to envisage a fundamentally transformed version of the agreed-upon rules that might govern human behavior—one that draws its principles instead from a tradition that has sustained humanity worldwide over millennia: the commons.

THE COMMONS AS A SOCIAL SYSTEM

If you've ever taken an introductory course in economics, chances are you've heard about a seemingly ironclad law called "the tragedy of the commons." This is the title of an academic paper published in 1968 by conservative ecologist Garrett Hardin, which became the most widely reprinted article ever published in a scientific journal. The article's success, however, had everything to do with its justification for neoliberal ideology, and nothing to do with its veracity. "Picture a pasture open to all," Hardin wrote. "It is to be expected that each herdsman will try to keep as many cattle as possible on the commons." Hardin's "tragedy" arises on account of the collective self-destruction of each herdsman's ruthless selfishness, causing them to ignore the common good while competing with one another for their own interests until the commons is utterly denuded. "Freedom in a commons," he concluded, "brings ruin to all."[2]

It was not until Elinor Ostrom appeared on the scene in 1990 with her seminal work, *Governing the Commons* (see chapter 6), that the deficiency of Hardin's argument was comprehensively revealed. As we know, Ostrom's groundbreaking research into how communities work together to manage collective goods depicted a world utterly different from Hardin's wretched purgatory—with the added benefit that Ostrom's arose from real-world experience rather than the product of a fevered imagination.[3]

A fundamental difference between these two versions of reality is that a true "commons" refers to something far more multifaceted than simply free access to an open resource. As summarized by commons advocate David Bollier, a commons is "a resource + a community + a set of social protocols." Commons, Bollier explains, "are living social systems through which people address their shared problems in self-organized ways." The design principles that Ostrom enumerated—including such parameters as clearly defined boundaries, collective-choice arrangements, community monitoring, graduated sanctions, and low-cost conflict resolution mechanisms—form a set of rules that enable communities to sustain themselves indefinitely with limited resources, while maintaining the health of their bioregion for future generations. The experience of living in community according to these behavioral norms, called by Bollier "commoning," is essentially aligned with evolved human principles of flourishing, but at odds with the overriding capitalist imperatives of extraction and exploitation.[4]

Ironically, while Hardin's fable had nothing to do with how communities enact the commons around the world, it is an eerily accurate depiction of the neoliberal world order that now dominates the global economy. For this reason, Bollier suggests, it should more properly be called "the tragedy of the market." At a deeper level, the difference between Hardin's and Ostrom's versions of the commons reflects a fundamental divergence in worldviews. At the heart of Hardin's tragedy is a belief in the elemental separation of each individual from their community and of humankind from the rest of life on Earth—the source of the Windigo virus described in chapter 3 that has since overwhelmed our world. Ostrom's depiction, by contrast, describes a living system driven by the same general parameters of life itself identified in chapter 5: dynamic self-organization with multiple feedback loops, the state of unity with differentiation known as integration, and mutually beneficial symbiosis—each parameter arising ultimately from the underlying principle that the relationship between parts of a system are frequently more important than the parts themselves.

Ostrom's principles, as we've seen, have been generalized in recent decades to apply to a proliferation of non-traditional commons incorporating such domains as knowledge, information, music, and software. The patterns of commoning that enable the success of such enterprises undergird many of the community-enhancing exemplars described in previous chapters including local currencies, agroecology, seed-sharing cooperatives, community land trusts, platform cooperatives, Fab Labs, and grassroots democratic governance. There are some important generalities to these cases. They are not organized according to a fixed blueprint imposed by an external authority; rather, their democratically developed practices respond to the specific demands faced by a particular set of circumstances. In contrast to the hierarchical organizational structures of the dominant system, in which power radiates downward while wealth is sucked upward, the organization of commons frequently resemble networked structures known as heterarchy.

Heterarchy is not the opposite of hierarchy. Rather, it combines some elements of hierarchy with the grassroots dynamics of peer-to-peer networks. In a heterarchy, power is distributed horizontally, allowing subgroups to make decisions that relate to their particular expertise, while decisions that affect the group as a whole are made collaboratively. This maintains a broader distribution of power with multiple decision-making centers, known as polycentric governance. As Ostrom's principles predict, multiple benefits arise: Decisions are made by those who best understand the issues; people feel a greater sense of ownership over what they do; and there is greater flexibility to change course when needed.

These informal but highly resilient norms have governed much human activity throughout history. As part of our evolutionary heritage, they allow people to experience actualized lives in community, playing their part in modifying and monitoring the rules when needed, and contributing to the overall health of the group. For millennia, these commons-based forms of self-organization survived worldwide even within larger structures of oppression and domination from centralized agrarian regimes. This uneasy equilibrium, epitomized by the Charter of the Forest, would however be swept away with the rise of the enclosure movement in early modern Europe.

THE INSTALLATION OF THE WEALTH PUMP

The modern assault on the commons had its roots in ancient times, most notably with the codification of law decreed by the Roman emperor Justinian in the sixth century. The Code of Justinian, completed in 534 CE, is considered the most consequential law book in history and forms the foundation of the Western legal tradition. The categories of property defined by Justinian created the conceptual structures for most major legal doctrines that followed.

A central concept was the *dominium*: the household of the Roman patriarch which included his wife, children, slaves, land, and livestock, all of which were utterly subject to his will and could be used, mistreated, and in some cases killed at his whim with impunity. There were important distinctions made between various forms of non-private ownership. Some property, such as public land, squares, and aqueducts were *res publicae*—belonging to the city. Certain things such as the air, sea, beaches, and rivers were considered *res communis omnium*—belonging to everyone by natural law, requiring shared use and accessibility for all people. The final category was *res nullius*—belonging to no one, until someone claimed it for themselves. This category, which covered wild animals or abandoned property, also crucially included land that had not yet been claimed by any legally recognized entity and was therefore open for the taking. From Justinian's time onward, the concept of *res nullius* would give legal justification for the violent seizure and enclosure of the commons in Europe and, with the rise of European colonialism, much of the Earth's land.[5]

The first centuries of the English enclosure movement, as landlords asserted rights over land that had previously been used as commons, can be understood as a contest between two conflicting interpretations of land: as *res communis omnium*, freely accessible for all to use—or *res nullius*, land waiting to be claimed for private ownership. There were no titles or land registries in those days, and disputes were frequently decided in court, mostly but not always in favor of the landlords, who would characterize commoners as rioters blocking their "improvements" which would bring prosperity to all. Landlords received significant support from the theories of philosopher John Locke in the seventeenth century, who argued that, by cultivating or "improving" land that was previously undeveloped, a proprietor earned the moral right to claim that land as his private property.

The changing tide in favor of landlords culminated in the Act of Settlement (1701) which, inspired by the new thinking of the Scientific Revolution, established the "rule of law" as a scientific truth to be discovered by professionally trained lawyers who would codify it using the scientific method. The "Settlement" referred, not to a settlement between landowners and commoners, but between Parliament (representing property owners) and the Crown. At this point, the entire idea of the commons, as represented by the Charter of the Forest, along with its informal, self-organized, community-based set of customary norms, disappeared from legal view. The idea that landowners had any obligations to those who used the land for sustenance was eradicated. William Blackstone, the first Oxford professor of English law, defined private property in 1765 as the "sole and despotic dominion which one man claims and exercises over the external things of the world, in total exclusion of the right of any other individual in the universe"—a definition that would set the foundation for modern law.

As European powers extended their "despotic dominion" over the rest of the world, they used the concept of *res nullius* to grant themselves legal justification for unlimited plunder and exploitation. A notary traveled with Columbus to witness that the land of the New World was *res nullius*, giving legal title to anyone who staked their claim to the gold and silver mines, along with the slaves used to extract the metals. The US Supreme Court ruled in 1823 that "discovery gave an exclusive right to extinguish the Indian title of occupancy either by purchase or by conquest"—thus transforming overnight the native peoples of the territory into illegal squatters on their land, and sanctioning their forceful removal into reservations so the land could be carved up and titled into settlers' private property. Recognizing this shameful history, prominent political scientists have described this process of state-making through legitimizing plunder as a form of organized crime writ large.[6]

With commoners and Indigenous peoples out of the picture, the structures of modern law formed primarily to protect private property from appropriation by government, while ensuring that property owners had the full force of legalized state violence to back them up whenever their rights might be compromised. Government, meanwhile, assumed to represent the common interest, was free to take property from the commons, either for itself or to transfer it to private ownership for further "development." Any transfer in the other direction, from the private sector to the public, can only rarely be done under stringent judicial review. In this way, modern law has institutionalized the wealth pump as an inherent structural design characteristic.

As the ultimate enforcer of property rights, the primary function of the state is to protect the interests of property-owners through core legal modules such as contracts, collateral rules, corporate protections, and bankruptcy law. The legal protections given to private property by the state are equivalent to a giant hidden subsidy allowing capital to enjoy lavish returns with minimal enforcement costs. Meanwhile, as "sole despotic" owners, land developers can exploit their land through reckless practices such as fracking or real estate speculation, regardless of how it might impact the well-being of others.

RELATIONAL LAW

Reclaiming our future in the form of an ecocivilization requires a recognition of this structural design of law and a conscious dismantling of the legally constructed wealth pump. What might an alternative look like? Recognizing that modern law is based, like Hardin's fable, on a worldview of separation, we can begin by exploring the potential framework of a legal system based, instead, on the relational principles underlying the commons—an "ecology of law" as envisioned by the legal system scholars Fritjof Capra and Ugo Mattei in a book by that name.

The legal theorist Alex May conceptualizes this alternative legal paradigm as "interconnected law" which emphasizes, above all, the value of the interconnected web of relationships that constitute a society—relations with each other as well as the living Earth. Law, he suggests, "should focus on the relationships that are the context and conditions within which individuals act. In general, law's goal should be looking to improve the web of relations we live in," rather than engaging in the zero-sum game of protecting one individual's rights against another. The aim would not be to abolish individual rights, but "to contextualize them in this relational web and have that be the focus instead."

Traditional Indigenous values, consistent with commons-based principles, offer a fundamentally different orientation for a relational system of rules. Indigenous groups worldwide hold in common the precept that, rather than "despotic dominion," rights always come with responsibilities. As explained by Sherri Mitchell, author of *Sacred Instructions: Indigenous Wisdom for Living Spirit-Based Change*, "demanding rights without taking responsibility creates a warped sense of entitlement." A right to clean water comes with the responsibility for protecting the water from contamination or overuse. A right to a healthy life is accompanied by responsibility for the lives already existing around us.[7]

This core concept is epitomized by the traditional Hawaiian term *kuleana*, which encompassed a sense of privilege, responsibility, and stewardship. *Kuleana* governed the people's relationship with each other and nonhuman island inhabitants, obliging direct personal contributions to society's flourishing, accountability for individual actions, and responsibility to the land and future generations. As a result, while the premodern Hawaiian population increased over centuries to 800,000, the island's biodiversity continued to thrive.[8]

Relational law would have a dynamic quality. Modern law, with its basis in reductionist ontology, is conceived as a fixed set of parameters, which can be interpreted by specialists but amended only by centralized legislation. Relational law, arising from the self-organized dynamics of living systems, would be more adaptable to changing local conditions. Just as the meaning of *kuleana* would unfold over time as individuals grew and acquired new roles in their community, so the rules governing communities' interactions would continually evolve as an adaptive process, based on core underlying principles with a solid foundation of equity and fairness, but contingent on specific conditions arising. Rather than relying on a specialized cadre of legally trained mercenaries to fight battles in court, disputes could be resolved by smaller versions of citizens' assemblies looking for resolutions that could restore more harmonious relations between disputants going forward.

The foundational concept of ownership coexisting with responsibility would have far-reaching practical ramifications for property law. In societies with scarce, overpriced housing and widespread homelessness, practices such as flipping empty homes for price speculation, charging exorbitant rents, or maintaining unoccupied second homes, would be unacceptable. Landowners would no longer have the right to keep people off their land at their whim. Such "trespass-free" conventions already exist in Norway, Sweden, and Finland where "right to roam" laws forbid fencing of private property, holding owners legally responsible to allow safe and open access to their land, including camping for a reasonable time period. More broadly, if vacant land held by absentee owners were responsibly cultivated for sustenance by local farmers (such as Brazil's MST movement described in chapter 14), they should customarily be granted provisional title which would evolve over time into a transfer of ownership.[9]

Relational law would involve a fundamental change in the conceptualization of the state. Consistent with the idea of the Partner State described in the previous chapter, the state's legitimacy would arise, not from its protection of private property, but from its fostering of the collective health of the entire society. While private property would continue to play a legitimate role as long as it served a generative purpose, when conflicts arose, the sovereignty and integrity of the common good would override that of private ownership rights. Examples of these changed priorities have been described extensively in earlier chapters, such as a triple bottom line requirement for corporations; a wealth cap and land value tax funding universal basic income, universal basic services, and commonwealth trusts; full-cost pricing on products; and fiat money allocated directly by governments according to need.

FROM INTELLECTUAL PROPERTY TO OPEN INFORMATION

A crucial aspect of law requiring transformation is the intellectual property (IP) regime, which represents a major frontline in the continuing enclosure of the commons. Intellectual property rights first emerged as a concept in fifteenth-century Venice, when artisans were required to register "new and ingenious devices" with authorities, allowing the city to use these devices "for its own use and needs" but in return prohibiting anyone else from using the same device without the artisan's permission. This quid pro quo between individual rights and the common good quickly evaporated as the idea spread throughout Europe to become a unilateral claim of ownership over intellectual property, enjoying the moral support of Locke's theory that cultivation of any *res nullius* justified ownership. A fundamental flaw in this theory is the fact that, as discussed in chapter 10, the innovations granted patents are nearly always mere tweaks representing what sociologist Lewis Mumford describes as "the last link in the complicated social process that produced the invention." This is true, not just of technological designs but also the music, art, and literature emerging from the cultural commons.[10]

The standard argument used by proponents of IP is that it promotes innovation, but this contention has been shown to be bogus. Studies have failed to demonstrate any correlation between innovation and stronger IP protections. Instead, it's widely recognized that corporate abuse of IP law stifles the very innovations it's supposed to generate. With global patents lasting for twenty years, and granted for a wide range of spurious inventions, major corporations invest heavily in armies of lawyers who claim or acquire patents as tactical fortifications to maintain monopolies by blocking or suing potential competitors. This has the paradoxical effect of reducing their need to innovate further.[11]

A hundred years ago, it was unthinkable for the commonwealth of human knowledge to be enclosed. US Supreme Court Justice Brandeis declared in 1918 that "the general rule of law is, that the noblest of human productions—knowledge, truths ascertained, conceptions, and ideas—become, after voluntary communication to others, free as the air to common use." When virologist Jonas Salk developed a vaccine for polio in 1954, he scoffed at a journalist asking him about ownership of the patent, saying: "There is no patent. Could you patent the sun?" Since then, neoliberal ideology has upended this priceless human heritage. An act of the US government in 1980 directed that any IP arising from government-funded research should be transferred from the public domain to private ownership, routinely appropriating public knowledge for corporate profits.

One of the greatest scientific achievements of the modern era has been the sequencing of the string of three billion nucleotides that make up the human genome. Our genetic code, shared by all humans, is open information freely available to all researchers. However, it very nearly became private property, controlled by a single company to monopolize for profit. Two groups competed in a race to finish the sequencing: The Human Genome Project, an international consortium of scientists from twenty different nonprofit and public institutions; and Celera Genomics, a private company launched by centimillionaire Craig Ventner with the aim of patenting the genome and exploiting it financially. It was a close race in which, as described by the Nobel prize–winning biologist John Sulston, "the whole future of biology came under threat. For one company was bidding for monopoly control of access to the most fundamental information about humanity, information that is—or should be—our common heritage."[12]

How can this pernicious enclosure of the knowledge commons—our irreplaceable human birthright—be stopped? Is there a way for innovators to be rewarded for their contributions without penalizing the rest of humanity? In a groundbreaking book, *The Open Revolution: Rewriting the Rules of the Information Age*, the economist Rufus Pollock shows that there is, in fact, a model that would make all the world's IP freely available while ensuring fair remuneration for creators.

IP is fundamentally different from physical property such as a house, in that it can be shared endlessly without obstructing the ability of the original owners to enjoy it—a characteristic described by economists as non-rivalrous. Frequently, in fact, the value of information increases the more it's shared. Watching the World Cup final wouldn't be much fun if you were the only person who knew it was happening.

Pollock lays out a framework for non-rivalrous property that would replace patents and copyrights with "remuneration rights," which would entitle creators to payment from a fund according to the value that their information generates. Songs could be valued according to how many times they're played; a medicine according to its measurable impact on improving health worldwide. In return, all information created and registered would be openly accessible to everyone.[13]

Instead of paying IP owners directly, people would pay collectively into trust funds that could be managed by trustees in a manner similar to the commonwealth trusts described in chapter 10. Different trusts would exist for different pools of IP such as software, music, film, and medicine. These trusts would allocate funds to creators based on algorithms developed to assign fair compensation. Pharmaceutical companies, for example, would receive compensation based on the demonstrated value of a particular innovation they registered, but would not have the right to hold humanity hostage based on a series of patents.

Significant issues arise from this model which would need to be resolved collectively. What should be the size of the entertainment fund versus the medicine fund? Initial sizes for each pool could be based on current parameters and modified over time by consensual debate using a citizens' assembly model. In the current neoliberal model, the market is supposed to determine these questions. In reality, however, the monopolistic practices of Big Pharma, Big Ag, Big Tech, and other concentrated industries have warped any pretense of market efficiency. Furthermore, as discussed in chapter 7, unrestrained market pricing inevitably optimizes resource allocation for wealthy elites rather than for humanity as a whole.

Other substantial issues would need to be resolved in such a radical metamorphosis of this legal framework. What is clear, however, is that in contrast to the artificial scarcity of the current IP protection regime, an open knowledge commons could create limitless abundance of information that would transform our world, increasing innovation, creativity, fairness of opportunities and outcomes, and global wealth. In an open model, every kind of information including science and technology, music, news, entertainment, and creative works would be shared by all humanity rather than held captive by profit-seeking corporations.

FROM RETRIBUTIVE TO TRANSFORMATIVE JUSTICE

The criminal justice system is another component of law needing fundamental restructuring. In medieval communities, people who breached acceptable standards of behavior generally received graduated sanctions (one of Ostrom's principles) ranging from reprimands to ostracism in severe cases. As the enclosure movement stripped people of their livelihood, "houses of corrections" were established for petty criminals and vagrants, which evolved in the eighteenth century into a new conception of imprisonment itself as a form of punishment.

Since then, incarceration has become a central part of the world's legal order, with over 11 million people held in penal institutions, an increase of more than 25 percent since 2000. The world leader in incarceration is the United States, accounting for more than 20 percent of the world's total number of prisoners. While politicians preoccupied with reelection strive to be perceived as "tough on crime," the dirty little secret of imprisonment is that it does not work. Rather than teaching offenders that "crime doesn't pay" and making society safer, mass incarceration has been shown to increase the likelihood that offenders will go on to commit further crimes.[14]

Systematic studies by criminologists conclude that prisons act more like a "crime school," severing previous social bonds, stigmatizing inmates, and fostering anger and resentment. As a result, offenders re-entering society are more likely to commit further crimes than if they had never been imprisoned. Studies show recidivism rates of about 70 percent within three to five years of release, significantly higher than the rate from noncustodial sanction.[15]

The current criminal justice paradigm views a crime essentially as an offense committed by an individual who must be punished. A relational approach, by contrast, would focus on the conditions that led to the wrongdoing and intervene to reorient people's lives into a more wholesome direction. Norway, once again, leads the world in a more enlightened response to those who have committed crimes. As reported by author Rutger Bregman, maximum security prisons such as Halden and Bastøy house drug dealers, sexual offenders, and murderers, but with a model that flips the conventional approach to incarceration. Inmates each have a room of their own with underfloor heating, a flatscreen TV, and a private bathroom. They have access to kitchens equipped with steel knives, a library, and a fully equipped music recording studio. Guards don't carry weapons, don't wear uniforms, and eat meals with the inmates sitting around the same table. Inmates grow much of their own food, chop wood, and do carpentry. The goal of these prisons, Rutger explains, "is not about preventing bad behavior, but preventing bad intentions . . . to prepare detainees, as best they can, for a normal life." The results are remarkable. Norway's recidivism rate is the lowest in the world, with Bastøy reporting just 16 percent. "It's really very simple," explains Bastøy's warden, Tom Eberhardt. "Treat people like dirt, and they'll be dirt. Treat them like human beings, and they'll act like human beings."[16]

In relational law, while the Norwegian model would be exemplary for occasions when imprisonment is required, more generally practices known as restorative and transformative justice would be paramount. Indigenous approaches to conflict resolution frequently use a council process, requiring an offender to face up to those they harmed, listen to their experiences, accept accountability, and make restitution. Drawing on these traditions, restorative justice methods go beyond the incarceration model with a mediated process involving perpetrator, victim, and others involved. In this framework, holding a wrongdoer accountable is not about punishment or retribution, but repairing broken relationships within the community and moving people's lives into a more healing direction. Restorative justice has been shown to benefit victims, offenders, and the broader community, resulting in lower recidivism rates and improved victim satisfaction, while fostering accountability and healing.[17]

RECLAIMING THE COMMONS

While the dominant world order is currently based on the antithesis of relational law, our evolved human drive toward mutual cooperation continues to imbue a broad and powerful commons movement thriving as a kind of subterranean mycelial network of subversive collaboration.

Commoning, as Bollier explains, is the natural form of human relationship, where solidarity and fellowship override the frenzied drive to exploit others for personal gain. The commons stands as an existential adversary of market economics, affirming a diametrically different standard of valuation. Rather than prioritizing profits and growth, commons enterprises value fairness, belonging, connection, security, and meaningful relationships. Together, these filaments of mutuality, many of which we've already encountered, have the potential to converge to form a worldwide movement—one with platform cooperatives empowering worker-owned enterprises partnering with community land trusts and enhanced by local currencies.

The voluntary sharing of information and low cost of mutual coordination offers the potential for commons-based enterprises to out-compete—or "out-cooperate"—market capitalism. In 2001, for example, when Wikipedia formed, Encyclopædia Britannica had been the world's dominant reputable reference source for two centuries; ten years later, people-powered Wikipedia was 85 times its size with comparable accuracy, and today has become the unrivaled global champion of peer-reviewed general information.[18]

Just as medieval peasants used to "beat the bounds" to keep at bay the onslaught of enclosure, so modern-day commoners beat back the encroachments of the market on our shared human heritage. In a world dominated by neoliberal capitalism, this is a never-ending struggle. As Kate Raworth observes (see chapter 7), markets are like fire, and commons-based entities need strong firewalls to protect themselves from the inferno. Investors and corporations, supported by nation-states, are engaged in a perpetual drive to enclose and commodify the remaining land, forests, water, culture, and genes that are still *res communis omnium*. Even sanctuaries of mutual cooperation are continually under assault from the market: Members of housing co-ops are tempted to cash out when market prices rise; a collaborative software development group might receive an irresistible acquisition bid from a Big Tech company. If just one person in a commons receives monetary payment for what others are freely contributing, other commoners will begin to feel unjustly treated and lose their motivation. Clear and enforceable rules are therefore required to defend the commons from market corrosion.[19]

Frequently, these rules are devised as "hacks" of the current legal system, using creative adaptations of laws designed for protection of private property and repurposing them in ways never imagined by lawmakers. A spectacularly successful example is the set of Creative Commons licenses used today by over 1.6 billion creative works. These simple and standardized licenses, conceived in 2001 by the Harvard legal scholar Lawrence Lessig, permit others to copy, share, and modify a creator's work as long as it's not used commercially, offering various fine-tuning conditions for a creator to select. The Creative Commons idea was itself derived from a General Public License for software, known as "copyleft," originally developed in the 1980s by the free software hacker Richard Stallman, which became pivotal to the open-source software industry.[20]

In these cases, the "despotic dominion" of private property is repurposed to establish rules that create firewall protection from market corrosion, but then voluntarily relinquished for the sake of *communis omnium*. Similar ingenious market firewalls have been erected to protect common housing from torrid real estate markets. A German federation of common housing, Mietshäuser Syndikat, manages 170 housing projects offering affordable homes to thousands of residents. People own their buildings but pay rent to themselves as a collective to maintain their properties. The temptation for a group of owners to capitalize on market effervescence and sell their property is prevented by a legal structure that gives the Syndikat veto authority before such a sale could take place. This mechanism, described as "capital neutralization," enables all residents to trust in the long-term maintenance of their community regardless of ambient market conditions.

Legal hacks such as these can be initiated by entire cities. In 2010, the people of Pittsburgh were alarmed by aggressive tactics of oil and gas companies acquiring land leases for fracking with the likelihood of long-term toxic effects on residents' health. While Pittsburgh's city council was unanimously against this development, they were hamstrung by legislation from the state of Pennsylvania which prohibited them from limiting or banning fracking. In response, the council adopted a Community Bill of Rights, claiming enforceable rights to clean water and air, recognizing nature's right to flourish, and reaffirming the power of local community to protect these rights.[21]

Galvanized by this example, other municipalities in Pennsylvania, Ohio, Colorado, California, and New Mexico have drafted and adopted similar legislation. Although many of these claims later get overturned by higher courts backed by powerful corporations, some remain in effect, particularly in tribal and local jurisdictions. In general, while these and other legal hacks subvert the dominant regime of private enclosure, a comprehensive reformulation of law would need the support of a Partner State, as described in the previous chapter, to coordinate a more symbiotic relationship between markets, the commons, and centralized authorities.[22]

A transformation to an ecocivilization will require a fundamental reimagining of our entire legal system. While widely accepted as a natural state of affairs, the law itself has been constructed over centuries as an imperceptible but potent force that permeates virtually every aspect of our social, political, and economic relations, imposing structures that inexorably pump wealth and power away from common people into the hands of a small, propertied elite. As we've seen from this chapter, an alternative formulation of law is not only feasible, but could create a framework more aligned with our evolved human attributes, one that empowers grassroots communities to regain their primacy as the foundation of sustainable human flourishing.

POSSIBLE SECOND AND THIRD HORIZON CONTOURS | LAW

SECOND HORIZON

"Right to roam" laws based on the Scandinavian model applied by nation-states around the world

Title to vacant land held by absentee landlords transferred to those who cultivate it responsibly for sustenance

IP from government-funded research belongs by default to the commons and cannot be transferred to private ownership

Prisons transformed based on Norway's model to treat inmates with dignity and prepare them for a law-abiding life after release

Laws amended where appropriate to support commons structures and strengthen firewalls to protect from market corrosion

Governments encourage a more symbiotic relationship between markets and the commons by decentralizing decision-making from central government to local communities

THIRD HORIZON

Relational law is the paradigm for a restructured legal system based on the precept that rights always come with responsibilities

The state's legitimacy arises, not from protection of private property, but from its fostering of the collective health of society

When conflicts arise, the sovereignty and integrity of the common good override that of private ownership rights

All information created and registered is openly accessible in an open knowledge commons

The IP regime is replaced by "remuneration rights" entitling creators to payment from a fund according to the value their information generates

Judicial process for wrongdoers is based on principles of restorative justice

FOR CONSIDERATION

What Second and Third Horizon ideas arise in your own mind inspired by this chapter?

CHAPTER 16

GLOBAL GOVERNANCE: GUIDING PRINCIPLES FOR STEERING A PLANETARY COMMUNITY

It was barely a month after the end of World War II. Over three nightmarish decades, the world had suffered unimaginable horrors: two world wars causing an estimated 75 million deaths; the industrialized extermination of Nazi concentration camps; the firebombing of entire cities; and the devastation of Hiroshima and Nagasaki from two atomic bombs. As a battered world vowed "Never Again," in the days approaching the launch of the United Nations, Albert Einstein and other notable thinkers published a letter in the *New York Times*—not to endorse the UN but to condemn it.

What Einstein and others saw as the UN's fatal flaw was that it affirmed full sovereignty for its members' governments without establishing any power over them—essentially the same structure that had led to the earlier failure of the League of Nations. Instead, they wrote: "We must aim at a Federal Constitution of the world, a working worldwide legal order, if we hope to prevent an atomic war." Later that year, Einstein published an essay with a warning that seems grimly prophetic eight decades later: "An individual state with sufficient military and economic power can easily resort to violence, and voluntarily destroy the entire structure of supranational security built on nothing but words and documents. Moral authority alone is an inadequate means of securing the peace."[1]

Einstein's proposal called for any individual state to "be prevented from making war by a supranational organization supported by a military power that is exclusively under its control." This could only happen if nation-states voluntarily ceded their sovereign power. While this idea may seem wildly utopian from today's vantage point, it commanded broad support in the immediate aftermath of World War II, even among such established politicians as Winston Churchill and Jawaharlal Nehru. In a 1947 poll, 56 percent of Americans surveyed agreed that "the UN should be strengthened to make it a world government," and in 1949 the House Committee on Foreign Affairs held hearings on a resolution cosponsored by 105 members of Congress to support the development of the UN into "a world federation open to all nations with . . . powers adequate to preserve peace and prevent aggression through the enactment, interpretation, and enforcement of world law."

This was the closest humanity has ever come to any form of organized world governance. It is notable that it took extraordinary horrors to awaken a popular desire for such transformative change. Before long, however, nationalistic power dynamics prevailed, and the worldwide system solidified into the configuration that has dominated the past eighty years, with sovereign nation-states agreeing to certain moral codes and then choosing whether to apply them to their own actions.

In the current era, with increasingly brazen authoritarian regimes discarding even the pretense of a rules-based world system, it's becoming clear that the global order of the past eight decades is disintegrating. It may take many years before its replacement clearly emerges. Meanwhile, an unsettled future beckons with the potential for cataclysms that could leave even last century's upheavals in the shade.

It is in this sobering context that this chapter will explore the contours of how global governance might plausibly steward a planetary community for sustained well-being. While some ideas considered may seem far-fetched by today's standards, it is important to remain mindful of the groundswell of support for Einstein's proposals in the years following World War II. When previously solid global norms crumble, the possibility exists that multitudes around the world will begin to recognize the need, like Einstein, for "some assurance that we shall not vanish into the atmosphere, dissolved into atoms, one of these days." Since Einstein's era, thinking about world governance has developed greater sophistication. In the precarious years ahead, this might just be the time when such ideas take root and spread more extensively than ever before.

THE WORLD AS A FAILED STATE

Throughout human history, multiple societies around the world have designed their own governance systems. It's estimated that, around 1,500 BCE, with the world's population at 50 million, thousands of different political units existed. To a large degree, these units were self-contained: What happened in Mesopotamia had no impact on a Chinese fiefdom. Gradually—then very rapidly—these separate polities became inextricably linked in a complex interdependent web until the number of autonomous units has arguably decreased to just one: the entire world system. There is no place to escape from climate breakdown or fallout from thermonuclear war.

However, we now suffer a numerical mismatch between autonomous units and governance systems. The fate of a single world system is subject to the chaotic interactions of roughly 200 sovereign nation-states, causing grievous dysfunction. If viewed as a single country, our world exhibits the anarchic turmoil generally characteristic of a failed state.

We're so accustomed to the system of sovereign nation-states that we might consider it to be a natural state of affairs, but its origin can be traced back just a few hundred years to the Peace of Westphalia that ended the Thirty Years War in Europe in 1648. This was the moment when the idea of sovereignty became paramount in international affairs. Sovereignty is different from authority and power, which can be assumed by any person or group strong enough to force their will on others. Rather, sovereignty is a collective assumption about power: an agreement by different states to recognize each other as the exclusive authority within their own territory. Since it arises through collective agreement, sovereignty can also be revised or even eliminated through collective decisions.[2]

To some degree, the sovereignty of nation-states has already been surrendered to a greater authority—but not the one that Einstein had in mind. As described in chapter 3, the Global Power Elite, a tight-knit group of roughly seven thousand people meeting in Davos and other exclusive sanctuaries, undermine nation-states' sovereignty through their control of global capital, frequently making decisions that national governments must implement. More broadly, transnational corporations, controlling operational empires larger than the economies of most nation-states, make executive decisions for their own benefit that dictate the priorities of national governments, bolstered by legal instruments such as intellectual property (IP) rights or threats of ISDS claims (see chapters 2 and 15). Adding a veneer of legitimacy to their unwarranted domination, they bring the notion of "multistakeholder governance" into global policy discussions, in which "stakeholder" refers to agribusinesses or Big Tech rather than the people affected by their decisions. Moreover, the dominance of the World Trade Organization (WTO) in enforcing corporations' claims over nation-states has led some observers to view it as "the actual existing world government"—one that exists, not for nations or their peoples, but for the benefit of global capital.[3]

The idea of the nation-state can also be traced back to seventeenth-century Europe, when elites realized they could consolidate their power by promoting a narrative of a single nation with a shared identity vying with its neighbors. The term is a hybrid of two concepts: "nation" indicates a people with common heritage and characteristics whereas "state" describes an organized political system holding sovereignty over a geographical area. Ruling elites quickly discovered that nationalism unleashed powerful forces they could harness, by creating a mythic family-like cohesion that allowed them to maneuver common people into sacrificing everything—even their own lives—for the national cause.

Throughout most of human history, the world map was a hodgepodge of city-states, principalities, unclaimed territory, and empires, which could be traversed without the need for passports. Creating nation-states did not come easily, since people naturally identified with their own regional, ethnic, and linguistic groups. As late as 1863, French was still a foreign language for half its citizens. However, in the twentieth century, as nations claimed independence in the wake of colonialism, the European model of nation-states became the default vehicle for governance.

It was the UN's backing of nation-state sovereignty that Einstein railed against so vehemently. Nevertheless, for all its faults, the UN's architects attempted to set a moral foundation to guide the future interplay of nations. The Universal Declaration of Human Rights, along with the Genocide Convention, both adopted in 1948, established a principle of universality: the axiom that everyone, without exception, is endowed with basic human rights, and nations have an obligation to respect these rights. This spawned a series of international conventions establishing norms for how to navigate the complexities of global conflicts consistent with upholding human rights. A major milestone was achieved in 2002 with the establishment of the International Criminal Court (ICC), the first permanent international court with jurisdiction to prosecute individuals for war crimes, genocide, and crimes against humanity.

While there have been numerous failures of this system, ranging from the Vietnam War to genocides in Cambodia and Rwanda, and frequent coups in the Global South sponsored by Western powers, there was a broadly understood sense of accountability. Those who flagrantly breached the norms had to defend themselves in the court of public opinion, even if they had the power to get away with it.

This rules-based system arguably began its retreat with the collapse of the Soviet Union in 1991, when the United States' attempt to claim global hegemony on the basis of overwhelming military force, economic dominance, and soft cultural power, caused some to view this moment erroneously as the "end of history." However, not everyone assented to this takeover. Ten years later, after the shock of 9/11, the United States unleashed its "war on terror" which explicitly excluded certain people from the moral protection of human rights, based on its government's sole discretion. Since then, governments around the world, mimicking the same rhetoric, have conveniently adopted this arrogation for their own ends.[4]

Even before the Trump regime assumed power in 2025, there was widespread recognition that the post-war rules-based system was unraveling. In 2024, UN Secretary-General António Guterres issued a stark warning that the world had entered an "age of impunity" as Israel's mass killings in Gaza—condemned as genocidal by respected international institutions and inducing arrest warrants by the ICC for its leading perpetrators—continued unchecked. "Today," Guterres declared, "a growing number of governments and others feel entitled to . . . thumb their nose at international humanitarian law. They can invade another country, lay waste to whole societies, or utterly disregard the welfare of their own people. And nothing will happen. We see this age of impunity everywhere." The disregard for previously functioning norms exhibited by the Trump administration is further dismantling the flimsy structure that remained. "The rules-based liberal international order," in the words of one observer, "has been consigned to the ashcan of history."[5]

This failure could not come at a worse moment for humanity. We face multiple existential crises. Ecological devastation and climate breakdown, gaping economic inequalities, socio-political fragmentation, and exponential technological change intensified by the rise of AI, all point to a world that needs, more than ever, a judicious and humane system of governance.

In the turbulent power struggles that lie ahead, the most terrifying threat is that of nuclear warfare. There are good reasons why the Bulletin of the Atomic Scientists set the Doomsday Clock in 2025 to the closest it has ever been to midnight. After decades of nuclear disarmament agreements mitigating such risk, we are entering an era defined by "the almost total absence of the security architectures that went before," in the words of Admiral Tony Radakin, the former chief of the United Kingdom's armed forces. As the United States and Russia invest in new nuclear capabilities, with China aggressively playing catch-up, erstwhile US allies now wonder whether they need their own nuclear deterrent.[6]

There has never been a greater need for world governance, even as its realization has rarely seemed more remote. Yet, as the experiences of last century demonstrate, it is precisely when the fear of annihilation looms large that radical demands for change intensify. Because of this, the ideas we are about to explore are not merely scenarios for a distant future. They may well become centerpieces of public discourse sooner than we might imagine.

PRINCIPLES OF WORLD GOVERNANCE

There is certainly no lack of proposals for a world government—it's estimated that over 150 proposed World Constitutions have been drafted. However, even if a change in global power dynamics opened up the possibility for a single planetary authority, many thoughtful observers shudder at this possibility. Suppose it became tyrannical? In the current world system, anarchic as it is, at least there is the potential to escape the clutches of an oppressive regime for a more amenable jurisdiction. In a single world order, there would be no place to go. Most advocates for world government, aware of this, propose a federal, multilayered, system of checks and balances between different centers of power. However, as the recent history of the United States demonstrates, even the most carefully conceived constitution can be undermined.

Nevertheless, the stakes for planetary welfare are too high to allow this risk to forestall the very idea of a world government. Instead, astute thinkers have attempted to establish certain foundations upon which a resilient system of governance might safely work. Researcher Paul Raskin, founder of the Tellus Institute, proposes three core principles which are consistent with those of an ecocivilization. First is the recognition that some issues, such as the health of the biosphere, human rights, fair use of planetary resources, and maintaining world peace, require a global level of governance: the *irreducibility principle.* The crucially important *subsidiarity principle*, however, strictly limits that global authority, devolving decision-making to the most local feasible level. Finally, the *heterogeneity principle* endorses the rights of regions to fulfill their global responsibilities in their own distinct ways.[7]

The principle of subsidiarity has appeared elsewhere in this book, but there is, perhaps, no place where it's more important than the realm of global governance. Recognizing this, authors Jonathan Blake and Nils Gilman of the Berggruen Institute propose planetary subsidiarity as a "fundamentally new architecture for the governance of the planet." They outline three scales for institutions: planetary for irreducibly global issues; national for large-scale effectiveness; and local for accordance with specific conditions and preferences. Their overriding doctrine is that authority should always be "allocated to the smallest-scale governing institution capable of managing the task effectively." Subsidiarity, they note, "aims to maximize local control within an overarching governance framework that retains the capacity to manage shared problems."[8]

How might this work in practice? The European Union (EU) is perhaps the closest real-word example of supranational governance, with nations voluntarily relinquishing some of their sovereignty for a vision enshrined as "ever-closer union among the peoples of Europe." As such, it offers a valuable case study that is both exemplar and warning. The EU's founding treaty was executed in 1992. During earlier debates in the 1980s, as nationalists raised concerns about centralization of power, advocates for European federation proffered the principle of subsidiarity to reassure them, with the result that it became one of the EU's founding principles. Since then, however, nation-states have yielded significant, binding powers to a central institution that can issue a common currency and debt, overturn national laws, and enforce wide-ranging standards and regulations. While most Europeans still view the EU favorably, they see it as out of touch with citizens' needs. Where did subsidiarity go? Blake and Gilman explain that, in essence, sovereignty has been yielded, not to elected representatives, but to neoliberal forces that wield the power to ensure that Europe-wide policy decisions work primarily for their benefit.

This highlights the overriding need—discussed in chapter 14—for true participatory democracy to replace the deeply flawed system of electoral democracy. Any system of global governance relying on electoral democracy will be subject to the same structural dynamics experienced in today's national systems, in which power inevitably gravitates toward moneyed elites intent on maintaining their control over the wealth pump. An authentic and sustainable system of planetary subsidiarity would require a worldwide extension of the fractal and grassroots democracy models sketched out in that chapter, in which power originates and persists in local people's assemblies, and cannot easily be hijacked by unrepresentative forces.

A FRAMEWORK FOR FRACTAL FLOURISHING

In today's globalized, commoditized world, where flows of information and material move faster, further, and at greater scale than ever before, the idea of concentrating power locally might seem quaint and even far-fetched. However, many pioneering thinkers have formulated alternative visions for how the world might be organized, not according to global networks, nor even nation-states, but based on bioregions.

Bioregionalism begins with the recognition that, in many cases, the boundaries of nation-states make no sense—they are merely the imposition of a geographical abstraction, frequently the historical result of violent conquest or an afterthought of colonial appropriation. Instead, bioregionalism seeks a renewed human relationship with the land, nurturing a deeper connection between the political, economic, and cultural design of communities and natural, place-based processes of weather, watersheds, and ecologies.[9]

While nature's borders are more fluid than geospatial coordinates drawn in longitude and latitude, they remain quite stable. The boundaries they form contain an internally consistent logic that blends human activity with the natural rhythms of the terrain. Names given to bioregions, such as Amazon Sacred Headwaters or Salmon Nation, frequently reflect a regional identity that emerges from this harmonization between humans and nature. The One Earth Project has mapped out the entire planet according to bioregions, identifying fourteen broadly defined biome "realms" incorporating a total of 185 unique bioregions, each with its distinctive natural features.[10]

From a global governance perspective, bioregions might be viewed as a more coherent organizing configuration for true subsidiarity, permitting large-scale planetary issues to be broken down to local levels where they can be more effectively managed for tangible impact. Culturally, a bioregional approach can offer profound reorientation, connecting people, not just to their physical space, but to deeper bonds with each other and the natural world, encouraging an ontological shift from the modernist worldview of separation to a lived experience of intimate interconnectedness—frequently informed by native Indigenous peoples for whom bioregionalism has always been an intrinsic form of organization. Economically, bioregions would prioritize local industry, with food production largely consistent with principles of agroecology (see chapter 9), accessing global markets mostly for products that are not locally available. Politically, some thinkers envisage a scenario in which the internal cohesion of bioregions makes the nation-state itself obsolete, leading to a potential Third Horizon scenario of a world constituted of bioregions instead of demarcated by today's political boundaries.

Such bioregions would still require planetary coordination for the world's irreducible problems. Recognizing this, some have extended the bioregional vision to embrace a synthesis of cosmopolitanism and localism, or *cosmolocalism*. The idea of cosmopolitanism can be traced back in the West to ancient Greece, when the philosopher Diogenes identified himself as a "citizen of the world." Many non-European traditions express similar ideas of the unity of humanity, such as the African term *bumuntu*, which denotes a virtuous person who respects the dignity of all life. In Europe, the cosmopolitan concept was later reimagined by the eighteenth-century philosopher Immanuel Kant, who laid out an early vision of world citizenship superseding local legal codes.[11]

The amalgam of cosmolocalism was conceived in the 1990s by the environmental thinker Wolfgang Sachs, in response to the homogenization of global capitalism, as a way to integrate the uniqueness of each culture and community within a planetary context. It might best be conceptualized as a global form of "commoning" (see chapter 15) whereby each community participates in a larger regional, and ultimately, planetary commons, with the same kinds of rights and responsibilities that inform any healthy assemblage of commoners. We've already seen, in chapter 12, how commons-based peer production can generate a network of cosmo-local enterprises, fabricating locally and cooperating with others worldwide. Cosmolocalism applies this proven model in cultural and political dimensions, offering a vision of robust democratic polycentric governance, from neighborhood councils extending fractally all the way to global citizens' assemblies accountable for managing irreducible global issues.

SETTING THE CONDITIONS FOR A GLOBAL COMMONS

There is, however, a major discrepancy between relationships in the successful commons described by Elinor Ostrom and those in today's global society. Ostrom's design principles work when commoners feel a sense of equivalency with each other, participating to modify rules when required and monitoring each other for appropriate behavior. Today's world, by contrast, exhibits grotesque structural inequities as a result of the five hundred years of colonialist and capitalist exploitation described in chapter 2. Until this prodigious injustice is resolved, there can be no solid basis for peaceful planetary coexistence.

The first step toward restorative justice (see chapter 15) is for the perpetrator to acknowledge wrongdoing—both culpability and the consequences of their actions. The injustice wrought on the Global Majority by colonial powers is immeasurable, but some heroic attempts have been made to at least apply a financial accounting. One estimate calculates that the financial benefits accrued from slavery in the United States until its abolition in 1865 amount to $97 trillion in today's dollars, roughly four times the nation's GDP. Similar assessments of the wealth Britain siphoned off from India during its centuries of colonialism come to $45 trillion.[12]

The enormity of this injustice continues today. As noted in chapter 2, financial drain from the Global South through unequal exchange since 1960 aggregates to $62 trillion. In the context of the climate crisis, attempts have been made to assign each country "fair shares" of the carbon budget required to limit global heating to 1.5°C. On this basis, Global North countries are on target to overshoot so dramatically by 2050 that they would owe $192 trillion to Global South nations for appropriation of their budgets.[13]

Understandably, there have been numerous calls for reparations for this gross injustice, which frequently get mired in controversies over calculations, how restitution would be made, and claims that current generations should not be held responsible for their ancestors' wrongdoing. As scholar Olúfémi Táíwò points out though, liability rather than responsibility should be the moral criterion. Historical inequities, he demonstrates, are intergenerational, structural, and racialized. Racially advantaged people from the Global North who have inherited unearned privilege, he concludes, "should bear more of the burdens of constructing the just world order, *not* because of the relationship that they, as *responsible moral agents*, hold to the injustices of the past . . . [but] because of the relationship that their *advantages* hold to that history."[14]

On this basis, proposals for global wealth redistribution accrue firm moral standing. As laid out in chapter 2, the sovereign economic development attempted by Global South nations in the post–World War II era was crushed by structural adjustment policies imposed by the IMF and World Bank. As a result, labor and resources of the Global South are now organized primarily for the benefit of wealthy nations, forcing Majority World countries into a vicious cycle of financial dependence. This is exacerbated by the worst debt crisis in history facing Global South nations (see chapter 11) with an overhang of $29 trillion compelling them to spend more on interest payments than on education or healthcare.

Numerous proposals have been advanced, each of which would bring enormous benefits by itself. Collectively, if implemented thoroughly, they would reshape the world, preparing it for a transition toward a functional global commons. A simple but significant step would be democratizing the governance of the World Bank and the IMF, giving fair and equal representation to Global South nations in the rule-making institutions currently controlled by the US and Europe.[15]

More broadly, economist Jason Hickel suggests guaranteeing a baseline of human dignity through a global minimum wage, which could be set at 50 percent of the country's median wage. Other proposals include placing a moratorium on the land grabs that systematically dispossess small farmers in the Global South, ending the stifling intellectual property regime enforced by the WTO, and disbanding the extortionate ISDS system legalizing corporate blackmail of nation-states.[16]

A comprehensive program of debt cancellation would be essential. The moral argument that is sometimes raised in response—that those who take out a loan should be obliged to repay it—has been shown to be flawed on multiple levels. In many cases, the original loans were initiated by unelected dictators, often as a result of US-assisted coups; after decades of interest payments, the loan principal has frequently been repaid three or four times over; and the economic policies often forced on countries through structural adjustment programs required for the loans have largely failed. There is no ethical reason why people scrabbling to survive today in Global South nations should continue to pay the price for these misdeeds with their health, education, and livelihood.

FRAMEWORK FOR A GLOBAL COMMONWEALTH

While these may seem like bold Second Horizon initiatives from the context of today's economic system, they might also be viewed as mere tentative steps toward the realization of Article 25 of the UN's Declaration of

Human Rights, which spells out in unequivocal terms:

> Everyone has the right to a standard of living adequate for the health and well-being of himself and of his family, including food, clothing, housing and medical care and necessary social services, and the right to security in the event of unemployment, sickness, disability, widowhood, old age or other lack of livelihood in circumstances beyond his control.

The moral foundations for a global commons have already been unanimously endorsed by the nations of the world—which then proceeded to institute economic and governance systems that ensured they would never be fulfilled.

What would a planetary ecocivilization upholding these foundational rights look like? This Third Horizon vision might best be envisaged by extending to a global scale ideas introduced in earlier chapters such as the Commonwealth, Universal Basic Income (UBI) and sovereign money issuance. Some pioneering thinkers have done just that, laying out proposals for a worldwide UBI as everyone's birthright, allocating to each person their fair share of the global Commonwealth.[17]

Half the world's population lives in countries with a national income too low to sustain UBI for their citizens at a level that could meet these basic standards. Recognizing this, financial theorists have called for an international monetary system that could redirect funds to where they are needed the most, not just for UBI but also to invest in solutions to planetary scale problems. A supranational revenue collection system could be instituted, levying nations for use of the global commons, such as ocean fishing, sea-bed mining, flight lanes, and the electromagnetic spectrum, as well as for activities that pollute the biosphere. Funds could be collected in a global trust, the beneficiaries of which were all human beings. We saw in chapter 11 how sovereign money issuance could facilitate the implementation of a UBI within a nation-state; similarly, an international currency could be issued by an independent supranational authority directing funds as needed based on allocations set by a global citizens' assembly selected by sortition for that purpose.[18]

While this system may seem remote, such a currency already exists in the form of special drawing rights (SDRs). Established by the IMF in 1967, SDRs are a stable "artificial" currency that is used as a unit of account by the IMF, World Bank, and the airline and other industries. It is exchangeable for other currencies and, like sovereign money, it can be created "out of thin air." The IMF is empowered to allocate SDRs to countries when needed, such as in 2021, when it issued $650 billion to counter the effects of the Covid pandemic. Most of the funds, however, were allocated to wealthy countries where they weren't needed. Many Global South countries are calling for SDRs to be issued to fund climate action, but as long as the IMF is controlled by wealthy nations, such calls are unlikely to be heeded. The financial technology already exists—it is the governance that needs changing.[19]

A global commonwealth would extend beyond financial considerations to include the right of every person to consider themselves a world citizen—a legal manifestation of cosmopolitanism. Interestingly, perhaps because of rising global interconnectedness, worldwide polls report that the majority of respondents see themselves primarily as "global citizens" and only secondarily national citizens. This is especially true of young people, only 13 percent of whom consider their national identity primary.

National borders, however, increasingly fortified and militarized, stand as a formidable obstacle to this cosmopolitan view. In fact, borders may be understood as the world's single greatest mechanism for maintaining inequality. An Australian laborer earning the minimum wage receives nearly a hundred times more each month than their counterpart in Nigeria. These disparities influence every aspect of life, including the very expectation for having one: A baby born in Afghanistan is seventy times more likely to die in infancy than one born in Iceland. If you're Japanese, you can expect to live more than 50 percent longer than if you live in Nigeria.[20]

There is no moral defense for this inequity. While it's nowadays widely agreed that discriminating purely on the basis of race is wrong, there is little debate about the egregious discrimination that persists on the basis of where someone happened to be born or the passport they hold. As the volume of climate refugees from the Global South rises in response to climate and ecological breakdown, migration is destined to become one of this century's most central concerns.

The legal scholar Ayelet Shachar advocates viewing citizenship as an inherited entitlement, similar to the way we view inheritance of wealth. The moral argument for significant taxation on inherited wealth applies equally to the inheritance of citizenship in an unequal world. Shachar's proposal is for a birthright privilege levy to be applied to the windfall recipients of citizenship in wealthy countries. This levy need not be paid individually, but in aggregate by nation-states based on annual birthrates; it could be collected in a commonwealth trust and reallocated to those born in poorer countries.[21]

Why have closed borders at all? EU citizens, as well as those living in the Mercosur bloc of Latin American countries (Argentina, Brazil, Paraguay, Uruguay, and Bolivia), can travel freely within their regions to live and work where they please, while retaining their original citizenship. For those in the Majority World, however, gaining residency or citizenship rights in affluent countries is an arduous, if not impossible, process. Shachar points to a legal theory implemented by the UN's International Court of Justice that assesses citizenship based on the level of integration someone has attained within a country. On this basis, she tenders a policy of allowing migrants to "ascend a scale of rights" toward full citizenship, "as they extend and deepen their actual participation in a polity over time."

Open borders are a desirable long-term goal, but they will never be the primary path to economic justice. While the number of international migrants has surpassed 150 million, nearly four billion people live in poverty, many of them too desperate to even consider international migration. For this reason, a conscious worldwide policy of wealth redistribution must be considered paramount for any meaningful transition toward a global commonwealth.

POTENTIAL PATHWAYS TO WORLD GOVERNANCE

Einstein's letter to the *New York Times* calling for a world parliament was published two months after the atomic carnage of Hiroshima and Nagasaki with a death toll as high as 250,000 people. It is a bittersweet proposition that it might require a twenty-first-century version of such catastrophes before the world wakes up to the need to transition to some form of global governance. What can be done to at least kickstart the journey we must take if humanity stands a chance of breaking through to a more robust planetary future?

Around the world, people are setting the foundations for grassroots Earth-centered democracy in bioregional communities. In the realm of international policy, political coalitions are striving to create the economic conditions for a fair world, with proposals around reparations, debt cancellation, and reform of the World Bank, IMF, and WTO. Is there a skillful way to advance transformative action around global governance itself?

Among proponents for world governance, there is a debate about whether to work within the UN or to bypass it entirely. The argument for bypassing has the same basis as Einstein's original letter. For all its lofty rhetoric, the UN was set up to represent the governments of sovereign nation-states, not their people. The General Assembly is functionally powerless and structurally undemocratic in the sense that Tuvalu, with a population of 10,000, has the same vote as China's 1.4 billion citizens. The Security Council, meanwhile, was designed from the outset to give permanent veto power to the winners of World War II. There is no chamber that represents actual people. In general, institutions are path-dependent, meaning that early decisions constrain later ones, with the result that, even if the UN adapts to changing conditions, it is unlikely to transform fundamentally from within.[22]

One creative attempt to bypass the UN is called Simpol (for "simultaneous policy"). Seeing global cooperation as the only solution to humanity's existential threats, Simpol advances policy frameworks confronting multiple planetary issues, then attempts to persuade politicians across jurisdictions to pledge support for the policy, with some success in countries such as the United Kingdom, Germany, and Ireland.

Most global governance advocates, however, believe that bypassing the UN is, in the words of Andreas Bummel, founder of Democracy Without Borders, "deeply misguided." While Bummel acknowledges that "the UN is fundamentally flawed," he asserts that "any alternative path that is not accepted by governments will be even more flawed." Bummel and others view the UN as an initial step in a longer journey. They see an opening in article 22 of the UN Charter, which allows the General Assembly—crucially, without needing the support of the Security Council—to establish, by a simple majority vote, any subsidiary body it deems necessary to support its functions.[23]

With this in mind, they campaign for a UN Parliamentary Assembly (UNPA) with members directly elected by ordinary people, which would make it "the first body in human history mandated to represent the world's citizens." With its greater legitimacy, they envisage a scenario in which the UNPA increases its relative power in stages, ultimately becoming a primary organ of the UN and evolving into a true world parliament. Endorsed by former UN Secretary-General Boutros Boutros-Ghali, the UNPA campaign has had some success, with support from national parliaments of Germany, Canada, and the Mercosur nations.

These proposals might seem like long shots in a world fragmenting into authoritarian power blocs competing for domination, trampling underfoot those who get in their way. In this precarious era, however, it becomes more important than ever to consider proposals and imagine new possibilities that would benefit the vast majority of human beings. Perilous as these times appear, there is no inevitability about the direction the world will take. There has never been a greater need for skillful planetwide measures that just might help to redirect us toward a global future that works for all.

POSSIBLE SECOND AND THIRD HORIZON CONTOURS | GLOBAL GOVERNANCE

SECOND HORIZON

SDRs issued by the IMF to fund climate action and other planetary solutions

Governance of the World Bank and IMF democratized, with equal representation for Global South nations

A global minimum wage set at 50 percent of each country's median wage

A moratorium placed on major land grabs throughout Global South

Dissolution of the global IP regime currently enforced by the WTO

Dismantlement of the ISDS system legalizing corporate blackmail of nation-states

A comprehensive program of debt cancellation for Global South nations

UN Parliamentary Assembly established to directly represent the world's citizens

Laws allow migrants to ascend a scale of rights toward full citizenship

THIRD HORIZON

Worldwide UBI apportions to every person their fair share of the global Commonwealth

Charges for use of the global commons collected in a trust, with all humans as beneficiaries

Birthright privilege levy applied to the windfall recipients of citizenship in wealthy countries

An international monetary system allocates funds for UBI and addressing planetary scale problems directed by a global citizens' assembly selected by sortition

Political boundaries drawn around bioregions instead of current nation-states

Open borders allow all people to live and work where they choose

Cosmolocalism: each community participates in the larger regional and planetary commons

Democratic polycentric governance adopted worldwide: from neighborhood councils extending fractally to global citizens' assemblies managing irreducible planetary issues

FOR CONSIDERATION

What Second and Third Horizon ideas arise in your own mind inspired by this chapter?

CHAPTER 17

LIVING EARTH: MUTUALLY BENEFICIAL SYMBIOSIS WITH ALL OUR RELATIONS

Following the first Earth Day in 1970, which mobilized 20 million participants in the United States alone, people around the world became increasingly aware of rising pollution and other environmental concerns. The UN's Conference on the Human Environment in 1972 kicked off a global discussion that led to a landmark document ten years later: the UN World Charter for Nature, adopted in 1982 by nearly all nations, with the United States as the only holdout voting against it.

During this same period, however, Ronald Reagan and Margaret Thatcher began spearheading the neoliberal takeover of the global economy. Most nations quickly forgot they signed the document as they grappled with the new economic order. Prominent environmentalists, realizing that nation-states were not about to change their ways any time soon, sensed that the world needed a new universal declaration laying out foundational principles to guide humanity in healing its relationship with the Earth. Mikhail Gorbachev, former president of the Soviet Union, and Maurice Strong, secretary general of the UN Rio Earth Summit held in 1992, decided to join forces and lead a collective effort by civil society to draft what became known as the Earth Charter.

Over several years, they championed what's considered to be the most inclusive and participatory process ever associated with an international declaration. It needed to be a "people's document," Gorbachev insisted, that would "stir people's souls," laying a moral foundation that could guide all people in their actions for generations to come: "A Ten Commandments for the future."[1]

It was a skillfully steered global effort designed to integrate the voices of multiple diverse groups frequently at odds with each other: Indigenous peoples, scientists, women's groups, policymakers, religious leaders, and business sectors. It was a boisterous yet inviting process. Yale professor Mary Evelyn Tucker, who participated in the drafting, recalls prominent feminist Bella Abzug rushing into a room after reviewing an early draft exclaiming: "We've got to have this for the women!"—and the document was changed to reflect her views. When the first "Benchmark Draft" was revealed at the Rio+5 follow-up conference, Tucker recounts seeing Indigenous representatives in the audience weeping with emotion as they witnessed their worldview included for the first time in a UN-sponsored declaration: "Earth, our home, is alive with a unique community of life."

The Charter's final version, completed at the UNESCO headquarters in Paris in 2000, has since been endorsed by over 6,000 organizations worldwide. Its sixteen principles are organized on four pillars: Respect and Care for the Community of Life; Ecological Integrity; Social and Economic Justice; and Democracy, Nonviolence, and Peace. Its preamble majestically declares:

> We stand at a critical moment in Earth's history, a time when humanity must choose its future . . . To move forward we must recognize that in the midst of a magnificent diversity of cultures and life forms we are one human family and one Earth community with a common destiny . . . Towards this end, it is imperative that we, the peoples of Earth, declare our responsibility to one another, to the greater community of life, and to future generations.[2]

With its all-embracing benevolent values, its devotion to the sacredness of life, and its solid scientific basis, the Earth Charter could be seen as the moral foundation for an ecocivilization. What will be its eventual fate? Will it ultimately become a broadly recognized "Ten Commandments for the future" or a forgotten relic of bygone hopes?

In this chapter, we will trace how the fractured relationship between humanity and the living Earth has spawned various movements that, sharing the Earth Charter's core values, are exploring ways to apply them in hallways of power through legal initiatives and visionary policy proposals. We will see how, through the chaos of this turbulent century, the principles underlying the Earth Charter and its associated movements could provide the moral bedrock humanity needs to make it through to a brighter future of mutually beneficial symbiosis with our Mother Earth.

LICENSE TO SLAUGHTER

Here in the throes of the Anthropocene, the relationship between humanity and the rest of life on Earth is characterized by untrammeled domination and desecration. *Homo sapiens*, comprising only 0.01 percent of Earth's biomass, has extinguished 83 percent of all wild animals, 80 percent of marine mammals, and about half the world's plant biomass. Humans, along with domesticated animals, now represent 96 percent of all land mammals by weight. Scientists repeatedly warn that wildlife populations are nearing "points of no return" and that we are on the verge of "shattering Earth's natural limits"—all to no avail. We are well on the way to the Sixth Great Extinction since life began on Earth—the only one caused by the conscious activities of a single species.[3]

The cattle, pigs, and chickens that have replaced wildlife are, meanwhile, enslaved in factory farms, brutally tortured, and mercilessly slaughtered for human convenience. Every year, 85 billion animals—each one a sentient creature with a nervous system as capable of registering excruciating pain as you or me—undergo the systematic torment of an unnaturally brief life of terror and misery.

How does the vast bulk of humanity accept this ongoing holocaust of life conducted in their name? There are a number of reasons already discussed in this book. One is the "distancing phenomenon" (see chapter 3) by which excruciating violence, such as that suffered by domesticated animals, is kept invisible to most people. Another is the hegemony of billionaire-owned mass media ensuring that, while nearly everyone knows the winner of the Super Bowl, very few are aware of nature's "Great Dying."

Underlying these, however, is a deeper reason: the all-embracing but unseen ideology of human supremacy which claims innate superiority of humans over all other life forms, rendering it morally acceptable to cause untold suffering to nonhuman life for any human convenience. As the ecological philosopher Eileen Crist explains, human supremacy turns living beings into mere resources to be exploited, reclassifying fish as "fisheries" and farm animals as "livestock." This anthropocentric doctrine gives moral license for humans to poison rivers, extirpate species, convert vibrant ecosystems into monocrop wastelands, and treat the entire Earth as a mere container of raw materials.[4]

This extreme form of anthropocentrism is a logical outcome of the dominant worldview that emerged in early modern Europe (see chapter 3) which understands nature as nothing more than a complicated machine, the design of which can be deciphered and controlled by human endeavor. Diametrically opposed to this worldview, Indigenous peoples around the globe have, for millennia, understood the world around them to be more like an extended family, a community of subjects rather than objects, of which humans are merely one lineage among others. The gulf between worldviews was summed up by Smohalla, a Wanapum medicine man in the nineteenth century, with these searing words:

> You ask me to plow the ground! Shall I take a knife and tear my mother's breast? Then when I die she will not take me to her bosom to rest. You ask me to dig for stone! Shall I dig under her skin for her bones? Then when I die I cannot enter her body to be born again. You ask me to cut grass and make hay and sell it, and be rich like white men! But how dare I cut off my mother's hair?[5]

Since Smohalla's time, modern scientific insights have demonstrated a remarkable confluence with the understanding of Indigenous knowledge and other non-European wisdom traditions. We are indeed related to all life forms, sharing more than 60 percent of our genes with fruit flies and bananas. Ontologically, the dominant worldview of separation has been contradicted by advances in systems sciences, complexity theory, cognitive science, and other fields. These disciplines point, instead, to a worldview of deep interconnectedness, seeing humanity as intricately embedded in a web of connectivity.

Important implications arise from seeing humans as part of nature, rather than separate from it. From a self-interested standpoint, it makes no sense to jeopardize the life support systems on which every human being relies. Beyond that, however, are moral implications. The collective knowledge of humanity, accumulated over millennia, has given our species enormous power to manipulate and destroy other life forms, but it does not bestow moral license to use that power for harm. Once we recognize there is no ethical basis for the assumption of human supremacy, this opens an entirely different perspective on the norms by which our society works. This is the great insight shared by the Earth Charter and other approaches to Earth jurisprudence that we will now explore.

RIGHTS FOR MOTHER EARTH

Earth jurisprudence begins with the realization that current laws will not protect the Earth from the harm caused by humans, because that's not their purpose. The law is entirely anthropocentric, reserving rights and privileges only to humans and their legal constructions (such as corporations) and reducing the rest of life on Earth to the status of property. There is, of course, environmental legislation that regulates how much ecological harm can be caused by industry, but Earth jurisprudence emerges from a different paradigm. It recognizes nature itself as a rights-bearing subject, rather than a mere object for human ownership and regulation.

This legal paradigm shift began in the West with a seminal article written by Christopher Stone in 1972, "Should Trees Have Standing?—Toward Legal Rights for Natural Objects," which proposed granting rights not only to natural entities but "to the natural environment as a whole." Although many jurists responded mockingly to such a radical suggestion, Stone's ideas remarkably found their way the same year into a legal dissent by Supreme Court Justice Douglas in a case involving the Sierra Club.[6]

From a philosophical perspective, the progenitor of the current worldwide movement for Earth jurisprudence is generally agreed to be the cultural historian Thomas Berry, who laid out in *The Great Work: Our Way into the Future* a framework for rights of nature, starting from an alternative ontological foundation:

> In reality there is a single integral community of the Earth that includes all its component members whether human or other than human. In this community every being has its own role to fulfill, its own dignity, its inner spontaneity. Every being has its own voice. Every being declares itself to the entire universe. Every being enters into communion with other beings. This capacity for relatedness, for presence to other beings, for spontaneity in action, is a capacity possessed by every mode of being throughout the entire universe.

In an interconnected world, Berry elaborated, "all rights are limited and relative." Humans have rights to nourishment, shelter, and well-being, but "no rights to deprive other species of their proper habitat" nor "to disturb the basic functioning of the biosystems of the planet." Consistent with the principle of fractal flourishing (see chapter 5), Earth jurisprudence recognizes that the well-being of the entire Earth system is paramount, and the needs of any particular member of this community of life cannot take precedence over the greater whole.[7]

Acknowledging nature's rights upends the paradigm of law with a Copernican-style transformation. As Berry explained, law becomes an extension of ecology, rather than ecology being subsumed under law. Instead of law facilitating the human destruction of nature, Earth jurisprudence grants nature the power to participate in the legal system, allowing it to make claims against individuals and corporations and demands for restoration and care.

In recent decades, a substantial body of jurisprudence has arisen to turn this theoretical revolution into practical implementation. The fact that trees, species, or ecosystems can't speak for themselves doesn't present a problem. The law is replete with analogous instances such as infants or comatose patients. In these examples, the court appoints guardians to represent them, as can be done for nonhuman entities.

A thornier issue arises over conflicting rights between different natural entities. Ecosystems contain complex webs of interrelationships, with diverse species and individuals cooperating and competing with each other. When biomes have been disrupted through human intervention, imbalances arise whereby protecting one species might entail culling another. How should nature's rights be applied in these cases? A crucial concept in resolving this type of question is that of *ecological integrity*. This doesn't presume trying to return ecosystems to an idealized pristine pre-human state, but aims instead to set the conditions that could allow a habitat to flourish sustainably as a complex, dynamic system of interrelating parts ranging all the way from top predators to underground fungal webs.[8]

Given the dominant anthropocentric legal paradigm, the most compelling way to effect this transformation is through changing a nation's constitution. In 2008, a historic milestone was achieved when Ecuador became the first country to recognize in its constitution the rights of Mother Earth ("Pachamama") to "maintain and generate its vital cycles, structure, functions, and evolutionary processes," granting nature legal standing to be protected by law and represented in court. In Ecuador, trees do indeed have standing, as exemplified in 2015 by a case in which the protection of mangrove trees compelled the removal of shrimp farmers encroaching on their territory.[9]

In 2010, Bolivia followed Ecuador's example, passing a law recognizing the Rights of Mother Earth as a collective subject. That year, Bolivia's first Indigenous president, Evo Morales, hosted a People's World Conference on Climate Change and Mother Earth's Rights, attended by 35,000 people from around the world. There, ten years after the Earth Charter's inauguration, seventeen working groups formed to articulate a shared perspective on how to respect the dignity of our common home. The result was a Universal Declaration of the Rights of Mother Earth, which recognizes Earth as an indivisible, living community of interrelated and interdependent beings with inherent rights, and defines fundamental human responsibilities to the community of life. A group is now organizing a global petition requesting the UN to adopt this declaration.[10]

There are other important ways in which Earth-defending jurists are engaging effectively with the legal system, ranging in scale from global legislation to the defense of individual animals.

The multifaceted Stop Ecocide movement is rapidly gathering momentum toward making the crime of ecocide—reckless and severe long-term damage to ecosystems—prosecutable under national, regional, and international law. The International Criminal Court (ICC) has jurisdiction to prosecute individuals for genocide, crimes against humanity, and war crimes. A model ecocide definition has been drafted and proposed for inclusion in the court's purview. It may take some years to enshrine at the ICC, but in the meantime domestic proposals of law have been submitted in dozens of countries with some already adopted (such as in Belgium, Chile, France, and Ukraine), while the EU has formalized a directive addressing "conduct comparable to ecocide." For senior executives of transnational corporations, who can currently direct the destruction of ecosystems around the world with impunity, these steps could have huge ramifications.[11]

A PLACE AT THE TABLE FOR NONHUMANS

At the other end of the scale, juridical activists have disrupted the anthropocentric paradigm by claiming legal personhood for specific animals, with attendant rights to pursue fulfilling lives rather than be used as property for human amusement. The conventional scientific approach to ethology has long denied any analogy between the subjective lives of animals and humans, even in the face of overwhelming evidence—a particular manifestation of human supremacy termed *anthropodenial* by primatologist Frans de Waal. Recent advances in ethology reveal the cognitive richness of animal lives, replete with elaborate social relationships, complex emotions, and cultural learning, rendering the basis for anthropodenial ever flimsier.[12]

From this solid ground, the Nonhuman Rights Project asserts personhood for their clients, who are mostly captive chimpanzees and elephants, soon to be joined by dolphins and whales. Because of their clients' proven social intelligence—elephants and dolphins have, for example, been shown to relate to each other by name—they view these cases as the "low hanging fruit" of nonhuman personhood. However, philosopher Martha Nussbaum notes that this "So Like Us" legal theory may be practical but risks neglecting other dimensions of nonhuman experience, such as echolocation, that can't easily be mapped onto human cognition.[13]

In fact, scientists are increasingly discovering evidence of consciousness in a wide array of animals, including birds, bats, and octopuses, even extending to reptiles, bees, and fruit flies. In 2024, forty leading experts assembled to sign the New York Declaration on Animal Consciousness, affirming "strong scientific support for attributions of conscious experience" to mammals and birds and "a realistic possibility of conscious experience in all vertebrates." They didn't shy away from the moral implications. "If there is a realistic possibility," they stated, "that an animal is conscious—for instance, that octopuses can suffer—then this possibility merits consideration in policy contexts—for instance, in decisions about whether to support octopus farming."[14]

Earlier in her career, Nussbaum had co-developed with Amartya Sen the capabilities approach to human welfare discussed in chapter 7, and she suggests applying a similar theoretical underpinning to animal wellbeing. A starting point, she proposes, should be to identify what actually matters to each animal. What are the conditions that enable them to flourish? For each species, we can then determine the "minimum threshold beneath which we should judge an animal's life to be unjustly thwarted" and construct our laws from that basis. A case in point is the court-ordered restriction on the US Navy's sonar program on the grounds that it impeded the foraging, breeding, and migration of whales, preventing them from realizing their full potential. Building on these ideas, a collaboration of scientists and specialists named "Animals in the Room" recognizes the species-specific need for proper representation and works intimately with animals to create video and audio testimony, bringing their authentic voices into a courtroom.[15]

Extending the purview to living systems that allow many beings to flourish, juridical campaigners have achieved success in attributing legal personhood to rivers, with associated rights to flow and maintain biodiversity. The Whanganui River in New Zealand (Aotearoa) was the first to be granted personhood in 2017 after 150 years of advocacy by the Whanganui tribe, which views it as an ancestor central to its identity. Guardians were appointed from both the Whanganui iwi and the government to act on behalf of the river, which is legally represented by two lawyers. Since then, similar attributions have occurred in nations worldwide including Colombia, Canada, India, and Bangladesh.

Another important, previously unrepresented group has recently begun to find a place at the policymaking table: future generations. Finland, in 1993, instituted a parliamentary "Committee for the Future" that reviews governmental policy for its impact on future generations. Since then, several countries have established similar departments, most notably in Wales, whose government in 2015 created a Future Generations Commissioner, charged with promoting sustainable development and long-term thinking across the nation. In Japan, the Future Design movement has pioneered a uniquely dramatic approach in which imaginary future generations, dressed in distinctive ceremonial costume, engage in policymaking debates asserting the viewpoint from 2060. Studies report that input from "future residents" leads to more radical and progressive municipal plans than otherwise.[16]

Future generations have also established legal standing in litigation. In the Philippines, timber licenses to cut down old-growth forest were retracted because they violated rights of posterity to a healthy environment; and, in a landmark ruling in 2019, the Dutch Supreme Court ordered its government to take more aggressive action to secure "the legal right to a safe climate and healthy atmosphere for all present and future generations."[17]

THE GREAT OCEAN ENCLOSURE

There is one constituency, comprising a large part of the living Earth, whose rights have been largely ignored by the vast bulk of humanity. Covering 71 percent of Earth's surface, and containing 97 percent of its water, the oceans are in deep crisis and yet are barely protected. Overuse of nitrogen fertilizers has created more than 700 ocean dead zones covering about 100,000 square miles. The Great Pacific Garbage Patch, a vast gyrating accumulation of plastic debris twice the size of Texas, contains nearly 2 trillion pieces of plastic. The ocean absorbs about one third of humanity's fossil fuel emissions, which has increased its acidity by over 30 percent, impairing shell and coral formation, which is further damaged by global heating. As a result of all this, it's been estimated that, by 2050, at current rates, up to 90 percent of corals will have died off and there will be more plastic in the ocean by weight than fish.[18]

The primary response of the world's decision-makers has been, not to protect the oceans, but to speed up its exploitation. In chapter 1, we discussed how scientists examining the increasing scale of humanity's impact on Earth have called the period since World War II the Great Acceleration. As terrestrial resources get exhausted, and technological advances make even remote marine areas accessible, governments and corporations see the next frontier for global capitalism in the ocean, launching a free-for-all scramble that scientists are calling the "Blue Acceleration." The numerous tentacles of this new Windigo onslaught extend across oil and gas production, mineral exploration, fish farming, factory trawlers, container shipping, tourism, desalination, and cable laying.[19]

Global regulation of marine activities is disjointed—overseen by various UN agencies that hardly talk to each other—and barely functioning, with only three percent of the ocean effectively protected. As far back as 1972, the UN initiated negotiations among countries to rationalize a regulatory framework. Most countries at that time claimed exclusive economic zones (EEZs) up to twelve nautical miles from their coastline; beyond that the high seas were available to all states for navigation and exploitation.[20]

After ten years of negotiation, the UN Convention on the Law of the Sea (UNCLOS) was signed in 1982 and ratified by sufficient countries in 1994 to become effective. However, rather than rationalizing regulation, UNCLOS legitimated a colossal appropriation of the oceans. The treaty massively extended nations' EEZs to 200 nautical miles, assigning to nation-states roughly 40 percent of the oceanic commons in what has been called "the biggest enclosure in history." This led to a bizarre process known as "ocean grabbing," whereby nations would claim that a rock or undersea ridge was part of their territory, thereby asserting rights over thousands of square miles of marine resources. The tiny Pacific archipelago of Kiribati, one of the smallest nations by landmass, became the twelfth largest measured by EEZs. These ecologically fragile islands are extremely vulnerable to predatory conglomerates with ambitions to mine their seabed for valuable manganese nodules, destroying deep sea ecosystems and ocean food webs in the process.[21]

The remainder of the high seas, defined by UNCLOS as Areas Beyond National Jurisdiction, was proclaimed grandly (and anthropocentrically) to be the "Common Heritage of Mankind," with weak and largely unenforceable regulatory protections. After two further decades of negotiation, an agreement on Biodiversity Beyond National Jurisdiction (BBNJ) was adopted in 2023 to lay down rules to create and protect marine reserves and require environmental impact assessment of economic expansion plans. This represents a significant step forward for marine conservation, but is unlikely, by itself, to reverse the devastating trends.

Some policy visionaries have proposed far more radical treatments that would set maritime conservation on a regenerative path. One proposal would make the entire BBNJ a marine protected area, free from fishing and off-limits to destructive industries. Another proposal suggests treating BBNJ as a right-bearing entity, analogous to New Zealand's Whanganui River, recognizing the ocean's rights to maintain its natural cycles, and empowering a "Council of Ocean Custodians" as legal guardians to protect it in court. More broadly, in *The Blue Commons*, the economist Guy Standing calls for taking the UNCLOS declaration of the "Common Heritage of Mankind" seriously: managing the ocean as part of the Commonwealth (see chapter 10), with trusts financed by levies on resource exploitation using their funds to regenerate and preserve the ocean into the future.[22]

NATURE NEEDS HALF

These proposals exemplify the scale of thinking required if we are to emerge from this century on a pathway toward an ecocivilization. It's estimated that just five percent of Earth's land surface remains unaffected by humans. Half of the world's habitable land is used for human purposes—mostly agriculture and livestock grazing, which is the greatest cause of habitat destruction—while only 17.5 percent of land is protected or conserved. Ever since the 1970s, conservation scientists have estimated that, to safeguard global biodiversity and prevent the Sixth Great Extinction, humanity must set aside triple that amount, or roughly half of Earth's surface area, as protected wilderness. A "Nature Needs Half" initiative was launched by a coalition of scientists and conservationists in 2009—an idea that was popularized by eminent biologist E. O. Wilson in *Half-Earth: Our Planet's Fight for Life,* published in 2016.[23]

This visionary movement doesn't contemplate restoring land to a mythical state of unblemished wilderness, but builds on the concept of ecological integrity, giving nature the chance to regenerate itself. Many areas currently set aside for conservation fail to do this because they are too small to sustain an integrated ecosystem; broken up by roads, agriculture, or settlements that prevent species from roaming widely; or used for logging and other human activities. By contrast, the prerequisites for true wilderness regeneration can be summed up in the simple phrase: "Big, connected, and free." Authentic conservation of nature requires the scale and autonomy for viable populations of wild animals and plants to flourish sustainably.[24]

The Nature Needs Half initiative, similar to the Rights of Nature movement, represents a paradigm shift from anthropocentrism. It sheds the conventional conservation approach of maintaining a patchwork of wilderness zones in a world organized for humans, replacing it with a vision of equitable coexistence with nonhuman life, imbued with respect for nature's power to renew itself if left alone. This level of natural restoration would have a dramatic effect on the overall health of Earth's living systems, protecting species, maintaining clean air and water, stabilizing climate extremes, and reducing climate breakdown by sequestering significant amounts of carbon.[25]

This ambitious movement has gained considerable traction in mainstream policymaking. A UN-sponsored treaty adopted in 2022 set a "30x30" target, aiming to conserve 30 percent of Earth's surface by 2030, as a step toward the stated 50 percent goal, while the EU has endorsed a plan to protect 50 percent of its ecosystems by 2050. Meanwhile, a vibrant rewilding movement has gained global momentum, with successful projects ranging from wolf reintroductions in Yellowstone National Park in the United States, to Patagonian landscape regeneration in Chile and Argentina, an antelope recovery project in Kazakhstan, and several major wildland restorations in the United Kingdom and Europe.

There are many challenges facing such a broad-based program. Critics worry that it could lead to massive human displacement, perhaps requiring militarized enforcement. It is true that environmental protection policies have sometimes been devastating for the local people, frequently Indigenous and tribal groups, living on targeted land. Cases have been reported in Africa and Asia of colonial-style seizure of territory designated a "National Park" or "Protected Area," with violent dispossession of villagers whose land is then turned into ecotourism or trophy-hunting destinations, and sometimes opened up for illicit logging or mining.

These issues are well understood by leading advocates of Nature Needs Half, who emphasize that it's essential to partner with Indigenous and local communities in and around protected areas. Indigenous peoples, sharing a worldview that sees nonhumans as family, are widely recognized as the most effective stewards of biodiversity, and generally adhere to time-honored traditions of intimate identity with their land, infused with respect, reverence, and reciprocity with nonhuman nature. "Territory is more than just the environment, territory is our whole lives," explains the Indigenous Brazilian educator Célia Xakriabá. "We sow hope, because we, ourselves, are the very Earth healing itself . . . Our body is the territory and the territory is our body."[26]

Many Indigenous communities want their land to be protected from industrial and agricultural encroachment—but crucially it must be done on their terms. Consistent with the principle of subsidiarity, Indigenous and local communities must be allocated decision-making powers in how conservation should be carried out within their own territories. In Peru and Ecuador, for example, the pioneering Amazon Sacred Headwaters Alliance, an Indigenous-led initiative, seeks to permanently protect 86 million acres of bio-culturally rich tropical rainforest as an autonomous bioregion allowing humans and nature to flourish symbiotically.[27]

Another concern raised by critics of Nature Needs Half is that such a program might undermine global food security. With world population expected to grow this century to roughly ten billion people, many of whom are already undernourished, some argue that any plan that circumscribes growth in agricultural production is untenable. Instead, they suggest, we should enhance protection of targeted areas with high biodiversity and explore "convivial conservationism" with shared landscapes intermingling agriculture and conservation. As described in chapter 5, in many parts of the world, agroecology demonstrates how crops can be sustainably cultivated in a way that harmonizes with the natural environment.[28]

However, as a strategy to regenerate wilderness and prevent mass extinctions, convivial conservation falls short. The unrelenting creep of Windigo, Inc. predicts that the inevitable outcome of such a strategy, no matter how well intentioned, will only lead to further wilderness loss. Instead, as chapter 9 highlights, the Nature Needs Half program may have the best chance of success if it is linked with technical advances in cell-based meat and precision fermentation that offer alternative sources of protein for mass consumption, allowing a drastic reduction in the amount of land allocated to grazing and soy cultivation for animal feed.

Ultimately, this issue raises another critical question that is frequently considered taboo, but needs to be examined thoroughly for an authentic investigation of the relationship between humans and the living Earth: What is the maximum human population that Earth can sustain in a way that allows for the continued flourishing of nonhuman nature?

A PATHWAY TO A THRIVING WORLD

Ever since eighteenth-century cleric Thomas Malthus warned that overpopulation would lead inevitably to mass starvation, debates about population have tended to generate more heat than light. After the biologist Paul Ehrlich's more recent prediction of mass starvation in *The Population Bomb*, published in 1968, failed to come about, many mainstream economists have dismissed such concerns, arguing that the market will always provide a solution. Most of these debates have been limited by an anthropocentric focus, however, concerned about what's best for humanity rather than the living Earth. A broader question, one that's integral to the vision of an ecocivilization, is: How many humans can live on Earth in a manner that is mutually beneficial with the nonhuman life sharing the planet with us?

It's already clear that eight billion of us here today are rapidly denuding Earth of its living treasures. Wealth inequality, however, drives differences in consumption patterns, with the result that the world's richest 20 percent, mostly in the Global North, consume more than 75 percent of its resources. On this basis, many argue that focusing on global population is misguided: It's more important to direct attention on reducing over-consumption in affluent nations. While this argument contains much truth, a sizable and growing global middle class understandably holds aspirations for the material-intensive consumer products, such as automobiles, refrigerators, washing machines, and TVs, that many of us take for granted. The question, therefore, must be framed accordingly: How many humans can live sustainably on a flourishing Earth while enjoying an adequate level of material convenience?

Various studies have investigated this question, generally by targeting a moderately affluent degree of consumption, such as the average European level, and analyzing the ecological footprint required to achieve this. Their results range between roughly 2 and 4 billion people, with substantial convergence around 3 billion. This seems plausible when we consider that the last time there were 3 billion humans on Earth was in 1960, when the Great Acceleration was taking off, and that in 1976, with a population around 4 billion, the world's ecological footprint began to exceed its sustainable biocapacity.[29]

With UN projections that the world's population will hit 10 billion by the end of this century, the idea of reducing it to 3 billion may seem implausible, barring scenarios of catastrophic civilizational collapse. However, a closer analysis demonstrates a realistic pathway to a world population of 3 billion by the middle of next century, based on a fertility rate of 1.7, somewhat lower than replacement-level fertility of 2.1 children per woman. Many countries are already below the 1.7 rate, including the United States, Brazil, Turkey, Malaysia, China, Japan, and most European nations. However, demonstrating the suicidal short-term thinking that characterizes much mainstream discourse, this is generally viewed negatively—a "dire demographic trajectory" in the words of the *Economist*—because of the increased economic burden of an aging population.[30]

Africa is the only continent where fertility rates remain high, with a population projected to triple by 2100 accounting for virtually all the world's growth. The root causes of rapid population growth are commonly identified as gender inequality, poverty, and child marriage—an astonishing 21 percent of young women globally are married before their eighteenth birthday, resulting in millions of unwanted pregnancies. In recent years, family planning interventions have accrued a bad reputation in some circles, as a result of forced sterilizations and coercive campaigns such as China's one-child policy. However, voluntary family planning programs based on empowerment of girls and women have demonstrated significant long-term success in countries such as Iran, Japan, Tunisia, and Thailand. Research shows that, when women are allowed to control their own fertility, they rarely choose more than one or two children. A pivotal factor is the education of girls: there is a high inverse correlation between the years of education a woman attains and the number of children she has—both worldwide and in Africa. In reality, population intervention and social justice go hand-in-hand: It's been estimated that strategies such as educating girls, eradicating gender bias, and giving women control over their own bodies could lead to a world population of 6 billion by the end of the century.[31]

Weaving together the approaches discussed in this chapter allows us to envision a fundamentally different world by next century. A world where our species has shed the fallacy of human supremacy, and been welcomed back into the family of living beings, coexisting with our nonhuman relations in a mutually beneficial manner. A world where the mass torture and slaughter of other sentient beings has been banished to the history books, and where the miracle of nature's abundance, accumulated over billions of years, once again plays a central role in Earth's flourishing.

The Earth Charter concludes its preamble with the following words:

> Everyone shares responsibility for the present and future well-being of the human family and the larger living world. The spirit of human solidarity and kinship with all life is strengthened when we live with reverence for the mystery of being, gratitude for the gift of life, and humility regarding the human place in nature.

It is up to all of us to ensure that the eventual fate of this document will not be as a forgotten relic, but as the moral foundation for a world that truly works for all—humans and nonhumans combined.

POSSIBLE SECOND AND THIRD HORIZON CONTOURS | LIVING EARTH

SECOND HORIZON

National constitutions acknowledge the rights of nature (following Ecuador's model)

A Universal Declaration of the Rights of Mother Earth adopted at the UN

Ecocide established as an international crime prosecutable by nation-states and the ICC

Animals assigned legal rights consistent with their level of consciousness and potential for suffering

Legal rights assigned to ecosystems (such as rivers) and to future generations

The high seas (BBNJ) declared a rights-bearing entity protected by legal guardians

Half of Earth's surface protected as wilderness under Indigenous and local stewardship

Mass education of girls and empowerment of women in Africa begins reducing world population

THIRD HORIZON

A paradigm shift in jurisprudence where law is seen as an extension of ecology

Systematic torture and slaughter of animals through factory farming is abolished worldwide

Oceans stewarded as part of the Commonwealth with trusts using levied funds to regenerate and preserve it into the future

Human supremacy gives way to a recognition of humanity as an integral part of the living Earth

Earth Charter broadly adopted as a moral foundation for an ecocivilization

FOR CONSIDERATION

What Second and Third Horizon ideas arise in your own mind inspired by this chapter?

CHAPTER 18

CULTURE AND COMMUNITY: CULTIVATING CARE, DIGNITY, AND PLANETARY CONSCIOUSNESS

Prussia, the epitome of the German nation, was in ruins, as the philosopher Johann Gottlieb Fichte saw it. In 1806, Napoleon's army advanced through Europe, occupying Berlin and forcing the Kaiser to flee in humiliation to Russia. In Fichte's view, Prussians needed to rediscover their national identity through a renewed sense of duty, discipline, and patriotism. In a series of lectures, he laid out a road map for how the Prussian educational system could create generations of proud Germanic warriors.

Fichte was a complex and subtle thinker, and his philosophy of education interwove ideals of love and morality with the Prussian fatherland. In his view, instilling a love of learning in a child would naturally lead him to strive for a perfect moral order that incorporated a strong national identity. "The new education," he argued, "on the soil whose cultivation it takes over, . . . completely annihilates freedom of will, producing strict necessity in decisions and the impossibility of the opposite."[1]

The "strict necessity" that Fichte believed in was an innate compulsion to act for the moral good. However, those who implemented his educational program took his call to "annihilate freedom of will" all too literally. What became known as the Prussian method, later augmented by new techniques of psychological behavior modification and social control, inverted Fichte's original intention by destroying the creative impulse in students and molding their minds to suit the national imperative.

Prussia was known as a centralized, authoritarian police state. As it metamorphosed from a marginal power to the dominant force of nineteenth-century Europe, its educational system became a model for other Western nations eager to produce their own militarized youth. Many educational features that we take for granted today, such as compulsory institutionalized schooling, surveillance and control of students, strict discipline, age segregation, a prescribed national curriculum, rote memorization, standardized testing with grades, and state certification for teachers, originated from the program first developed in Prussia.

Consider what you might observe today in a classroom almost anywhere in the world. Pupils aren't allowed to talk or move around without permission. They must sit obediently at geometrically arranged desks and silently absorb the teachings of an established authority. Rather than follow their personal interests, they must complete tasks imposed on them with strict deadlines, measuring their progress in tests that pit them against their peers through a competitive system of rewards and punishments. Although it's well established that curiosity promotes learning far more effectively than fear, our mainstream educational system is built on principles of command and control initially developed in Prussia. It's a system that still functions, primarily, to extinguish the free will of children, eradicate their creative impulse, and churn out generations of obedient citizens conforming to whatever role the hegemonic system assigns them.

It is rather astonishing to realize that the standard approach to educating children—something we take for granted—developed as a prescription for building a militarized state. In earlier chapters, we've encountered equally unexpected sources for the development of other institutions that structure our lived reality, including money, governance, and law. In this chapter, we'll investigate how the defining characteristics of today's dominant culture were similarly contrived.

The foundational intention of an ecocivilization is to set the conditions for all beings to flourish on a regenerated Earth. By contrast, as we'll see, the dominant cultural milieu, beginning from birth, far from enabling people to achieve their full potential, contorts and inhibits the natural development of each human being. Equipped with that knowledge, and digging deeply into evolutionary history to ascertain humankind's naturally evolved needs, we'll be better able to discern the possibility of an alternative set of cultural norms.

A PATHOLOGICAL CULTURE

Every human born today brings with them a complex panoply of instincts, needs, and drives resulting from millions of years of evolutionary adaptation. In the seven million years since the hominid evolutionary niche diverged from our primate cousins (see chapter 5), we developed a unique set of characteristics honed for our particular social and bioregional conditions. Many of our core biological and psychological drives—our need for companionship, moral emotions such as guilt and shame, and a collective sense of identity transcending the self—evolved to maximize our chances of success living in small nomadic bands of foragers in the African savanna.

Humans thrive when this mélange of evolved needs are authentically met throughout the arc of life from infancy to old age. However, modern industrialized society violates our evolutionary heritage in multiple ways. Some of these mismatches are unintended byproducts of a technologically advanced, globally connected world. Most people live in isolated nuclear families with no extended kin. Instead of measuring ourselves against a few dozen peers, we are bombarded by media portraying idealized models of glamorous superstar celebrities and find ourselves lacking, anguished by self-deprecating envy.

In the past century, however, capitalist consumer culture has weaponized this mismatch, preying cynically on evolved human needs to manipulate them for profit. Our desire for sugar, salt, and fat has been exploited by corporations designing scientific algorithms to target our "bliss point"—the irresistible reaction to food precisely engineered to maximize flavor—leading to a global epidemic of obesity and diabetes. The healthy instinct to be respected by peers is transformed by consumer culture into a desperate need to make a good impression, trapping people on a hedonic treadmill as they grasp perpetually at status symbols acquired through their clothing, automobiles, and gadgets.

The rise of neoliberalism has further exacerbated this onslaught on the human condition, causing widespread suffering in its wake. Many surveys have reported significant increases in rates of anxiety, depression, and suicidality over the past fifty years, in tandem with increasing materialist and individualist values. The ascendancy of social media has aggravated these trends, especially among younger people, driving a narcissistic focus on self-esteem that generates performative shows of "happiness." Most people learn to adapt to this toxic culture from an early age by distorting their own nature, emphasizing those aspects of themselves, such as competitiveness and egotism, that lead to successful outcomes, at the expense of other evolved human qualities. As summarized by the physician Gabor Maté in *The Myth of Normal*, "what passes for normal in our society is neither healthy nor natural . . . To meet modern society's criteria for normality is, in many ways, to conform to requirements that are profoundly abnormal in regard to our Nature-given needs—which is to say, unhealthy and harmful."[2]

After analyzing dozens of studies on values and well-being across many different cultures, the psychologist Tim Kasser has identified two different clusters of values and goals held by people worldwide. One of these, a cluster of extrinsic, self-enhancement values (henceforth abbreviated "extrinsic"), prioritizes money, possessions, and status. An opposing cluster of intrinsic, self-transcendent values (abbreviated "intrinsic") prizes "benevolence" (helping family and friends), personal growth and self-acceptance, "universalism" (caring about the broader world), and community. Virtually everyone holds both value clusters, but surveys demonstrate that one cluster is usually dominant in a person. The crucial finding arising from this research—documented in wide-ranging samples of people from diverse cultures, age groups, and wealth brackets—is that extrinsic values undermine psychological health and personal well-being, whereas intrinsic values lead to greater well-being and self-actualization. Those holding extrinsic values are more likely to diminish the well-being of others, act more manipulatively and competitively, experience less compassion, and engage in fewer prosocial activities such as sharing or helping. Extrinsic values have also been shown to correlate with higher levels of stress and concomitant health risks arising from greater expression of inflammatory genes.[3]

From an evolutionary perspective, it is not surprising that intrinsic values, aligned with our evolutionary heritage, would engender human flourishing. The globally prevailing culture, however, is designed to reward handsomely extrinsic values which, when dominant, tend to diminish both personal and community well-being.

A pervasive belief underlying our "myth of normal"—one that emerged with the rise of capitalism and has been sanctified by the ideology of neoliberalism—is that competition plays a central role in advancing human progress. A wide range of studies, however, suggests that a predominant focus on competition—the requirement that one person or group must fail so that another can succeed—can be intrinsically counterproductive.

In *No Contest: The Case Against Competition*, the education researcher Alfie Kohn elucidates why this is the case. As a hypersocial species, humans evolved to rely primarily on cooperation, rather than competition, to survive and thrive. Beyond creating a state of anxiety, which inhibits performance, competition prevents people from exchanging their ideas or sharing skills with each other, which is the hallmark of humankind's evolutionary success. Furthermore, competition distracts people from whatever is their primary task, forcing them to focus attention on beating their opponent rather than achieving excellence. Kohn cites more than 120 empirical studies that validate this theoretical understanding.

Why, then, would the dominant culture obsessively promote competition? One answer is that competition performs a crucial function for capitalism by creating scarcity out of nothing. Whereas cooperation usually produces win-win scenarios where everyone benefits, a competitive contest establishes victory itself as a goal, thereby creating a structure in which everybody else loses.

Competition, however, existed as a cultural leitmotif long before the rise of capitalism. Its genesis as a prevalent feature of the human experience can be traced back thousands of years to the rise of settled agrarian communities (see chapter 3). The increased value placed on material possessions motivated aggressive groups to steal from and conquer neighboring communities, spawning cultures that prized machismo, violence, and competition. The cultural historian Riane Eisler, who has spent her life studying these dynamics, distinguishes between two opposing cultural complexes—domination systems and partnership systems—with contrasting sets of values that align with Kasser's extrinsic and intrinsic value clusters.

Extreme domination systems in modern history span the political spectrum, including examples such as Hitler's Germany, Stalin's USSR, and Afghanistan's Taliban regime. They are characterized by rigid hierarchies with strict ranking of males over females, while venerating attributes stereotypically viewed as masculine such as power and control. Violence and mistreatment, ranging from spousal abuse to warfare, is culturally accepted as a means to maintain dominance. Underlying these systems is the belief that such features are normal and morally justified.

Partnership systems, by contrast, support relations based on respect, reciprocity, and accountability. They orient toward democratic governance structures, valuing both women and men, as well as qualities associated more with feminine stereotypes, such as compassion, caregiving, and nurturance. Cruelty and violence may not be completely absent from partnership systems, but they are considered abnormal and not institutionalized.

While the prevailing world order may be characterized broadly as a domination system, there have been clear trends over generations toward the partnership constellation of values. These may be seen most strikingly in the Nordic nations where women are well represented in political and economic power, government policies support nurturance, and boundaries defining masculine and feminine stereotypes are less rigid.

THE MULTILAYERED SCOURGE OF INEQUALITY

Beyond the direct harm caused to the wellbeing of virtually everyone trapped in a domination system, an inevitable outcome of such systems is the inequality that pervades our world. As discussed earlier (chapters 1 and 10) the level of equality within a country is a more powerful predictor of wellbeing than a nation's wealth—even for those who are relatively well off. More equal societies also generate greater trust, with people in Sweden more than six times likelier to trust others than those in highly unequal nations.

For those at the lower ends of the income scale, inequality undermines not just psychological wellbeing but also physical health. As the biologist

Robert Sapolsky has pointed out, it "is not so much about being poor as feeling poor." Long-term studies of civil servants with equivalent access to healthcare have shown that low job status, more than differences in lifestyle, correlates with higher risk of heart, lung, and gastrointestinal disease, cancer, depression, and suicide. This is largely attributable to greater levels of stress on those whose lives are controlled by others, leading to increased inflammation throughout the body causing faster aging and impairing brain function.[4]

For those whose skin color or ethnicity causes them to be assigned by the dominant culture to a marginalized racial group, the negative effects of income inequality are greatly amplified. Like other widely accepted presumptions that are rarely questioned, the very concept of race is a cultural construction with origins in early modern Europe. To rationalize their exploitation and enslavement of Africans and Indigenous peoples, Europeans developed pseudo-scientific theories that certain groups were naturally inferior. This became the basis for the pseudo-scientific racism that still surfaces in more sophisticated forms to this day.

In fact, scientific evidence shows that most genetic variation occurs within so-called racial groups, not between them. However, while race itself is merely a cultural construct, racism—after 500 years of institutionalized transmission—has become an ever-present social reality. The philosopher Olúfẹ́mi O. Táíwò describes the "cumulative disadvantage" of the structural racism that pervades the United States, where someone racialized as Black has to "fight an uphill and sometimes unwinnable battle to muscle their way past their better-positioned rivals." The journalist Ta-Nehisi Coates searingly recalls the fear and suppressed outrage of his childhood in Baltimore:

> We could not get out. The ground we walked on was tripwired. The air we breathed was toxic. The water stunted our growth. We could not get out . . . Not being violent enough could cost me my body. Being too violent could cost me my body. We could not get out.[5]

Many Black Americans find themselves trapped in a self-reinforcing loop of racially biased urban policing and a punitive criminal justice system, generating what is known as the school-to-prison pipeline. As a result, one in five young Black men is likely to experience imprisonment in his lifetime. In 1961, civil rights activist James Baldwin declared that "to be a Negro in this country and to be relatively conscious, is to be in a rage almost all the time." Even after decades of civil rights legislation, his words still hold true, not just in the United States but in many countries around the world.

Of all forms of inequality, perhaps the deepest and most pervasive is patriarchy: gender inequality that automatically places men in a position of power over women. Patriarchy is abnormal for the human species—anthropologists find no trace of it in forager cultures resembling those of our early ancestors. It emerged, along with concepts of wealth and patrimony, with the rise of sedentary agrarian societies. The historian Mary Beard memorably points to an iconic episode in Homer's *Odyssey*, when Odysseus's wife Penelope is told by their son, Telemachus, to retire from public discourse: "Mother," he says, "go back up into your quarters, and take up your own work, the loom and the distaff . . . speech will be the business of men, all men, and of me most of all; for mine is the power in this household."[6]

Throughout world history, patriarchy has persisted as a relentless form of oppression, forcing half the human species into subordinate roles, frequently through violence and institutionalized cruelty. From the agonizing foot binding that crippled Chinese women for a thousand years, to the witch hunts of early modern Europe that terrorized women, keeping them isolated and confined to their homes, patriarchy has been one of the world's greatest impediments to human flourishing. In the words of the feminist researcher Heide Göttner-Abendroth, "Women are always aliens in the patriarchal system, invisible and unheard; they are always 'the other.'"[7]

Patriarchy pervades every aspect of the human experience, from intimate family life to economic, social, and political dynamics. In spite of marginal steps made in recent generations toward a partnership cultural system, surveys report that roughly 90 percent of people still hold prejudices against women, believing that men make better political and business leaders and should have more rights to higher education and employment. Strikingly, demonstrating the internalized oppression that results from cultural hegemony (see chapter 3), nearly as many women hold these prejudices against their own gender as men.[8]

Beyond silencing women and making them invisible, ubiquitous discrimination against women engenders misogyny, which frequently leads to direct physical and sexual violence. The United Nations reports that one in five women worldwide will be a victim of rape or attempted rape in her lifetime. Each year, more than two million girls undergo the painful trauma of genital mutilation, suffering severe physical and psychological effects throughout their lives. In many cultures, beating a woman for not obeying her husband is considered acceptable behavior, and in some regions, horrific acts such as throwing acid in a girl's face for rejecting a suitor go unpunished.[9]

The oppression of women is starkly reflected in economic injustice and frequently intersects with racial discrimination to create even more severe distortions. Worldwide, men own 50 percent more wealth than women, and 98.6 percent of all financial assets under management in the United States are controlled by firms owned by white men. Women's worldwide share of income from work remains less than 35 percent and fewer than 20 percent of landowners are women. Political imbalances parallel the economic: Only 25 percent of parliamentary seats are held by women, and in just 13 percent of countries do women serve as heads of state.[10]

It is important to recognize the pernicious effects of patriarchy on men as well as women. From early childhood, boys are trained to define their identity in contrast to girls. They are taught to emphasize "masculine" behaviors such as expressions of anger, competitiveness, and strength, while rejecting qualities such as nurturance, compassion, and empathy as "effeminate." Girls, meanwhile, are socialized into accepting that the "manly" behaviors encouraged for boys are off limits for them. Through this conditioning, both sexes are progressively cast into gender identities to which they are expected to conform throughout their lives, creating a false binary that invalidates the lived experience of those who don't fit neatly into one or the other. "In our culture," explains the therapist Terry Real, "we 'turn boys into men,' through disconnection. To learn to disconnect from your feelings, from your vulnerabilities, and from others is what we call autonomy and independence. That's a traumatic wound, a hidden one because it's culturally normative." Although culturally hidden, male-specific traumas frequently express themselves in harmful ways: Men have significantly higher rates of substance abuse and alcoholism than women, and account for roughly 80 percent of violent crimes, suicides, and homicides.[11]

It doesn't have to be this way. History demonstrates that, even in patriarchal eras, alternative partnership systems can flourish. Sometimes referred to as matriarchies, they are not simply the mirror image of patriarchies in which women hold power over men. Rather, they are gender-egalitarian societies constructed around values such as collaboration, nurturance, and nonviolent conflict resolution.

For two thousand years, the ancient Minoan culture of Crete illustrated the stability and resilience of such a society. Their cities had no fortified walls and there are no depictions of war or violence in their art. Instead, the fecundity of nature is featured, celebrating animals, vegetation, and physical pleasure. Women conduct their activities bare-breasted, images of female divinity are common, and men, when they appear, are usually depicted in positions of awe or reverence.[12]

Several matriarchal societies flourish today, despite the influence of neighboring patriarchal cultures. Societies such as the Khasi of northeastern India, the Mosuo of southwestern China, and the Minangkabau of Sumatra demonstrate functioning models of systems that value women while offering men alternative, nonviolent identities. While each society is unique, characteristic patterns have been identified. Socially, they are non-hierarchical and matrilineal, with naming and clan identity passed down through the mother. Culturally, the whole world is regarded as sacred, with Mother Nature often seen as a goddess giving birth to the Earth. Economically, there is no private property but people have usage rights over the land, which is worked communally, and exchanges are conducted primarily through a gift economy. Politically, decision-making is driven by consensus with the clan matriarch as the facilitator. Larger-scale decisions are made by local delegates meeting in regional councils until a broader consensus is reached.[13]

As we've seen in this book, similarly structured partnership systems exist worldwide without being classified as matriarchies. The gender-balanced assemblies of Rojava, the grassroots councils of the Zapatistas, and the enlightened Kudumbashree movement of Kerala demonstrate that they can occur anywhere in the world where people consciously reconnect with core human values and assert them politically.

CONDITIONED BY THE MARKET, FOR THE MARKET

The disconnection from core human values that plagues modern society is a process that begins with infancy. As the evolutionary psychologist Darcia Narvaez explains, every species has an "evolved nest": a development process honed by evolution to meet psychological, social, and biological needs unique to that species. Humans are born highly immature compared to other species, requiring extensive nurturing over decades to develop optimally. When we are infants, our evolved nest includes essential elements such as near constant touch from mother and other caregivers, frequent breastfeeding on request, extensive affection, and self-directed play.[14]

In forager societies, a community of caregivers shares these responsibilities, providing the support needed to cultivate secure attachment for the growing infant. Children enjoy freedom to play as they please throughout the day with mixed groups comprising girls and boys of different ages. They learn primarily by observing their elders and pitching in or mimicking their activities in play, through which they acquire and practice the skills required for successful adulthood. While adults rarely initiate teaching, they are usually willing to aid children seeking their help and allow them to join their activities. Corporal punishment of children is considered abhorrent. Narvaez cites a Jesuit missionary reporting an incident in 1633 in which Algonquin adults were horrified to see a French child about to be whipped for wrongdoing. One of the Indians threw his robe over the child and presented his bare back to the Frenchmen, crying, "Strike me if you will, but you will not strike him." The missionary notes with concern that this refusal to punish children is ubiquitous throughout the Americas, adding, "How much trouble this will give us in carrying out our plans of teaching the young!"[15]

Most elements of humankind's evolved nest are lacking or absent in modern society. Infants are frequently immobilized in carriers or strollers, with prescribed eating and sleeping schedules, fixed times for structured play, and limited touch. Isolating infants to a separate bedroom at night and ignoring their distress cries is a species-atypical practice considered cruel by most non-Western cultures, instilling dysregulated behaviors such as tantrums and emotional shutdown that develop into adult patterns of anger and emotional numbness. In affluent, developed countries, roughly two thirds of adults have experienced one or more adverse childhood experiences, which can inhibit healthy physiological and psychological development.

Although detrimental to a child's healthy development, the cultural norms inculcated in children boost the capitalist economy by conditioning them to become lifelong consumers. Advertisers see infants and children as a lucrative and vulnerable market, and deliberately sabotage childhood development by linking corporate brands with social esteem and identity, thereby reinforcing extrinsic values. Studies estimate that the average American child watches 40,000 television advertisements a year—and that number has ballooned exorbitantly with social media. Until they reach the age of about eight, most children are unaware of the persuasive intent behind advertising. As they enter adolescence, spending more time with their screens than with their parents, their increasing social anxiety creates further opportunities for predatory advertisers. "You open up emotional vulnerabilities," confessed one ad agency president, "and it's very easy to do with kids because they're the most emotionally vulnerable." The Danish marketing guru Martin Lindstrom concurs, noting, "We are forcing the brain in the wrong direction."[16]

As we've seen, the mainstream educational system has been designed to consolidate the early conditioning inculcated from infancy, directing the developing minds of children toward those avenues that will prepare them to serve the hegemonic culture. Building on the Prussian model, conventional schooling trains children to suppress their natural curiosity, unquestioningly accept tasks imposed by authority figures, compete relentlessly with their peers, and orient their lives around achieving rewards for work they would frequently rather not do.

The rise of neoliberalism in the modern era has added a further twist to this contortion of childhood by transforming the traditional view of education as a public service into yet another market opportunity. Historically, as a healthier counterpoint to the Prussian model, liberal arts philosophy traditionally viewed the primary goal of education as providing students with a broad foundation of knowledge while cultivating critical thinking, ethical reasoning, and communication skills. However, in the early 2000s, the institutionalized emphasis on Science, Technology, Engineering, and Mathematics (STEM) in education began displacing this view by asserting education's role as, above all, preparing students to become effective contributors to the growth economy. Powered further by the rise of digital technology, an EdTech floodgate has since opened, allowing dominant tech companies to shape educational policy for profit. In the words of the distinguished retired history professor Rashid Khalidi, "higher education has developed into a cash register—essentially a money-making, MBA, lawyer-run, hedge fund–cum-real estate operation, with a minor sideline in education, where money has determined everything, where respect for pedagogy is at a minimum."[17]

REIMAGING EDUCATION

A redirection of society toward an ecocivilization will require a deep and extensive reorientation of values from the present consumerist alignment. Of all the transitions explored in this book, there is perhaps none more important for the multi-generational shift required than a transformation of education. Rather than suppressing children's creativity and training them to become enablers of Windigo Inc., we may re-envision the purpose of education as cultivating the discernment, emotional maturity, and wisdom required for each student to embark on a lifelong journey to fulfill their unique potential and contribute to the health of their community, society, and the living Earth. What might this look like?

By nurturing innate human collaborative tendencies, education can become a catalyst for behavior that builds healthy communities. It can reshape patriarchal and competitive cultural conditioning by emphasizing prosocial values. It can foster social and emotional skills such as empathy, mindfulness, compassion, and resilience, as encapsulated by the Spanish term *convivencia*—the art of living together in benevolent coexistence. Its methods would emphasize cooperative, team-based learning, engaging students in exploring answers to their own questions and developing their unique aspirations. It would also cultivate participatory and democratic practices and values for consensual decision-making.

Beginning in the early twentieth century, visionary educators have developed educational alternatives to the dominant system, which help us imagine what education might look like in an ecocivilization. The Waldorf method, initiated by Rudolf Steiner in 1919, takes a holistic approach to education, giving teachers significant autonomy and emphasizing qualitative assessments over standardized testing. Montessori schools, originally developed by Maria Montessori in 1907, focus on self-directed, experiential learning with mixed-age groups, encouraging children's intrinsic motivation and respecting each child's unique psychological development. Both traditions now include thousands of schools worldwide that serve diverse populations in dozens of countries.

An important characteristic—one almost entirely missing from today's educational syllabus—would be an emphasis on ecological literacy ("ecoliteracy") and systems thinking. Understanding core ecological principles can help students recognize human embeddedness within Earth systems and develop mental models embracing complex interrelationships and systems dynamics that apply to virtually all aspects of life and society. Nature-based learning, such as familiarizing children with their local "neighborwood," cultivates a sense of stewardship and reverence for all life. For inner-city schools without easy access to wildlife, a sense of wonder at natural expressions of life can be encouraged with simple incitements such as fish tanks in the classroom or a butterfly hatchery on the campus.

Rather than focusing only on conceptual and analytical skills, education would foster holistic learning. In general, education is far more effective when embodied, rather than focusing solely on the intellect. This approach utilizes the full range of human faculties, going beyond the rational and cognitive to include experiential, intuitive, and relational aspects of learning. Teachers would be encouraged to create spaces that welcome creativity and playfulness, experimentation, passion—and tears.

The natural human tendency toward empathy and compassion can be further cultivated within an educational context. The psychologist Daniel Goleman, who popularized the term "emotional intelligence," has developed a Kindness Curriculum beginning with age-appropriate mindfulness exercises for four-year-olds. Children are encouraged to practice helping each other and expressing gratitude. Scandinavian countries are leading the way in these respects. Some schools have mandatory classes in empathy, teaching schoolchildren to share emotional problems and collaborate non-judgmentally with others in finding solutions—thus establishing a "partnership" ethos at the sensitive time when children internalize ethical norms into their moral intuition.[18]

An important distinction from the dominant paradigm is that education would become far more self-directed and self-designed, allowing children to learn through their own evolved curiosity. Children, in the words of Loris Malaguzzi, creator of the groundbreaking Reggio Emilia educational philosophy, can be "authors of their own learning." This entails a shift of the center of authority from the teacher to the learning community as a whole, while the role of the educator moves from being a transmitter of information to a mentor, resource, and catalyst for the child's innate curiosity. Instead of being trained to compete with each other, children are encouraged to learn collaboratively, wherein the practice of teamwork itself becomes a fundamental part of pedagogy.[19]

Some of the most innovative educational practices in this regard are found in the "unschooling" movement, in which children are offered a rich context and support for self-designed learning instead of a set curriculum, assignments, and tests. Visionary "democratic schools" have overturned the original Prussian paradigm, granting students educational freedom and democratic governance—even the right to hire and fire the staff. Rather than leading to unruly behavior, this approach encourages a deeper sense of personal and group responsibility among students. In general, students from these schools demonstrate improved learning skills and psychological wellbeing. As they develop, students are driven by a powerful self-motivated desire to learn, resulting in greater achievement in higher education and enhanced flourishing in adult life compared with those from conventional schools. In addition to the Reggio Emilia example, successful models include the Sudbury Valley School in Massachusetts, the Agora School in the Netherlands, and a network of Agile Learning Centers with dozens of learning communities worldwide.[20]

Finally, an ecocivilization would re-envision schools as hubs for community engagement, with students acting as leaders in building healthier learning communities beyond the school itself. Pathbreaking institutions, such as Swaraj University in Rajasthan and LEAP Schools in South Africa, exemplify new concepts such as "Ecoversities" and "Communiversities," where students and staff work side-by-side cleaning and maintaining buildings, cooking and washing dishes, and growing food. These institutions are dissolving the boundaries of higher education, expanding it to underserved rural villagers and even prisoners. Building on these innovations, the anthropologist Aninhalli Vasavi lays out a vision of "Integrated Learning Centers" that could serve the most marginalized regions of the Global South, breaking down barriers between theory and practice so that learning and implementation become interconnected. As she envisions, "exercises in assessing crop growth can also be an exercise in maths; a lesson in language learning can be a lesson on history and culture; a lesson in history and culture can be a part of knowing the ecological history of a place; identifying specific species of flora or fauna can also be a way of learning to write."[21]

Through these re-imagined designs, schools might become centers for vibrant community life, promoting intergenerational learning and helping nurture new generations, naturally inclined to contribute to the overall health of their communities, to realize their full potential in an ecocivilization.

We may envisage, in the diverse cultures of an ecocivilization, a greater level of communal trust and well-being arising from living in partnership systems where the scourges of extreme income inequality, racism, and patriarchy have been banished to the history books. From this backdrop, we might envisage communities thriving from the realization of Third Horizon ideas proffered in earlier chapters: universal basic income enabling people to pursue their dreams rather than be bound to mindless wage slavery; urban environments promoting conviviality; worker-owned cooperatives providing meaningful collaborative work; and grassroots democratic institutions giving everyone a stake in determining their society's future.

AN EXPANDED PLANETARY CONSCIOUSNESS

A fundamental characteristic of an ecocivilization would be an ontological shift from an anthropocentric worldview to one that recognizes humanity an integral part of the extended family of life on Earth. How might that manifest in cultural terms?

As we saw in the previous chapter, the Earth Charter has already laid a foundation for a broader moral and spiritual reckoning with the entangled relationship between humanity, nonhuman nature, and the living Earth that is our shared home. Alongside this majestic document, pioneering thinkers in each of the major world religions are grappling with reexamining their own spiritual traditions in light of the calling to heal the relationship between humanity and the rest of life on Earth.

In 2015, Pope Francis issued a landmark encyclical, *Laudato Si'*, subtitled "On Care for Our Common Home," which was an impassioned appeal for ecological stewardship, social justice, and a new ethos of global solidarity. Combining theological authority with sophisticated scientific insight, this historic document emphasized the deep interconnectedness of all creation, showing how ecological, political, and cultural issues are intrinsically linked, and framing ecological care as a moral and spiritual duty for governments, businesses, and individuals alike. "A true ecological approach," Francis wrote, "always becomes a social approach; it must integrate questions of justice in debates on the environment, so as to hear both the cry of the earth and the cry of the poor."[22]

Trailblazers are similarly expanding the discourse of other spiritual traditions to a broader metaphysical spectrum, bringing religious thought into conversation with ecological consciousness. The Greek Orthodox Patriarch Bartholomew, referred to as the "Green Patriarch," has been a leader for decades in calling out "crimes against creation" and "ecological sin." A consortium of respected Islamic authorities released in 2024 a declaration called *Al-Mizan: A Covenant for the Earth*, drawing on the Holy Quran and the teachings of Islam to issue a global call mobilizing the world's 1.8 billion Muslims toward a powerful environmental ethic and set of practices. In China, the New Confucian movement, led by influential scholars such as Tu Weiming and Yao Xinzhong, has played a role in shaping modern Chinese culture, showing how traditional Confucian values such as *tianren heyi* ("the unity of humankind and nature") can be understood to refute anthropocentrism and inspire a greater sense of ecological ethics and planetary responsibility. Leading Buddhist practitioners, from the Dalai Lama to the

Vietnamese monk Thích Nhât Hanh, have emphasized the deep interconnectedness of all life, which Hanh calls "interbeing," teaching practices that open up the heart, inviting practitioners, in Hanh's words, "to hear within us the sounds of the Earth crying."[23]

The Parliament of the World's Religions, a global interfaith organization, regularly convenes thousands of representatives from different religions, including Hinduism, Buddhism, Jainism, Judaism, Christianity, and Islam, to find common ground based on ethics of justice, peace, and ecological care. In 1993, it issued a landmark declaration "Toward a Global Ethic," that outlined a moral compass transcending individual religions, which was updated in 2015 with a Declaration on Climate Change that closed with these words: "The future we embrace will be a new ecological civilization and a world of peace, justice, and sustainability, with the flourishing of the diversity of life. We will build this future as one human family within the greater Earth community."[24]

These shimmering strands of Earth-centric consciousness emerge from a broader historic lineage that has been called by the scholar Bron Taylor "dark green religion"—a core belief that nature is sacred, has intrinsic value, and is therefore due reverent care. As we've seen, Indigenous cultures have shared this perception from earliest times, but with the rise of monotheism, followed by the ascendancy of the modern mechanistic worldview, it was banished from the European thought tradition until more recent times. Taylor traces the beginnings of its reawakening in the Romantic movement of the eighteenth and nineteenth centuries, with its iconic expression in the transcendentalist writings of Henry David Thoreau, following it through to modern visionaries such as David Suzuki, Carl Sagan, and Thomas Berry, and its landmark articulation in the Earth Charter.

In particular, Thomas Berry influenced many present-day changemakers with his call for a new story of the universe incorporating evolution and spirituality to inspire mutually enhancing human–Earth relations. The Yale Forum on Religion and Ecology has further amplified his work over three decades, launching a new academic field resulting in thirty graduate programs in North America along with multiple publications, online classes, and a *Journey of the Universe* multimedia project spreading these ideas worldwide.[25]

Could this broad movement provide a cosmological underpinning for an ecocivilization? In *Becoming Gaia: On the Threshold of Planetary Initiation*, the philosopher Sean Kelly suggests that our planetary crisis might have the potential to catalyze a new form of planetary awareness: a "Gaian consciousness" characterized by an awakening to our deeper nature as sentient manifestations of the living Earth, or Gaia. From this perspective, Gaia itself is envisaged as the ultimate locus of belonging and spiritual participation, with the world's conventional religions as metaphysical tributaries offering specific viewpoints grounded in a deeper, shared nexus of meaning.

This expanding planetary consciousness is paralleled by a similar scientific trajectory. Concepts of ecology, ecosystems, and biosphere, which arose in the late nineteenth century, have developed into mature disciplines such as Earth science, allowing humanity to contemplate the Earth as a complex living system, and leading to the concept of the Anthropocene—the current precarious era in which the planet is dominated by human activity. Even as wanton collective human behavior devastates the Earth, sophisticated technology replete with satellites, sensors, cameras, and computers enables us to measure our own destruction with extraordinary precision, awakening a planetary awareness available to all who choose to attend to it.

Similarly, the internet has made available an unprecedented connectivity of the human family, allowing awareness of events in one locality to spread virally almost instantaneously across the world. As discussed in chapter 12, the internet's potential for planetary connectedness has currently been hijacked by Big Tech corporations and largely contorted into a morass of epistemic chaos. In an ecocivilization, however, we may envisage online networks that have already achieved scale, such as Facebook, being turned over to the commons, so that rather than manipulating users to maximize advertising dollars, the internet could become primarily a vehicle for humanity to further develop a planetary consciousness.

Following nature's model of a hub-and-spoke network of communication, we can visualize the local community as the basic building block of society, with face-to-face interaction regaining ascendance as a crucial part of human flourishing. At the same time, building on a prosocial, commons-based internet, an overriding ethos of cosmopolitanism might be the defining character of a global identity that would celebrate diversity between cultures while recognizing the deep interdependence that binds all people into a single moral community with a shared destiny.

We've seen in the past twelve chapters that a beneficial alternative future for humanity is available to us. There is an internally consistent and functionally realizable life-affirming world system, spanning every major domain of society, that could set the conditions for all to thrive on a healthy, living Earth. It is not a utopian dream, but rather an achievable future that can serve as a magnet for those who desire a better world for future generations.

The vision of an ecocivilization is, however, a long way from the daily realities we face as the dominant world system unravels. Major obstacles stand in the way of this aspiration: embedded systems of beliefs, practices, laws, and material infrastructures that currently obstruct any significant movement toward this Third Horizon. Additionally, there are powerful elite groups who believe they are served well by the current domination system and may be expected to use their power to oppose those striving for the changes required.

The forces moving us in the wrong direction frequently appear unstoppable. How might they be overcome? Is it feasible that humanity might emerge through these darkening times on a pathway to a desirable future? And if so, what are the most skillful means to achieve that outcome? These are the crucial questions we will now turn to in the final section of the book.

POSSIBLE SECOND AND THIRD HORIZON CONTOURS | CULTURE & COMMUNITY

SECOND HORIZON

Structures of racial and gender inequality are dismantled

Education reoriented around prosocial values, emphasizing cooperative, team-based, and holistic learning to cultivate emotional intelligence

Teaching methods such as Waldorf, Montessori, and Reggio Emilia become dominant worldwide

Major world religions center ecological care and social justice as primary virtues

THIRD HORIZON

Societies structured as partnership systems supporting relations based on respect, reciprocity, and accountability

Women and men have equal access to wealth and power, eliminating gender inequality

"Democratic schools" are widespread, granting students educational freedom and autonomy to follow their own learning pathways

Schools are centers for vibrant community life, promoting intergenerational learning

Earth-based spirituality infuses traditional religions with a shared nexus of meaning

Humanity forms a cosmo-local planetary consciousness, with local communities connecting globally in recognition of our shared destiny

FOR CONSIDERATION

What Second and Third Horizon ideas arise in your own mind inspired by this chapter?

SECTION 4

HOW DO WE GET THERE?

CHAPTER 19

HOW CHANGE HAPPENS: MODELS OF SOCIETAL TRANSFORMATION

The top 1-percenters in the United States might think they've never had it so good, but their relative wealth pales in comparison with that of the Japanese plutocrats of the 1930s. In 1938, the wealthiest one percent of Japanese garnered 20 percent of their nation's income—a third more than American one percenters today. Over the next decade, however, most of that bounty disappeared. Their share of Japan's income declined by more than two-thirds, while the value of the top one percent of Japanese estates was almost wiped out, dropping by 98 percent. What happened?

The answer, of course, is revealed by the dates. Japan entered what would become World War II, invading China and setting up a colonial empire that rivaled the British Empire at its peak, wielding power over half a billion people. In an embattled world, Japan employed total war to defend its empire, conscripting a quarter of all Japanese males into the military and orienting its entire economy around military operations. By the end, with roughly 10 percent of its population killed and its cities destroyed by American bombers with the final devastation of two atomic explosions, Japan surrendered unconditionally to American military occupation.

Total war leading to total defeat was the primary cause of Japan's drastic reduction in inequality. Mass mobilization required emergency measures by the state, such as intervening in industrial production, doubling income taxes, restricting dividends, and requisitioning merchant ships. This, alongside the ensuing inflation and widespread destruction of property, obliterated most of the elite's wealth. The US occupiers, instead of restoring to the elites what they had lost, further consolidated this leveling of Japan's economy. The primary objective of the US occupation was to eliminate the hierarchical power structures its planners perceived as the source of Japan's imperialist aggression. As a result, they launched a massive program to dismantle Japan's wealth pump, enforcing a "Basic Directive" manifesto that called for a "wide distribution of income and of the ownership of the means of production and trade." They systematically organized labor into powerful unions, dissolved family-owned business conglomerates, and imposed progressive property taxes with a marginal rate of 90 percent on assets, essentially confiscating most of the elites' wealth that remained. In one of the great ironies of history, the policies they imposed on Japan were more radical than many of those that, in later decades, would cause the US military to depose leaders in the Global South who attempted redistribution programs in their own countries. The ultimate beneficiaries of these structural reforms were ordinary Japanese people, who still reside in a relatively egalitarian economy compared to other OECD nations.

The Japanese experience is the poster child for a decidedly grim theory of transformative change in history laid out compellingly by historian Walter Scheidel in *The Great Leveler: Violence and the History of Inequality from the Stone Age to the Twenty-First Century*. Scheidel's thesis is as simple as it is disheartening. Stable times, he argues, invariably cause elites to accumulate wealth at the expense of ordinary people. Historically, he maintains, only cataclysmic systemic shocks have reduced inequality, in the form of what he calls "the Four Horsemen of Leveling": war, revolution, pandemics, and state failure. Even these four "horsemen" only achieve leveling if they are apocalyptic in scale, rupturing society's bonds with extraordinary levels of violence, suffering, and misery.[1]

Scheidel's research is extensive and authoritative. If his thesis is correct, the implications are daunting. It suggests that the only pathway to an ecocivilization is a blood-soaked one, littered with bodies. In the words of historian Roman Krznaric, "no historical thesis could be more disempowering," because it renders futile all well-intentioned efforts to transform society by peaceful means.[2]

Is apocalypse, indeed, our only gateway to a better future, or are there alternative routes that might avert calamitous suffering? The bulk of this book has sketched the contours of an attractive potential future for humanity and the living Earth—one that creates conditions for all to flourish. In this final section, we'll investigate how we might possibly get from here to there. How can we transform our currently ruinous system into one that's beneficial for all? What are the most effective strategies that might enable such a transition to happen?

In this chapter, we'll explore some theoretical underpinnings to these crucial questions, and in the final chapter, we'll examine how they might be applied. As we probe the complexities of these issues, we'll discover how, concealed within the broad brushstrokes of Scheidel's narrative, potential opportunities exist that might just prove his thesis wrong.

NO SECOND CHANCE

To some observers, Scheidel's thesis might be seen as a source of optimism rather than despair. Increasing numbers of people have analyzed the dominant civilization through a lens similar to this book's approach, recognizing how its internal contradictions are structurally unsustainable. To some, however, civilizational collapse is not merely one potential scenario, but our society's inevitable fate.

In 2018, sustainability professor Jem Bendell published a paper, "Deep Adaptation: A Map for Navigating Climate Tragedy," that went viral and was downloaded roughly a million times within a couple of years. Bendell's paper broke academic taboos by predicting that "we face inevitable near-term societal collapse," and therefore need to prepare for "civil unrest, lawlessness, and a breakdown in normal life." His arguments were critiqued by a number of climate experts but, as climate statistics have continued to worsen beyond most predicted parameters, the question of the inevitability of collapse has become an ever more widely discussed topic.[3]

Although dismissed by many as "doomsters," those who foresee impending collapse believe they are providing a critical service to humanity. "The sooner we confront our situation," writes Ray Scranton, author of *Learning to Die in the Anthropocene*, "and the sooner we collectively accept it, the better prepared we will be to adapt to its unavoidable consequences." In a similar vein, French authors Pablo Servigne and Raphaël Stevens have called for a new scientific discipline of "collapsology," which they define as "the transdisciplinary study of the collapse of our industrial civilization, and what might succeed it."[4]

As a historical phenomenon, societal collapse has been studied extensively for over a century. In *The Collapse of Complex Societies*, published in 1988, anthropologist Joseph Tainter proposed a convincing general theory of collapse that continues to influence the field. As a civilization becomes more complex, he posits, it needs ever more energy to maintain its growth, and will keep doing whatever it's done successfully in the past to sustain itself. A military power such as the Roman Empire will conquer more nations; modern capitalism will rely on new technologies to accelerate extraction and exploitation. At a certain point, however, the society finds itself spending increasing amounts of resources for ever more meager returns. In effect, as the society gets more complex, it finds itself having to run harder and harder just to stay in the same place, until the entire system collapses under its own weight.[5]

It's easy to see how this theory applies to the current world system. As the ecological and climate crises worsen, fossil fuel companies double down on their investments. As economic inequality ruptures the bonds of civic cohesion, Big Tech wields its dominance to sow epistemic chaos, further fueling the rise of regimes based on fear and hatred. For reasons such as these, Bendell has since amplified his original prediction to say that, not only is collapse inevitable, but it's an irreversible process that has already begun. "The cracks," he writes, "appearing on the surface of most modern societies worldwide since 2016 are symptoms of a widespread fracturing within the foundations of societies that cannot be reversed. Because those foundations are all breaking together, and slowly cascading into each other, it means that few, perhaps none, are reversible."[6]

For Bendell and other predictors of collapse, however, there is a silver lining. We've repeatedly seen in this book how inbuilt structures of the dominant system have systematically resisted and shut down virtually all attempts at positive transformation. "Collapse," he writes, "comes also as an opportunity . . . As the systems of modern society were so impervious to these tactics over decades," Bendell suggests, "if they were not collapsing now then there would be no chance of any real change."[7]

There is a certain cogency to this argument. However, further analysis tarnishes even this silver lining. There is an important difference between the collapse of historical civilizations and that of the current world system. Previously, no matter how catastrophic it felt to those experiencing it, a collapse was limited in scope. People were closer to the land, and could readily turn to farming, hunting, and gathering to feed themselves. Gradually, they could rebuild from the ruins of the old, while geographically distant civilizations followed their own separate destinies. By contrast, today's civilization is, in the words of political scientist Thomas Homer-Dixon, "a single, tightly coupled human social-ecological system of planetary scope." Collapse in the modern era would almost certainly entail the disintegration of our entire global civilization, shattering the elaborately interconnected latticework of sub-systems such as mining, agriculture, industry, shipping, technology, and communications that keep most people sheltered and fed. Like a colossal house of cards, it would most likely all come crashing down. In its wake, we should anticipate a holocaust beyond anything humanity has ever experienced: billions of deaths from starvation, violence, and disease.[8]

It gets worse. Over the past five thousand years, humankind has already used up the more easily accessible energy sources and raw materials on Earth. Even in the aftermath of the carnage, it is highly unlikely that future generations of humans or any other species would ever be able to rebuild a society to an advanced level of scientific and technological sophistication. "With coal gone," observes astronomer Fred Hoyle, "oil gone, high-grade metallic ores gone, no species however competent can make the long climb from primitive conditions to high-level technology. This is a one-shot affair. If we fail, this planetary system fails so far as intelligence is concerned."[9]

The stakes could not be higher for humanity. If modern civilization collapses, the human race will likely continue, but we're most likely condemning our descendants for time immemorial to lives bounded by the limitations and values of agrarian norms, where draft animals and enslaved or indentured humans become the energy fodder for small, powerful elites.

BEFORE THE TIPPING POINT

Given this dire outlook, there is an overriding moral imperative for those alive today, with any capacity to effect change, to find and advance an alternative path. Where can we look for it? In this exploration, it is helpful to recognize that, from a systems perspective, human society is a particular instance of a larger category of complex, self-organized adaptive systems. Scientists have extensively studied the process of change in complex systems, and their insights merit attention. In particular, an interdisciplinary group of hundreds of scientists has spent decades developing what is known as the Adaptive Cycle model of change, which applies to all kinds of complex systems, from cells to ecosystems, and is equally applicable to human systems.

The Adaptive Cycle describes a life cycle consisting of four phases that virtually every living system experiences. It begins with a rapid *growth phase*, where innovative strategies can exploit new opportunities—think of entrepreneurs developing new products or businesses targeting new markets. Gradually, the system settles into a stable *conservation phase*. This phase can last for a long time, during which the future seems quite predictable, but as time passes the system becomes increasingly brittle and resistant to change. At some point, a tipping point causes a phase transition, known as the *release phase*. Think of lightning igniting a forest fire, coral reef bleaching—or civilizational breakdown. Following the system's collapse, a period of chaos ensues and uncertainty rules. New opportunities for creativity emerge, which is why the final stage in the cycle is called the *renewal phase*. In this period, small chance events can drastically shape the future.[10]

Applying this model to modern civilization, we might place our current era somewhere in the late conservation phase. Ever since colonialism established Western control over the rest of the world, the dominant worldview has generated an interdependent set of legal, financial, and cultural institutions maintained by technologies and infrastructure that are mutually reinforcing. The increased connectivity of the modern era has further entrenched this schema, imposing economic and cultural uniformity, consolidating the power of dominant groups, and making transformative change almost unthinkable. Through cultural hegemony, the system's dominant institutions deflect popular attention from its structural defects, while economic inequality protects the elites from experiencing the detrimental effects of the impending release phase.

So far, the Adaptive Cycle model seems to validate predictions of imminent collapse. However, the period progressing from conservation to release phases warrants further attention. First, we must ask how close we are to the release phase. There are alternative plausible scenarios for this century that build on the dominant civilizational framework to maintain the conservation phase into the distant future. In *Navigating the Polycrisis: Mapping the Futures of Capitalism and the Earth*, political theorist Michael J. Albert provides a grounded, fact-based, systems-informed exploration of these various potential pathways. While most scenarios he outlines avoid civilizational collapse, many are troublingly dystopian. They range from a neo-feudal "Fortress World" with global elites ruling over impoverished populations bereft of most rights and resources, to a "Techno-Leviathan" world of high-tech authoritarian oppression, in which elites reap the fruits of continuous technological advance, a racialized underclass is subject to pervasive surveillance and mobility constraints, and the world's ecological biodiversity is lost to monocrop agriculture.

Albert does depict one relatively favorable scenario combining degrowth, demilitarization, and a transformed international economic order—resembling a Horizon 2 pathway to an ecocivilization. This outcome, he avers, "will be contingent on the capacities of activists, intellectuals, and progressive policymakers to formulate compelling narratives that resonate with people during the 'far-from-equilibrium crisis' situations that will emerge with greater frequency in the coming years, thereby nudging them toward alternative worldviews."[11]

With this reference to "far-from-equilibrium crisis situations," Albert points to a crucial systemic phenomenon that generally occurs prior to the release phase, which contains clues to a potential way out of the predicament we face. The phase transition from one stable state, such as civilization's conservation phase, to another is known as a tipping point. When a system approaches that point, even a small disturbance can have enormous consequences, catalyzing strongly reinforcing feedback effects that are difficult or impossible to reverse. Scientists who study systems prior to a tipping point have discovered certain distinctive phenomena that have significant implications for our time.

The "far-from-equilibrium" situations that Albert mentions typify systems as they approach a tipping point. Conditions begin to fluctuate erratically, going from one extreme to another with increasing frequency. This process, known as "flickering," is considered an early-warning signal and has been observed in changing glacial periods, epileptic seizures, asthma attacks, overexploited fish stocks, and lakes shifting from a clear to turbid state. Along with flickering, another crucial signal is "critical slowing down" behavior: When the system experiences disruption, it takes increasingly longer to get back to the former equilibrium. Eventually, the old equilibrium is forever lost as a tipping point sends the entire system through a period of chaos until it reaches a new and transformed state: the renewal phase of the Adaptive Cycle model.[12]

As our world swings from crisis to crisis, and previously reliable norms are shattered, this far-from-equilibrium state seems to accurately depict the current era. And it is here, in the deteriorating chaos of our time, that the opportunity may exist to break out of the inevitability trap posed by the "four horsemen" hypothesis.

REWEAVING SOCIETY'S FABRIC

Imagine you own a rug, but you don't like the pattern that's woven into it. Try as you might, the weave is so tightly braided that you can barely isolate a thread, never mind transform its design. Now imagine that, as in a magic fable, the rug begins to unweave itself spontaneously, loosening its knots and randomly releasing its assorted threads. All of a sudden, you have an opportunity to reweave the rug into the desired pattern before it entirely unravels. This corresponds to the potential that the current moment presents to us: to reweave society's fabric even as it unravels from its own internal contradictions.

Change theorists Richard Heinberg and Asher Miller helpfully identify two typical stages of this unraveling prior to collapse: "destabilization" and "breakdown." In a stock market, for example, destabilization might describe a pattern of repeated market crashes and rebounds, forcing investors to adapt by changing their trading practices. A breakdown describes more severe disruptions, leading to "a profound loss of function or structure." In this case, numerous traders might abandon the market, causing illiquidity and further destabilization. A stock market collapse might occur if a critical mass of companies consequently chose to delist, causing its permanent closure.[13]

The world system is comprised of multiple subsystems. In the current era, different components of the world order, and different regions, are experiencing varying degrees of destabilization, breakdown, and collapse. Many political systems are encountering destabilization. The public sphere, overwhelmed by the epistemic chaos of social media, might be characterized as undergoing breakdown. Meanwhile, ordinary people living in Haiti, Gaza, or Sudan are already suffering the full onslaught of collapse, while Indigenous peoples worldwide have endured for generations the aftermath of their own near-annihilation. Overall, as the world undergoes "flickering" and "critical slowing down," we might anticipate a decades-long lurching decline in material and ethical standards, with some societies collapsing while others struggle on.

This bleak scenario nevertheless opens up greater possibilities for a swerve toward an ecocivilization pathway. As the flickering worsens, new generations will increasingly recognize that the system is dying. Many will turn, as they're already doing, to tribalism and authoritarianism. However, as the coherence of the dominant civilization unravels, its cultural hegemony begins to lose its grip. Young people, rejecting the failed narratives of previous generations, will likely become increasingly open to radically different alternatives that offer a life-enhancing future.

In *History for Tomorrow: How the Past Can Inspire Our Future*, Roman Krznaric has laid out a model of this critical juncture in society, which he calls the Disruption Nexus. The nexus is composed of three elements: crisis, movements, and ideas. The rapid, transformative change that's needed will only occur when all three are in place and reinforcing each other. As we've seen, a *crisis*, or series of crises, is required to destabilize the system from the equilibrium of its conservation phase. Along with this, powerful *movements* must arise composed of large numbers of people alienated from the dominant system and challenging those who hold power. And finally, the movements need to wield visionary *ideas* offering a coherent and radically alternative set of policies and practices from those that predominated in the old system.[14]

Reweaving society's fabric even as it's unraveling, through a deft intertwining of movements and ideas, defines the challenge facing all those who desire a better future. It is a task fraught with difficulties, and there is no guarantee of its success. The psychic distress caused by social breakdown frequently engenders feelings of panic, fear, and rage, which can lead people further into the sway of authoritarian strongmen fueling those very emotions. While grassroots movements for systemic change have spontaneously emerged in recent times, such as Occupy, Black Lives Matter, and #MeToo, they have not yet achieved the fervent worldwide adoption with staying power required for civilizational transformation. Alternative ideas already exist—as this book has attempted to demonstrate—but the task of multiple groups, frequently working in isolation, weaving them into a cohesive fabric, in the face of ever-worsening dislocations, presents a daunting challenge.

Difficult as it is, this is nevertheless the calling that the times demand. Now that we've investigated the current crisis, let us turn our attention to the other two essential elements comprising the Disruption Nexus: the ideas and the movements.

LEVERAGE POINTS IN A SYSTEM

There are plenty of well-intentioned advocates working to make the world a better place by promoting and implementing new ideas. The problem however, is that most of those ideas will never lead to the transformation required. They may solve particular issues within the system, but frequently this merely allows the system to extract and exploit its way to the release phase even more effectively. For example, researchers have responded to the worldwide collapse of butterfly and bee populations from habitat loss, pesticide use, and climate breakdown, by designing tiny airborne drones to pollinate trees instead, thus further enabling the systems that cause ecological collapse.[15]

Donella Meadows's influential analysis, "Leverage Points: Places to Intervene in a System," discussed in chapter 4, helps identify which types of ideas will likely have the most leverage in achieving systemic transformation. The least leveraged ideas, such as taxes, regulations, and technical fixes, are the kind that dominate mainstream political and economic discourse. More powerful than these are the rules of the system: constitutions, legal codes, laws, punishments, and incentives. Even more effective than the system's rules, is the capacity to make the rules themselves—a power surpassing all the previous intervention points.[16]

Many ideas in this book revolve around changing the system's rules and power structures from triple bottom–line requirements for corporations, rights of nature legislation, and citizens' assemblies. However, Meadows goes further and identifies two places to intervene in the system with even greater leverage.

The first of these is changing the goals of the system. Meadows notes that when President John F. Kennedy famously stated, in 1961, "Ask not what your country can do for you—ask what you can do for your country," he was instantiating a value system that placed social welfare above individual pursuits. Twenty years later, President Ronald Reagan launched the neoliberal takeover of the economy when he declared in his inaugural address, "Government is not the solution to our problem; government is the problem." The goal of the system was changing from national wellbeing to individual wealth maximization.

When the wrong goals are pursued, no amount of efficiency improvements will take us to the desired destination. Meadows quotes systems scientist Jay Forrester describing how, as a consultant, he would identify a leverage point in a company. "Then," he related, "I've gone to the company and discovered that there's already a lot of attention to that point. Everyone is trying very hard to push it IN THE WRONG DIRECTION!" In the current system, the relentless pursuit of economic growth as measured by GDP, as a goal in itself, is an iconic example of this misdirection.

Meadows goes on to identify the highest leverage point, even more powerful than the system's goals, which is the paradigm holding the society's entire set of values, ideas, and policies. As described in chapter 3, the mechanistic paradigm that emerged in early modern Europe, epitomized by Francis Bacon in his dictum "Knowledge itself is power," established the cognitive framework for a system that reduces everything to a resource to be exploited. Underlying the vision of an ecocivilization is an alternative paradigm—one that begins and ends with the dignity of all life.

Meadows's model of leverage points, however, raises a new conundrum. The most leveraged methods to achieve systemic transformation are also the most difficult to accomplish. It's relatively simple to legislate taxes or regulations, but changing the mindset of an entire culture is a process that—if it's achievable at all—requires considerable time. And as we've seen, we are rapidly running out of time. How do we resolve this?

The Three Horizons model introduced in chapter 4 helps us work through this conundrum. Paralleling Meadows's model of leverage points, the first horizon tends to contain the least leveraged solutions; the second horizon invites more radical solutions around the system's rules and power structures; while the third horizon entails a shift in the system's goals or paradigm. The types of change agents involved in each horizon are sometimes characterized, accordingly, as managers, entrepreneurs, and visionaries.[17]

It is important to recognize that each horizon plays an essential role in the path toward transformation. The only way to access the third horizon (H3) is by traversing the first two. However, the discernment used in selecting which initiatives to support within each horizon is critically important. Some may lead naturally to the next horizon, whereas others will move us in the wrong direction. This is particularly significant when considering second horizon (H2) ideas. Change theorists using the Three Horizons model characterize these initiatives as either H2- (leading back to the first horizon) or H2+ (leading toward the third horizon). For example, in response to climate breakdown, scientists are calling for investments in geoengineering to reflect the sun's rays back into space. This is a prime example of H2- thinking: a radical "solution" that enables systemic harm to nevertheless continue unabated, while creating new centralized technological infrastructures requiring continual maintenance to avoid catastrophic rebound effects.[18]

Frequently, contentious disputes can arise between change advocates immersed in different horizons. Someone from Horizon 1 (H1) can see H2 ideas as too risky and H3 as irrelevant. From Horizon 2, H1 actions may appear too limited and H3 as too idealistic. From a Horizon 3 perspective, H1 actions may appear self-defeating and H2 as reinforcing the wrong paradigm. By contrast, achieving systemic transformation will require those working in each horizon to coordinate with one another, creating off-ramps and on-ramps that allow initiatives to transition seamlessly from one horizon to the next.

The Sentience Institute, an animal rights advocacy group, internally debated their horizon-based activities. For example, would reforms such as cage-free farming legislation merely give moral justification to meat-eating practices? Would activists feel the problem had been solved and become complacent? After investigating the British antislavery movement as a case study, they concluded that the opposite was true. Incremental reforms created momentum rather than complacency, allowing activists to focus attention on further targets.[19]

How can effective coordination between those working in different horizons be achieved? How can momentum be created that impels mass movements toward a third horizon that few people have even considered? Let us now consider movements—the third element of the Disruption Nexus.

FOSTERING TRANSFORMATION

Sociologists have studied in detail the manner in which innovations diffuse through a population. A seminal model first developed by Everett Rogers tracks the uptake of new ideas as an S-curve beginning with a small number of Innovators, then expanding to Early Adopters, representing roughly 15 percent of a population. Once an Early Majority accepts the innovation, it's just a matter of time until more skeptical groups adopt it and it becomes commonplace. How does this apply to movements pushing for political change?

In 2013, political scientist Erica Chenoweth gave a TED talk describing her research on grassroots campaigns over the previous century that had led to the overthrow of a government or liberation of a territory. No campaign, she reported, failed once it had achieved the active and sustained participation of just 3.5 percent of the population (slightly greater than Rogers's category of Innovators). Her findings went viral and inspired the tactics of the Extinction Rebellion movement founded in 2018, among others. However, as Chenoweth has herself noted, the 3.5 percent rule applied to a particular context and is frequently misinterpreted as a universally applicable formula which can generate unrealistic expectations.[20]

More recently, sociologist Damon Centola developed an empirical model to identify the tipping point required to change embedded social norms. In *Change: How to Make Big Things Happen*, Centola describes a series of online experiments to determine the critical mass needed for a minority group to overturn established conventions and bring a population to a new equilibrium. He found that, once a coordinated group of committed changemakers reached 25 percent of the population, they predictably transformed the dominant behavior. In Rogers's terms, this would represent Innovators, Early Adopters, and a modest number of the Early Majority.[21]

Centola's research is particularly valuable by virtue of his insights into how behavioral change spreads from a small population of innovators to a broader minority, thus achieving critical mass. He makes an important distinction between simple memes such as a dance move or hashtag, and complex ideas that require significant personal investment in new norms. Simple ideas, just like viruses, spread as a function of the number of casual connections, and are most effectively dispersed by well-known celebrities. As soon as Oprah Winfrey or Beyoncé adopts a new fashion, millions of people around the world might embrace it. Complex ideas, however, especially those that require meaningful behavioral change, spread in a very different manner.

Centola studied a variety of complex innovations requiring behavioral changes, such as the uptake of Facebook or Twitter, including those involving some personal risk, such as the Arab Spring movement, new farming techniques in Malawi, or new birth control methods in Korean villages. These innovations encountered significant barriers to adoption. Some (including Facebook, Twitter, and the Arab Spring movement) only worked when large numbers of people coordinated their behaviors. Others, such as new birth control methods and farming techniques, required social approval and credibility about their safety and effectiveness. They also needed some degree of emotional contagion, when one person's enthusiasm energizes another.

He discovered that these more demanding innovations succeeded through a very different pathway. Rather than large numbers of loose connections, they required shared commitment from a nucleus of tightly knit community members, who would reinforce each other's behavioral changes through approval and emulation. The *percentage* of people we know embracing something new, rather than the total number, Centola explains, has the predominant influence on how likely we are to adopt it. "Real social change," Centola concludes, "is about creating entrenchment." These findings are further validated by social change theorist Leslie Crutchfield, who studied the most successful popular movements in recent US history, spanning the political spectrum from the National Rifle Association to Mothers Against Drunk Driving. She found that the success of these movements arose primarily from the collective commitment held by their members, who were driven by deeply felt common values bolstered by extensive social contact.[22]

These findings lead to key principles for the early development of a transformational movement. Rather than prioritizing broad-brush campaigns, it's more important to nurture innovative practices in close-knit groups, which are likely to be on the periphery of mainstream networks. Communities of changemakers must be incubated from corrosion by established norms, allowing them to create resilient pockets of legitimacy. And it's crucial to encourage strong relationships of trust and shared values among members at the grassroots level, whose ideas are frequently the most effective. Once these ideas become well-established among groups of Innovators and Early Adopters, then more widespread campaigns can hope to encourage uptake of an Early Majority.

As mentioned in the Introduction, Nobel prize–winner Ilya Prigogine famously described how complex systems transition from one state to another through "small islands of coherence in a sea of chaos" that have "the capacity to lift the entire system to a higher order." As described throughout this book, these "islands of coherence" already exist worldwide in the form of grassroots movements and community initiatives motivated by shared values, laying down pathways toward a life-enhancing future.

How can these islands of new ideas, practices, and norms transform into something resembling a new landmass? It would require augmenting their growth as autonomous entities, in the face of headwinds from the mainstream culture. Meanwhile, networks of connections would need to form between them, so that as the dominant system unravels, a new continent of Second and Third Horizon possibilities can emerge in its place.

When Krznaric critiqued Scheidel's "Four Horsemen" theory as disempowering, he went on to rebut it with real-world examples of transformative change accomplished more peacefully. One example he cites is the Indian state of Kerala which, as described in chapter 14, transformed itself from a backward, caste-ridden society to the nation's leader in most measures of well-being. Other exemplars are the Nordic states of Finland, Norway, Sweden, and Denmark, which metamorphosed from being the least developed in Europe in the nineteenth century—impoverished, parochial, and undemocratic—to becoming the undisputed regional leader for quality of life as measured by the World Happiness Report.

How might this kind of dramatic, yet relatively peaceful, transformation be accomplished, not just in one or two regions, but throughout the entire world system? In the final chapter, we will examine the practical steps that might, even against tremendous odds, enable such a process to succeed.

CHAPTER 20

MAKING CHANGE HAPPEN: MOVING TOWARD AN ECOCIVILIZATION

The world was heading perilously in the wrong direction, in Friedrich Hayek's opinion, and he was determined to change its course. Born in Vienna, Hayek had joined the London School of Economics in 1931, where he quickly became recognized as a leading economic theorist. He viewed with dismay the polarizing battles between fascism and communism that defined the period, rejecting the totalitarian philosophy espoused by both sides. However, the Keynesian middle ground that dominated Western economies during that era was, in his view, equally dangerous. In *The Road to Serfdom*, published in 1944, he argued that any government control of economic decision-making would lead inevitably to the destruction of individual liberty.[1]

To Hayek and like-minded thinkers such as Milton Friedman and Ludwig von Mises, it was as though they were shouting unheard in the wilderness. In 1947, forty of them from both sides of the Atlantic met at a hotel near Mont Pèlerin, Switzerland. They spent ten days discussing what had gone wrong with the world and how to change it. By the end, they agreed to set up a society and issued a "statement of aims" beginning with the somber words, "The central values of civilization are in danger."[2]

The Mont Pelerin Society, formed during those fateful days, is arguably the most successful change-making entity in modern history. The policies they espoused, promoting individual liberty, free markets, and limited government, form the foundation of the neoliberal ideology which has since taken over the world. At that time, though, success at such a scale would have been unthinkable. The group's founders were considered fringe crusaders, unmoored from economic reality. Liberals and conservatives alike agreed that government intervention was a prerequisite for economic and political stability. The only serious debate was over when, and how much, governments should intercede in the market. Nearly twenty-five years after the Mont Pelerin Society formed, Republican president Richard Nixon could still proclaim in 1971 that "we are all Keynesians now."

Within a few years, however, all that would change. Beginning with the military coup of General Pinochet in Chile (see chapter 2), the forces of neoliberalism were unleashed on the world. Consolidating in the corridors of power after the elections of Ronald Reagan and Margaret Thatcher, the ideas propagated by the Mont Pelerin Society went on to conquer the rest of the world, generating the system that has led to the devastation we experience today. How did they do it?

The set of ideas deemed acceptable to mainstream thinking is known as the Overton window, named after a neoliberal policy analyst, Joseph Overton. During the decades following the launch of the Mont Pelerin Society, its advocates set about assiduously shifting the Overton window toward its constellation of preferred ideas, such as slashing regulations, marketizing public services, and crushing trade unions. They accomplished this through a series of coordinated, interconnected strategies. They built academic hubs, most famously at the University of Chicago, to further develop and give intellectual credence to their ideas. They pioneered the creation of numerous think tanks, launching entities such as the Cato Institute, the Heritage Foundation, and the American Enterprise Institute, to transmute their theories into practical policy proposals. They circulated ideas through media outlets such as the *National Review*, *Reader's Digest*, and the *Saturday Evening Post*, to influence the general public. And they systematically developed alliances with the business community, churches, and broadcast media, converting influential organizations to their way of thinking. All this was generously funded by wealthy philanthropists and foundations who stood to gain by the instillation of free market economics into increasingly broad swathes of society.[3]

Their success was the result, not just of these strategies, but of a larger set of overarching principles. Above all, they were driven by an overriding moral commitment to their long-term vision. As Hayek wrote in 1949, "We need intellectual leaders who are willing to work for an ideal, however small may be the prospects of its early realisation. They must be men who are willing to stick to principles and to fight for their full realisation, however remote." As a result, they remained uncompromising in their core values.[4]

At the same time, however, they exhibited unswerving pragmatism, pouncing on every crisis as an opportunity to score even partial victories. As Friedman famously wrote, "Only a crisis—actual or perceived—produces real change. When that crisis occurs, the actions that are taken depend on the ideas that are lying around." Their ability to exploit each crisis was, nevertheless, the result of exhaustive preparation. When Reagan became president in 1981, the Heritage Foundation presented him with a 1,000-page manual called "Mandate for Leadership," filled with concrete proposals for instituting neoliberal policies, which Reagan handed out at his first cabinet meeting. It's estimated that 775 of these proposals were subsequently adopted.

What can we learn from the success of the Mont Pelerin Society as we face into the metacrisis of our time? There are, of course, significant differences between their approach and what is needed now. The society consisted of mostly elite white males, with ready access to significant sources of funds from wealthy benefactors and institutions that would profit handsomely from their success. By contrast, a movement for an ecocivilization would naturally be more distributed, incorporate widely diverse populations, and emphasize different nodes for dissemination of its ideas. Most importantly, its source of power would not so much be financial as in the hearts and minds of the billions of people around the world who desire a better future for themselves and their offspring.

In this chapter, we'll consider what can be learned from the success of the Mont Pelerin Society and other movements that have achieved social transformation. There are currently innumerable groups around the world composed of caring, engaged people working to create alternatives to the dominant system. In spite of all their efforts, though, forces of destruction remain predominant. What can be done to enable these life-enhancing movements to come together and generate something powerful enough to change humanity's trajectory before it's too late? And what is the role that each of us can play in helping to make that happen? These are the all-important questions we must contemplate as we ponder how the ideas this book has attempted to convey can potentially influence and transform the wider world.

A SHARED MANIFOLD OF MEANING

Looking back at the success of the Mont Pelerin Society, it might appear as though its activities were the result of a focused master plan, but that was not the case. There was no central command post. On the contrary, its members disagreed over many issues, both theoretical and tactical, and argued constantly over crucial principles around government, markets, and democracy. In hindsight, the neoliberal narrative appears far more cohesive than it did as it was being formed. There was, however, a shared overriding motif that provided a central manifold of meaning: a belief in the preeminence of individual liberty. The same was true of their operations. Individuals and institutions frequently acted autonomously, both competing and collaborating with each other, with some fading away while others rose to prominence, but they were driven by a shared overarching vision. Their collective actions formed a vigorous, evolving ecosystem that spurred innovation and nurtured the most successful ideas and approaches.

If this sounds reminiscent of the evolution of life itself (see chapter 5), this is no coincidence. Many successful change-making movements follow a principle that characterizes all living systems, known as *reciprocal causality*. Each component pursues its own path, integrating with other elements to create the system as a whole, while the holistic identity of the system coheres the activities of each part. The whole and the parts thus exert a reciprocal causal effect on one another. We experience this in our own bodies, where each cell and organ is differentiated but nevertheless acts in a coordinated way according to a shared overall identity and purpose.

Reciprocal causality is a major factor in some of the most transformative movements in history. In early modern Europe, for example, a rare set of characteristics emerged, such as a sophisticated economy with paper currency, productive agriculture, movable-type printing, the use of gunpowder, a network of roads and canals, large-scale iron production, and cosmopolitan cities. This was rare but not unprecedented. The same set of conditions had previously arisen in Song dynasty China in the eleventh century. However, they had little effect on China's historical trajectory, whereas in Europe they led to the transformation of the Scientific Revolution. A major reason for this contrast is the shared manifold of meaning that arose in Europe around the vision of "conquering nature," as championed by Francis Bacon and other contemporary philosophers. This overarching and revolutionary narrative integrated the various breakthroughs occurring in mathematics, philosophy, and empirical science into a new coherence that led to one of the great phase transitions of history.

The potential exists for the shared vision of a life-affirming civilization to similarly cohere the various movements around the world that are currently pursuing their goals as separate threads of a tapestry yet to be woven. While the term *ecocivilization* is used in this book to give a name to this manifold of meaning, the name is not as important as the common set of values and principles embraced by all who participate in the effort. As we've seen, the multiple strands of this vision include Indigenous traditions such as *buen vivir* and *ubuntu*, insights from ecological economics and commons theory, principles from the cooperative, degrowth, and agroecology movements, and learnings from exemplary models such as Mondragón, Rojava, and Kerala. The vision reflects the spiritual underpinnings of Deep Ecology, engaged Buddhism, Gandhian *swaraj*, and Christian ecotheology, among others. It embraces ideas from groups building a solidarity economy, pursuing social and racial justice and LGBTQ rights, and championing the Rights of Nature.

Reciprocal causality arises when the system as a whole and the activities of its separate parts coexist in a balanced dynamic equilibrium. The project of the Mont Pelerin Society would likely have failed if its founders had tried to exert too much control or demanded greater coordination. However, it may never have succeeded without consistently expressing the overarching vision of individual liberty. Advocates saw themselves as part of a larger movement and were therefore willing to support one another, share their learnings, and build on others' successes. But they acted independently and were driven by their own unique confluence of personal and philosophical motivations.

When the various elements of a complex system cohere through reciprocal causality, the power of the system as a whole becomes significantly greater than the sum of its parts. For a popular movement, this needs, at a minimum, a shared overarching vision, but it also requires an intentional process of coordination to catalyze the connections and increase the amplitude of its collective effect.

CATALYZING TRANSFORMATION

Frequently, activist groups working on a campaign become so focused on achieving their objective that they view with distrust fellow activists trying to achieve related but different objectives. A crucial aspect to catalyzing transformation is therefore to reduce the friction between related groups, revealing areas of mutual synergy and thereby motivating different groups to work collaboratively and more effectively.

Social change theorist Leslie Crutchfield recounts the striking experience of the LGBTQ community in the campaign for marriage equality in the United States. The outlook for same-sex marriage looked grim after President Clinton had signed into law the 1996 Defense of Marriage Act banning federal recognition of same-sex marriage. Yet within twenty years, the US Supreme Court established marriage as a fundamental right guaranteed to same-sex couples nationwide. How did this turnaround happen?

When a leading group of LGBTQ activists met in 2005, the movement was fragmented. In some states, popular opinion was more conducive to full LGBTQ rights, whereas in other states the opposite was true. Some activists wanted full legal marriage equality, others thought it more practical to merely push for civil union arrangements, and others wanted to focus on reducing discrimination more generally against the entire LGBTQ community. Their breakthrough was to embrace each of these tactics for different states, depending on what seemed doable, while coordinating them as part of a global strategy to move the entire country toward LGBTQ equality. In some states, activists would simply focus on rolling back discriminatory laws and policies; in others, they would advocate for stronger civil union recognition; whereas in the more receptive states they would push for full marriage equality. The working plan they developed, endorsed by major LGBTQ rights groups, gave a differentiated but meaningful role to every party, ensuring they were all pulling together across the entire spectrum of tactics.[5]

How might such an approach be applied to the worldwide movement for transformative change? The Three Horizons model offers a helpful framework. Consider the Second and Third Horizon contours suggested at the end of the chapters of this book. In many cases, it's possible to map a plausible set of pathways leading from current First Horizon political campaigns to Third Horizon targets that could ultimately shift the Overton window and generate an essential component of an ecocivilization. If different groups focusing on each horizon were to coordinate their activities as part of a larger arc, this could generate a more cogent overall trajectory. Let us examine four major Third Horizon cornerstones which, if fully established, could form a solid foundation for systemwide transformation: Universal Basic Income (UBI); a triple bottom line requirement for corporations; Rights of Nature; and Citizens' Assemblies.

In the case of UBI, First Horizon initiatives already demonstrate the efficacy of direct wealth redistribution to impoverished groups. In Mexico, for example, in 2018, the Morena administration implemented a system of cash transfers to all citizens over sixty-five years of age and other demographic segments. In the first six years since they began implementation, the number of people living below the poverty line dropped by 13.4 million, a reduction of more than 25 percent. Successful outcomes like this open the Overton window to more radical Second Horizon ideas such as national UBI pilot programs funded by a wealth tax or land value tax. The Third Horizon, meanwhile, can validate these innovations by offering a transformed moral paradigm. Currently, debates about UBI usually revolve around whether they are an effective way to use scarce government funding for improving public welfare. However, by positing the notion of the "commonwealth" as a cumulative historical legacy belonging to everyone (see chapter 10), Third Horizon thinking can reframe such initiatives as the moral birthright of each human, so that rather than being seen as government handouts, they are recognized as the rightful distribution of everyone's social dividend.

Similar patterns can be seen in each of the other three pillars. In the case of corporations, First Horizon campaigns might take the form of requiring corporations merely to report the social and environmental impact of their operations. While this would not, by itself, change the corporate fixation on shareholder returns, it would establish reporting frameworks and allow views into the impact of corporate activities, providing an opening for Second Horizon requirements for multiple stakeholders to be included in decision-making. A Third Horizon perspective can meanwhile provide an alternative paradigm by reframing the corporate charter as a temporary license bestowed by society only to those entities convincingly demonstrating that they exist for the benefit of society as a whole.

The Rights of Nature movement (see chapter 17) is already a multifaceted phenomenon making strides in each horizon, achieving recognition of personhood for animals and ecosystems in courtrooms, with glimmers of Second Horizon breakthroughs in reformulated national constitutions and the campaign to establish ecocide as a prosecutable international crime. In this case, the Earth Charter already exists as a Third Horizon landmark, providing a broadly sanctioned moral foundation for a paradigm shift in jurisprudence that replaces human supremacy with a recognition of humanity as an integral part of the living Earth.

The rise in adoption of citizens' assemblies around the world is another development that could potentially create a central pathway leading from immediate problem solving to a Third Horizon transformation of democracy. The current electoral system is losing its veneer of legitimacy as people increasingly recognize it as little more than oligarchy by consent. However, in the face of disturbingly large numbers of people giving up on democracy itself and surrendering to authoritarianism, deliberative democracy offers a transformative solution available to any regional or national government caring to listen to its citizenry. From local municipalities to international bodies, citizens' assemblies have the potential to reconfigure the system based on increasingly popular moral legitimacy.

A recurring pattern in these cases is that the Third Horizon doesn't just exist in the distant future. Rather, its ideas can be injected into current policy debates and germinate there. As discussed earlier in the book, transformational change isn't about fixing the dominant system, which isn't broken but is doing exactly what it was intended to do. However, Third Horizon ideas can help to transform the system from within, as long as they can be coordinated with more immediate and mid-range objectives. In each case, it is critical to distinguish between "fixes" that only further instantiate the dominant system and approaches that generate the potential to reweave elements of the system into an alternative fabric.

In the jostling give-and-take of current political debate, the vision of an ecocivilization can act as a moral compass, establishing the direction of true north and orienting our activities in the here and now. Keeping that vision constantly in mind can help reinforce a crucial lesson from the success of the Mont Pelerin Society: Be pragmatic and exploit opportunities, but don't compromise on your fundamental values.

The importance of coordination across ranks extends to the tactics chosen by activist groups. Frequently, conflict can arise between established groups working incrementally to change public opinion on an issue and more radical groups attempting to raise awareness through provocations designed to garner media attention. Studies have shown, however, that a spectrum of methods can achieve greater effect than one standalone approach. Provocative actions by a "radical flank" tend to raise awareness of an issue, leading to increased public support for groups with the same political agenda that appear more "reasonable" in their tactics.[6]

Another important axis of coordination extends across different sectors of society. A crucial motif of this book is that Third Horizon ideas in one sector can be far more effectual when combined with those in other sectors, thus interweaving a robust matrix for an alternative system. The same can hold true of the movement for transformative change. Examples of this kind of cross-fertilization can be seen in how Extinction Rebellion (nominally focused on responding to climate change) utilizes citizens' assemblies to bolster the legitimacy of its demands. Similarly, agroecology gains much of its potency through its deep integration of regenerative farming techniques with community empowerment and overcoming gender inequality.

ISLANDS OF COHERENCE

Along with a shared vision and intensive collaboration, the movement for transformative change requires living exemplars of Third Horizon possibilities which, if scaled accordingly, could successfully replace the dominant system. In the words of Buckminster Fuller, "You never change things by fighting the existing reality. To change something, build a new model that makes the existing model obsolete." While Fuller's aphorism might downplay the necessity of resisting the onslaught of destructive forces, it highlights the transformative potential of creating meaningful alternatives. These living exemplars might also be understood as the "islands of coherence" mentioned in the previous chapter which, in Prigogine's depiction, have "the capacity to lift the entire system to a higher order."

We can think of islands of coherence as communities of practice already prefiguring the world of an ecocivilization—in bioregions, neighborhoods, commons-based groups, and cooperative networks, among others. They are groups that have chosen to live or work (sometimes both) according to principles consistent with those underlying an ecocivilization, such as emphasizing cooperation over competition, respecting the intrinsic value of all life and the dignity of all people, and a shared commitment to justice, diversity, and subsidiarity.

Since these communities function according to a different set of criteria than those of the dominant system, they tend to face persistent pressure from external forces, which sometimes place their very survival under threat. Identifying these communities and supporting their collective flourishing is therefore a critically important factor in successfully steering the world system in a positive direction.

Islands of coherence can be found in a wide range of sizes, and in rural and urban settings. Some of the most compelling examples are Indigenous communities consciously living according to their traditional values rather than acceding to the values and practices of their colonizers. The Amazon Sacred Headwaters Alliance, for instance, spanning 74 million acres in Ecuador and Peru, was formed by twenty-five Indigenous nations working with trusted allies to permanently protect the Amazon's headwaters in two major river basins. Through Indigenous-led governance and stewardship, they have developed a "Bioregional Life Plan" inspired by the principle of *buen vivir*, envisioning a future based on "recognition and respect for Indigenous peoples' collective rights, the rights of nature, and the pursuit of collective wellbeing." In 2019, they issued a declaration calling on their respective governments to halt the expansion of new fossil fuel projects, mining, and large-scale industrial development in the headwaters regions. Their goal is to permanently protect the bioregion as off-limits to the resource extraction that has caused deforestation, biodiversity loss, and the decimation of Indigenous populations.[7]

More broadly, and virtually unseen by standard economic statistics, it's estimated that up to 2.5 billion people still live and work according to traditional community-based land ownership systems, covering roughly half of Earth's landmass. Groups such as La Vía Campesina representing over 200 million people in eighty-one countries—perhaps the world's single largest island of coherence—help many of these communities pursue food sovereignty through principles of agroecology, in the face of existential threats including land grabs by powerful financial interests. Several other major groupings exist, including the Indigenous and Community Conservation Areas Consortium, which organizes tens of millions of people to document, sustain, and defend the biological and cultural diversity of what they call "Territories of Life" around the world.[8]

In the Global North, some of the most inspiring islands of coherence have arisen in urban wastelands left behind in capitalism's frenzied rush to greener pastures. In Jackson, Mississippi, a city struggling to overcome deindustrialization, disinvestment, and crumbling infrastructure, Cooperation Jackson formed with the vision of a comprehensive and just transition toward a localized, cooperatively owned future. With a community land trust managing commercial spaces and residential housing units, and a number of successful workers' cooperatives, such as an urban farm and small-scale manufacturing, catering, and graphic design enterprises, they envision turning Jackson into a globally recognized model of radical transformation.[9]

Along similar lines, Evergreen Cooperatives in Cleveland, Ohio, is a network of worker-owned businesses revitalizing the city's low- and middle-income neighborhoods. They have pioneered what's known as the Cleveland Model, a scalable and replicable method for building worker co-ops as part of a larger strategy of systemic change. Focusing on majority employee ownership, quality jobs, and profit-sharing, with support from anchor institutions such as hospitals and municipal governments, their approach has been emulated, with measurable success, by other cities such as Preston in England.[10]

Some of the most innovative and diverse islands of coherence can be seen in enterprises that consciously organize themselves according to principles of the commons. As discussed in chapter 12, distributed networks such as Fab Labs demonstrate the promise of commons-based peer production as an alternative form of economic organization. We've seen, in chapter 15, how Mietshäuser Syndikat, a German federation of common housing, has structured a way to reclaim housing from the tyranny of the market. In the Netherlands, a commons-based enterprise named Buurtzorg (Dutch for "neighborhood care") has reinvented home care, with more than 14,000 nurses caring for tens of thousands of patients nationwide with no middle managers or hierarchical planning. It relies on small, self-guided autonomous teams who plan their own schedules, manage their own training, and pool their knowledge. They prioritize spending as much time with their patients as they need rather than cost-cutting, which paradoxically results in lower overall cost and a 30 percent reduction in emergency room visits, while generating far higher staff and client satisfaction than other providers.[11]

In every domain of society, islands of coherence are creating Third Horizon portals, offering glimmers of the life-enhancing future that's possible by shedding layers of the dominant system of extraction and exploitation. For example, a networked community of over 400 transformative learning spaces in forty countries, known as the Ecoversities Alliance, is reinventing education from a Third Horizon perspective. Their diversity of forms encompasses formal university communities of practice dedicated to sustainability; farmversities connecting farmers, researchers, and enthusiasts; a Free Home University for refugees, artists, and land activists; and a jailversity reigniting self-esteem, leadership, and life vision for prisoners.[12]

However, for these islands of coherence to be collectively powerful, their impact must be visible and transmissible through a process of *fractal scaling*, whereby successful principles of an initiative can be reproduced elsewhere, while each particular manifestation remains unique to its specific locality and community. To bring about global systemic change, these transformative practices need to be amplified by a cohesive framework that can augment their power and support their diverse trajectories.

In decades to come, as the dominant system unravels, there is a potential for these islands of coherence to become self-sustaining and build bridges between "archipelagoes" of related islands. Ultimately, if successful, these archipelagoes might join together to form a new "continent of coherence"—a living, growing, sociopolitical, cultural, and conceptual platform for an emerging new civilization.

PERSONAL ENGAGEMENT

Is such a positive outcome possible in the face of the unyielding destructive forces of contemporary capitalism? As we flounder from incessant news media transmitting the ruthless violence of authoritarian regimes and corporate power trampling on human dignity, it's only too easy to surrender to hopelessness about the future. In those moments, it is crucial to realize that the future is not a spectator sport. It is something that we are all co-creating as part of the interconnected web of our collective thoughts, ideas, and actions. The future is not an edifice constructed by others, but by the collective choices each of us makes daily: choices of what to ignore, what to notice, and what to do about it.

As much as we co-create the future, many of us are also implicated in the very structures of violence that have led to the suffering of billions of our fellow beings, both human and non-human. Those of us who are born into unearned privilege, whether through gender, race, geography, wealth, educational access, or any combination of these, especially need to recognize the ethical implications of our intimate connection with the systems causing such harm.

The dominant culture is designed to make its structural violence virtually invisible to those holding privilege, and many people spend their lives blissfully unaware of the part their actions play in it. For those who open themselves to it, this realization can lead to a disturbing sense of guilt, sometimes too difficult to bear, leading some to turn their attention back to more agreeable pursuits. However, there is no need to suffer a burden of guilt at this initial juncture. Once we realize our entanglement in these systems of oppression, we can choose to accept the ethical imperative to channel that very privilege into the activities that might transform those systems. It is only if we continue to shut our eyes to this truth, even after realizing it, that we become morally implicated. "The trouble is that once you see it, you can't un-see it," writes author Arundhati Roy. "And once you've seen it, keeping quiet becomes as political an act as speaking out. There's no innocence. Either way, you're accountable."[13]

The structures of violence causing worldwide harm have deep roots that are both tangible and cognitive. The tangible impacts of 500 years of colonization are ubiquitous, affecting almost every person and activity on the planet. The cognitive impacts are subtler but ultimately more insidious. They arise from the dominant worldview, which infiltrates people's minds from infancy, shaping the presumptions and implicit values that direct most people's actions and relationships. These range from an orientation to self-seeking behaviors and consumerism to deeper inclinations toward the power dynamics of patriarchy and viewing others as objects for exploitation. Working to identify these oppressive patterns of cognition within ourselves, and repatterning them, is sometimes referred to as "decolonizing our minds" and is a continuous, life-enhancing journey of self-discovery and empowerment. This is a crucial aspect of working to transform the dominant system since, without it, we are liable to re-create similar structures of oppression in any alternative approaches that we might pursue.

Opening our hearts and minds further to the vastness of the devastation wrecking our planetary home can be another gravely difficult experience, potentially leading to existential despair. Medical ethicists David Schenck and Larry Churchill, who encountered the realization of the metacrisis late in their careers, helpfully published a paper offering "Ethical Maxims for a Marginally Inhabitable Planet." These include precepts such as working hard to grasp the immensity of the situation and cultivating radical hope—

the kind of hope that doesn't attach to measurable outcomes or probabilities of success, but rather to the faith that arises from doing what you know is right. It is the kind of hope described sublimely by dissident statesman Václav Havel as "a state of mind, not a state of the world . . . A deep orientation of the human soul that can be held at the darkest times . . . an ability to work for something because it is good, not just because it stands a chance to succeed."[14]

TURNING TO ACTION

Ultimately, this means opening ourselves to feeling the Earth's heartbreak, along with the collective suffering of billions of fellow humans, and embracing the moral imperative to work toward a better outcome for humanity and all life on Earth. You know that you've reached this place when you realize you are drawn to action—not because you think you *should* do something, but because you are *impelled* to do it. What is the most skillful way to follow that imperative?

We are all integral parts of complex systems, and the ecosystem for transformative change is no exception. Each of us must find our particular niche within the system where we can be most effective as a result of our unique mix of skills and interests. It's essential to engage in something we feel passionately about, because only fierce devotion will overcome the setbacks that inevitably ensue.

In every domain of civilization, change-making groups are active in each of the three horizons. As discussed earlier, each horizon has its own critical role to play in the transition to an ecocivilization. However, the level of activity already occurring is disproportionately weighted toward the First Horizon, and to a more limited degree, the Second Horizon. Since few people are even aware of the Third Horizon as a possibility, never mind working toward it, your personal engagement is likely to have more impact to the extent you focus on Third Horizon outcomes. Consider the Second and Third Horizon contours laid out at the end of each chapter of this book. Which ones strike a chord in your own heart? What other Third Horizon possibilities galvanize you that I may not have covered?

However you choose to engage, you will quickly find that you're not alone. In fact, most people around the world are profoundly aware of the predicament we face and would like to be part of a solution. Ipsos MORI, a global market research company, conducted a survey in 2021 of roughly 20,000 people across the G20 nations covering the majority of the world's population. Of those polled, 58 percent were "extremely worried" or "very worried" about the current state of the planet, and nearly three-quarters felt that Earth is close to tipping points because of human action. Those in the Majority World have significantly higher awareness of these risks than Global North populations, and in many countries, more than 90 percent want to do more to protect nature. Three-quarters of people want to see their country's economic priorities move beyond increasing GDP and focus more on wellbeing and ecological protection.[15]

Because mainstream media is dedicated primarily to enforcing the cultural hegemony of global capitalism, people are generally unaware that these views are shared by most others around them. Even in the United States, people reject greed, but don't realize others feel the same way. A report entitled *Yearning for Balance*, based on a national survey of Americans, revealed that most people want to "move away from greed and excess toward a way of life more centered on values, community, and family" but feel isolated because they believe these priorities are not shared by most of their compatriots. When people discussed these issues in focus groups, they were "surprised and excited to find that others shared their views."[16]

This is crucially important, because it will require a worldwide mass movement to create the future most of us want. This highlights the critical difference between the achievement of the Mont Pelerin Society and the potential success story available to us now. The neoliberal takeover was well funded but required deceiving most people into supporting policies that worked against their better interests. The movement for an ecocivilization may be relatively short of funds, but can appeal to the hearts and minds of billions of people around the world who desire a better future for their children on a regenerated Earth.

None of us are likely to see the full realization of an ecocivilization within our lifetime, but we can choose to play a part in helping sow the seeds and cultivate the shoots for its eventual fruition. In the words of ecological visionary Wes Jackson, "If your life's work can be accomplished in your lifetime, you're not thinking big enough."

In medieval Europe, when architects embarked on a project to build a cathedral, they knew they would never be around to see the result. Over the centuries that followed, generations of workers pooled their resources toward a shared vision of something great that transcended their own lives. At the age of sixteen, Greta Thunberg, speaking to the British Parliament, called on leaders to exhibit similar cathedral thinking. "We must lay the foundation," she declared, "while we may not know exactly how to build the ceiling." While we're not likely to see cathedral thinking from our elected politicians any time soon, each of us can choose to be part of a movement that lays the foundations for a life-enhancing future that might not come to fruition until generations from now.[17]

Above all, the manner in which we interact with others is crucial. In contrast to the old adage that "the end justifies the means," a more ecological reality is that there is no end—simply a continued organic unfolding of whatever means becomes the predominant mode of operation. As a result, the only way our engagement will lead to an ecocivilization is if we consistently act according to its key principles of collaboration, solidarity, respect for the inherent dignity of others, and reverence for the intrinsic value of life.

In closing, let us reflect on a paradox. Even as we engage in cathedral thinking, we don't actually need to leave the achievement of an eco-civilization to the distant future. Just as Third Horizon ideas can germinate within current policy debates, so each of us can choose to create with others collective islands of coherence, generating a field of life-affirming values and practices that resonates beyond our direct relationships. Every day of our lives, in the decisions we make and the actions we take, we can choose to *be* the future we aspire to, even while we're creating it together.

EPILOGUE:

TOWARD THE SYMBIOCENE

Enrico Fermi was visiting his colleagues at Los Alamos. It was 1950, and the center, famous for building the first atomic bomb, had become one of the world's most advanced scientific research hubs. Fermi, an acclaimed physicist who had created the first nuclear reactor, was renowned for posing simple but seemingly unanswerable questions. The scientists were having lunch together when, out of the blue, he suddenly asked aloud: "But where is everybody?"

The rest of the table burst out laughing. They immediately understood where Fermi's mind had taken him. He wasn't asking about their other colleagues, but was posing a profound cosmological question. Given that there are billions of stars in the Milky Way, many of which are probably orbited by Earth-like planets, why have we never encountered any convincing evidence of extraterrestrial civilizations?[1]

Fermi's paradox, as it became known, has captivated people ever since. Numerous answers have been floated, ranging from the possibility that complex life is an extremely rare phenomenon, to a suggestion that advanced extraterrestrials may have communication technologies that we can't detect. One possibility, however, discussed in a hypothesis known as the Great Filter, haunts the conversation. Suppose there have been many complex civilizations that attained similar technological prowess to ours, including the potential to annihilate themselves, and that in every case they have succumbed to the inevitability of self-destruction. Could that also be our fate? And if so, is there any way to avoid it?[2]

A helpful way to frame this question uses the evolutionary theory of multilevel selection discussed in chapter 5. The basis of that theory is that within a group, individuals that outcompete others tend to be successful, but groups predominantly composed of cooperators tend to outcompete groups of more selfish individuals. This theory convincingly explains the major evolutionary transitions of life on Earth. Over four billion years, there have only been a few significant episodes when the complexity of life jumped to a higher level: when basic cells developed a nucleus; when those nucleated cells became multicellular; when groups of cells specialized to permit the emergence of complex organisms; and when social animals evolved. In each case, these transitions occurred only with a breakthrough in cooperation, when individual entities discovered life's great secret of mutually beneficial symbiosis—a form of cooperation that works to the advantage of each party. The rarity of such jumps shows how difficult it is to find that winning formula—but when it occurs, its effect is spectacular.[3]

Applying this theory to the present era, we can consider humanity to have reached a crossroads in its own evolutionary path. Imagine there were a multitude of Earths where a species had developed our level of advanced technology. Those that were dominated by competitive forces would ultimately self-destruct, consistent with the Great Filter hypothesis. But the occasional species that discovered a way to organize itself that elevated cooperation above competition would survive and prosper.

This defines the challenge facing humanity today. Can we find ways to organize ourselves that foster prosocial behavior over competitive forces? Our evolutionary heritage is a propitious factor. Humans evolved to become super-cooperators with an innate sense of morality and a propensity to group identity. On the other hand, as we've seen, the dynamics of the past few thousand years have systematically intensified the competitive streak within us, leading to the dire situation we face today. And of course, as far as we know, there are not multiple Earths—just our single solitary venture. There is no margin for error. We either get this right through intentional collective effort, or we may succumb to the Great Filter.

The vision of an ecocivilization offers glimmers of possibility for how we might break through this conundrum. In many of the Third Horizon possibilities I have suggested in this book, we see forms of organization that enhance cooperative behaviors over competitive ones. When we consider deliberative democracy, acknowledgment of everyone's right to partake in the commonwealth, relational law, convivial technologies, or polycentric global governance, we're envisioning pathways toward a phase transition that could escape collective self-annihilation.

The mutually beneficial symbiosis we need applies equally to the relationship between humankind and the nonhuman beings comprising most of life on our shared home. Even if humans learned to cooperate among themselves, this would not lead to sustained well-being as long as the belief in human supremacy remains predominant. Once again, the contours of an ecocivilization reveal prospects for a harmonious partnership with all our relations. These possibilities include agroecology, a circular economy, the Rights of Mother Earth, setting aside half the planet for nature, and an expanded identity that sees life as sacred and ourselves as one human family within the greater Earth community.

In all these cases, the outlines of the Third Horizon remain just that: They are rough guidelines, imprecise and blurry, offering hints of a landscape still to be charted. While its foundational principles are solid, one person's view of an ecocivilization may look different from another's, and the closer we get there, the more finely we will be able to distinguish its parameters. What is most important at this time is not for us to settle on the solutions, but to be asking the right questions, and exploring potential answers through experimentation and further inquiry.

We currently live in the Anthropocene, a dangerously unstable era when human activities have broken through Earth's safe operating space in multiple dimensions. If we can make it through this turbulent phase, an ecocivilization has the potential to set us on a steadier course of symbiotic flourishing, a fundamentally different era that has been termed the Symbiocene. This period, which might be very long-lasting, would be one where the human species could embark on the learning required to integrate deeply enough with our planet's cohabitants that we could ultimately develop a truly planetary intelligence.[4]

This possibility hints at one other possible solution to Fermi's paradox. Could there have been numerous instances of advanced species that have reached a technological prowess similar to ours and survived self-annihilation—but instead of using technology to leave their planet and conquer the universe, they chose to stay within their planetary boundaries, cultivate their shared home, and enjoy perpetual mutual flourishing?

Humanity is at a turning point in its story. We happen to have been born at a fateful time when we can influence which direction it will take. We may never know the ultimate outcome of our collective actions at this juncture here on Earth, but we can devote ourselves to this calling with the knowledge that there is nothing we can do that is more deeply meaningful.

ENDNOTES

INTRODUCTION

1 Francis Fukuyama, *The End of History and the Last Man* (New York: Penguin, 1992).
2 WWF. "Living Planet Report 2024—a System in Peril," Gland, Switzerland: WWF, 2024; William J. Ripple et al., "World Scientists' Warning to Humanity: A Second Notice," *BioScience* 67, no. 12 (2017): 1026–28.
3 Emanuele Rigitano, "COP24, the Speech by 15-Year-Old Climate Activist Greta Thunberg Everyone Should Listen To," *Lifegate Daily*, December 17, 2018.
4 Ilya Prigogine, "Biographical," The Nobel Prize, nobelprize.org.

CHAPTER 1

FURTHER READING

Mark Lynas, *Our Final Warning: Six Degrees of Climate Emergency* (London: HarperCollins, 2020).
Will Steffen, et al., "The Trajectory of the Anthropocene: The Great Acceleration," *The Anthropocene Review* 2, no. 1 (2015): 1–18.

1 David B. Yaden et al., "The Overview Effect: Awe and Self-Transcendent Experience in Space Flight," Psych*ology of Consciousness: Theory, Research, and Practice* 3, no. 1 (2016): 1–11.
2 Will Steffen et al., "Trajectories of the Earth System in the Anthropocene," *PNAS* 115, no. 33 (2018): 8252–59.
3 Sarah Kaplan, "By 2050, There Will Be More Plastic Than Fish in the World's Oceans, Study Says," *Washington Post*, January 20, 2016.
4 Jason Hickel, *Less Is More: How Degrowth Will Save the World* (London: William Heinemann, 2020), 113.
5 Jason Hickel, *The Divide: Global Inequality from Conquest to Free Markets* (New York: W. W. Norton & Company, 2017), pp. 15–16.
6 Lucas Chancel et al., "World Inequality Report," World Inequality Lab, 2022.
7 Dylan Matthews, "You're Not Imagining It: The Rich Really Are Hoarding Economic Growth," *Vox*, August 8, 2017.
8 David Leonhardt, "Our Broken Economy, in One Simple Chart," *New York Times*, August 7, 2017.
9 Oxfam, "Pandemic Creates New Billionaire Every 30 Hours—Now a Million People Could Fall into Extreme Poverty at Same Rate in 2022," May 23, 2022.
10 Richard Wilkinson and Kate Pickett, *The Spirit Level: Why Greater Equality Makes Societies Stronger* (New York: Bloomsbury Press, 2009).
11 Josaphat and the Baghdad slum-dweller quoted in Mike Davis, "Slum Ecology," *Orion*, March 6, 2006.

CHAPTER 2

FURTHER READING

Jason Hickel, *The Divide: Global Inequality from Conquest to Free Markets* (New York: W. W. Norton & Company, 2017).
Fabian Scheidler, *The End of the Megamachine* (Alresford, UK: Zero Books, 2020).
Karl Polanyi, *The Great Transformation: The Political and Economic Origins of Our Time* (Boston,

MA: Beacon Press, 2001).
Richard H. Robbins, *Global Problems and the Culture of Capitalism* (Boston: Pearson Education, 2008).

1 Quoted in Hickel, *The Divide,* Kindle locs. 1263–1272; also in Raj Patel, *Stuffed and Starved: The Hidden Battle for the World Food System* (London: Portobello Books, 2007), ch. 4.
2 Scheidler, *The End of the Megamachine*, 92–3.
3 Fernand Braudel, *Capitalism and Material Life, 1400–1800* (New York: Harper and Row, 1967).
4 Polanyi, *The Great Transformation*, 37.
5 John Restakis, *Civilizing the State: Reclaiming Politics for the Common Good* (Gabriola Island, BC, Canada: New Society Publishers, 2022), 51–4.
6 Henry Phelps Brown and Sheila V. Hopkins, *A Perspective of Wages and Prices* (Routledge, 2013).
7 Fritjof Capra and Ugo Mattei, *The Ecology of Law: Toward a Legal System in Tune with Nature and Community* (Oakland, California: Berrett-Koehler, 2015), 90.
8 Jason Hickel, *Less Is More: How Degrowth Will Save the World* (London: William Heinemann, 2020), 47–50.
9 Quotations from Michael Perelman, *The Invention of Capitalism: Classical Political Economy and the Secret History of Primitive Accumulation* (Durham, NC: Duke University Press, 2000).
10 Polanyi, *The Great Transformation*, 81–2; Rutger Bregman, *Utopia for Realists: How We Can Build the Ideal World* (New York: Little, Brown and Company, 2017), 89–90.
11 Ugo Mattei and Laura Nader, *Plunder: When the Rule of Law Is Illegal* (Malden, MA: Blackwell Publishing, 2008) 20–1.
12 William Dalrymple, *The Anarchy: The Relentless Rise of the East India Company* (London: Bloomsbury, 2019), iBook ed., Introduction.
13 Wangari Maathai, *Unbowed: A Memoir* (New York: Anchor Books, 2007), Kindle locs. 218–25.
14 George Kennan, document PPS 23, in *Foreign Relations of the United States*, 1948, vol. 1, 509–29.
15 Marc Pilisuk and Jennifer Achord Rountree, *The Hidden Structure of Violence: Who Benefits from Global Violence and War* (New York: Monthly Review Press), 181–2.
16 Dylan Sullivan and Jason Hickel, "Capitalism and Extreme Poverty: A Global Analysis of Real Wages, Human Height, and Mortality since the Long 16th Century," *World Development* 161 (2022): 106026.
17 John Perkins, *The New Confessions of an Economic Hit Man* (Oakland, CA: Berrett-Koehler, 2016).
18 George Monbiot, "Neoliberalism—the Ideology at the Root of All Our Problems," *Guardian*, April, 15, 2016.
19 Oliver Stone, *Wall Street* (20th Century Fox, 1987).
20 Dennis J. Snower and David Sloan Wilson, "Rethinking the Theoretical Foundation of Economics I: The Multilevel Paradigm," edited by Evolution Institute, 2022.
21 Milton Friedman and Rose D. Friedman, *Capitalism and Freedom* (Chicago: University of Chicago Press, 2009), xiv.
22 Hickel, *The Divide*, 148–50.
23 Manfred Max-Neef, "The World on a Collision Course and the Need for a New Economy," *Ambio* 39 (2010): 200–10.
24 Patel, *Stuffed and Starved*, 34–51; Garry Leech, *Capitalism: A Structural Genocide* (New York: Zed Books, 2012), 45–52.
25 Jason Hickel, "Aid in Reverse: How Poor Countries Develop Rich Countries," *Guardian*, January 14, 2017.
26 Jason Hickel, Dylan Sullivan, and Huzaifa Zoomkawala, "Plunder in the Post-Colonial Era: Quantifying Drain from the Global South through Unequal Exchange, 1960–2018," *New Political Economy* 26, no. 6 (2021): 1030-47.
27 Robbins, *Global Problems*, 86–8.
28 Al Gore, *The Future: Six Drivers of Global Change* (New York: Random House, 2013), iBook edition, ch. 3.
29 David R. Boyd, "Paying Polluters: The Catastrophic Consequences of Investor-State Dispute Settlement for Climate and Environment Action and Human Rights," United Nations General Assembly Report, 2023.
30 Joe Myers, "How Do the World's Biggest Companies Compare to the Biggest Economies?," World Economic Forum, Agenda, October 19, 2016.

31 Joel Bakan, *The New Corporation: How "Good" Corporations Are Bad for Democracy* (New York: Vintage Books, 2020), 57.
32 Paul Mazur and Edward Bernays, cited in Gore, *The Future*, ch. 4.
33 David T. Courtwright, *The Age of Addiction: How Bad Habits Became Big Business* (Cambridge, MA: Belknap Press, 2019).
34 FIAN International, "Rogue Capitalism and the Financialization of Territories and Nature." FIAN International; Transnational Institute; Focus on the Global South, 2020.
35 Daniela Gabor, "The Wall Street Consensus," *Development and Change* 52, no. 3 (2021): 429–59.
36 Marjorie Kelly, *Wealth Supremacy: How the Extractive Economy and the Biased Rules of Capitalism Drive Today's Crises* (Oakland, CA: Berrett-Koehler, 2023), 70–1.

CHAPTER 3

FURTHER READING

Amitav Ghosh, *The Nutmeg's Curse: Parables for a Planet in Crisis* (Chicago: University of Chicago Press, 2021).

Jeremy Lent, *The Patterning Instinct: A Cultural History of Humanity's Search for Meaning* (Amherst, NY: Prometheus, 2017).

Luke Kemp, *Goliath's Curse: The History and Future of Societal Collapse* (New York: Alfred A. Knopf, 2025).

Raj Patel and Jason W. Moore, *A History of the World in Seven Cheap Things: A Guide to Capitalism, Nature, and the Future of the Planet* (Oakland, CA: University of California Press, 2017).

Marc Pilisuk and Jennifer Achord Rountree, *The Hidden Structure of Violence: Who Benefits from Global Violence and War* (New York: Monthly Review Press, 2015)

1 Jason Hickel, *The Divide: Global Inequality from Conquest to Free Markets* (New York: W. W. Norton & Company, 2017), 67–8.
2 Quoted in Ghosh, *The Nutmeg's Curse*, 55.
3 Robin Wall Kimmerer, *Braiding Sweetgrass: Indigenous Wisdom, Scientific Knowledge and the Teachings of Plants* (Minneapolis, MN: Milkweed Editions, 2013), 304–9.
4 Columbus's journal cited in Patel and Moore, *Seven Cheap Things*, 60–1.
5 Quoted in Ghosh, *The Nutmeg's Curse*, 75.
6 Bacon cited in Ghosh, *The Nutmeg's Curse*, 26; Mill cited in Marjorie Kelly, *Wealth Supremacy: How the Extractive Economy and the Biased Rules of Capitalism Drive Today's Crises* (Oakland, CA: Berrett-Koehler, 2023), 73.
7 James C. Scott, *Against the Grain: A Deep History of the Earliest States* (New Haven: Yale University Press, 2017), xi–xii, 1–2, 138.
8 Peter Turchin, *End Times: Elites, Counter-Elites, and the Path of Political Disintegration* (New York: Penguin, 2023), 134.
9 Walter Scheidel, *The Great Leveler: Violence and the History of Inequality from the Stone Age to the Twenty-First Century* (Princeton: Princeton University Press, 2017), 5–6.
10 David Korten, "Ecological Civilization: From Emergency to Emergence." 2021.
11 Cited in Sally Dugan and David Dugan, *The Day the World Took Off: The Roots of the Industrial Revolution* (London: Channel 4 Books, 2000), 142.
12 Garry Leech, *Capitalism: A Structural Genocide* (New York: Zed Books, 2012), 4..
13 Jan Coen quoted in Ghosh, *The Nutmeg's Curse*, 42–4. Silvia Federici, *Caliban and the Witch: Women, the Body, and Primitive Accumulation* (Brooklyn, NY: Autonomedia, 2004).
14 Economist. "What Two Crimes Reveal about Violence against Indian Women." *Economist*, November 29, 2022.
15 David Dean, "Roots Deeper Than Whiteness: Remembering Who We Are for the Well-Being of All," *White Awake* 2018.
16 Bauman cited in David Whyte, *Ecocide: Kill the Corporation before It Kills Us* (Manchester: Manchester University Press, 2020), 33–4.
17 Pilisuk and Rountree, *The Hidden Structure of Violence*, 81–2.
18 Mark Anielski, "An Economy of Well-Being," in *Thrive: Fundamentals for a New Economy*, ed. Kees Klomp and Shinta Oosterwaal (Netherlands: Business Bibliotheek, 2021); Manfred Max-

Neef, "The World on a Collision Course and the Need for a New Economy," *Ambio* 39 (2010): 200–10.

19 Ludvig Wier and Gabriel Zucman, "$1 Trillion in the Shade – the Annual Profits Multinational Corporations Shift to Tax Havens Continues to Climb and Climb," *The Conversation*, February 23, 2023.

20 Culture Hack Labs, "Territories of Transition," 2022.

21 Peter Phillips, ed., *Giants: The Global Power Elite* (New York: Seven Stories Press, 2018), 11, 19–22. *Violence*, 151–5.

22 Martin Gilens and Benjamin I. Page, "Testing Theories of American Politics: Elites, Interest Groups, and Average Citizens," *Perspectives on Politics* 12, no. 3 (2014).

23 Edward S. Herman and Noam Chomsky, *Manufacturing Consent: The Political Economy of the Mass Media* (New York: Random House, 1988).

24 Ghosh, *The Nutmeg's Curse*, 75.

CHAPTER 4

FURTHER READING

Thomas Homer-Dixon, *The Upside of Down: Catastrophe, Creativity, and the Renewal of Civilization* (Washington, DC: Island Press, 2008).

Marjorie Kelly, *Wealth Supremacy: How the Extractive Economy and the Biased Rules of Capitalism Drive Today's Crises* (Oakland, CA: Berrett-Koehler, 2023).

Jeremy Lent, *The Web of Meaning: Integrating Science and Traditional Wisdom to Find Our Place in the Universe* (Gabriola Island, BC, Canada: New Society Publishers, 2021).

1 Emma Graham-Harrison, Saeed Kamali Dehghan, and Zeinab Mohammed Salih, "Hajj Pilgrimage: More Than 700 Dead in Crush near Mecca," *Guardian*, September 24, 2015.

2 William J. Ripple et al., "The 2023 State of the Climate Report: Entering Uncharted Territory," *BioScience* 73, no. 12 (2023).

3 William J. Ripple et al., "World Scientists' Warning to Humanity: A Second Notice," *BioScience* 67, no. 12 (2017): 1026–8.

4 Oliver Burkeman, "Is the World Really Better Than Ever?," *Guardian*, July 28, 2017.

5 Jeremy Lent, "Steven Pinker's Ideas About Progress Are Fatally Flawed. These Eight Graphs Show Why," *Patterns of Meaning*, May 17 (2018).

6 Dylan Sullivan and Jason Hickel, "Capitalism and Extreme Poverty: A Global Analysis of Real Wages, Human Height, and Mortality since the Long 16th Century," *World Development* 161 (2022): 106026.

7 Timothée Parrique, "Decoupling Debunked: Evidence and Arguments against Green Growth as a Sole Strategy for Sustainability," *European Environmental Bureau*, July (2019); Jason Hickel and Giorgos Kallis, "Is Green Growth Possible?," *New Political Economy* 25, no. 4 (2019): 469–86.

8 Christopher L. Magee and Tessaleo C. Devezas, "A Simple Extension of Dematerialization Theory: Incorporation of Technical Progress and the Rebound Effect," *Technological Forecasting and Social Change* 117, no. April (2017): 196–205.

9 Adam Vaughan, "Inside the Race to Scale up CO^2 Capture Technology and Hit Net Zero," *New Scientist*, August 18, 2021; Kai Kuhnhenn, "Economic Growth in Mitigation Scenarios: A Blind Spot in Climate Science. Global Scenarios from a Growth-Critical Perspective." Heinrich Böll Stiftung, 2018.

10 *Economist*, "Political Economy Suggests That Geoengineering Is Likely to Be Used," *Economist*, April 27, 2019.

11 Douglas Rushkoff, "The Super-Rich 'Preppers' Planning to Save Themselves from the Apocalypse," *Guardian*, September 4, 2022.

12 Garrett Hardin, "Lifeboat Ethics: The Case against Helping the Poor," *Psychology Today*, September, 1974.

13 Paul K. Piff, "Wealth and the Inflated Self: Class, Entitlement, and Narcissism," *Personality and Social Psychology Bulletin* 40, no. 1 (2013): 34–43.

14 Thomas Homer-Dixon, *Commanding Hope: The Power We Have to Renew a World in Peril* (Toronto: Alfred A. Knopf, 2020), 252–5.

15 Ainhoa Ruiz Benedicto, Mark Akkerman, and Pere Brunet. "A Walled World: Towards a

Global Apartheid," Transnational Institute, 2020.
16 Peter Phillips, *Giants: The Global Power Elite* (New York: Seven Stories Press, 2018) 135–40, 155–8.
17 Donella Meadows, "Leverage Points: Places to Intervene in a System," *Sustainability Institute* 1999."
18 Daniel Christian Wahl, *Designing Regenerative Cultures* (Axminster, England: Triarchy Press, 2016), 62–4.

CHAPTER 5

FURTHER READING

Fritjof Capra and Pier Luigi Luisi, *The Systems View of Life: A Unifying Vision* (New York: Cambridge University Press, 2014).
Jeremy Lent, *The Web of Meaning: Integrating Science and Traditional Wisdom to Find Our Place in the Universe* (Gabriola Island, BC, Canada: New Society Publishers, 2021).
Christopher Boehm, *Hierarchy in the Forest: The Evolution of Egalitarian Behavior* (Cambridge, MA: Harvard University Press, 1999).

1 Richard Dawkins, *The Selfish Gene: 30th Anniversary Edition* (London: Oxford University Press, 2006), 2; Ghiselin quoted in Mary Midgley, *Evolution as a Religion: Strange Hopes and Stranger Fears* (London: Routledge, 2002), 3.
2 Dawkins, *Selfish Gene*, 3.
3 Lynn Margulis and Dorion Sagan, *Microcosmos: Four Billion Years of Microbial Evolution* (Berkeley: University of California Press, 1997).
4 David Sloan Wilson and Edward O. Wilson, "Rethinking the Theoretical Foundation of Sociobiology," *The Quarterly Review of Biology* 82, no. 4 (2007): 327–48.
5 Simon A. Levin, "Ecosystems and the Biosphere as Complex Adaptive Systems," *Ecosystems* 1, no. 5 (1998): 431–36.
6 Jorge Moll, et al. "The Neural Basis of Human Moral Cognition," *Nature Reviews: Neuroscience* 6, no. October (2005): 799–809.
7 Michael Tomasello, "The Human Adaptation for Culture," *Annual Review of Anthropology* 28, (1999): 509–29.
8 Joseph Henrich, *The Secret of Our Success: How Culture Is Driving Human Evolution, Domesticating Our Species, and Making Us Smarter* (Princeton, NJ: Princeton University Press, 2016).
9 Christopher Boehm, *Moral Origins: The Evolution of Virtue, Altruism, and Shame* (New York: Basic Books, 2012).
10 Dennis J. Snower and David Sloan Wilson. "Rethinking the Theoretical Foundation of Economics I: The Multilevel Paradigm." edited by Evolution Institute, 2022.
11 Lent, *Web of Meaning*, 342–4; David Sloan Wilson, "Evaluating Narratives of Conscious Evolution," *This View of Life*, March 26 2022.

CHAPTER 6

FURTHER READING

Elinor Ostrom, *Governing the Commons: The Evolution of Institutions for Collective Action* (New York: Cambridge University Press, 1990).
Four Arrows (Don Trent Jacobs) and Darcia Narvaez, *Restoring the Kinship Worldview: Indigenous Voices Introduce 28 Precepts for Rebalancing Life on Planet Earth* (Berkeley, CA: North Atlantic Books, 2022).
Pluriverse: A Post-Development Dictionary, ed. Ashish Kothari et al. (New Delhi: Tulika Books, 2019).

1 David Sloan Wilson, "The Woman Who Saved Economics from Disaster: Who Is Elinor Ostrom?," *Evonomics*, February 1, 2016.
2 David Sloan Wilson, Elinor Ostrom, and Michael E. Cox, "Generalizing the Core Design Principles for the Efficacy of Groups," *Journal of Economic Behavior and Organization* 90S (2013): S21–S32.

3 La Donna Harris and Jacqueline Wasilewski, "Indigeneity, an Alternative Worldview: Four R's (Relationship, Responsibility, Reciprocity, Redistribution) Vs. Two P's (Power and Profit). Sharing the Journey Towards Conscious Evolution," *Systems Research and Behavioral Science* 21 (2004): 489–503.
4 Christopher Boehm, *Hierarchy in the Forest: The Evolution of Egalitarian Behavior* (Cambridge, MA: Harvard University Press, 1999), 68; Fabian Scheidler, *The End of the Megamachine* (Alresford, UK: Zero Books, 2020), 208.
5 Robin Wall Kimmerer, *Braiding Sweetgrass: Indigenous Wisdom, Scientific Knowledge and the Teachings of Plants* (Minneapolis: Milkweed Editions, 2013), 27–8.
6 Arrows and Narvaez, *Kinship Worldview*, 69–71; Daniel L. Everett, "Cultural Constraints on Grammar and Cognition in Pirahã: Another Look at the Design Features of Human Language," *Current Anthropology* 46, no. 4 (2005): 621–46.
7 Darcia Narvaez and G. A. Bradshaw, *The Evolved Nest: Nature's Way of Raising Children and Creating Community* (Berkeley, CA: North Atlantic Books, 2023), 32.
8 M. Kat Anderson, *Tending the Wild: Native American Knowledge and the Management of California's Natural Resources* (Berkeley, CA: University of California Press, 2005), 55; Kimmerer, *Braiding Sweetgrass*, 179–87.
9 Eduardo Gudynas, "Buen Vivir: Today's Tomorrow," *Development* 54, no. 4 (2011): 441–7.
10 Alfie Kohn, *No Contest: The Case against Competition* (Boston: Houghton Mifflin Company, 1992).
11 Arran Gare, "Ecological Civilization: What Is It and Why It Should Be the Goal of Humanity," *Culture of Sustainability* 27, no. 1 (2021): 8–23.

CHAPTER 7

FURTHER READING

Kate Raworth, *Doughnut Economics: Seven Ways to Think Like a 21st Century Economist* (White River Junction, VT: Chelsea Green, 2017).

Michael J. Sandel, *What Money Can't Buy: The Moral Limits of Markets* (New York: Farrar, Straus and Giroux, 2013).

Jason Hickel, *Less Is More: How Degrowth Will Save the World* (London: William Heinemann, 2020).

Thrive: Fundamentals for a New Economy, ed. Kees Klomp and Shinta Oosterwaal (Netherlands: Business Bibliotheek, 2021).

David Barmes and Fran Boait, "The Tragedy of Growth." Positive Money, 2020.

Christine Corlet Walker and Tim Jackson, "Measuring Prosperity—Navigating the Options," Guildford, UK: Centre for the Understanding of Sustainable Prosperity, 2019.

1 Kate Raworth. "Doing the Doughnut at the G20?" *Blog: Exploring Doughnut Economics*, December 1, 2018.
2 Jason Hickel, "Is It Possible to Achieve a Good Life for All within Planetary Boundaries?," *Third World Quarterly* 40, no. 1 (2019): 18–35; Jason Hickel, "Want to Avert the Apocalypse? Take Lessons from Costa Rica," *Guardian*, October 7, 2017.
3 Andrew L. Fanning et al., "The Social Shortfall and Ecological Overshoot of Nations," *Nature Sustainability* 5 (2022): 26–36.
4 Mariana Mazzucato, "It's a Myth That Entrepreneurs Drive New Technology," *Slate*, September 1, 2013.
5 Clare Coffey et al., "Time to Care: Unpaid and Underpaid Care Work and the Global Inequality Crisis." Oxford: Oxfam International, 2020; Anna Fälth and Mark Blackden, "Gender Equality and Poverty Reduction," UNDP Policy Brief, October, 2009.
6 Dennis J. Snower and David Sloan Wilson, "Rethinking the Theoretical Foundation of Economics I: The Multilevel Paradigm," *Economics* 18, no. 1 (2024); Jasper O. Kenter, et al., "Ten Principles for Transforming Economics in a Time of Global Crises," *Nature Sustainability* 8 (2025): 837–47.
7 John B. Fullerton, *Regenerative Economics: Revolutionary Thinking for a World in Crisis* (Gabriola Island, BC, Canada: New Society Publishers, 2025).
8 Giorgos Kallis, "In Defence of Degrowth," *Ecological Economics* 70 (2011): 873–80; Jason Hickel,

"What Does Degrowth Mean? A Few Points of Clarification," *Globalizations* 18, no. 7 (2020): 1105–11.

9 Peter Metcalf, "The Poverty of 'Economic Growth,'" *Aljazeera*, June 10, 2021.

10 Ida Kubiszewski et al., "Beyond GDP: Measuring and Achieving Global Genuine Progress," *Ecological Economics* 93 (2013): 57–68.

11 Manfred Max-Neef, *Human Scale Development: Conception, Application and Further Reflections* (New York: Zed Books, 1991).

12 Rutger Hoekstra, "Towards a WiSE Society: How to Move Beyond GDP," in *Thrive:* ed. Klomp and Oosterwaal.

CHAPTER 8

FURTHER READING

David Whyte, *Ecocide: Kill the Corporation before It Kills Us* (Manchester: Manchester University Press, 2020).

Paddy Le Flufy, *Building Tomorrow: Averting Environmental Crisis with a New Economic System* (First Light Books, 2023).

John Restakis, *Humanizing the Economy: Co-Operatives in the Age of Capital* (Gabriola Island, BC, Canada: New Society Publishers, 2010).

Sandra Waddock, *Transforming Towards Life-Centered Economics: How Business, Government, and Civil Society Can Build a Better World* (New York: Business Expert Press, LLC, 2020).

Nick Romeo, *The Alternative: How to Build a Just Economy* (New York: Hachette/Public Affairs, 2024).

Christian Felber, *Change Everything: Creating an Economy for the Common Good* (London: Zed Books Ltd, 2015).

William McDonough and Michael Braungart, *Cradle to Cradle: Remaking the Way We Make Things* (New York: North Point Press, 2002).

Ellen Macarthur Foundation. "Towards the Circular Economy: Economic and Business Rationale for an Accelerated Transition." 2013.

1 Max Tegmark, *Life 3.0: Being Human in the Age of Artificial Intelligence* (New York: Alfred A. Knopf, 2017), 13–23, 136–7.

2 Richard Register, *Ecocities: Rebuilding Cities in Balance with Nature* (Gabriola Island, BC, Canada: New Society Publishers, 2006), 87–9; Katie Surma, "Their Lives Were Ruined by Oil Pollution, and a Court Awarded Them $9.5 Billion. But Ecuadorians Have yet to See a Penny from Chevron," *Inside Climate News*, December 18, 2022.

3 Le Flufy, *Building Tomorrow*, 69–93.

4 David Korten, "Ecological Civilization: From Emergency to Emergence," 2021.

5 Guy Dauncey. "The Economics of Kindness: A Ten-Year Transition to a New Ecological Civilization." Ladysmith, BC, Canada, 2021, 43–6; Restakis, *Humanizing the Economy*, 118–9.

6 Georgia Kelly, "The Mondragón Model: The Ethics and Values of Cooperative Culture in the Basque Region of Spain," Praxis Peace Institute, 2023.

7 Janine M. Benyus, *Biomimicry: Innovation Inspired by Nature* (New York: HarperCollins, 1997).

8 Freya Mathews, "Towards a Deeper Philosophy of Biomimicry," *Organization and Environment* 24, no. 4 (2011); Freya Mathews, "Biomimicry and the Problem of Praxis," *Environmental Values* 28, no. 5 (2019): 573–99.

9 Simon Black, Ian Parry, and Nate Vernon, "Fossil Fuel Subsidies Surged to Record $7 Trillion," *IMF Blog*, August 24, 2023; Rockefeller Foundation, "True Cost of Food: Measuring What Matters to Transform the US Food System," Rockefeller Foundation, 2021; Sheryl Hendricks et al., "The True Cost of Food: A Preliminary Assessment," in *Science and Innovations for Food Systems Transformation*, ed. Joachim von Braun, et al. (Springer, Cham, 2023).

10 Eckart Wintzen, "Re-Engineering the Planet: Three Steps to a Sustainable Free-Market Economy," in *Creating a Sustainable and Desirable Future: Insights from 45 Global Thought Leaders*, ed. Robert Costanza and Ida Kubiszewski (Singapore: World Scientific Publishing, 2014), 299–303.

CHAPTER 9

FURTHER READING

Raj Patel, *Stuffed and Starved: The Hidden Battle for the World Food System* (London: Portobello Books, 2007).

George Monbiot, *Regenesis: Feeding the World Without Devouring the Planet* (London: Penguin Books, 2022).

Nicole Negowetti, *Feeding the Future: Restoring the Planet and Healing Ourselves* (Washington, DC: Georgetown University Press, 2026).

1 *Economist*, "Technology Can Help Deliver Cleaner, Greener Delicious Food," *Economist*, September 28, 2021. Tim Benton quoted in Damian Carrington, "Global Food System Is Broken, Say World's Science Academies," *Guardian*, November 28, 2018.

2 M. Crippa et al., "Food Systems Are Responsible for a Third of Global Anthropogenic GHG Emissions," *Nature Food* 2 (2021): 198–209.

3 Kirtana Chandrasekaran et al., "Exposing Corporate Capture of the UNFSS through Multistakeholderism," Food Systems 4 People, 2021.

4 FAO, "The 10 Elements of Agroecology: Guiding the Transition to Sustainable Food and Agricultural Systems," Food and Agriculture Organization of the United Nations, 2018.

5 Maywa Montenegro, "Agroecology Can Help Fix Our Broken Food System. Here's How," *Ensia*, June 17, 2015.

6 Miguel A. Altieri, "The Scaling up of Agroecology: Spreading the Hope for Food Sovereignty and Resiliency," SOCLA, 2012.

7 David Bollier, "Hacking the Law to Open up Zones for Commoning," in *The Great Awakening: New Modes of Life Amidst Capitalist Ruins*, ed. Anna Grear and David Bollier (Punctum Books, 2020).

8 EAT/Lancet Commission. "Food, Planet, Health: Summary." *The Lancet*, 2019.

9 Catherine Tubb and Tony Seba. "Rethinking Food and Agriculture 2020–2030." RethinkX, 2019.

10 Kenny Torrella, "Why Florida and Alabama Banned a Kind of Meat That Doesn't Really Exist," *Vox*, May 9, 2024.

11 *Economist*, "Microbes Are Being Used More and More to Make Delicious Food." *Economist*, September 28, 2021.

12 Tubb and Seba, "Rethinking Food."

13 Monbiot, *Regenesis*, 187–92.

14 Chris Smaje, *Saying NO to a Farm-Free Future: The Case for an Ecological Food System and against Manufactured Foods* (London: Chelsea Green Publishing, 2023).

15 Jonathan Watts, "Move to Sustainable Food Systems Could Bring $10tn Benefits a Year, Study Finds," *Guardian*, January 29, 2024.

CHAPTER 10

FURTHER READING

Richard Wilkinson and Kate Pickett, *The Spirit Level : Why Greater Equality Makes Societies Stronger* (New York: Bloomsbury Press, 2009).

Guy Standing, *Plunder of the Commons: A Manifesto for Sharing Public Wealth* (London: Penguin Random House, 2019).

Peter Barnes, *Ours: The Case for Universal Property* (Cambridge, UK: Polity Press, 2021).

Guy Standing, *Basic Income: And How We Can Make It Happen* (London: Pelican Books, 2017).

1 Marina Koren, "Jeff Bezos Knows Who Paid for Him to Go to Space," *The Atlantic*, July 20, 2021.

2 Dylan Matthews, "AOC's Policy Adviser Makes the Case for Abolishing Billionaires," *Vox*, July 9, 2019.

3 Rebecca Riddell et al., "Inequality Inc: How Corporate Power Divides Our World and the

Need for a New Era of Public Action," Oxford: Oxfam International, 2024.

4 Wilkinson and Pickett, *The Spirit Level*, 40–53.

5 Mukesh Sud and Craig V. VanSandt, "Of Fair Markets and Distributive Justice," *Journal of Business Ethics* 99, no. 131–142 (2011).

6 Ingrid Robeyns, *Limitarianism: The Case against Extreme Wealth* (New York: Astra House, 2024); Christian Felber, *Change Everything: Creating an Economy for the Common Good* (London: Zed Books Ltd, 2015), 78–82.

7 Rupert Neate, "Tax Our Wealth, Super-Rich Tell Politicians at Davos," *Guardian*, January 17, 2024.

8 Marti-Brehm Christensen et al., "Survival of the Richest: How We Must Tax the Super-Rich Now to Fight Inequality," Oxford: Oxfam, 2023.

9 Gabriel Zucman, "A Blueprint for a Coordinated Minimum Effective Taxation Standard for Ultra-High-Net-Worth Individuals," Brazilian G20 Presidency, 2024.

10 Christensen et al., "Survival of the Richest."

11 Lucas Chancel et al., "World Inequality Report." World Inequality Lab, 2022.

12 Standing, *Plunder of the Commons*, 322.

13 Robeyns, *Limitarianism*, 122.

14 Milena Büchs, "Sustainable Welfare: How Do Universal Basic Income and Universal Basic Services Compare?," *Ecological Economics* 189 (2021): 107152.

15 George Monbiot and Peter Hutchison, *Invisible Doctrine: The Secret History of Neoliberalism* (New York: Crown, 2024), 155–8.

16 Standing, *Basic Income,* 19–25.

17 Ibid.

18 Nick Srnicek and Alex Williams, *Inventing the Future: Postcapitalism and a World without Work* (London: Verso, 2016), 137; Rich Whitney, "How Universal Basic Income Can Help Build a Solidarity Economy," *Nonprofit Quarterly*, Summer, 2021.

19 Rutger Bregman, *Utopia for Realists: How We Can Build the Ideal World* (New York: Little, Brown and Company, 2017).

20 Sigal Samuel, "A Canadian Study Gave $7,500 to Homeless People. Here's How They Spent It.," *Vox*, September 2, 2023.

21 Rebecca Hasdell, "What We Know About Universal Basic Income: A Cross-Synthesis of Reviews," Stanford, CA: Stanford Basic Income Lab, 2020.

22 Standing, *Basic Income*, 105–7.

23 Standing, *Basic Income*, 71–3.

CHAPTER 11

FURTHER READING

Mary Mellor, *The Future of Money: From Financial Crisis to Public Resource* (London: Pluto Press, 2010).

Richard Douthwaite, *The Ecology of Money* (Cambridge: UIT Cambridge, 2012).

Ben Dyson et al., "Sovereign Money: An Introduction," London: Positive Money, 2016.

Bernard Lietaer and Jacqui Dunne, *Rethinking Money: How New Currencies Turn Scarcity into Prosperity* (San Francisco: Berrett-Koehler, 2013).

James Robertson, *Future Money: Breakdown or Breakthrough?* (Totnes, Devon: Green Books, 2012).

1 Galbraith quoted in Marcus M. Dapp, "From Fiat to Crypto: The Present and Future of Money," in *Finance 4.0—Towards a Socio-Ecological Finance System*, ed. Marcus M. Dapp, Dirk Helbing, and Stefan Klauser (Cham, Switzerland: Springer, 2021), 1.

2 David Barmes and Fran Boait, "The Tragedy of Growth," Positive Money, 2020.

3 Michael McLeay, Amar Radia, and Ryland Thomas, *Money Creation in the Modern Economy*, Bank of England Quarterly Bulletin, Q1, London, Bank of England, March 14, 2014; Lord Stamp quoted in Douthwaite, *The Ecology of Money*, 11.

4 Erik Kobayashi-Solomon, "Climate Change Investing: Discounting the Future," *Forbes*, March 27, 2019; Ramsey quoted in Roman Krznaric, *The Good Ancestor: A Radical Prescription for Long-*

Term Thinking (London: WH Allen, 2020), 64–8.
5 Ellen Brown, "It's the Interest, Stupid! Why Bankers Rule the World," *Truthout*, 2012.
6 UNCTAD, "A World of Debt: A Growing Burden to Global Prosperity," Geneva, Switzerland, 2024; Patricia Cohen, "$29 Trillion: That's How Much Debt Emerging Nations Are Facing," *New York Times*, June 14, 2024.
7 Dyson et al., "Sovereign Money."
8 Thomas Hanna, Mathew Lawrence, and Nils Peters, "A Common Platform," Common Wealth, Democracy Collaborative, 2020.
9 David Barmes and Fran Boait, "The Tragedy of Growth," Positive Money, 2020.
10 David Korten, "Eco-Nomics for an Ecological Civilization," March 31, 2024.
11 David Bollier, "Beyond Finance Capitalism (Unpublished Manuscript)," Commons Strategies Group, 2021.
12 Paddy Le Flufy, *Building Tomorrow: Averting Environmental Crisis with a New Economic System* (First Light Books, 2023), 163–9.
13 Lietaer and Dunne, *Rethinking Money*, 199.

CHAPTER 12

FURTHER READING

The Consilience Project, "Technology Is Not Values Neutral: Ending the Reign of Nihilistic Design," Consilience Project, 2022.

Thomas Hanna, Mathew Lawrence, and Nils Peters, "A Common Platform," Common Wealth, Democracy Collaborative, 2020.

E. Glen Weyl and Audrey Tang, *Plurality: The Future of Collaborative Technology and Democracy* (Independently Published, 2024).

1 Greg Brockman and Ilya Sutskever, "Introducing OpenAI," *OpenAI*, December 11, 2015.
2 Greg Brockman and Ilya Sutskever, "OpenAI LP," *OpenAI*, March 11 2019.
3 Sara Morrison and Peter Kafka, "What to Know About OpenAI's Failed Coup," *Vox*, November 22, 2023.
4 Sigal Samuel, "OpenAI as We Knew It Is Dead," *Vox*, September 26, 2024.
5 John Perry Barlow, "A Declaration of the Independence of Cyberspace," *Electronic Frontier Foundation*, February 8, 1996.
6 The Consilience Project, "How Big Tech Is Reshaping Governance," Consilience Project, 2021.
7 Zephyr Teachout, "The Boss Will See You Now," *New York Review of Books*, August 18, 2022.
8 Tristan Harris, "Re-Aligning Technology with Humanity," in *The New Possible: Visions of Our World Beyond Crisis*, ed. Philip Clayton et al. (Eugene OR: Cascade Books, 2021).
9 *Economist*, "China Invents the Digital Totalitarian State," *Economist*, December 17, 2016.
10 Ivan Illich, *Tools for Conviviality* (London: Marion Boyars, 2009), 6–29.
11 Jathan Sadowski et al, "Everyone Should Decide How Their Digital Data Are Used—Not Just Tech Companies," *Nature* 595 (2021): 169–71.
12 Yochai Benkler, "The Political Economy of Commons," *Upgrade* IV, no. 3 (2003).
13 Ralph Horat and Jan Baeriswyl, "Cosmo-Localism: Outlines of a New Model of Civilization," *Whitepaper 1.0* (2021).
14 Khushboo Balwani, "Fab Labs: Peer Production for a New Commons Economy" in *Sharing Cities: Activating the Urban Commons* (Shareable, 2018).
15 Neal Gorenflo, "How Platform Cooperatives Can Beat Death Stars Like Uber to Create a Real Sharing Economy," *Shareable*, November 4, 2015.
16 Trebor Scholz, "Platform Cooperativism: Challenging the Corporate Sharing Economy," New York: Rosa Luxemburg Stiftung, 2016.
17 David Rozas et al., "When Ostrom Meets Blockchain: Exploring the Potentials of Blockchain for Commons Governance," *Sage Open* 1–14, no. 1 (2021): 1.
18 Primavera De Filippi and Xavier Lavayssière, "Blockchain Technology: Toward a Decentralized Governance of Digital Platforms?," in *The Great Awakening: New Modes of Life Amidst Capitalist Ruins*, ed. Anna Grear and David Bollier (Punctum Books, 2020)
19 Mio Tastas Viktorsson and Saoirse Gowan, "Revisiting the Meidner Plan," *Jacobin*, August 22, 2017.

CHAPTER 13

FURTHER READING

Jonathan F. P. Rose, *The Well-Tempered City: What Modern Science, Ancient Civilizations, and Human Nature Teach Us About the Future of Urban Life* (New York: HarperWave, 2016).

Paul Chatterton, *Unlocking Sustainable Cities: A Manifesto for Real Change* (London: Pluto Press, 2019).

Sheila R. Foster and Christian Iaione, "Ostrom in the City: Design Principles and Practices for the Urban Commons," in *Routledge Handbook of the Study of the Commons*, ed. Dan Cole et al. (New York: Routledge, 2020).

Richard Register, *Ecocities: Rebuilding Cities in Balance with Nature* (Gabriola Island, BC, Canada: New Society Publishers, 2006).

1 Jonathan Kwitny, "The Great Transportation Conspiracy," in *Controlling Technology: Contemporary Issues*, ed. W. B. Thompson (Buffalo, NY: Prometheus Books, 1991), 265–74.

2 Mark Swilling et al., "The Weight of Cities: Resource Requirements of Future Urbanization," United Nations Environment Programme, 2018.

3 Gemma Burgess, et al., "Flourishing Systems: Re-Envisioning Infrastructure as a Platform for Human Flourishing," Cambridge, UK: Centre for Digital Built Britain and Centre for Smart Infrastructure and Construction, 2020.

4 Aleksandar Sasha Zeljic, "Polycentric Cities: The Future of Sustainable Urban Growth," *Gensler*, 2018.

5 Herbert Girardet. "Regenerative Cities—Making Cities Work for People and Planet": Cooperative Research Centre for Low Carbon Living, 2017.

6 Henri Sulku. "Urban Landscapes in the 21st Century: Can Eco-Cities Tackle Climate Change and Pollution?" *Resilience*, October 23, 2024.

7 Chatterton, *Unlocking Sustainable Cities*, 12–36.

8 Luke Taylor, "'The Tranquility Frees You': Bogotá, the City That Shuts out Cars Every Week," *Guardian*, May 30, 2024.

9 Janis Birkeland, "Eco-Positive Design," in *Pluriverse: A Post-Development Dictionary*, ed. Ashish Kothari et al. (New Delhi: Tulika Books, 2019).

10 Francesca Mari, "Imagine a Renters' Utopia. It Might Look Like Vienna," *New York Times Magazine*, May 23, 2023.

11 David Bollier, "An Atlas for Urban Commons of the World," *Resilience*, October 21, 2024.

12 Subin Dennis, "How Women Beedi Workers Set up Asia's Largest Housing Cooperative," *Open Democracy*, April 17, 2018.

13 Joshua Frank, "'Where California Goes, There Goes the Nation,'" *Resilience*, August 14, 2024.

14 Paddy Le Flufy, *Building Tomorrow: Averting Environmental Crisis with a New Economic System* (First Light Books, 2023), 54–8.

15 Oliver Wainwright, "The Tate Modern Privacy Ruling Could Lead to a Worrying Future for Cities," *Guardian*, February 1, 2023.

16 Sheila R. Foster and Christian Iaione, "The City as a Commons," *Yale Law & Policy Review* 34 (2016): 281–349.

CHAPTER 14

FURTHER READING

John Restakis, *Civilizing the State: Reclaiming Politics for the Common Good* (Gabriola Island, BC, Canada: New Society Publishers, 2022).

Brett Hennig, *The End of Politicians: Time for a Real Democracy* (London: Unbound, 2017).

Hélène Landemore, *Open Democracy: Reinventing Popular Rule for the Twenty-First Century* (Princeton: Princeton University Press, 2020).

1 Wes Enzinna, "A Dream of Secular Utopia in Isis' Backyard," *New York Times*, November 24, 2015.

2 Hennig, *The End of Politicians*, 47–8.

3 James Madison, "Federalist No. 10," *The Federalist Papers* (1787).

4 George Zarkadakis, *Cyber Republic: Reinventing Democracy in the Age of Intelligent Machines* (Cambridge, MA: MIT Press, 2020), 3–10. Juncker quoted in "The Quest for Prosperity."

Economist, March 15, 2007.

5 John S. Dryzek, "The Crisis of Democracy and the Science of Deliberation," *Science* 363, no. 6432 (2019): 1144–46.

6 Graham Smith, *Democratic Innovations: Designing Institutions for Citizen Participation* (Cambridge: Cambridge University Press, 2009), 76–145.

7 Mauricio Mejia, "2023 Trends in Deliberative Democracy: OECD Database Update," *Participo*, December 7, 2023.

8 Claudia Chwalisz, "A Movement That's Quietly Reshaping Democracy for the Better," *Noema*, May 12, 2022.

9 Terry Bouricius, *The Trouble with Elections: Everything We Thought We Knew About Democracy Is Wrong* (Substack, 2023), chapter 2.6 "What About Electing a Chief Executive?"

10 Laura Giesen, "DemocracyNext: Replacing Elections with Deliberation: An Interview with Claudia Chlawisz," *Democracy Technologies*, September 20, 2022.

11 Indra Adnan, *The Politics of Waking Up: Power and Possibility in the Fractal Age* (London: Perspectiva Press, 2021).

12 Ted Trainer, "Kurdist Rojava: A Social Model for Our Future," *Resilience*, January 3, 2020.

13 Restakis, *Civilizing the State*, 123; Trainer, "Kurdist Rojava."

14 Ryan Mallett-Outtrim, "Two Decades On: A Glimpse inside the Zapatista's Capital, Oventic," *Links International Journal of Socialist Renewal*, August 13, 2016.

15 Anna Rebrii, "30 Years Later, the Zapatista Struggle Continues," *Truthdig*, May 20, 2024.

16 Ann Louise Deslandes, "Crossing the Storm: EZLN Marks 30 Years with a 120-Year Plan," *Nacla*, January 19, 2024.

17 Miguel Carter, "The Landless Rural Workers Movement and Democracy in Brazil," *Latin American Research Review* 45 (2010): 186–217.

18 Richard Flyer, "Sri Lanka's Untold Story of Resilience: Sarvodaya's Pathway Can Work Anywhere," *Shareable*, October 6, 2022.

19 Roman Krznaric, *History for Tomorrow: Inspiration from the Past for the Future of Humanity* (London: WH Allen, 2024), 178–9.

20 Restakis, *Civilizing the State*, 100–106.

21 Ibid., 159, 165–7.

22 OECD. "Open Government and Citizen Participation" OECD, 2021.

23 Ismael Peña-López, "Decidim.Barcelona, Spain: Case Study," *IT for Change* (2017).

24 Audrey Tang and E. Glen Weyl, "Plurality: Technology for Collaborative Diversity and Democracy," *Radical Xchange*, September 15, 2022; The Consilience Project, "Taiwan's Digital Democracy," *Consilience Project*, June 6, 2021.

25 Dmytro Khutkyy, "Participatory Budgeting: An Empowering Democratic Institution," *Eurozine*, October 31, 2017.

CHAPTER 15

FURTHER READING

Fritjof Capra and Ugo Mattei, *The Ecology of Law: Toward a Legal System in Tune with Nature and Community* (Oakland, California: Berrett-Koehler, 2015).

Katharina Pistor, *The Code of Capital: How the Law Creates Wealth and Inequality* (Princeton: Princeton University Press, 2019).

David Bollier and Silke Helfrich, *Free, Fair and Alive: The Insurgent Power of the Commons* (Gabriola Island, Canada: New Society Publishers, 2019).

Alex May, "Interconnected Law: A Paradigm Shift in Legal Thinking," *OpenDemocracy*, 27 November, 2020.

Ugo Mattei and Laura Nader, *Plunder: When the Rule of Law Is Illegal* (Malden, MA: Blackwell Publishing, 2008).

Rufus Pollock, *The Open Revolution* (A/E/T Press, 2018).

1 Guy Standing, *Plunder of the Commons: A Manifesto for Sharing Public Wealth* (London: Penguin Random House, 2019), 1–6.

2 Garrett Hardin, "The Tragedy of the Commons," *Science* 162 (1968): 1243–48.

3 Elinor Ostrom, *Governing the Commons: The Evolution of Institutions for Collective Action*

(New York: Cambridge University Press, 1990.
4 David Bollier, *Think Like a Commoner: A Short Introduction to the Life of the Commons*, 2nd. ed. (Gabriola Island, BC, Canada: New Society Publishers, 2025).
5 Capra and Mattei, *The Ecology of Law*, 77–83.
6 Charles Tilly, "War Making and State Making as Organized Crime," in *Bringing the State Back In*, eds. Peter Evans, Dieter Rueschemeyer, and Theda Skocpol (Cambridge: Cambridge University Press, 1985), 169–91; Mancur Olson, "Dictatorship, Democracy, and Development," *American Political Science Review* 87, no. 03 (1993): 567–76.
7 Sherri Mitchell cited in Wahinkpe Topa (Four Arrows) and Darcia Narvaez, *Restoring the Kinship Worldview: Indigenous Voices Introduce 28 Precepts for Rebalancing Life on Planet Earth* (Berkeley, CA: North Atlantic Books, 212).
8 J. B. MacKinnon, *The Once and Future World: Nature as It Was, as It Is, as It Could Be* (New York: Houghton Mifflin Harcourt, 2013), 165–77.
9 Samuel Firman, "Trespassing for the Common Good," *Noema*, December 10, 2024; Patrick Barkham, "'Get on My Land': The Farmers Who Want Strangers Wandering Their Fields," *Guardian*, January 8, 2025.
10 Lewis Mumford, *Technics and Civilization* (Chicago: University of Chicago Press, 2010), 142.
11 Thomas Hanna, Dana Brown, and Miriam Brett, "Democratising Knowledge: Transforming Intellectual Property and Research and Development," Common Wealth/Democracy Collaborative, 2020.
12 Pollock, *The Open Revolution*, 53–70.
13 Rufus Pollock et al., "Remuneration Rights: An Innovative Two-Part Payment System for Funding Medicines," Rockefeller Foundation, 2017.
14 Francis T. Cullen, "Prisons Do Not Reduce Recidivism: The High Cost of Ignoring Science," *The Prison Journal* 91, no. 3 (2011): 48S–65S.
15 Madalyn Hayden, "Recidivism Rates in the United States Versus Europe: How and Why Are They Different?," ScholarWorks at Western Michigan University Honors Theses, no. 3665 (2023).
16 Rutger Bregman, *Humankind: A Hopeful History* (New York: Little, Brown and Company, 2019), 328–46.
17 Denise C. Breton, "Decolonizing Restorative Justice," in *Unsettling Ourselves: Reflections and Resources for Deconstructing Colonial Mentality* (Minnesota: Unsettling Minnesota Collective, 2009).
18 Michel Bauwens, "Peer-to-Peer Economy and New Civilization Centered around the Sustenance of the Commons," in *The Wealth of the Commons: A World Beyond Market and State*, ed. David Bollier and Silke Helfrich (Levellers Press, 2012).
19 Janelle Orsi, "Three Legal Principles for Organizations Rebuilding the Commons," in *Law and Policy for a New Economy: Sustainable, Just, and Democratic*, ed. Melissa K. Scanlan (Cheltenham, UK: Edward Elgar Publishing, 2017).
20 David Bollier, "Hacking the Law to Open up Zones for Commoning," in *The Great Awakening: New Modes of Life Amidst Capitalist Ruins*, ed. Anna Grear and David Bollier (Punctum Books, 2020).
21 Ben Price, "CELDF and Pittsburgh's Community Bill of Rights Banning Fracking" in Shareable, *Sharing Cities: Activating the Urban Commons* (Shareable, 2018).
22 Erin Ryan et al., "Environmental Rights for the 21st Century: A Comprehensive Analysis of the Public Trust Doctrine and Rights of Nature Movement," *Cardozo Law Review* 42, no. 2447 (2021).

CHAPTER 16

FURTHER READING

Oded Gilad and Dena Freeman, *Global Democracy: The Key to Global Justice* (Berlin: Democracy Without Borders, 2022).

Jonathan S. Blake and Nils Gilman, *Children of a Modest Star: Planetary Thinking for an Age of Crises* (Stanford: Stanford University Press, 2024).

Andreas Bummel, "Towards a Planetary Polity: The Formation of Global Identity and State Structures," in *Expanding Worldviews: Astrobiology, Big History and Cosmic Perspectives*, ed. Ian Crawford (London: Springer, 2021).

Gideon Kossoff, "Cosmopolitan Localism: The Planetary Networking of Everyday Life in Place," *Cuadernos del Centro de Estudios en Diseño y Comunicación* 19, no. 73 (2019).

1 Gilad and Freeman, *Global Democracy,* 124–33.
2 Derek Croxton, "The Peace of Westphalia of 1648 and the Origins of Sovereignty," *The International History Review* 21, no. 3 (1999): 569–91.
3 Wolfgang Sachs and Tilman Santarius, *Fair Future. Resource Conflicts, Security and Global Justice* (London: Zed Books, 2007).
4 Agnès Callamard, "Gaza and the End of the Rules-Based Order," *Foreign Affairs*, February 15, 2024; Francis Fukuyama, *The End of History and the Last Man* (New York: Free Press, 1992).
5 Sharon Zhang, "UN Chief: World Has Entered 'Age of Impunity' as Israel's Aggression Spreads," *Truthout*, September 24, 2024; Nathan Gardels, "Looking Ahead to the 19th Century," *Noema*, February 21, 2025.
6 Joshua Keating, "The World Has Entered the Third Nuclear Age," *Vox*, February 5, 2025.
7 Paul Raskin, "Scenes from the Great Transition," in *Creating a Sustainable and Desirable Future: Insights from 45 Global Thought Leaders*, eds. Robert Costanza and Ida Kubiszewski (Singapore: World Scientific Publishing, 2014), 59.
8 Blake and Gilman, *Children of a Modest Star*, 9.
9 Eileen Crist, "For Cosmopolitan Bioregionalism," *Ecological Citizen* 3 (Supp C) (2020): 21–9.
10 Samantha Power, "From Nation States to Nature States: The Case for Bioregioning, Birthing New Stories, and Building the World We Want to Live in without Delay," *Medium*, November 6, 2024.
11 Kossoff, "Cosmopolitan Localism."
12 Jason Hickel, *The Divide: Global Inequality from Conquest to Free Markets* (New York: W. W. Norton & Company, 2017), 71; Economic Times, "Independence Day: How the British Pulled Off a $45 Trillion Heist in India," *India Times*, August 15, 2023.
13 Andrew L. Fanning and Jason Hickel, "Compensation for Atmospheric Appropriation," *Nature Sustainability*, no. 6 (2023): 1077–86.
14 Olúfémi O. Táíwò, *Reconsidering Reparations* (New York: Oxford University Press, 2022), 81–2, 123–4.
15 Winne van Woerden, "Why the Climate Justice Movement Should Put Decoloniality at Its Core," *Resilience*, July 29, 2022.
16 Hickel, *The Divide*, 251–5.
17 Mohammed Sofiane Mesbahi, *Towards a Universal Basic Income for All Humanity* (Share the World's Resources, 2017).
18 James Robertson, *Future Money: Breakdown or Breakthrough?* (Totnes, Devon: Green Books, 2012), 144–5.
19 Michael Franczak and Olúfémi O Táíwò, "Here's How to Repay Developing Nations for Colonialism—and Fight the Climate Crisis," *Guardian*, January 14, 2022.
20 Rutger Bregman, *Utopia for Realists: How We Can Build the Ideal World* (New York: Little, Brown and Company, 2017), 219–21.
21 Ayelet Shachar, *The Birthright Lottery: Citizenship and Global Inequality* (Cambridge, MA: Harvard University Press, 2009), 96–105.
22 John S. Dryzek, "Institutions for the Anthropocene: Governance in a Changing Earth System," *British Journal of Political Science*, no. December (2014): 1–20.
23 Andreas Bummel, "A World Parliament and the Transition from International Law to World Law," *Cadmus* 2, no. 3 (2014).

CHAPTER 17

FURTHER READING

Eileen Crist, *Abundant Earth: Toward an Ecological Civilization* (Chicago: University of Chicago Press, 2019).

Cormac Cullinan, *Wild Law: A Manifesto for Earth Justice* (Totnes: Green Books, 2011).

Thomas Berry, *The Great Work: Our Way into the Future* (New York: Three Rivers Press, 1999).

1 Steven C. Rockefeller, "Ecological and Social Responsibility: The Making of the Earth Charter," in *Responsibility*, ed. Barbara Darling-Smith (New York: Rowman & Littlefield, 2007).

2 Earth Charter, Preamble, 2000.
3 Damian Carrington, "Humans Just 0.01% of All Life but Have Destroyed 83% of Wild Mammals—Study," *Guardian*, May 21, 2018.
4 Crist, *Abundant Earth,* 44–8, 67–9.
5 Liz Sonneborn, *Chronology of American Indian History* (New York: Infobase Publishing, 2007), 152.
6 Joshua C. Gellers, "Earth System Law and the Legal Status of Non-Humans in the Anthropocene," *Earth System Governance* 7 (2021): 100083.
7 Berry, *The Great Work*, 4–5.
8 Geoffrey Garver, "A Systems-Based Tool for Transitioning to Law for a Mutually Enhancing Human-Earth Relationship," *Ecological Economics* 157 (2019): 165–74.
9 Cormac Cullinan, "Nature Rights," in *Pluriverse: A Post-Development Dictionary*, ed. Ashish Kothari et al. (New Delhi: Tulika Books, 2019).
10 Rights of Mother Earth: https://www.rightsofmotherearth.com/.
11 Stop Ecocide International: https://www.stopecocide.earth/.
12 Frans de Waal, *Are We Smart Enough to Know How Smart Animals Are?* (New York: W. W. Norton, 2016), 25.
13 Nonhuman Rights Project: https://www.nonhumanrights.org/; Martha C. Nussbaum, "What We Owe Our Fellow Animals," *New York Review of Books*, March 10, 2022.
14 Kristin Andrews et al., "The New York Declaration on Animal Consciousness." April 19, 2024.
15 Animals in the Room: https://animalsintheroom.org/.
16 Roman Krznaric, *The Good Ancestor: A Radical Prescription for Long-Term Thinking* (London: WH Allen, 2020), 144–50.
17 Thomas Hale, "A Declaration on Future Generations Could Bring the Changes We Need," *New Scientist*, September 18, 2024.
18 Christina Conklin and Marina Psaros, *The Atlas of Disappearing Places: Our Coasts and Oceans in the Climate Crisis* (New York: The New Press, 2021), 15–25.
19 Jean-Baptiste Jouffray, et al., "The Blue Acceleration: The Trajectory of Human Expansion into the Ocean," *One Earth* 2, no. 1 (2020): 43–54.
20 Graham Lawton, "How the 'Blue Acceleration' Is Supercharging Ocean Exploitation," *New Scientist*, April 20, 2022.
21 Guy Standing, "How Private Corporations Stole the Sea from the Commons," *Open Democracy*, July 28, 2022.
22 Guy Standing, *The Blue Commons: Rescuing the Economy of the Sea* (London: Penguin, 2022).
23 Nature Needs Half: https://natureneedshalf.org/; Edward O. Wilson, *Half-Earth: Our Planet's Fight for Life* (New York: Liveright Publishing, 2016).
24 Eric Dinerstein, "An Ecoregion-Based Approach to Protecting Half the Terrestrial Realm," *BioScience* 67, no. 6 (2017): 534–45.
25 Eileen Crist et al., "Protecting Half the Planet and Transforming Human Systems Are Complementary Goals," *Frontiers in Conservation Science* 2, no. 761292 (2021).
26 Culture Hack Labs. "Territories of Transition." 2022.
27 Amazon Sacred Headwaters Alliance: https://cuencasagradas.org/.
28 Bram Büscher and Robert Fletcher, "Radical: Misdirections, New Directions," *Great Transition Initiative:* Conservation at the Crossroads (2022).
29 Theodore P. Lianos and Anastasia Pseiridis, "Sustainable Welfare and Optimum Population Size," *Environment, Development and Sustainability* 18 (2016): 1679–99.
30 *Economist*, "Global Fertility Has Collapsed, with Profound Economic Consequences," *Economist*, June 1, 2023.
31 Nandita Bajaj and Kirsten Stade, "Challenging Pronatalism Is Key to Advancing Reproductive Rights and a Sustainable Population," *Population and Sustainability* 7, no. 39–69 (2023).

CHAPTER 18

FURTHER READING

Darcia Narvaez and David Witherington, "Getting to Baselines for Human Nature, Development, and Wellbeing," *Archives of Scientific Psychology* 6 (2018): 205–13.

Gabor Maté, *The Myth of Normal: Trauma, Illness and Healing in a Toxic Culture* (New York: Penguin Random House, 2022).

Alfie Kohn, *No Contest: The Case against Competition* (Boston: Houghton Mifflin Company, 1992).

Riane Eisler and Douglas P. Fry, *Nurturing Our Humanity: How Domination and Partnership Shape Our Brains, Lives, and Future* (New York: Oxford University Press, 2019).

Osprey Orielle Lake, *The Story Is in Our Bones: How Worldviews and Climate Justice Can Remake a World in Crisis* (Gabriola Island, BC, Canada: New Society Publishers, 2024).

Peter Gray, "Self-Directed Education—Unschooling and Democratic Schooling," *Oxford Research Encyclopedia of Education* (2017).

Bron Taylor, *Dark Green Religion: Nature, Spirituality, and the Planetary Future* (Berkeley: University of California Press, 2010).

Sean Kelly, *Becoming Gaia: On the Threshold of Planetary Initiation* (Revelore Press, 2021).

1 Gregory Moore, ed. *Fichte: Addresses to the German Nation* (Cambridge, UK: Cambridge University Press, 2009).

2 Maté, *The Myth of Normal*, 2–8.

3 Tim Kasser, "Values and Human Wellbeing," Bellagio Initiative, 2011.

4 Robert M. Sapolsky, *Behave: The Biology of Humans at Our Best and Worst* (Penguin, 2017), 290–5.

5 Olúfẹ́mi O. Táíwò, *Reconsidering Reparations*, 2nd ed. (Chicago: Haymarket Books, 2025), 24–8; Ta-Nehisi Coates, *Between the World and Me* (New York: Spiegel & Grau, 2015), 27–8.

6 Quoted in Mary Beard, *Women and Power: A Manifesto* (Liveright, 2017), 3–5.

7 Heide Goettner-Abendroth, "Re-Thinking 'Matriarchy' in Modern Matriarchal Studies Using Two Examples: The Khasi and the Mosuo," *Asian Journal of Women's Studies* 24, no. 1 (2018): 3–27.

8 Lake, *The Story Is in Our Bones*, 112.

9 Lake, *The Story Is in Our Bones*, 111–12; Eisler, *Nurturing Our Humanity*, 285–6.

10 Clare Coffey et al., "Time to Care: Unpaid and Underpaid Care Work and the Global Inequality Crisis," Oxford: Oxfam International, 2020.

11 Maté, *The Myth of Normal*, 341–2.

12 Sophie Strand, *The Flowering Wand: Rewilding the Sacred Masculine* (Rochester, VT: Inner Traditions, 2022).

13 Heide Goettner-Abendroth, "Re-Thinking 'Matriarchy.'"

14 Darcia Narvaez and G. A. Bradshaw, *The Evolved Nest: Nature's Way of Raising Children and Creating Community* (Berkeley, CA: North Atlantic Books, 2023).

15 Darcia Narvaez, "Grounding Moral Psychology in Evolution, Neurobiology, and Culture," in *The Cambridge Handbook of Moral Psychology*, eds. Bertram Malle and Philip Robbins (Cambridge: Cambridge University Press, 2025).

16 Maté, *The Myth of Normal*, 188–9; Jeremy Lent, *The Web of Meaning: Integrating Science and Traditional Wisdom to Find Our Place in the Universe* (Gabriola Island, BC, Canada: New Society Publishers, 2021), 220–3.

17 Razia Iqbal, "Rashid Khalidi, America's Foremost Scholar of Palestine, Is Retiring: 'I Don't Want to Be a Cog in the Machine Any More,'" *Guardian*, October 8, 2024.

18 Daniel Goleman and Richard J. Davidson, *Altered Traits: Science Reveals How Meditation Changes Your Mind, Brain, and Body* (New York: Penguin, 2017), 279–80.

19 Rob Hopkins, *From What Is to What If: Unleashing the Power of Imagination to Create the Future We Want* (White River Junction, VT: Chelsea Green, 2019), 93–103.

20 Gray, "Self-Directed Education"; Rutger Bregman, *Humankind: A Hopeful History* (New York: Little, Brown and Company, 2019), 289–9.

21 A. R. Vasavi, "Rethinking Mass Higher Education: Towards Community Integrated Learning Centres," Paris: UNESCO, 2020; Swaraj University: https://www.swarajuniversity.org/; Ecoversities: https://ecoversities.org/.

22 Pope Francis, "Laudato Si': On Care for Our Common Home," *Our Sunday Visitor* (2015).
23 Othman Llewellyn, Fazlun Khalid, et al., "Al-Mizan: Covenant for the Earth" (Birmingham, UK: The Islamic Foundation for Ecology and Environmental Sciences, 2024); Tu Weiming, "Beyond the Enlightenment Mentality: An Anthropocosmic Vision," In *Civilizations and World Orders* (Istanbul: Foundation for Sciences and Arts, 2006); Hanh quoted in Joanna Macy and Molly Brown, *Coming Back to Life* (Gabriola Island, BC, Canada: New Society Publishers, 2014).
24 Parliament of the World's Religions, "Towards a Global Ethic," *Parliament of the World's Religions*, 1993.
25 Journey of the Universe: https://www.journeyoftheuniverse.org/.

CHAPTER 19

FURTHER READING

Roman Krznaric, *History for Tomorrow: How the Past Can Inspire Our Future* (London: WH Allen, 2024).

Thomas Homer-Dixon, *Commanding Hope: The Power We Have to Renew a World in Peril* (Toronto: Alfred A. Knopf, 2020).

Michael J. Albert, *Navigating the Polycrisis: Mapping the Futures of Capitalism and the Earth* (Cambridge, MA: MIT Press, 2024).

Damon Centola, *Change: How to Make Big Things Happen* (New York: Little, Brown Spark, 2021).

1 Walter Scheidel, *The Great Leveler: Violence and the History of Inequality from the Stone Age to the Twenty-First Century* (Princeton: Princeton University Press, 2017), 6–8,115–28.
2 Krznaric, *History for Tomorrow*, 175.
3 Jem Bendell, "Deep Adaptation: A Map for Navigating Climate Tragedy," *IFLAS Occasional Paper* 2 (2018).
4 Ray Scranton, *Learning to Die in the Anthropocene: Reflections on the End of a Civilization* (San Francisco: City Lights Books, 2015), 23.
5 Joseph A. Tainter, *The Collapse of Complex Societies* (Cambridge: Cambridge University Press, 1988).
6 Jem Bendell, *Breaking Together: A Freedom-Loving Response to Collapse* (Bristol: Good Works, 2023), 149–151, 281.
7 Ibid., 24–5.
8 Thomas Homer-Dixon et al., "Synchronous Failure: The Emerging Causal Architecture of Global Crisis," *Energy and Society* 20, no. 3 (2015): 6.
9 Cited in R. C. Duncan (1991). *The Life-Expectancy of Industrial Civilization.* Paper presented at the Proceedings of the 1991 International System Dynamics Conference.
10 Lance H. Gunderson and C. S. Holling, eds. *Panarchy: Understanding Transformations in Human and Natural Systems* (Synopsis). (Washington, DC: Island Press, 2002).
11 Albert, *Navigating the Polycrisis*, 108.
12 Marten Scheffer et al., "Early-Warning Signals for Critical Transitions," *Nature* 461 (2009): 53–9.
13 Richard Heinberg and Asher Miller, "Welcome to the Great Unraveling: Navigating the Polycrisis of Environmental and Social Breakdown," Post Carbon Institute, June 2023.
14 Krznaric, *History for Tomorrow*, 241–4.
15 Rachael Lallensack. "Could This Pollinating Drone Replace Butterflies and Bees?" *Science* (2017).
16 Donella Meadows, "Leverage Points: Places to Intervene in a System," *Sustainability Institute* 1999.
17 Bill Sharpe, *Three Horizons: The Patterning of Hope* (Axminster, UK: Triarchy Press, 2013).
18 Daniel Christian Wahl, *Designing Regenerative Cultures* (Axminster, England: Triarchy Press, 2016), 62–4.
19 Sigal Samuel, "Should Animals, Plants, and Robots Have the Same Rights as You?," *Vox*, April 4 (2019).
20 Erica Chenoweth, "My Talk at TedXBoulder: Civil Resistance and the '3.5% Rule.'" *RationalInsurgent*, 2013.
21 Damon Centola et al., "Experimental Evidence for Tipping Points in Social Convention,"

Science 360 (2018): 1116–19.

22 Leslie R. Crutchfield, *How Change Happens: Why Some Social Movement Succeed While Others Don't* (Hoboken, NJ: John Wiley, 2018).

CHAPTER 20

FURTHER READING

Leslie R. Crutchfield, *How Change Happens: Why Some Social Movement Succeed While Others Don't* (Hoboken, NJ: John Wiley, 2018).

1 Edward Chancellor, "The Naturalist," *New York Review of Books*, December 7, 2023.

2 Larry Kramer. "Beyond Neoliberalism: Rethinking Political Economy." Hewlett Foundation, 2018.

3 Richard Roberts, "Limits to Growth at 50: The Groundbreaking Study That Failed to Change the World," *Medium*, May 14, 2022.

4 Cited in Daniel Stedman Jones, *Masters of the Universe: Hayek, Friedman, and the Birth of Neoliberal Politics* (Princeton: Princeton University Press, 2012), iBooks ed., ch. 2.

5 Crutchfield, *How Change Happens*, 53–8.

6 Brent Simpson et al., "Radical Flanks of Social Movements Can Increase Support for Moderate Factions," *PNAS Nexus* 1, no. 3 (2022).

7 Atossa Soltani, "The Pandemic: Portal to a Living Earth Paradigm," in *The New Possible: Visions of Our World Beyond Crisis*, eds. Philip Clayton et al. (Eugene OR: Cascade Books, 2021), 26–8. Amazon Sacred Headwaters Alliance website: https://cuencasagradas.org/en/.

8 La Vía Campesina: https://viacampesina.org/en/; ICCA Consortium: https://www.iccaconsortium.org/defending-territories-of-life/.

9 Cooperation Jackson: https://cooperationjackson.org.

10 Pamela Haines, "How Worker Ownership Builds Community Wealth and a More Just Society," *ZNet*, February 4, 2023.

11 David Bollier and Silke Helfrich, *Free, Fair and Alive: The Insurgent Power of the Commons* (Gabriola Island, Canada: New Society Publishers, 2019), 20–1, 318–36, 344.

12 Ecoversities: https://ecoversities.org/.

13 Arundhati Roy, *Power Politics* (South End Press, 2001), 7.

14 David Schenck and Larry R. Churchill, "Ethical Maxims for a Marginally Inhabitable Planet," *Perspectives in Biology and Medicine* 64, no. 4 (2021): 494–510; Václav Havel, *Disturbing the Peace* (Faber & Faber, 1990).

15 Owen Gaffney and Zoe Tcholak-Antitch, "Global Commons Survey: Attitudes to Planetary Stewardship and Transformation among G20 Countries," Global Commons Alliance, 2021.

16 Richard Wilkinson and Kate Pickett, *The Spirit Level: Why Greater Equality Makes Societies Stronger* (New York: Bloomsbury Press, 2009).

17 Greta Thunberg, "'You Did Not Act in Time'": Greta Thunberg's Full Speech to MPs,' *Guardian*, April 23, 2019.

EPILOGUE

1 Eric M. Jones. "'Where Is Everybody.' An Account of Fermi's Question," *OSTI.gov*, February 28, 1985.

2 David Grinspoon, *Earth in Human Hands: Shaping Our Planet's Future* (New York: Grand Central Publishing, 2016), 342–51.

3 David Sloan Wilson, "Evaluating Narratives of Conscious Evolution," *This View of Life*, March 26 2022.

4 Glenn Albrecht, "Exiting the Anthropocene and Entering the Symbiocene," *Psychoterratica*, December 17, 2015.

ACKNOWLEDGEMENTS

In many ways, this entire book serves as an acknowledgement of the important and inspiring work that has already been done, and continues to unfold across the world among thought leaders and communities laying down pathways toward an ecocivilization.

My own path toward the vision of civilizational transformation, and the concomitant desire to write this book, began with David Korten, who was the first person to introduce me to the idea of an ecological civilization. I was immediately struck both by its scope—the realization that every major aspect of our civilization needed to change—and its hint that the source of this transformation was life itself: the core principles that have allowed ecosystems to flourish resiliently over eons. David introduced me to the Institute for Ecological Civilization, co-founded by Philip Clayton and Andrew Schwartz and inspired by John B. Cobb, Jr., which has since become a part of my own life's arc.

Once I formed the conception for this book, more than five years ago, I began a multi-year research project to immerse myself in the ideas and accomplishments of pathfinders blazing trails toward a better future, which I have attempted to portray in the preceding chapters. Some whose writings were foundational to my own sense-making are, in no particular order, Kate Raworth, Jason Hickel, Darcia Narvaez, David Sloan Wilson, David Bollier, Fritjof Capra, and John Restakis—each of whom has generously given me feedback on specific chapters.

Other luminaries whose ideas have been integral to this book include Amitav Ghosh, Rutger Bregman, Riane Eisler, Raj Patel, Sandrine Dixson-Declève, Michael Sandel, Hélène Landemore, Guy Standing, Ugo Mattei, Audrey Tang, George Monbiot, Damon Centola, and Fabian Scheidler.

In addition to those already mentioned, I'm indebted to the following friends and colleagues who reviewed various chapters and offered many constructive suggestions: Sean Kelly, Mary Evelyn Tucker, Stewart Wallis, Mirian Vilela, Marjorie Kelly, Thomas Homer-Dixon, Ashish Kothari, Helena Norberg-Hodge, Eileen Crist, Nafeez Ahmed, Roman Krznaric, Paddy Le Flufy, Georgia Kelly, David Korten, Sandra Waddock, Manish Jain, Aaron Frank, Jojo Mehta, Michael Pawlyn, Jonathan Rose, Bron Taylor, Richard Heinberg, John Perkins, Jem Bendell, Michael Albert, Tim Kasser, Paul Chatterton, Howard Switzer, Herman Greene, Brian Hoffstein, Fran Korten, and Neal Gorenflo.

I'm grateful for the many generative conversations on the topics of the book that have helped me in formulating my ideas, with those already mentioned along with numerous other friends including Mamphela Ramphele, Yuka Saito, Douglas Rushkoff, Osprey Orielle Lake, Atossa Soltani, Troy Lush, Indra Adnan, Pat Kane, Rupert Read, Samantha Power, Janelle Orsi, Gus Speth, and Paul Raskin.

I thank my agent, Anthony Arnove, and Melville House editor, Mike Lindgren, for their excellent work in helping to bring this book into the world.

More generally, there have been no end of expansive conversations on themes related to this book that have occurred in the feed and live monthly meetings of the Deep Transformation Network, and I'm filled with gratitude for the committed work of the Ecocivilization Coalition and its Advisory Partner network, who are sowing the seeds that may one day turn this book's vision into a reality.

Finally, I reserve my greatest measure of appreciation for my beloved life-partner, Lisa Ferguson, who has been my first reader and editor for each chapter, and has supported me lovingly every step of the way.